SYNGRESS®

1 YEAR UPGRADE
BUYER PROTECTION PLAN

Webmaster's Guide to the Wireless Internet

Ryan Fife

Wei Meng Lee

Dan A. Olsen Technical Editor

KEY	SERIAL NUMBER
001	NJ48USDNFV
002	MBLAU4TPTR
003	WDP9FUV3GB
004	56LNSXDKMF
005	2SNF438BMF
006	KGF8E45SJF
007	KXMPER9T3E
008	AMGPE94FGY
009	LE49ETVD9R
010	CERUT3HNTR

PUBLISHED BY
Syngress Publishing, Inc.
800 Hingham Street
Rockland, MA 02370

Webmaster's Guide to the Wireless Internet

Printed in the United States of America

1 2 3 4 5 6 7 8 9 0

ISBN: 1-928994-46-6

Technical Editor: Dan A. Olsen
Technical Reviewer: Richard Weeks
Co-Publisher: Richard Kristof
Acquisitions Editor: Catherine B. Nolan
Developmental Editor: Kate Glennon
Freelance Editorial Manager: Maribeth Corona-Evans
Cover Designer: Michael Kavish
Page Layout and Art by: Shannon Tozier
Copy Editors: Darren Meiss, Jesse Corbeil, and Adrienne Rebello
Indexer: Robert Saigh

Distributed by Publishers Group West in the United States and Jaguar Book Group in Canada.

Acknowledgments

We would like to acknowledge the following people for their kindness and support in making this book possible.

Richard Kristof and Duncan Anderson of Global Knowledge, for their generous access to the IT industry's best courses, instructors, and training facilities.

Ralph Troupe, Rhonda St. John, and the team at Callisma for their invaluable insight into the challenges of designing, deploying, and supporting world-class enterprise networks.

Karen Cross, Lance Tilford, Meaghan Cunningham, Kim Wylie, Harry Kirchner, Kevin Votel, Kent Anderson, and Frida Yara of Publishers Group West for sharing their incredible marketing experience and expertise.

Mary Ging, Caroline Hird, Simon Beale, Caroline Wheeler, Victoria Fuller, Jonathan Bunkell, and Klaus Beran of Harcourt International for making certain that our vision remains worldwide in scope.

Anneke Baeten and Annabel Dent of Harcourt Australia for all their help.

David Buckland, Wendi Wong, Daniel Loh, Marie Chieng, Lucy Chong, Leslie Lim, Audrey Gan, and Joseph Chan of Transquest Publishers for the enthusiasm with which they receive our books.

Kwon Sung June at Acorn Publishing for his support.

Ethan Atkin at Cranbury International for his help in expanding the Syngress program.

Gene Landy at Ruberto, Israel, & Weiner for his support and his honesty—and for occasionally picking up the tab. Thank you for your friendship Gene.

Contributors

Ryan Fife is a Technical Architect for Yospace where he is building their developer outreach program. Yospace has a strong market reputation for the development and deployment of high quality, working wireless data solutions that add value even at the earliest stages of this market. Ryan is working to maintain this prestigious reputation and expand the number of developers who use Yospace products to build quality applications.

He has been building wireless solutions for more than two years for clients that include large wireless companies such as Nokia and Ericsson. Prior to joining Yospace, Ryan co-founded AnywhereYouGo.com, a wireless portal for developers that covered WAP, J2ME, SMS, i-Mode, and PDA technologies. Ryan also has architected and built large e-commerce systems in Java as a consultant for Electronic Data Systems (EDS).

Ron Herardian is a leading expert in wireless software technology and messaging presently serving as Director of Product Strategy for ClickServices, Inc., a venture-backed Silicon Valley startup funded by Cisco Systems. Ron previously founded a wireless software startup, 3minder, Inc., that developed an integrated wireless and Internet messaging technology and which merged with ClickServices, Inc., in May of 2000. Before entering the wireless field, he served for five years as CEO and Chief Systems Architect for Global System Services Corporation (GSS), an infrastructure systems consulting firm providing a range of services in the areas of electronic messaging, directory services, and groupware. At GSS, Ron provided technology strategies for Fortune 500 clients, as well as software and solution architectures for ISPs and infrastructure software vendors such as Netscape Communications. A California native, Ron holds various technical certifications and is the author of numerous technical papers and articles on wireless technology and electronic messaging, as well as a book on LAN-based e-mail. He holds a bachelor's degree from Santa Clara University and a master's degree from Stanford University.

Rory Lysaght is a Mobile Device Specialist at Ripcord Systems, a wireless startup based in Seattle and London. At Ripcord, Rory put together one of the first wireless GSM iPAQs in Europe. He has worked in Web and wireless development in the United States, Europe, and Japan. He has contributed articles to several online and paper publications, including Web Review and the EE Times. Prior to this, Rory worked as a photojournalist, publishing numerous documentary stories in magazines in the same three continents. He is a member of the WAP forum and the Palm developer network. Rory is also a contributor to Syngress Publishing's *Palm OS Web Application Developer's Guide* (ISBN: 1-928994-32-6). He lives in Seattle, WA.

Wei Meng Lee is Series Editor for Syngress Publishing's .NET Developer Series. He is currently lecturing at The Center for Computer Studies, Ngee Ann Polytechnic, Singapore. Wei Meng is actively involved in Web development work and conducts training for Web developers and Visual Basic programmers. He has co-authored two books on WAP and holds a bachelor's degree in Information Systems and Computer Science from the National University of Singapore. The first book in the .NET series, *VB.NET Developer's Guide* (ISBN: 1-928994-48-2), is currently available from Syngress Publishing.

Technical Editor and Contributor

Dan A. Olsen is an independent Web technology consultant based in San Francisco, CA. He specializes in helping nonprofit organizations and small business people utilize Internet technology to make their internal processes more efficient and to communicate with their clients more easily. Dan formerly worked as an application developer and usability engineer for Informano Networks, a wireless Managed Services Provider located in Emeryville, CA. In this capacity, he handled all aspects of client-side development for a wide variety of devices including WAP and wireless mobile phones, PDAs, and desktop Web browsers.

Prior to his venture into the world of wireless technology, Dan spent two years with Cox Interactive Media (CIM) as a Multimedia Developer and Web Technical Lead. During his tenure with CIM, he was the in-house technical resource for BayInsider.com, a San Francisco Bay Area portal. Under the umbrella of CIM, he developed, built, and maintained several Web sites for various local media partners and local events. Dan studied anthropology and new media communications at the University of Washington in Seattle.

Technical Reviewer and Contributor

Richard Weeks (B.Sc.) is Managing Director of brightfluid (www.brightfluid.com), a research consultancy that is studying the behavioral patterns of the users of mobile communications—the social and psychological triggers that accompany mobile phone usage. Richard's background includes key positions at Grey Interactive Services Ltd. (UK) where he helped launch the Cartoon Network's WAP site and AnywhereYouGo.com in the UK where he was Business Development Manager. Richard is a frequent contributor to various consumer and professional mobile publications and has appeared on CNN Financial as an expert in the field. His expertise extends from mobile phone technologies such as SMS and WAP through to wireless LAN, satellite communications, and in-flight information delivery resulting in an all-round appreciation for all aspects of the wireless Internet phenomenon.

Contents

Answers to Your Wireless Questions

Q: Will I have to learn different programming if i-Mode comes to the United States?

A: i-Mode uses a subset of HTML called Compact HTML (cHTML). Anyone familiar with HTML should have no problem learning this. However, there are signs that the industry may move towards XHTML as the preferred markup language for these devices.

Using the Short Message Service

The Short Message Service (SMS) allows you to send and receive messages of about 160 characters via your mobile phone using a GSM network. This is a relatively old technology but is still quite popular.

Exploring the <postfield> Element

The <postfield> element specifies a name and value pair that will be sent to the server as part of a URL request. The following are attributes for the <postfield> element:

- **name** The name of the field.
- **value** The value of the field.

Examining WMLScript Data Types

WMLScript supports five built-in data types:

- Integer
- Floating Point
- String
- Boolean
- Invalid

Using the Nokia WAP Toolkit 2.1

The Nokia WAP Toolkit is an environment for developing, viewing, and testing WAP applications. It includes:

- Editing, validating, and viewing WML decks
- Editing and debugging WMLScript files
- Viewing and changing WML variables inside the WAP browser
- Examining debug messages from the WAP browser
- Creating and editing WBMP images

Creating a Web Clipping Project with the WCA Builder

The WCA Builder has three main options from the File menu: Open Index, Rescan HTML, and Build PQA.

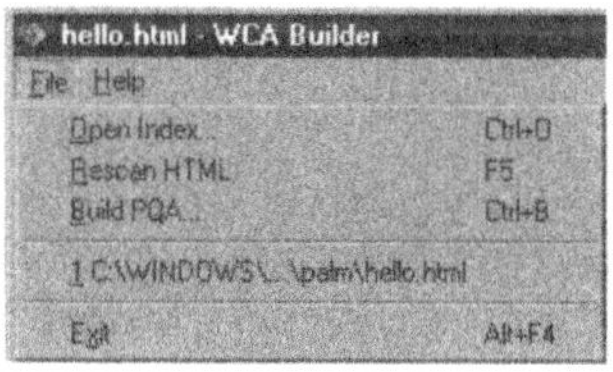

Avoiding the Common Mistakes Made by Webmasters

Some of the more common mistakes made by Webmasters include:

- Wasting bandwidth
- Forgetting task-based design
- Providing too many options or too much information
- Using branded, Web-like terminology instead of plain language

Choosing Mobile Content

One of the first steps to building any site is choosing what content to display on the site. The primary questions that arise in adapting a large existing site to the wireless Internet are:

1. What content/services might our users want to access while they are mobile?
2. What limitations are there to the existing mobile interfaces that we must consider?

The Architecture of ASP.NET

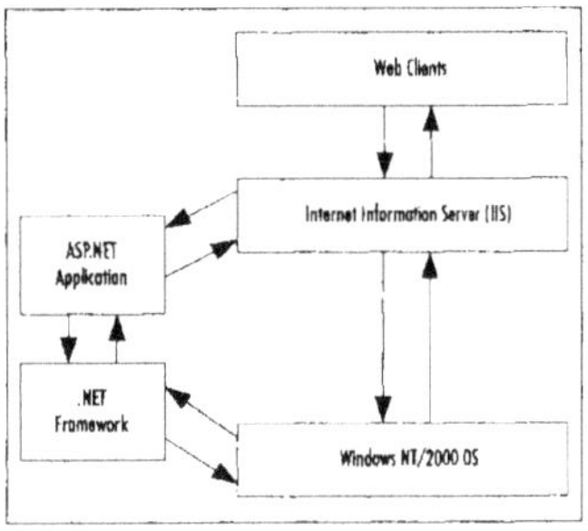

Understanding the Seven Layers of Point-to-Point Security

Point-to-point security can be broken down into seven layers, corresponding to the steps in the communication path between mobile devices and Web servers or applications:

1. Embedded Security Technology
2. Secure Air-Connect Technologies
3. Mobile Operator Network Security
4. Secure Mobile operator Gateways
5. Authentication
6. Data Center and Network Security
7. Secure Application Interfaces

Foreword

Over the past several decades, advances in computing technology have created widespread changes in the way that the world operates and the means by which we deal with information. Computing has revolutionized the way that business is done, bills are accounted for, and how records are stored. The invention of the underlying sets of protocols to enable communication between computers in the early 1970s and the advent of the personal computer in the 1980s, has helped to sow the seeds for the most recent communications revolution—the Internet. In the mid-1990s, as the World Wide Web matured to include graphics and multimedia components and more and more individuals gained access to affordable computers and Internet accounts, the popularity of the Internet exploded and the number of Web sites and people online grew at an exponential rate. Since then, many Web sites have come and gone and use of the Internet is something that many people in the United States take for granted. In the case of individuals whose livelihood is enabled by the Internet, such as Webmasters, it is something that we cannot live without.

We have also seen, over the past two decades, widespread adoption of mobile devices that are capable of enabling communication. Cellular phones are now being used by millions of individuals worldwide, and, in some areas, mobile phones are more reliable and used more often than land-based telephone communications systems. Recently, many phones and other handheld devices now have the ability to access the Internet and send messages between subscribers. These capabilities often include e-mail and the ability to send and receive data via the Hypertext Transfer Protocol (HTTP), although not all of these devices can view the type of HTML that has been associated with the World Wide Web of recent years. The advent of ubiquitous mobile Internet computing promises to be another revolution in the ways that human beings interact with each other, manage information, and interact with data applications. This revolution also promises a new landscape in which Webmasters may apply their skills and learn some new ones.

One common characteristic that most handheld wireless devices share, regardless of the device category, is a relative lack of processing power, memory, and display capabilities as compared to a desktop computer. Wireless networks, in addition, feature a mere trickle of bandwidth compared with a modem, let alone a DSL or T1 connection. It is very important to keep these constraints in mind as you build your content and applications.

Furthermore, your wireless users will most likely be accessing your Web site while they are mobile. This fact makes it imperative for you to consider the needs of a mobile user as you consider what types of content you should make available, or what kinds of applications make sense for a mobile user. Also, your user interface should take into account the small viewpoint of the devices that will be accessing your Web site and should also consider the difficulty that often exists with user input on these devices.

Webmaster's Guide to the Wireless Internet is intended to give you, the Webmaster, the skills and knowledge that you will need to add wireless Internet capability to your existing Web site, to build new wireless applications, and to help you understand the issues, both global and domestic, that exist with deploying wireless Internet solutions. The primary geographical focus of this book is the United States, but Webmasters in other countries will certainly find the information useful. *Webmaster's Guide to the Wireless Internet* is not a lengthy work on the wide variety of protocols that are used to deploy wireless technologies, nor does it focus unnecessarily on the minute details of emerging technologies that are volatile in nature and constantly changing. Rather, it focuses on hands-on examples that will allow you to adapt your existing skills in HTML and server-side scripting to deploy content and applications to a wireless audience using WML, WMLScript, and, in some cases, lean HTML. This book is intended to demystify the wireless landscape and provide you with answers on how to get your wireless Web site up and running quickly.

Chapter 1 covers the basics of what makes up the wireless Internet, and how it contrasts with the World Wide Web.

Chapter 2 covers the basic architecture of the wireless architecture and provides a comprehensive overview of the components of the wireless Internet and how they fit together.

Chapter 3 explains the nuts and bolts of the Wireless Markup Language, the client-side, XML-based markup language that allows devices using the Wireless Application Protocol (WAP) to display Internet content. This chapter will give you an understanding of how this language differs from HTML and will give you the skills to start building your own wireless content.

Chapter 4 explains how to add client-side scripting to your WML pages. WMLScript is loosely based on ECMAScript, which is the language that gave rise to both JavaScript and Jscript. Users familiar with these scripting languages will notice a similar syntax and structure, but the means of deployment will differ. Depending on the market in which you want to deploy your content, you may or may not be able to make much real-world use of WMLScript.

Chapter 5 explains how to install and use the many Software Development Kits (SDKs) supplied by wireless browser programmers and handset manufacturers to provide you with an emulator and debugger to develop your content or application.

Chapter 6 provides an introduction to the proprietary system that allows users of Palm-powered handheld devices to access content located on the Internet. This chapter will give you the information that you will need to start building Web Clipping Applications (WCAs). These special HTML-based applications can be integrated with local applications or interact with Web servers located on the Internet.

Chapter 7 explains the issues surrounding usability on wireless devices. This chapter will help you build effective small-viewpoint navigation and give you some handy tips on how to make your wireless site more user-friendly by working within the constraints of narrow bandwidth and limited user input.

Chapter 8 will give you information and guidelines on how to add wireless capabilities to your existing Web site and choose content that is of interest to mobile users. It also covers how to detect wireless devices and discusses the issues surrounding automated or on-the-fly conversion of your content for wireless users.

Chapter 9 explains how you can use the Microsoft Mobile Internet Toolkit and Mobile Web Forms to deploy content to a wide variety of devices using the same code. It covers how you can maintain state during a wireless or Web transaction and how you can integrate Microsoft's ActiveX Data Object (ADO) technology to provide interfaces to your data to many different devices.

Chapter 10 discusses the technology used to provide secure transactions for wireless devices and covers the issues surrounding security as it applies within the wireless landscape. Point-to-point and end-to-end security models and the various pitfalls surrounding both models are discussed.

The wireless revolution, like any revolution, is not without its challenges. The global market for wireless Internet technologies is highly diverse, with different rates of adoption, competing protocols and technologies, and existing infrastructures that are in some cases more economical to use in the short term than building a new global wireless communications architecture. At present in the United States, there exists a fragmented landscape of telecommunications companies that offer mobile phone service and not all of them are yet capable of offering wireless Internet access (but most are). In Europe, standardized networks and compatible handsets have enabled the wireless Internet to become popular very quickly. Asia has seen similar growth in the use of the wireless Internet, most notably in Japan with NTT/DoCoMo's iMode system. Many individuals in these markets find that the wireless Internet is an indispensable part of their lives, while the U.S. market has been slow to adopt the technology. There are many reasons for this, including legacy handsets, widespread Internet access via personal computers, and a telecommunications market that features competing incompatible protocols and technologies.

This book, while comprehensively covering the technologies that already exist on the wireless Internet (and the general principles behind them), does not attempt to address developing technologies that are not yet deployed. There has recently been much speculation and hype about so-called third generation, or 3G networks, which are "just around the corner." In addition, handset manufacturers have promised many new developments in wireless technology, and, in particular, location-based services. These dreams, at the time of this writing, are not yet a reality.

However, the wireless Internet is up and running and more subscribers join in every day. The future certainly promises to be interesting, and *Webmaster's Guide to the Wireless Internet* holds much value for Webmasters who wish to add the ability to develop wireless-accessible Web sites to their toolkit. The first step to the future begins today, and we can only expect that the number of mobile devices that are capable of accessing the Internet will grow as time progresses. It's your job to make sure that there is something worthwhile for individuals to access on the wireless Internet, and this book provides the hands-on examples and explanations that will allow you to do so!

—Dan A. Olsen
Technical Editor and Contributor

Chapter 1

Moving from the Web to Wireless

Solutions in this chapter:

- Explaining Wireless
- Types of Wireless Connectivity
- Evolving Mobile Devices
- Something Old, Something New
- Moving from a Wired to a Wireless Internet
- ☑ Summary
- ☑ Solutions Fast Track
- ☑ Frequently Asked Questions

Introduction

The past century has brought about many changes in information and communications technology, from the invention of the telephone and broadcast technologies to the invention of the personal computer and the Internet. These changes have enabled us to exchange information with other individuals and to retrieve data from vast databases practically instantly. You, as a Webmaster, are certainly familiar with these changes and have most likely played a role in developing some of the content accessible via the Internet and allowing users to connect with each other through time and space.

The wireless Internet is a new revolution upon us, one that will affect the world on a scale similar to that of the wired Internet. We have seen it grow in Europe and Asia, and North America appears to be the next frontier of this expansion.

We now live in a world populated with various devices that are capable of exchanging information at unprecedented rates of speed, measured on the scale of milliseconds. We have mobile telephones, pagers, personal digital assistants (PDAs), and laptop computers, all capable of being connected to the Internet. It is truly an exciting time to be alive.

In this book, we help you learn the tools and technologies to expand and adapt your current Internet offerings to the wireless Internet. As much as is possible, we provide analogies to technologies that you will already be familiar with as a Webmaster for the traditional Internet. However, you need to remember that you are dealing with a new space in which to exchange information, with new constraints and methodologies to building a successful site and/or application.

In this chapter, we provide a brief overview of wireless technology, discussing some of the devices that are currently connectable. We also cover in brief some of the similarities and differences between the wired and wireless Internet. We briefly discuss the concept of mobile versus fixed wireless and provide some examples of these different types of wireless connectivity in action.

Explaining Wireless

Wireless is one of those terms that would seem to be self-descriptive: *without wires*. However, in terms of the Internet, wireless actually encompasses a whole host of technologies that you need to understand if you want to move from the wired world. In the traditional Internet, you didn't have to concern yourself much with how your visitors actually arrived at your Web site. Of course, you did have to account for slower modem speeds and deal with different browser capabilities, but the actual connection itself wasn't of much concern, because every user reached your site in the same way: via a computer connected to the Internet.

The term *wireless* by itself is somewhat of a misnomer; a more precise term might be *mobile wireless*. Broadcast television is wireless, but for the most part not mobile. The emphasis on mobility is one of the defining characteristics of this new paradigm. From a Webmaster's point of view, this mobility—not simply the lack of wires—is likely to be the most important aspect.

So how do people connect wirelessly to the Internet? At the most basic level, someone with a wireless device—cell phone, pager, laptop—uses a radio frequency connection to a base station, which then makes a wired connection to the traditional Internet backbone. However, the actual technologies involved differ quite a bit depending on the wireless device and can have a large impact on how your content is delivered.

What are the potential impacts of having visitors to your site from wireless devices? If you've been in this business long enough to remember the "browser wars," when competing browser standards made it necessary to jump through hoops to make your content display effectively on multiple systems, the bad news is that, for the foreseeable future, it's likely to be much worse in the wireless arena; low bandwidth, differing standards, multiple network carriers, and a multitude of radically different devices means that the job of the wireless Webmaster just got immensely more complicated. However, the good news is that the amount and variety of available projects is also likely to increase significantly. As companies look, initially, to extend traditional applications into the wireless realm there will be a high demand for those skilled in both traditional Internet and wireless. This first generation of the wireless Web—translating existing applications to wireless—will gradually give way to new, native applications, things that are possible and make sense only on the wireless Internet.

The myriad of wireless devices is probably the first aspect that the wireless Webmaster will have to deal with. You've probably, at some stage, used some form of scripting, whether client-side or server-side, to detect the browser or operating system (via the HTTP_USER_AGENT header) of the requesting client, and you then formatted your content accordingly. Although it is certainly possible to do this with wireless devices, the sheer variety of possible device types makes it unlikely that you'll want to write custom code for each and every one. Where you may use this technique, however, is to detect which family of devices your visitor is using. For instance, if it's a Palm OS–based device, you can assume that the screen size is limited to 150 pixels wide and is probably monochrome, and the device does not support cookies. If the user-agent indicates it's in the Pocket PC family, chances are that this device can display full-color images at 0.25 VGA resolution, and it also supports JavaScript. Conversely, if it's a Wireless Application Protocol (WAP) phone, you need to ensure that data is sent to the device in chunks under 1.5KB and will need to be marked up using Wireless Markup Language (WML), rather than Hypertext Markup Language (HTML).

Types of Wireless Connectivity

The mobile wireless landscape is in a state of rapid change right now. After a period where pretty much your only option was to jury-rig some kind of connection through your mobile phone, you now have multiple options for giving all sorts of devices a mobile Internet connection. The sudden proliferation of mobile devices—especially those based on the Palm OS and Pocket PC, has prompted service providers to bring a wide array of wireless connection options to market.

The first widely available method of accessing Internet content from a mobile device was Wireless Application Protocol. WAP (which is covered in detail in Chapter 5) is a method of viewing specially formatted content on a mobile phone.

Back in 1995, Unwired Planet (now Phone.com) developed the Handheld Device Markup Language (HDML). HDML was a stripped-down version of HTML, designed specifically for displaying Web content on small devices. Recognizing that they needed the support of the large handset manufacturers to make this a success, in 1997 they joined forces with Ericsson, Nokia, and Motorola to form the WAP Forum. This was the body which came up with the WAP specification, part of which was WML. As the first company with a wireless product for carriers, Phone.com's gateway server—UP.Link—is still in place at a large percentage of global wireless operator facilities. Phone.com also made the first widely distributed microbrowser for mobile phones—the UP.Browser. Because their products were developed and integrated into a lot of handsets before the WAP specification was finalized, a large percentage of handsets out there, particularly in the U.S., still support HDML, rather than WAP. WAP gateways enable these legacy browsers to understand WML content.

WAP was slow to take off in the U.S., even though it was available almost a year earlier in Europe. Unfortunately, marketers in the U.S. didn't learn much from the mistakes of those in Europe, where WAP was trumpeted as "The Internet in your Pocket" and heavily hyped as providing the equivalent of a full Internet experience. Users were quick to realize that the reality was much, much less; slow speeds, dropped connections, high call charges, and the sheer difficulty of the user interface all led to a fairly rapid backlash against WAP. This was compounded by a severe lack of available WAP sites. After being promised access to the Internet, subscribers found that not only could they not access any of the existing Web sites, but they were also locked into *walled gardens*, closed portals providing links only to WAP sites which had signed a marketing agreement with the carriers; in many cases, there was no way to enter URLs into the phone's microbrowser.

Another wireless service, an information service often overlooked in the U.S., is Short Message Service (SMS). Also referred to as *text messaging*, SMS is a complementary service that comes with all European mobile phones. With it, users can send short text messages to each other at a fraction of the cost of a voice call. Users enter messages on the number pad of the phone. Although this input method is difficult for some people, particularly those accustomed to a computer keyboard, younger users in Europe became quite adept at it, and in some case even developed their own shorthand codes. SMS costs mere pennies per message, and doesn't require you to answer the phone to receive the message. As a result, SMS has become a huge success in Europe, especially in the youth market. Europeans send over a billion text messages a month!

Developing & Deploying…

One Web, but Not One Wireless Network

One reason for the delayed introduction of WAP in the U.S., and coincidentally the reason why the U.S. in general trails Europe in terms of wireless innovation, is that European countries all share a common wireless transmission standard, a legacy of Europe's former state-run telecom monopolies. Continent-wide availability of Global System for Mobile Communications (GSM) means that a mobile phone user from Helsinki can fly to London, turn on his phone on arrival at Heathrow Airport, and immediately get a connection. This also leads to economies of scale for the handset manufacturers. The same handset that sells in Stockholm can be sold in Dublin with no modifications. European handsets also use a Security Identity Module (SIM) chip—a thin sliver of plastic containing a memory chip—to store both network billing information and users' personal phone numbers. This allows users to easily

Continued

transfer their account from one phone to another, and consequently users upgrade their phones much more frequently. To sell consumers on WAP, European carriers just needed to persuade them to upgrade to a data-capable phone.

By contrast in the U.S., where handsets are subsidized to a lesser degree, most people spend a considerable amount of time inputting all of their personal phone numbers into the handset. To upgrade to a WAP phone, an early adopter would have had to buy a relatively expensive phone, from a small range of available models, and then re-enter all of her personal numbers, not to mention learn a totally new user interface. It didn't help that, when they did finally get WAP phones, U.S. users found themselves in the very same walled garden situation as their European counterparts.

Compounding this problem, the U.S. suffers from a mish-mash of competing and incompatible wireless standards. As a result, wireless innovation in the U.S. is severely restricted. One consequence of this for the wireless Webmaster is that you'll need to be much more rigorous in your testing. Due to differences in the WAP gateway configuration, and the particular microbrowser installed on the handset, a WAP page that displays perfectly on an AT&T Nokia phone may behave quite differently on the same handset on the Verizon network.

SMS wasn't initially made available in the US. The usual reason given is that the carriers didn't feel American consumers would respond well to having to enter messages on a tiny nine-button numeric keypad. Given that they need to use exactly this method to use WAP, this argument was a little hard to fathom. SMS is gradually becoming available on U.S. wireless phone plans, although in a limited fashion. Many service plans allow you to receive text messages, but not to send them, which sort of limits its usefulness. SMS is closely linked to WAP. As well as being used for sending text messages, SMS can also be used to send configuration settings to your phone.

In Japan, NTT DoCoMo is often pointed to as one of the most successful launches of a mobile data service. Within a year of its launch in 1999, the service, known as *i-Mode*, had gathered 10 million subscribers. I-Mode users browse a huge range of Web sites with cheap, full-color handsets that maintain an always-on connection to the Internet. Users pay per kilobyte downloaded, not based on how long they're connected. A key component in making m-commerce a success in a country where e-commerce has had a hard time taking hold is that users can purchase items from DoCoMo-approved sites and have the charges appear on their phone bill, avoiding the need to send credit card details over the air.

The walled garden approach of the network carriers, and the relative shortage of compelling WAP content, coupled with the usability problems inherent to the device itself, may ultimately doom WAP. In the short term, it remains the only viable option for presenting information to mobile phones, but as new phone/PDA hybrids begin to appear, this advantage may be short-lived. Many analysts have noted that the success of i-Mode has as much to do with Japanese cultural factors as with its technology, and that this model isn't necessarily transplantable abroad. However, NTT has recently made significant investments in several European and U.S. carriers (it owns 16 percent of AT&T Wireless), so it could present itself as an alternative to WAP at some stage, although it hasn't yet made an appearance outside of Japan.

The European wireless standard, GSM, is available on a limited basis in the U.S. Carriers such as VoiceStream and AT&T Wireless offer this service in various areas, which means that a European visitor with a Tri-Mode phone can use his mobile here in the U.S. and vice versa.

All of the major carriers worldwide are now readying their networks for an upgrade to a system called General Packet Radio System (GPRS). GPRS will offer higher data speeds and an always-on connection. It is already available in some European countries and on a trial basis in a few U.S. cities.

Although the ability to access the Internet via a mobile phone was indeed a technological marvel, most users quickly realized that it was of limited use. The next evolution was to wirelessly enable the popular PDAs. After a few false starts (the Apple Newton being a notable example), Palm, Inc. eventually got it right with the hugely successful Palm OS line of devices. The field has recently been expanded with the addition of several devices running Microsoft's Pocket PC operating system. Although these devices have gained wide consumer acceptance, only recently have options for giving them a wireless Internet connection begun to appear. Companies such as OmniSky and Sierra Wireless offer various options for adding wireless capability to devices such as the popular Palm V as well as Pocket PC–based PDAs. These generally use a packet-switched network called Cellular Digital Packet Data (CDPD), which offers speeds twice as fast as mobile phones.

Small handheld devices aren't the only mobile devices. Laptops have been mobile from the beginning, so it was also a natural to extend their reach by providing a wireless connection. Options for this are varied, although they generally use the Personal Computer Memory Card International Association (PCMCIA) slot, generically referred to as the PC Card slot, found on all laptops. Manufacturers have also begun to introduce models with integrated wireless capability, and it's likely that before long, integrated wireless will be as commonplace as built-in modems are today.

The newest frontier in mobile wireless is convergent devices such as combination mobile phone/PDAs or the Tablet PC. Although the first generation of these consists of bolted-together hybrids of existing devices, the pace of innovation is accelerating, and new devices come to market regularly. The combination of cheaper and more powerful processors, faster wireless networks and new mobile-centric operating systems means that new devices born on the wireless Internet are bound to change the landscape of mobile computing in the years to come.

What this means for the wireless Webmaster is that you'll need to develop techniques for dealing with a wide variety of device types and connection speeds. Some devices, such a WAP phones, will require you to format your content with specific markup languages. Others will accept regular HTML but severely limit your design options, whereas wireless laptops will have regular browsers but be constrained by extremely slow connection speeds.

Mobile Phones as Wireless Modems

One of the earliest methods of getting a wireless connection for your PDA or laptop was to use a cable to connect it to your mobile phone. Many mobile phones are capable of serving as wireless modems, and software is also available to install a *soft modem* on your laptop for those handsets that don't have a data feature. You can even do the same by means of the infrared link built into most PDAs and laptops, although this requires you to keep your device and phone precisely aligned. In either case, you then use your phone to dial up a regular Internet Service Provider (ISP) and establish an Internet connection. However, both of these methods limit you to the 9.6 Kbps data rate of your phone. This is, however, an option if you have an older PDA, such as a Palm III, that doesn't have a wireless modem available. It may also be a fallback option if you regularly find yourself traveling outside of the coverage areas of some of the other wireless services we look at next. In Europe, it's not uncommon to find people sitting at train stations and airports with a mobile phone velcroed to the lid of their laptop, and a cable running to the serial port on the back.

The first widely available integrated wireless option for laptops (and subsequently PDAs) in Europe was basically a mobile phone shrunk to the size of a PCMCIA card—the Nokia Card Phone. With this card in a laptop or PDA, the user essentially got a mobile dial tone. She would then use the cellular modem just as if it were a regular wire line modem to dial up an ISP. Ubinetics manufactures a similar GSM modem that clips onto the back of a Palm V. Once connected to an ISP, the user has a regular Internet connection, although the speed is limited to about 28.8 Kbps. To achieve these speeds, carriers use a technique known as High-Speed Circuit-Switched Data (HSCSD). HSCSD combines several wireless channels, each of which has a rated speed of only 9.6 Kbps, and bundles them together to achieve higher speeds. This is analogous to wiring two dial-up modems and two phone lines together to get a faster dial-up connection. HSCSD is offered only by a few carriers and only in a handful of European countries. It is unpopular with carriers because it uses up more than one voice channel, thus reducing their capacity, but they can't charge accordingly for the extra channel. Although it is still an effective way of getting a wireless connection in Europe, HSCSD is likely to fade in importance as services such as GPRS become more widespread. Although this system is theoretically possible in the U.S., to date no carriers have offered it.

Packet Switched Networks

A more recent option for wireless connectivity in the U.S. is Cellular Digital Packet Data (CDPD), which is a relatively old packet-switched network originally built for pager and fleet-tracking applications. *Packet-switched* means that data is broken up into packets or short chunks, which are sent independently, then re-assembled at the receiving end, very much like the methods used by Transmission Control Protocol/Internet Protocol (TCP/IP) to transfer data over the wired Internet. By contrast, telephones are circuit switched, meaning a dedicated circuit is established between the two ends of the connection for the duration of the call. Unlike cellular phones, CDPD is an always-on connection, meaning that you don't need to initiate a connection each time you request a URL. With certain services, this also opens the possibility of pushing data out to devices, rather than waiting for them to initiate communication.

The Sierra Wireless AirCard is a CDPD modem that operates at 19.2 Kbps, and a variety of service plans are available from companies such as Go.America and AT&T Wireless. Some wireless Internet service providers (WISPs) also offer proprietary compression technologies that promise to boost access speeds. One advantage of this model is that, with the correct drivers, you can use the exact same card in your PDA or in your laptop. The card fits into any standard Type II PCMCIA slot. Novatel manufacturers a similar card called the Merlin, which also operates on CDPD. Compaq's iPAQ and the @migo from URThere (manufactured by Palmax) both have the option to accept these and other PC Card modems.

Companies such as Pocket, Enfora, and Glenayre make CDPD modems in the Compact Flash (CF) format that is standard on many PDAs. CDPD modems are also available as a clip-on for the Palm V and to fit in the expansion slot of the popular HandSpring Visor, a Palm OS–based PDA.

Palm also makes a model with an integrated CDPD modem, the Palm VII. Although it is chunkier than the newer Palm models and runs at a lower data speed, the all-in-one design is convenient. Because it also runs on AAA batteries, it doesn't require a charger, making it one of the few truly wireless mobile wireless solutions.

Apart from its speed, the major drawback of CDPD is limited availability. Coverage maps available from the main service providers (AT&T, GoAmerica, Bell Atlantic, and GTE) reveal that signals are concentrated around the main population centers in the U.S. Although carriers maintain that service is available to over 80 percent of the U.S. population, that is little consolation to residents outside of those areas, or traveling professionals needing coverage at client sites en route.

Future Networks

You may have seen the terms 2.5G and 3G mentioned in relation to wireless. The first generation (1G) was the original analog cellular phone services. Although we are currently at 2G (all-digital service) in most of the developed nations, it's worth noting that close to 40 percent of mobile voice traffic in the U.S. still travels over analog networks. The next generation of wireless connectivity, sometimes also referred to as 2.5G, includes services such as GPRS. These services are already available in Europe, but U.S. rollout has been delayed by squabbling among the various carriers over which incompatible standard to choose. AT&T already has GPRS service available in its home city, Seattle, and Sprint and Verizon promise rollouts by 2002. GPRS promises data speeds of up to 200 Kbps, and early proponents talked about wireless multimedia applications such as full-motion videoconferencing. The reality is that most services will initially offer speeds of between 64 to 144 Kbps, which is not much faster than a traditional wired modem, although still quite a step up from today's meager speeds. However, as a packet switched service, the always-on nature of the connection and relatively workable speeds are sure to launch a host of new wireless services and applications. As GPRS service becomes more widely available, modems will no doubt be offered in both PC Card and CF formats.

Carriers in Europe, Japan, and Australia have begun to cautiously roll out these services, although early trials have been plagued by technical delays, a shortage of available handsets, much slower actual data speeds, and lackluster reception in the marketplace.

Carriers around the world have spent vast sums of money to purchase blocks of the wireless spectrum to use for so-called 3G services. 3G (3rd Generation) promises high speeds and always-on connections, and is expected to usher in an age of wireless broadband, with mobile devices capable of downloading information at high speeds, enabling such services as video e-mail and downloading music files to your mobile phone. The path to 3G however, will not be easy. It requires huge investments in new transmission equipment, and a complete replacement of all current handsets. Japan is already conducting trials of 3G services and handsets, but industry analysts expect it will be at least 2005 before full 3G service is available in Europe and the U.S.

In Europe, the government-mandated ubiquity of GSM as a mobile communications standard has meant the ready availability of a large potential audience for mobile wireless applications. The situation in the U.S. is somewhat more fragmented, with several major wireless carriers each promoting their own proprietary standards. Rather than uniting around a common standard, which would provide economies of scale for manufacturers of both handsets and networking hardware, and greater freedom of choice for consumers, U.S. carriers continue to bicker amongst themselves over which standard should form the basis of the next generation of wireless networks. Interestingly, while there was considerable experimentation in mobile phone designs in Europe, until quite recently PDAs were scarce. Conversely, in the U.S., PDA options have proliferated rapidly, but only recently have wireless options started to appear on the market.

Local and Personal Networks

Two other wireless standards are worth noting here. The first is the rather poorly named 802.11b, which is sometimes also referred to as wireless LAN (WLAN). A consortium of companies that manufactures the hardware is now trying to introduce it to consumers under the more marketing-friendly WiFi brand. 802.11b has found ready acceptance as a short-range radio replacement for traditional Ethernet connections. It uses an unlicensed portion of the radio spectrum to offer data speeds of up to 11 Mbps—comparable to older wired Ethernet connections. Transmitters are available as either a PC card, for use on a laptop or PDA, or as an internal or USB-connected option on a desktop computer. Although its short range—typically no more than 500 meters (about 1500 feet)—doesn't make it truly mobile, it does have application in such environments as warehouses, where wireless PDA-equipped workers can roam freely about the warehouse while maintaining a high-bandwidth connection to inventory systems. The system has recently become more popular with home users wishing to create a wireless home network; there is no need to drill holes in walls, floors, and baseboards, and no costly Ethernet cable to run. It is also suitable for older office buildings where cable cannot be run and is popular for setting up ad hoc networks at events and tradeshows. Paired with the broadband digital subscriber line (DSL) and cable modem services now available, 802.11b allows you to lounge in your garden or on the deck and surf the Internet at high speeds. Several companies have adapted the system to provide wireless coverage in areas where large numbers of business travelers typically congregate, such as airport lounges and the larger hotel chains. Café chains are also looking at this as a way to encourage business users to frequent their establishments; the Starbucks coffee chain recently installed wireless access in almost all of their outlets. The next version of this standard, 802.11a, will up speeds to the 50 Mbps range.

Bluetooth is another short-range wireless standard gaining ground recently. Bluetooth is quite a bit slower than 802.11b and has a shorter operational range—about 10 meters (39 feet). It uses the same unlicensed area of the radio spectrum as 802.11b (2.4 GHz) and offers data speeds of up to 1 Mbps. Originally envisioned as a cable replacement technology—the first commercial product was a wireless mobile phone headset from Ericsson—Bluetooth has expanded to a complete networking standard. Bluetooth *nodes* are each capable of operating as either a client or a server. In a PDA setting, one scenario is that you would walk into the lobby of a major hotel or an airline's frequent-flyer lounge. The Bluetooth chip in your PDA would automatically discover the Bluetooth network, negotiate your access rights and give you a network connection.

Bluetooth is also envisioned as enabling a personal area network (PAN), where the multiple electronic devices carried by a mobile user—mobile phone, PDA, laptop, digital camera—would communicate constantly and share functions. In this setting, your PDA would detect that your 3G phone had the best available network connection while on the road and use it to download your latest schedule from your office server. On arrival back at your office, the PDA would immediately detect the office network and use it to update your server with new data gathered while on the move.

While Bluetooth is still in the early stages of development, several manufacturers—including IBM, 3Com, and Toshiba—have PC card units commercially available now, and Compact Flash versions are in development by several more. IBM and others will soon begin shipping laptops with integrated Bluetooth chips and antennas. British Rail has already launched a trial service on some of their trains that combines Bluetooth and Wireless LAN (802.11b) to provide Internet connectivity to passengers.

Fixed Wireless Connectivity

Fixed wireless is an alternative to other broadband Internet services becoming available in several areas. The typical speed, for consumer services, is about 10 Mb (megabits per second). By contrast, the T1 lines that feed many businesses provide a 1.5 Mb connection, and consumer DSL connections typically provide about 256 Kb. A small dish installed on the roof picks up and transmits signals to a central antenna. A line of sight is usually required between the antennas, so this kind of connection is not suitable in all areas, but the service is usually not affected by bad weather. Fixed wireless is also finding a niche in providing Internet connectivity to rural areas beyond the reach of other broadband solutions, such as DSL and cable Internet.

Fixed wireless is also marketed to businesses as an alternative to costly leased lines for connecting several buildings of a corporate campus. In this configuration, dishes on the roofs of adjacent buildings serve the same purpose as a wired connection, linking disparate portions of a corporate local area network (LAN) but without the need to run expensive fiber and dig up roadways. These kinds of installations use higher-powered equipment and consequently can provide much higher bandwidth connections.

Because it's a broadband connection, fixed wireless won't generally have any relevance to the role of the wireless Webmaster; for all intents and purposes, fixed wireless is equivalent to a high-speed wired connection. You may be already serving fixed wireless users on your existing Web site, because fixed wireless is not tied to WAP, HDML, or any particular device.

Table 1.1 summarizes some of the available connectivity options and the data speeds of each. Note that these are rated top speeds. Variables such as distance from the radio tower, number of simultaneous users in the cell, and the general overhead involved in the HTTP connection means that actual available data speeds are likely to be much lower.

Table 1.1 Connectivity Options and Speeds

Device	Network	Data Speed
Palm VII	Mobitex	8 Kbps
Mobile phone	All carriers	9.6 Kbps
Nokia Card Phone II w/ HSCSD	Orange (UK)	28.8 Kbps
Palm V w/ OmniSky modem	CDPD	19.2 Kbps
Pocket PC w/ Sierra PCMCIA modem	CDPD	19.2 Kbps
RIM 957 (Blackberry)	Mobitex	19.2 Kbps
Wireless LAN (802.11b)	Local	11 Mbps
Fixed wireless	Proprietary	10 Mbps

Evolving Mobile Devices

The mobile landscape today is in a state of continual change. We hear of new devices introduced to the market almost weekly, and wireless access options continue to multiply. So how is the aspiring wireless Webmaster to deal with developing content for so many disparate devices? Although detecting the exact device accessing your server is possible in most cases, the sheer variety of different devices makes it very unlikely you will want to format content for each one. The good news is that most of the devices likely to be accessing your site wirelessly fall into three broad categories—mobile phones, PDAs, or laptop computers. Each has its own unique advantages and disadvantages. Although there are significant differences between devices in each category—PDAs in particular come in a wide variety of configurations—the three main categories are differentiated by connectivity, screen size, memory, and processing power.

The most widely available wireless devices are mobile phones. Their primary purpose, of course, is voice communication. With the addition of data services from the wireless carrier, they also work well for short text messages (using SMS) and sometimes for reading e-mails, but the difficulty of entering text makes them cumbersome for sending e-mail. WAP phones also allow you to access specially formatted Internet pages.

Personal digital assistants (PDAs) have been used by traveling professionals for several years now to track schedules, store contact information, and enter expenses while on the road. With the addition of a wireless connection, their usefulness is increased. With larger screens and handwriting recognition interfaces, they are suitable for short e-mails and can also be used to access the Internet.

Laptops have always been mobile, of course. Laptops with a wireless modem in the PC Card slot eliminate the need to search for phone jacks, fiddle with wires and connectors, or huddle in public phone booths. One advantage laptops, and some PDAs, have over wireless phones is that the wireless component is upgradeable, so that as better, faster options become available, users don't need to discard the whole device. With the current pace of development in the wireless Web, this is probably a sensible precaution, if you have the option.

Several other devices are available that seek to combine aspects of each category—a mobile phone with an integrated Palm screen, PDAs that can be used as phones, and laptop-size devices without keyboards that you use by writing directly on the screen.

Wireless Phones

The first and still most prevalent device today is the data-enabled cellular phone. Almost all of the major cellular carriers now offer data services as well as the traditional voice service. All of the major handset manufacturers—Nokia, Motorola, Ericsson, Mitsubishi, Alcatel, and others—offer data-capable phones, and before long, this will be standard on all new phones. These are typically the same size as regular cell phones, but with a screen capable of displaying specially formatted text. They use the WAP protocol. WAP was developed as an alternative to Hypertext Transfer Protocol (HTTP) to deal specifically with the restrictions of the current generation of wireless, that is, with low speeds and high latency. For display on WAP phones, content needs to be coded in WML. WAP phones don't connect directly with WML Web servers. They communicate with special WAP gateways, typically operated by the carriers, which then forward the request to the content server on their behalf. The WML content returned is then compiled into a special compressed format before being sent back to the WAP phone, where an application called a microbrowser decodes and displays it.

Basic Mobile Phone Properties

Mobile phones are, first and foremost, phones. Their primary purpose is to enable the original *killer app*: voice communication. As such, they need to be small and light and have minimal requirements for memory and processing power:

- **Connectivity** 9.6 Kbps digital cellular
- **Screen size** Typically 3 x 2.5 cm (1.25 x 1 in.) equivalent to 5 lines of text, about 15 characters per line

- **Memory** Minimal
- **Processing power** Minimal

Mobile Phone Connectivity

A data-enabled mobile phone uses the same radio-frequency (RF) connection as your voice calls to connect with its base station. This is typically a cell tower somewhere within a few miles. Although it depends on a number of factors, such as distance from the cell tower and number of users within that cell, the rated data speed in most cases is 9.6 Kbps (some services offer 14.4 Kbps). Compared to a 56 Kbps dial-up modem, the minimum connection speed most Web sites are designed for, you can see this is quite slow. In addition to low bandwidth, the current cellular networks suffer from high latency—that is, a significant delay occurs between the time a user hits a Submit button and when the resulting content is sent back to the device. It's also not uncommon for the signal to be dropped in the middle of a transaction as the user drives into a tunnel or the radio shadow of a large building.

The signal between the handset and the base station is encrypted and compressed. From there, the signal is routed over regular landlines to a special server called a WAP gateway. The segment of the call from the handset to the gateway is done using Wireless Session Protocol (WSP), a protocol defined within WAP. The WAP Gateway then acts on the phone's behalf to request the page from your server using traditional HTTP. The concept of the WAP gateway may be unfamiliar to you if you're accustomed to the traditional Internet client/server model. The gateway is basically acting as an agent or proxy for the wireless device and also translates from the WAP protocol stack to the TCP/IP stack used on the Internet. This is quite important to remember: A mobile phone never communicates directly with your Web server; it is always a WAP gateway acting on its behalf. Because the gateway can have a significant effect on how your content is displayed, looking at this a little more closely is worthwhile.

When a user requests some content (either by typing a URL directly into the phone's microbrowser or by clicking on a link), the following series of steps occurs:

1. The handset establishes a connection with its base station.
2. Once this connection is set up, the microbrowser then initiates a connection to a WAP gateway predefined in the phone's configuration.
3. The microbrowser requests a URL from the WAP gateway. This is done via a compact binary encoded request.

4. The gateway translates this request into an HTTP request and sends it over the wired Internet to the specified content server.
5. The content server responds by sending a page of WML content, which may also contain WMLScript (similar to JavaScript) and special graphics in WBMP format.
6. The gateway compresses the response into a special binary format optimized for low-bandwidth networks, then sends it back to the microbrowser. It also compiles any WMLScript found in the response.
7. The microbrowser decodes the compressed signal, and attempts to display it, if possible.

As you can see, there are quite a few steps between a visitor and your content, and each of the components along the way can have a significant effect on the format of your content. It's important to understand the effect each can have on the data you send to your visitors. To add to this, the same components but by different manufacturers can behave quite differently. This is analogous to the early days of the Web, when you had to contend with different manufacturers' browsers displaying your HTML in different ways. A WAP phone contains a microbrowser, which is similar in function to the familiar desktop browser. However, several major microbrowsers are in circulation, and though each conforms to the WAP specification, the specification allows for quite a lot of flexibility in how they actually display content.

The gateway, which is typically housed at the cellular carrier's premises, may also alter the content somewhat on its way through. Some gateways, for instance, store and pass cookies, whereas some do not. The gateway can also add special header fields, and it sometimes removes header information. The gateway will also cache information on behalf of the phone, because most phones don't have enough local memory to save much data. Again, this varies from one gateway to another, so you generally can't rely on it.

Mobile Phone Screen Size

The size and resolution of the display screen is probably the biggest hurdle you'll face in developing Web sites for WAP phones. This is similar to the early days of the Web, when you could never be sure of the screen resolution or color capability of visitors' monitors. There is a mechanism whereby phones can send capabilities information—such as pixel count, number of lines of text, and number of soft keys—to your server. Unfortunately, not all phones provide this information, and not all gateways pass it on.

A typical phone screen is 3 x 2.5 cm (1.25 x 1 in.) and usually has a monochrome LCD capable of displaying only black or white. Most current phone screens are limited to displaying about 5 lines of text, with about 15 characters per line. A few models have slightly larger screens, and some are even smaller. It is possible to detect the incoming User Agent (the microbrowser in the phone), compare this to a database of known phone configurations, and then format your content accordingly, but the sheer variety of possible handset configurations makes it very problematic to try to format your content for specific models of phone. Most people will choose a lowest common denominator format that has been tested to work satisfactorily on most common phones.

The minimal screens mean that you'll need to rethink the amount of content you put on pages meant for WAP users. People can always scroll up and down, of course, but reading in this manner is difficult. Long text pieces simply don't work in this form, so you'll need to cut down drastically on the amount of text on your pages. Fitting navigation menus on there as well becomes a difficult task. WML actually contains some features to help in this regard. Because most phones have a number of *soft keys* (buttons below the screen to which you can assign menu items), some of the navigational elements, such as *home*, *back*, and *next*, can be shifted off the main screen. However, the utility of this feature is reduced significantly by the fact that each manufacturer has chosen to implement these soft keys in very different ways, both physically and logically. Because you won't know exactly how the buttons will implement your interface on all phones, designing interfaces becomes something of a guessing game.

Mobile Phone Memory

Most wireless handsets have little or no memory available for storage. They do have some storage for personal phone numbers, but this varies from phone to phone, which means that you have to be very careful how much data you send to a handset at one time. Gateways compress your WML before sending to the device, but how much compression happens varies by gateway. In particular, because you typically won't know how much data the phone can handle, you'll need to pick a safe limit you're sure will work on most phones. Because it's difficult to gauge how much compression different carrier gateways will provide, this may take some trial and error, but as a general rule it's best to keep your pages, or WML decks, under 1.5 Kb total. This may mean developing special server code if you're doing things such as returning database record sets; you'll need a way to measure the size of the record set returned by a query and then split it up into WAP-sized chunks.

However, WML does allow for something that generally doesn't exist on the Web: persistent client-side variables. This means that you can capture form entries on one page and then pass them to another page without requiring a trip back to the server. You could, for instance, ask a visitor for some input on one card of a multicard deck and use their responses to determine which card to navigate them to next. This kind of conditional branching is very difficult to achieve via HTML alone. Another potential use might be to store a visitor's answers to a question from one page, then refer back to these answers several pages later, without needing to transfer the data back to the server and store it there. Again, these variables are limited by available handset memory, but they are session-independent, meaning they will be stored on the handset, even after your visitor navigates away from your site. However, as new data arrives, these variables may be pushed out and replaced. Furthermore, it is possible for any site to clear *all* of the variables on the phone.

SECURITY ALERT!

Unlike cookies on the Web, which can only be accessed from the same domain that set them, WML client variables are available to any Web site as long as they remain in memory. So if, for instance, you were to set a variable and value *"password=abc123"*, the potential is raised for a malicious WAP site to access and save this.

Mobile Phone Processing Power

The current crop of mobile phones has minimal processing power—basically just enough to run an embedded operating system, and a few simplistic games. Bear this in mind if you've got very complicated WMLScript that you expect to be processed on the device. Heavy-duty computation tasks are better handed back to the server to process. Higher powered phones capable of downloading and running Java programs are beginning to appear on the market, particularly in Japan, but these are so far not widely available in the US.

PDAs

The next step up in device size is the PDA. These come in many different forms, but typically have a larger screen, more memory, and more processing power than mobile phones. A PDA generally refers to a device small enough to hold in the palm of the hand, but with a larger screen than the typical mobile phone. Current PDAs evolved from gadgets designed to help you manage your contacts and calendar—essentially electronic FiloFaxes—and were relative latecomers to the wireless Internet. The market for PDAs is split mainly between those running the Palm operating system from both Palm, Inc. and its licensees (Handspring, IBM, Sony, and Symbol), and devices based on Microsoft's Windows CE, with a couple of niches occupied by other alternatives such as Symbian's EPOC and other devices.

Developing & Deploying...

Blackberry: Pager or PDA?

A device that has become quite popular, particularly with corporate "road warriors," is the RIM 957—popularly known as the Blackberry—from Canadian firm Research in Motion. This pager-like device features a miniscule keyboard and an always-on connection to corporate e-mail systems, such as Microsoft Exchange. The first version of this device had a small three-line screen, but the RIM 957 added a screen with the same dimensions and resolution as the Palm. Corporate users in the U.S. have found this device almost addictive. Utilizing North American CDPD networks, the device constantly polls a dedicated Blackberry server connected to the corporate mail server for new e-mails and downloads them automatically, giving the impression of always-on, anytime, anywhere e-mail access. First rolled out in North America, the Blackberry was such a success that it is now being made available in Great Britain in partnership with British Telecom, utilizing their GPRS service.

One thing to bear in mind with PDAs is that, even if the units are company-supplied, these are fundamentally personal devices. People carry these with them constantly, and use them to track personal schedules, birthdays, grocery lists, and address books, just as much as they do company work. Businesses have been slow to adopt these devices, although that is now beginning to change. In fact, these devices first began to enter corporations when people brought their own devices to work and began synching up with their corporate calendars and address books.

Palm OS Devices

Although there were earlier attempts, Palm, Inc.'s device was the first commercially successful PDA. When it was introduced in 1996, the Palm Pilot was an instant success due to its ease of use, intuitive user interface, and small size. Although the casings have changed quite a bit since then, and more memory has been added, the actual Palm operating system has changed very little over the years. A large community of developers has grown up around it, so a huge variety of programs are now available. Until quite recently, Palm, Inc.'s primary market was individual users. Even though Palm device users tend to be extremely loyal, Palm, Inc. has realized that to maintain their market position they need to develop enterprise-level applications and market to large corporations. To make their PDA acceptable to corporate IT managers, they also need to address concerns of security and support, and they need to beef up its meager memory and processing power to make it capable of running enterprise-class applications.

Palm, Inc. also licenses its OS to several vendors. Handspring, founded by the original developers of the Palm OS, took a leaf from Apple Computer's book and released a series of very stylish devices in the Visor line. Although the basic OS remains almost the same, Handspring sells Visors with a variety colorful translucent cases and developed a unique, proprietary expansion slot called the SpringBoard, which allows other manufacturers to make add-on modules for functions such as wireless access, Global Positioning System (GPS), and even a module that turns the Visor into a mobile phone. Sony's Clié adds a special jogwheel that allows for improved navigation around the screen, and also has a model with a higher screen resolution. IBM rebrands the Palm OS as its WorkPad line, which it markets into corporations. Symbol and a few other companies take the basic Palm device and encase it in a rugged, weather-resistant housing, adding an integrated barcode scanner and wireless LAN access to make units for use in warehouse management and other industrial applications.

Palm OS–based PDAs access the Internet via either a built-in modem (in the case of the Palm VII), or by means of a clip-on external modem, such as the one available for the Palm V from OmniSky. In the U.S., these modems typically use the packet-switched CDPD network mentioned earlier, whereas in Europe they use the GSM cellular standard. Most Palm devices currently on the market use low-resolution monochrome LCD screens, although Palm, Inc. and a number of its licensees have recently released some color models.

Palm, Inc.'s designers felt that the best solution to the limited screen size, and the very slow data speeds of wireless, was to do away with the concept of browsing as we understand it on the wired Web. Instead, they envisioned a way to give people quick access to targeted information, stripped of all embellishments. Palm, Inc. refers to this as Web Clipping. Rather than connecting directly with your content server, Palm devices generally use an intermediary server called a proxy. This is similar in concept to the WAP gateway, but it has quite different capabilities. Web Clipping uses a subset of HTML 3.2 with a few notable changes: It doesn't support frames, nested tables, or a lot of the formatting options of regular HTML.

Developing & Deploying...

How Can I Validate the HTML in My Web Clipping Application?

The full Document Type Definition (DTD), which describes in detail the acceptable tags and attributes, is available at www.palm.com/dev/web-clipping-html-dtd-11.dtd. You can specify this DTD in your document and validate your code using the W3C validator at http://validator.w3c.org.

The Palm.net proxy reads Web pages on behalf of the device, and then it compresses them before sending over the air. It will also rewrite any HTML that doesn't conform to the specification, including removing graphics wider than the Palm device screen size. However, the results of this translation are seldom what you had in mind. In most cases, you'll need to either construct new pages specifically for Palm OS, or reformat your existing pages so they work on both formats.

Visitors using the Palm OS generally won't type a URL into a conventional browser to access your site. Generally, they'll download a special Web Clipping Application (WCA, also previously referred to as a Palm Query Application [PQA]) from your regular Web site, then install this on their Palm device. WCAs are simply HTML pages compiled into a special binary format using an application that developers can obtain freely from Palm, Inc. One potentially useful feature of Web Clipping that differs substantially from traditional Web authoring is the ability to precompile graphics into the WCA, then later refer to these graphics from your online pages. Because the graphics are already resident on the Palm device, there is no need to download them over a slow wireless connection, which enables you to create extremely efficient applications. The drawback to this approach is that, because Web Clipping is a proprietary technology, you then can't use the same HTML for Pocket PC devices, which at present don't support this feature.

Pocket PC Devices

Pocket PC–based PDAs are a more recent addition to the mobile device arena, but they are gaining popularity because of their relatively higher-resolution color screens and greater processing power. Microsoft Pocket PC is a special version of Windows designed specifically for smaller devices, and it comes with familiar applications such as Outlook and Internet Explorer. In contrast to WAP phones and Palms, these devices generally make a direct HTTP connection with your server, without any intervening proxies.

After a few false starts with earlier versions, Microsoft's Pocket PC 3.0 revolutionized the PDA market when it was introduced in 2000. Although its market share is still considerably less than Palm's, it has raised the bar on functionality and continues to advance the state of the art in mobile wireless devices. The first and most obvious attribute is a higher resolution color screen (grayscale models are available, but these are largely confined to industrial units). Most models also have a backlit screen, making the display extremely bright and crisp. The Pocket PC operating system includes pocket versions of popular Microsoft applications, such as Word and Excel. It also has a version of Outlook that, with Microsoft ActiveSync, allows mobile users to sync the unit with their desktop or laptop Outlook. Most significantly for the wireless Webmaster, it features a browser that's very similar to Internet Explorer 3.2.

Rather than manufacture devices itself, Microsoft licenses its OS to any manufacturer that can meet the minimum technical requirements. These include a screen with 240 x 320 pixels of resolution, and memory of at least 16MB. 32MB is more common, and Compaq's iPAQ 3670 comes with 64MB. Pocket PC devices typically also have a more powerful CPU, allowing for more on-board processing.

One feature of Pocket PCs that's especially relevant to wireless is that most come with an industry-standard expansion slot; either CF or PCMCIA Type II (the same PC Card slot found on virtually every laptop computer). This immediately gives these devices a huge base of possible expansion options. When Compaq introduced their wildly popular iPAQ Pocket PC in 2000, other companies were quick to produce wireless options for the device, either writing software drivers for existing PCMCIA cards, or in some cases developing completely new PC cards.

Although technical features are obviously important, style has proven to be just as much of a selling point. When Compaq introduced their iPAQ, it was in such demand that units were back-ordered for months; it was practically impossible to get one through regular retail channels. At one point, iPAQs were selling on eBay for well over their retail value. Hewlett Packard makes a Pocket PC model, the Jornada 548, that's functionally very similar, but sales have slumped compared to the Compaq's superior visual appeal. At tradeshows and technology demonstrations throughout 2000 and 2001, the sleek and shiny iPAQ was *the* cool device to have.

Pocket PC–based PDAs have found ready acceptance too in the industrial market. Symbol, Intermec, iTronix and others make more rugged models based on the OS, usually with integrated barcode scanners and wireless connection options. The increased memory and more powerful CPUs make these devices suitable for applications that require more processing power on the handheld, such as mobile field service automation and sales force automation.

There is another class of mobile PDA device, sometimes referred to as Handheld PC or *clamshell* form factor. These are devices that feature a horizontal display aspect ratio, rather than the more common vertical format. Microsoft makes a version of its Windows CE operating system specifically for these devices. Known as Handheld PC 2000 (sometimes abbreviated to just H/PC), this comes with pocket versions of popular Microsoft Office applications such as Word and PowerPoint. The major difference from Pocket PC is that the screen resolution is 640 x 240 pixels—0.5 VGA—and that most devices come with a dedicated keyboard. Although not widespread among general consumers, handheld PCs are popular in industrial settings. iTronix makes a rugged, waterproof version for use in harsh environments. Microsoft isn't the only option here; Psion makes a range of consumer devices based on the EPOC operating system. These are mainly popular in the UK and Europe, but they don't seem to have made much impression in the US.

Basic PDA Properties

Mobile phones come in a seemingly endless variety of case designs, but their basic underlying characteristics are the same. PDAs, by contrast, come in a wide range of configurations. Models based on Palm OS and Pocket PC have radically different features, but the general package tends to be similar. Because these are meant to be handheld units, most have roughly the same physical dimensions:

- **Connectivity** 9.6 Kbps to 19.2 Kbps CDPD
- **Screen size** 5.7 cm x 5.7 cm (2.25 x 2.25 in.) (Palm); 6 cm x 8 cm (2.25 x 3 in.) (iPAQ).
- **Resolution** 160 x 160 pixels (Palm) to 240 x 320 pixels (Pocket PC)
- **Memory** 8MB (Palm) to 32MB (iPAQ)
- **Processing power** 16 MHz (Motorola Dragonball) to 206 MHz (Intel StrongARM)

PDA Connectivity

PDAs have perhaps the widest array of connection options of any mobile wireless device. One very popular wide-area network (WAN) option for any device with a PC card slot is the Sierra Wireless AirCard. As mentioned earlier, several companies also make CDPD modems in the CF format.

Another option for a mobile connection is to use your mobile phone as an external modem for your PDA. Cables are available to connect several popular mobile phone models to various PDAs. However, this will limit you to the data speed of your mobile phone, typically 9.6 Kbps, and makes your phone unavailable for regular voice calls. Although this is an interim option, or suitable for people who regularly find themselves traveling outside the coverage areas of CDPD, it's likely to become less useful as easier, better integrated wireless solutions become more commonplace.

The first commonly available integrated wireless PDA was the Palm VII, which had a built-in CDPD modem and a flip-up flexible antenna. In the U.S., the Palm VII and VIIx operate over the BellSouth CDPD network, rebranded as Palm.net, but they are limited to a data speed of about 8 Kbps. The Palm VII is quite a chunky device compared to models like the sleek Palm V. When Palm V users began clamoring for wireless options, a company called OmniSky responded with the Minstrel modem, a thin device that clips onto the back of the Palm. This also uses a CDPD network, although the data speeds are faster than Palm.net—about 19.2 Kbps. In Europe, Ubinetics markets a similar clip-on for the Palm V that uses GSM, with the maximum data speed limited to about 14.4 Kbps.

Rather than connecting directly to a Palm device, a special proxy server requests content from your site, and then reformats it especially for display on the Palm's limited screen. Pocket PC devices, by contrast, generally make a direct HTTP connection with your Web server. One important point to note is that, regardless of the connection type, the communication with your content Web server is still via conventional HTTP. This is true for Palm Web Clipping, Pocket PC browsers, and WAP phones. There may be intermediate gateway or proxy servers between the device and your server that perform protocol translation, but it is always a HTTP request that is made of your server.

PDA Screen Size

Palm OS–based devices have a screen approximately 5.7 cm x 5.7 cm (2.25 x 2.25 in.), with a resolution of 153 pixels wide by 144 pixels high (the actual screen resolution is 160 x 160 pixels, but the lower portion is reserved for Palm's handwriting recognition area, and a few pixels at the side are reserved for a vertical scroll bar). Although color models are available, the majority of devices on the market right now are monochrome. Most have a color depth of 2 bits, meaning they can display only four shades of gray. Although this is a big step up from the tiny WAP phone screen, for a Webmaster designing pages for such a device, this is obviously quite limiting, and you'll need to be creative in how you reformat your pages. Bear in mind also that, prior to Palm OS 4.0, no option for horizontal scrolling was available.

One other device we mentioned earlier, the RIM 957 or Blackberry, also contains a microbrowser. This browser is unique in that it can display both WAP and HTML content. When in HTML mode, it behaves very much like a Palm. In fact, it understands most of the Palm Web Clipping HTML extensions. The screen is also 160 x 160 pixels, although it can display only black or white. For the most part, you can use exactly the same pages for either Palm or Blackberry devices. The one restriction is that the Blackberry does not use the precompiled graphics capability of Web Clipping. If you're targeting pages for both devices, you'll need to be aware of this.

Some Pocket PC devices, by contrast, have much higher resolution full-color screens. Most can display 240 pixels wide by 320 pixels high (0.25 VGA). This is obviously much less limiting for a Webmaster. Pocket PC devices include a version of Internet Explorer 3.2, allowing you to create pages that more closely resemble your standard Web site. In fact, if you take care to allow for the smaller screen and slower connection speeds, you can use the same content for both traditional and wireless users.

PDA screens fall somewhere in between a WAP phone and a full-size laptop. Although WAP browsers are available for Palm and Pocket PC, WAP doesn't take full advantage of the larger screens, easier navigation, and availability of color. Conversely, content formatted for a large screen won't generally look good on a PDA. For instance, left-side navigation bars are a common and intuitive interface on conventional Web sites. A typical navigation bar might be 125 pixels wide, leaving the rest of the screen for content. However, on a Palm, this would leave just 28 pixels for content! Moreover, most navigation bars are constructed with nested tables—something not supported in the version of HTML used for Palm Web Clipping. Although Internet Explorer does a much better job of displaying regular Web sites on Pocket PC, it generally still requires an excessive amount of horizontal and vertical scrolling.

Handheld PCs and devices such as the Psion Revo have a horizontal screen. The Revo and other models have relatively low-resolution monochrome LCD screens, while most devices running Microsoft Handheld PC (H/PC) 2000 have full color screens capable of 640 x 240 pixel resolution. A typical H/PC device screen is 16.5 cm (6.5 in.) wide.

PDA Memory

Most Palm OS devices top out at 8MB of memory, and quite a few still get by on just 2MB. Pocket PC devices, by contrast, usually have at least 16MB of RAM. Many have 32MB, and Compaq's new iPAQ 3670 model comes standard with 64MB. Most Pocket PC devices feature an expansion slot that can accommodate extra memory. The two most common expansion options on Pocket PC devices are PCMCIA (the same PC card slot found on all laptops) and CF.

CF memory modules are available in various sizes, from 8MB up to 256MB. IBM even makes its 1GB MicroDrive in CF; rather than the solid-state memory of most CF cards, this is actually a miniscule spinning hard drive. Because CF is a popular storage option for many digital cameras, this makes it easy to move digital images from camera directly to PDA. You can also insert CF cards into laptops, or a PDA with PC card slot, by using a cheap adapter.

Some PDAs accept PCMCIA cards, either directly or via an expansion sleeve. Because this is exactly the same slot found on all laptops, this means that you can use the same cards on both, as long as the manufacturer provides a Pocket PC driver. IBM makes the MicroDrive in this format, which is basically a miniaturized spinning hard disk on a PC card, in capacities from 500MB to over 2GB. If you need to transport large amounts of data on your PDA, and you regularly exchange this data with a laptop, PC card storage is a good and cost-effective option.

Another storage option becoming more popular is the Secure Digital (SD) card. The newer Palm models accept this format, as do several digital cameras and other devices. These are similar to CF, but much smaller—not much bigger than a postage stamp. They come in various denominations, currently available up to 64MB.

PDA Processing Power

Due to the simplicity and efficiency of the Palm OS, these devices are able to perform adequately with relatively slow processors. However, as Palm devices are called on more and more to perform as sophisticated enterprise tools, there's a need to bump up the power. Motorola has announced that they will be doubling the power of the Dragonball chips used in all Palm devices.

Pocket PCs generally come with much more processing power. The OS itself requires more power, but these devices were designed from the outset to perform much more powerful onboard processing tasks. Even the slowest models come with a 66 MHz CPU. The Compaq iPAQ features a powerful Intel StrongARM chip that runs at 206MHz. Table 1.2 lists the processor speed and memory specifications of several popular PDAs.

Table 1.2 CPU Speeds and Memory of Mobile Devices

Maker	Device	Processor	Memory	Speed
Palm	Palm VII	Motorola Dragonball	2MB	16 MHz
Palm	Palm Vx	Motorola Dragonball EZ	8MB	20 MHz
Palm	Palm m505	Motorola Dragonball	8MB	33 MHz
Handspring	Visor Prism/ Platinum	Motorola Dragonball VZ	8MB	33 MHz
Compaq	iPaq 3650	Intel StrongARM	32MB	206 MHz
Sony	Clie (with Palm OS 4.00)	Motorola Dragonball VZ	8MB	33 MHz
IBM	Workpad	Motorola Dragonball EZ	4MB	16 MHz
Hewlett Packard	Jornada 548	Hitachi SH3	32MB	133 MHz
Symbol	PPT 2800 (Pocket PC)	Intel SA1100	32MB RAM / 32MB ROM	206 MHz
Symbol	SPT 1733 (Palm OS)	Motorola Dragonball	8MB	16 MHz

Laptop Computers

Laptops have been mobile from the beginning, but they have only recently acquired the capability to be wireless. This is a natural fit. Business travelers typically find themselves spending quite a lot of time in places such as airports, on trains, or in hotel rooms lacking a phone jack. The availability of a wireless connection in these areas immediately makes the time spent there more productive. A traveler can download e-mail or the latest Powerpoint presentation before boarding a plane, work on it en route, then upload again upon touching down.

Several manufacturers, such as IBM, HP, and Apple, have begun shipping laptops with built-in wireless LAN (802.11b) cards, with antennas integrated into the casing. These same manufacturers will soon begin offering Bluetooth-equipped laptops. As Wireless LAN and Bluetooth networks become more common in public spaces, it may soon be possible, in airports and large metro areas, to remain constantly connected to the Internet or your corporate systems, wirelessly. Several major airlines have recently announced plans to provide onboard wireless access, so even the time spent in the air may soon be connected.

The recent introduction of more powerful Pocket PC–powered PDAs opens the possibility that many mobile professionals will forego entirely the weight and bulk of laptops in favor of a wireless PDA, perhaps with a lightweight portable keyboard, as their only computer. Another OS option, Handheld PC from Microsoft, is a step up from Pocket PC, and offers functionality closer to a full-blown laptop system, but in a much more portable, instant-on package. With larger screens, keyboards, and more memory and storage, Handheld PCs are beginning to offer a viable alternative to bulky laptops.

Basic Laptop Properties

Laptops are an established product, and everyone from college students to traveling professionals now uses them. Increasingly, both groups are adding wireless communications options. Although larger and heavier than PDAs, they have the advantage of more power, memory, and storage. Because most all laptops feature at least one PCMCIA (PC Card) slot, this has been the natural way to add wireless connectivity.

- **Connectivity** 9.6 Kbps (mobile phone) to 19.2 Kbps (CDPD) or 11 Mbps (wireless LAN)
- **Screen size** Typically a minimum of 25 cm (10 in.) wide
- **Resolution** Minimum 640 x 480, usually 800 x 600 pixels and higher
- **Memory** Typically 64MB to 128MB
- **Processing power** Typically 450 MHz to 1 GHz

Laptop Connectivity

Because virtually every laptop comes with at least one PCMCIA slot, this is still the most popular method for adding wireless capability. Although you can purchase a cable to connect your laptop to your mobile phone, just like a PDA, at least in the U.S. this is probably a last resort for those outside the coverage areas of other faster options.

The Sierra Wireless AirCard mentioned earlier gives you a wireless connection rated at 19.2 Kbps in most metropolitan areas. Another advantage of the AirCard, or similar models such as the Novatel Merlin, is that you can eject the card from your laptop and stick it straight into your PDA. As with the PDA, a variety of service plans are available, from flat-rate monthly plans to usage-based plans that bill according to how much data you download. In Europe, travelers can get wireless connections of up to 28.8 Kbps using the Nokia Card Phone or a Ubinetics card on the GSM network in their PC Card slot.

Several manufacturers also make Wireless LAN PC cards, allowing you to access your company or home network wirelessly. As mentioned earlier, Wireless LANs are becoming increasingly common in the places traveling professionals tend to congregate. As these connection points become more widespread and corporate MIS departments implement Virtual Private Networks (VPNs), it may soon be possible for mobile professionals to access their corporate network, at LAN speeds, from almost anywhere in most major cities.

Although you can detect the type of device accessing your site, in most cases you won't be able to infer the speed of a visitor's connection from this. Just because your visitor is using a 5.0 browser, doesn't mean they're on a high-speed wired connection. You therefore need to make sure that your content is optimized for low-bandwidth connections. To add to the complication, some desktop browsers can also view WML content. The Opera browser can view both HTML and WML, and Klondike is a dedicated WAP browser for desktop PCs.

Laptop Screen Size, Memory, and Processing Power

Most laptops on the market today have a color screen that allows for at the very minimum 800 x 600 pixel resolution, with most newer models showing 1024 x 768 pixels. You can generally rely on them having enough memory and processing power to run browser-based applications, so from a Webmaster's perspective, you don't need to do anything special to serve content to laptops, apart from being aware that their connection speed may be low.

Convergent and Future Mobile Wireless Devices

The devices we've mentioned so far are all basic variations on established device families—the mobile phone, the PDA, the laptop. As we've shown, each has inherent limitations for mobile wireless use. Next up the rung are convergent devices that seek to merge aspects of each technology. The first devices to take advantage of GPRS will be hybrid phone/PDA units, similar to those currently available in Europe from Mitsubishi and Sagem, or the Kyocera Smartphone sold in the US. Although these hybrids can sometimes compensate for the limitations of single devices, they are still essentially old technology. The Swiss Army Knife approach of trying to force more and more functions into a single device will rapidly run up against basic physical restrictions in devices meant to be small, mobile, and easy to use. Industrial design guru Donald Norman envisions a key ring style solution, where you would have a basic communications module, then add other modules as needed for a desired task. Bluetooth and its concept of a personal area network could very well be the enabling technology that makes this a reality. This would also allow the form of devices to more closely match their function. For instance, most people want a mobile phone to be small, light, and simple to use. Bolting on a PDA seriously compromises all of these attributes. But because your phone is basically a communications module, why not have your PDA use it to provide a wireless connection, using Bluetooth to communicate between the two?

As we move into the future, we can expect to see a variety of convergent devices and technologies. At present, a few mobile phone models break with the traditional vertical form factor of the typical mobile phone. Nokia's Communicator looks at first like a rather chunky phone, but the entire front swings open like a clamshell to reveal a larger horizontal screen and a full, although miniaturized, keyboard. This phone's microbrowser can display both WML and HTML content. A newer version, the Communicator 9210, features a color screen and runs the EPOC operating system from Symbian, bringing it closer to a PDA.

Ericsson's R380 also has a larger screen. When closed, only one end is visible, making it look like a traditional phone, but swing the keypad open, and the display switches immediately to a horizontal, touch-sensitive screen with an intuitive graphical user interface operated with a stylus.

The Kyocera Smartphone takes an innovative approach of combining a phone with a Palm device. When closed, the top half of the screen is visible, and looks like a regular—if somewhat large—phone. But swinging the keypad down reveals a full, but slightly reduced, Palm handheld screen.

Another technology that looks set to change the landscape of mobile phones is Microsoft's new Stinger phone. Microsoft is not making the actual hardware itself, leaving that to several major OEMs, but they have designed a totally new operating system for them. Stinger is first and foremost a mobile phone, with every feature of the interface optimized for one-handed use. But it will also allow users to access the Internet, as well as connect directly to their Outlook inboxes. Stinger relies heavily on Microsoft's Mobile Information Server (MIS), a new enterprise server application designed specifically for the mobile Internet. One interesting feature of MIS that attempts to compensate for the slow data speeds of current networks is the ability to have the server selectively remove certain portions of a piece of content, thus cutting down on the amount of data sent. For instance, if you're on a particularly slow connection and in a hurry, you might choose to have it remove all articles and prepositions from your e-mail messages. It's even possible to remove all white space. While this might initially sound bizarre, condensed e-mails are actually quite readable, at least enough to decide whether you want to download the entire message.

There are also optional modules available for the Handspring Visor PDA that allow you to attach a microphone and speaker to the device, and use it as a phone. As PDAs become more expandable, we can reasonably assume that, provided there is demand for it, more devices will be capable of this cross-functionality.

Occupying a space somewhere between the laptop and a PDA, the Tablet PC is a recent arrival on the scene. Wireless by nature, this is basically a large, touch-sensitive screen, roughly the size of a small laptop screen, and less than an inch thick. Data input is via either handwriting recognition, or an on-screen virtual keyboard. While this device was initially introduced almost a decade ago, it failed then due to a lack of applications, low power, and user-interface problems. With recent advancements in both processors and memory, and new operating systems optimized for the form factor, the tablet is poised to become popular with traveling professionals.

Although all of these devices are innovative in their own way, they still share one underlying paradigm; communication is through visual display, with feedback and interaction with the user interface via touch screen or keypad. This method of interaction, however, isn't optimal or convenient for people who are actually mobile—in motion—as they use the device. One interface technology that looks set to change the face of mobile computing is voice recognition and synthesis. Voice Markup Language (VoiceML) is an XML-compliant markup language that, used in conjunction with a voice server, can enable people to interact with Web sites through voice alone.

Further down the line, no one can say what new devices may emerge once high-speed wireless networks become ubiquitous, and users come to expect and rely on constant connectivity. In several countries, wireless Internet users already outnumber wired users. As Moore's Law continues to drive the size and cost of computing power down, more and more devices—such as cars, refrigerators, utility meters, and personal music players—will begin to sport wireless Net connections. All of these devices will introduce their own unique capabilities and interface requirements to the wireless Web mix. It's impossible to say where this may lead, but one thing is certain: The job of the wireless Webmaster will continue to be new, exciting, and challenging.

Something Old, Something New

Although the devices and technologies of the wireless Internet are new, many things should be familiar to the Webmaster, and most of the skills you've developed to deal with the wired Internet are directly transferable to this new world. For one thing, you'll still be dealing with familiar markup languages. Palm's Web Clipping uses a subset of HTML 3.2, although with a few significant limitations. The browser preinstalled on Pocket PC devices is functionally equivalent to IE 3.2, so it should present no serious challenge to an experienced HTML coder. You can think of a Pocket PC device as a regular browser that just happens to have an extremely small screen (0.25 VGA, in fact).

Probably the most significant change, both in terms of device capabilities and markup, is the introduction of WAP. WAP phones require you to code your content in WML. WML is an application of Extensible Markup Language (XML). If you've kept your skills current, chances are you're already familiar with XML. To a coder familiar with HTML and the requirements of XML in terms of well-formed and valid code, the switch to WML shouldn't be difficult.

What may require some rethinking of your existing applications is that WML uses a new mode of content organization and navigation that differs significantly from the traditional page-based model of the Web. WML organizes content into *decks of cards*, collections of related pages that are downloaded to the client all at once, to minimize slow over-the-air transmissions. One of the problems of the traditional Web is that the same markup can look quite different in different browsers. Each of the major browsers is also quite tolerant of sloppy—or just plain illegal—markup. By contrast, WML, as an application of XML, is required to conform rigidly to the defined standard. Even a slight typo or incorrect tag usage will cause the WAP gateway to refuse to process it, or in extreme cases can even crash the phone. No more sloppy markup!

At least in the first generation of the wireless Internet, you'll need to pay attention to an issue that many Web developers had begun to forget about: slow connection speeds. Quite a few of the mobile devices out there connect at speeds of between 8 Kbps and 19.2 Kbps, slower than even the slowest modem you're likely to find today. (When was the last time you saw a 14.4K modem?) Network congestion and the overhead involved in maintaining the connection probably means that real throughput is significantly lower. This will begin to improve somewhat with the introduction of 2.5G systems such as GPRS. But it's likely that GPRS won't be widely available until at least 2003, and even then speeds are likely to be not much higher than current dial-up—in the 56 to 64 Kbps range. As 3G systems begin to appear towards the middle of the decade, we may finally begin to approach the promised marketing nirvana of wireless broadband, but the wireless landscape is changing so rapidly that it's impossible to say what may or may not be possible by then.

One thing that is likely to be very similar is markup. HTML has proven to be a very adaptable language, scaling from the early days of left-aligned text on a gray background to today's multimedia-rich, highly interactive Web applications, growing all the while to incorporate new and more complex media types. The next evolution of HTML, Extensible HTML (XHTML), with its modular design and capacity to negotiate capabilities with the requesting device, is positioned quite well to be the markup language of choice on both the wired and wireless Web.

WAP and WML may continue to serve a niche role on smaller devices such as mobile phones, although there's some evidence that their role may be diminishing. Japan's NTT DoCoMo service, i-Mode, was one of the most phenomenally successful wireless Internet services from the moment of its launch in 1999. Rather than use WAP, NTT chose to go with Compact HTML (cHTML), a proprietary subset of regular HTML. The advantage is that i-Mode's several million subscribers can visit regular Web sites, not just i-Mode ones, on their small, full-color, always connected handsets. NTT has begun to take significant stakes in several international telecom providers, and recently purchased 16 percent of AT&T Wireless, so there's a fair likelihood that i-Mode may soon be an addition to the wireless Web landscape in the U.S. and Europe.

Old Stuff: The Existing Internet

One of the most impressive things about the Internet—the underlying protocols of which were designed over 40 years ago—is how it has been able to continuously adapt to significant changes in technology and usage. Not very long ago, a user would have required expensive hardware, a large and difficult-to-use computer, and an even more expensive and hard-to-get connection to access the Internet at 300 bits per second. Today, you can surf the Net and retrieve your e-mail at 128 Kbps at 75 miles per hour in a car or train, with an inexpensive PC card in a mobile device, for not much more than the cost of your mobile phone plan. However, the underlying protocols are the same TCP/IP designed by the Defense Advanced Research Projects Agency (DARPA) pioneers in the early 1970s. That TCP/IP has been able to adapt and grow with the increasing demands of the Internet is a testament to the foresight and skill of its early designers.

Both the Palm and Pocket PC use the same HTTP to communicate with your content server. The portion of the connection that travels over the wireless link, known as the air interface, uses different protocols, but these are for the most part invisible to the Webmaster, and have no effect on how you design your content.

HTML has also proven to be extremely adaptable and long-lasting. When Tim Berners-Lee designed it for exchanging technical documents between research labs, he could hardly have imagined that in just a few years people would be cruising graphics-rich Web sites and downloading streaming media in coffee shops, on small portable devices with multiples of the processing power of a standard server of the time. The next evolution of markup, XHTML, is based on the concept of modularity. Instead of all devices having to support the entire standard, a device will be able to tell a server which portions of the standard it is capable of using. Servers would then send only the content appropriate to the device.

Another Web concept that has been maintained in the wireless realm is the browser. Pocket PC–based devices come with a version of Internet Explorer that's almost identical to IE 3.2. Once you take account of the reduced screen dimensions (0.25 of VGA size), coding for these devices is basically the same as for a regular browser. The Document Object Model (DOM) is the same, so most existing JavaScript should work with minimal modifications. There is, however, no support for CSS in the current version. WAP phones use a microbrowser installed on the phones to display WML pages. WAP also specifies a scripting language, WMLScript, which gives you more or less the same capabilities as you have with JavaScript.

New Stuff: Mobile Connectivity

When they designed Wireless Application Protocol, the engineers at Phone.com realized that HTTP had some drawbacks for use over cellular networks. HTTP is a "chatty" protocol, meaning that there is a lot of back and forth communication between the client and server as they negotiate each others' capabilities. Because it is also a sessionless protocol, this means that the connection has to be set up and broken down for each and every communication between the client and server. This leads to a lot of overhead that would slow communications to an unacceptable level over a wireless link. Because wireless links also frequently break, the resulting back and forth to establish communication would be unusable.

To alleviate these problems, they designed WAP, a protocol optimized for wireless transmission. The important thing to remember, for a Webmaster, is that WAP provides for a mapping between all layers of HTTP and the corresponding layers of WAP. This translation is performed transparently by the WAP gateway, so as a Webmaster you really don't have to worry too much about it. You can, for instance, implement secure communications using the Internet-standard Secure Sockets Layer (SSL) simply by having your visitors connect via a URL beginning with *https://*. The WAP gateway will then perform a translation to Wireless Transaction Layer Security (WTLS) before sending data to a wirelessly connected handset.

Currently the microbrowsers installed on mobile phones tend to be proprietary to the handset manufacturer and impossible to change, but in the future the browsers will likely coalesce around a common standard and be user-changeable. In Europe, some phones on the market use Microsoft's Mobile Explorer browser. Symbian, a consortium of companies including Nokia, Motorola, and Ericsson, is developing EPOC, an alternate operating system for mobile phones and other devices. Nokia already has a mobile phone based on EPOC for the U.S. market.

If you've ever analyzed the log files from your Web server, you may have seen reports on the geographic location of your visitors. This is generally a best guess, based on the location of their dial-up ISP connection, and generally can't get much more detailed than listing the closest major city. Beyond that, you generally can't know—or need to know—the exact geographical position of your visitors. However, mobile phones and other devices that communicate via cellular networks do have this capability. Cellular base stations have to know where a phone is in order to route calls. A switched-on phone is constantly communicating with a range of base stations to remain accessible. When a phone enters a particular cell tower's coverage area, it registers with that tower's controlling base station. The Federal Communications Commission (FCC), the agency responsible for licensing wireless carriers in the U.S., has mandated that all cellular networks in the U.S. put in place the capability to locate the exact coordinates of a mobile phone, to within 50 to 150 meters.

Carriers can accomplish this automatic location identification (ALI) by means of handset- or network-based technologies. Network-based solutions work by combining the signals from multiple base stations to triangulate the position of the phone. Handset-based solutions generally embed a GPS chip within the phone. GPS uses a network of satellites to precisely locate the geographical position of a device to within a few meters. The U.S. government's recent declassification of this system allowed small, relatively cheap, dedicated GPS devices to be much more accurate, spawning an entire industry. GPS units are now available as add-ons for most of the major PDAs and laptops. As GPS chip prices fall, expect this technology to disappear inside of these devices, until eventually all mobile devices will be capable of determining their exact physical location and, if their owner permits, communicating this information to the Internet sites they visit.

Developing & Deploying...

Privacy and E911

The impetus behind the FCC's ALI mandate—generally known by the term E911—was to provide emergency services with the ability to determine the location of callers in distress, just as they currently can with wired phones. This would enable fire departments to respond to a motorist trapped in a car wreck, for instance, or enable search and rescue teams to locate lost hikers. By October, 2001 all U.S. carriers are required to put in place technology that allows emergency services to locate the position of a cellular emergency call to within 50 meters for 67 percent of calls and 150 meters for 95 percent of calls for handset-based solutions (or 100 and 300 meters, respectively, for network-based solutions).

Privacy advocates, however, are concerned that this information could also be misused, either by the government and security services, or by marketers. Those concerned with government surveillance liken the ability to track mobile phones to the ankle bracelets used on paroled convicts, raising the specter of a Big Brother government tracking citizens' every move. Others fear that we will be bombarded with e-coupons and other wireless spam. A fast food restaurant might shoot a coupon for a burger and soda to your phone as you approach their location, or a department store might detect that you're in the music department and offer a CD discount coupon. Although these examples

Continued

might be simply annoying, it's a short step to imagining how this information might be misused, especially when it becomes possible for people to track when you're in places you'd rather not have them know you've been. Marketing companies are already notorious for correlating personal data with Web surfing behavior. Adding the ability to track your physical location and movements into this mix raises some serious invasion-of-privacy concerns.

Those charged with responding to emergency calls rightly claim that this information can be vital in saving lives and protecting property. As is the case with many new technologies, we need to balance the needs of public safety against the individual's right to privacy. Several bills have been introduced to require that carriers inform people before making this information known, but the outcome of this legislation is unknown and probably unlikely to satisfy everyone.

You can read the FCC's E911 documentation at www.fcc.gov/e911/.

The purpose of the FCC's E911 mandate was to enable emergency services to pinpoint the location of callers in distress. But wireless entrepreneurs were quick to spot other uses for this information, and a whole industry has sprung up around what has become known as location-based services. A simple example would be that a traveler in a strange city with limited time would pull up a listing of all restaurants within a two-block radius of his location, without having to know where he actually was. Marketers have also proposed the idea that merchants would be able to broadcast a special time-sensitive offer only to shoppers within the immediate area. Because location-based services are still in the formative stages, it's too early to tell whether privacy concerns will allow such applications to flourish, but the capability will be there very shortly, and it will undoubtedly lead to location-based applications we haven't even dreamed of yet.

Moving from a Wired to a Wireless Internet

The shift from the wired to wireless Internet has the potential to be every bit as revolutionary as the shift from print to Internet was. Predictably, it is also following a similar path. In the early days of the Internet, and particularly of the Web, many publishers simply ported existing print content and concepts to the Web. This resulted in a rash of atrocious, and unusable, brochure-ware sites. It has taken us several years to come to the realization that the Web is a new medium, demanding its own style of writing and content presentation. Early Web designers sometimes had difficulty letting go of their print sensibilities and adapting to the unique constraints and possibilities of HTML-based design. We now have a generation of designers whose natural medium is the Web, who understand its unique characteristics, and have no print-world baggage to contend with. Web site usability is an established (although still not always perfect) subject, with well-known practitioners and a wealth of research available.

In many ways, we are once again at that early stage. Most wireless Web sites out there are simply repurposed wired Web sites (or in many cases, exactly the same sites, with no accommodation made for wireless devices at all). Users of the first generation of wireless sites, WAP phone owners, were understandably less than impressed. Usability of most sites was appalling, content was generally unsuitable for the devices, and crashes and dead-ends were frequent.

So how is the wireless Webmaster to approach this problem? The first step is to realize that this is truly a new medium, not simply the same old Internet on new hardware. This consequently requires a change in perspective from a large-screen desktop browser to a small mobile device with limited user-interaction mechanisms and, for now, a slow wireless connection. One key point to keep in mind about wireless users is that they tend to be mobile. This has quite important consequences for how the wireless Webmaster presents both content and user interfaces. In addition to having a small screen and very slow connection, your visitors are most likely going to be using your site while actually moving—whether in their cars or when walking down the street. And, most likely, they'll be using it one-handed while simultaneously engaged in some other activity, whether taking notes or eating their lunches. This is quite a departure from the wired Web, where you can usually assume that your users are sitting comfortably at a large, high-resolution color screen, with a full-size keyboard and mouse.

Rethinking User Interface and Interaction

User-interaction is another area where you will need to rethink a lot of what you learned on the Web. Most current wireless devices have severely constrained interaction mechanisms. Most have touch-sensitive screens, for instance, but this is not the same as a mouse, the standard navigation device on the Web. Consequently, there is no concept of rollovers, one of the most useful—and abused—navigation aids. Data input is also problematic, because most wireless devices don't have keyboards.

Users on mobile phones must enter text by repeatedly pressing a number key. Punctuation characters are even more difficult, and differ considerably from phone to phone. For that reason alone, it's advisable to keep your URLs as short as possible—don't make visitors enter long strings of subfolders just to reach your WAP content, or you may find yourself without any visitors at all. PDA users have it a little easier—they can use either some form of handwriting recognition or a virtual onscreen keyboard. Entering long strings of text is still difficult, however, so the same advice on URLs holds true here.

Probably the main adjustment Webmasters will need to make to the wireless Web is to realize that users of mobile devices need quick access to relevant information only. This is quite different from the wired Web, where users tend to browse for the information they need, and they are content to follow links from a large array of choices. At least for the foreseeable future, you'll need to bear in mind that online time, and downloaded content, costs mobile users serious money. Personalization, discussed in the upcoming section "Adding Personalization," is one way to decrease the amount of time users need to spend searching for the content they need, but just as important is to optimize your user interface to meet the needs and limitations of mobile users.

Obviously quality assurance (QA) testing is important for any Web application, but the sheer variety of mobile wireless devices makes this a crucial task for the wireless Webmaster. It's not enough to convert your site to WML, check it on the WAP Emulator on your desktop, and assume that it looks fine. The degree of flexibility of interpretation allowed within the WAP specification means that content can look and act differently on different handsets. You'll need to test and verify your code on a variety of handsets, through as many carrier gateways as you can. Similarly, Web Clipping applications can look quite different depending on the transcoding proxy server used. On Pocket Internet Explorer, you'll need to test how your content looks with the different view settings and different user preferences. For instance, users may turn off graphics to increase response time, so you'll need to ensure your user interface (UI) is usable in text-only mode.

Recognizing Device Limitations

Just as Web designers eventually realized that people simply couldn't—and wouldn't—read the same amount of text on a cathode ray tube (CRT) screen as on the printed page, you need to realize that the volume of text that works on a Web page just won't be readable on a wireless device, with its limited screen size. Some early wireless Web tools offered to translate your content on the fly to wireless formats, but this approach simply doesn't work. Content will need to be specifically edited and formatted for small screens and wireless interfaces.

Many Webmasters have already come to the realization that the best way to deal with differing browser capabilities, and build a truly scalable Web site publishing system, is to completely separate content from presentation. This approach is one that will benefit those intending to publish wireless content; in fact, it may be a requirement, to deal with the constantly expanding variety of wireless devices. Cascading Style Sheets (CSS) was one good approach to this on the Web. However, most current wireless devices don't support CSS, so developing server-side solutions will be necessary. XML, coupled with some form of device detection, may be the answer to this particular problem. Before you cringe, thinking of the enormous task of formatting separate content for every wireless device out there, the good news is that most of these fall into just a few families of device types, so you won't need to worry about coding for particular device models. As a bare minimum, you might want to consider detecting and formatting for WAP, Palm OS, and Pocket PC.

Adding Personalization

Personalization on the wired Web has been used mostly as a tool for marketing. On the wireless Web, personalization takes on a new meaning and importance. To deal with slow connections and limited power, it makes sense to send a wireless user only the information she needs at any particular time, rather than making her select from among a huge array of mostly irrelevant choices. For instance, if a visitor to your traffic information site repeatedly asks for the traffic conditions on the Interstate 5/Interstate 90 intersection, presenting that choice at the top of the listings on his next visit makes sense. Because he also probably works in either Seattle or Bellevue, reordering subsequent choices—filtering locations in the Pacific Northwest to the top and favoring those in the Seattle region—would probably be helpful.

Location information is one emerging area where you can use personalization to offer an enhanced user experience. A typical Web application to search for a restaurant might first make the visitor choose a state, then a city, then an area, and then a culinary style. However, if you already know, from data supplied by my device, that I'm in New Orleans, Louisiana, then why not move that choice to the top, even if Alabama comes first alphabetically. Taking that a step further, if you know from my usage patterns that I have a fondness for Thai cooking, why not start my listings with Thai restaurants in the XXX area of New Orleans? Tools and application server software are already available to enable this sort of learning or adaptive interface on Web sites, but wireless access makes this a priority.

Above all, the major shift in perspective required of the wireless Webmaster is to realize that you're authoring for a mobile audience, not just mobile devices. Rather than simply using portable devices, visitors to your site may actually be on the move, whether walking down the street or in a vehicle. They're probably not donating 100 percent of their attention to the screen, and likely only have one hand for navigation. In this situation, the browsing model of the wired Web will not work. Users need simplified, quick access to just the information they need, in a concise format that downloads quickly. This is not simply a matter of shortening text and optimizing graphics; successful mobile Web sites need to provide mobile users immediate access to just the information they need, when they need it, from anywhere and from any device.

Summary

The wireless Web represents a revolution in access to online information that will have profound impact on our society—greater even than the Internet revolution of the past decade. Although the skills learned by Webmasters over the short but tumultuous life of the Web will provide a solid foundation for this new world, new skills will have to be developed and some old habits changed.

The sheer variety of different mobile devices is the first big change a Webmaster will have to deal with, making the "browser wars" of the last few years seem like child's play. However, you'll find that devices fall into a few general families with similar characteristics, simplifying the presentation task somewhat. Device detection, coupled with on-the-fly, server-side generation of markup is one way to solve this problem. Here, XML transformed to appropriate markup via XSL, provides a future-proof option.

How users connect to your site can be as important as which device they use. The majority of current mobile devices are limited to wireless speeds of between 9.6 Kbps to 19.2 Kbps, with few exceptions. These connections are also inherently unreliable, with long call setup times and latency. You'll need to modify your content and navigation to compensate for these limitations. The *walled garden* approach of carriers, coupled with the inevitable backlash against WAP when users discovered it didn't live up to the early hype, has left a lot of users disillusioned with WAP, but newly available wireless options for PDAs and laptops have revived interest in mobile computing. With the huge surge in interest in wireless data services—particularly from corporate users—carriers continue to offer newer and faster connectivity options. 2.5G services such as GPRS are already being rolled out worldwide, and we can look forward to the much higher data speeds of 3G introducing a world of broadband wireless within the next two to four years.

For the purposes of the wireless Webmaster looking to provide content for mobile users, mobile wireless devices can be classified into three families: mobile phones, PDAs, and laptops. Mobile phones have tiny screens and slow data speeds—9.6 Kbps is the current top speed on most networks. User interaction is difficult, requiring users to enter data with a nine-key numeric keypad. However, these are still the most prevalent wireless devices in circulation. In the U.S. and Europe, WAP is the predominant means of delivering Internet content to mobile phones. WAP compiles content to optimize transmission over wireless connections, but it is still slow and difficult to use on current networks. Japan has had huge success with a similar service called i-Mode, but as yet this doesn't seem to have made much impact outside of Japan.

PDAs are a step up in functionality, providing relatively larger screens, color display, and support for both handwriting recognition and virtual keyboards. Currently, PDAs are split into the subclasses of either Palm OS or Pocket PC, each of which has different display capabilities, memory, and processing power. PCMCIA and Compact Flash modems are widely available for both varieties of PDA, offering data speeds up to 19.2 Kbps or even 28.8 Kbps.

The same wireless options available to PDA users also offer the possibility of wireless Internet access to laptop users. Here, users have the benefit of large, full-color screens and full keyboard/mouse interaction, but you'll still need to be aware of their relatively slower data speeds and adapt your content to suit.

The mobile wireless landscape is in a state of rapid flux, with new devices announced almost monthly. Hybrid devices attempt to combine the mobility and voice capabilities of mobile phones with the organizational capabilities of PDAs. Unfortunately, these tend to compromise the capabilities of each. Microsoft Stinger is one device to watch, although its impact is still uncertain. Tablet PC holds some promise as a next-generation mobile device, but is not yet available to end-users. Voice interaction is another emergent technology that could radically affect the job of the wireless Webmaster.

Despite the wide range of new devices and connection options, a certain amount of overlap still exists with the skills Webmasters have developed on the wired Web. HTML, with some modifications, is still a very viable option for both Pocket PC and Palm OS PDAs, and WML should present no major problems for a competent Web coder. XHTML, XML, and XSL are the next evolution in markup, and wireless Webmasters would do well to become proficient in these technologies. Location-based services are another new area worth exploring, utilizing technologies such as GPS to customize content for a users physical location. Personalization is another option for users with less time and limited screen sizes and access speeds.

Perhaps the largest change required of Webmasters is to adapt UI and presentation to suit the different needs of mobile users, who need rapid access to targeted information, rather than the browsing paradigm of the wired Web. In most cases, this means rethinking both content presentation and user interaction, rather than simply formatting with a new markup language. QA testing is important, to ensure a satisfactory user experience.

Solutions Fast Track

Explaining Wireless

☑ The emphasis on mobility is one of the defining characteristics of this new wireless paradigm, and from a Webmaster's point of view this mobility, not simply the lack of wires, is likely to be the most important aspect you have to deal with.

☑ Low bandwidth, differing standards, multiple network carriers, and a multitude of radically different devices means that the job of the wireless Webmaster just got immensely more complicated.

Types of Wireless Connectivity

☑ The Wireless Application Protocol (WAP) is the first widely available method of accessing Internet content from a mobile device. WAP gateways enable legacy browsers to understand WML content. However, due to differences in the WAP gateway configuration, and the particular microbrowser installed on the handset, a WAP page may display differently on different handsets.

☑ With Short Message Service (SMS), users can send short text messages to each other at a fraction of the cost of a voice call. SMS can also be used to send configuration settings to your phone. SMS is a huge success in Europe, and it is gradually becoming available on U.S. wireless phone plans, although in a limited fashion.

☑ Japan's NTT DoCoMo mobile data service i-Mode offers users the ability to browse a huge range of Web sites with cheap, full-color handsets that maintain an always-on connection to the Internet. It could possibly become an alternative to WAP but currently is in use only in Japan.

☑ The European wireless standard, Global System for Mobile Communications (GSM), is available on a limited basis in the US. The General Packet Radio System (GPRS) will soon offer higher data speeds and an always-on connection worldwide; it is already available in some European countries, and on a trial basis in a few U.S. cities.

- ☑ A recent option for wireless connectivity in the U.S. is Cellular Digital Packet Data (CDPD), a packet-switched network this is an always-on connection. The major drawback of CDPD is limited availability.
- ☑ The 802.11b standard has found ready acceptance as a short-range radio replacement for traditional Ethernet connections. Bluetooth is another short-range wireless standard.

Evolving Mobile Devices

- ☑ The three main categories of mobile devices, mobile phones, PDAs, and laptop computers, are differentiated by connectivity, screen size, memory, and processing power.
- ☑ Data-capable phones use the WAP protocol, and content needs to be coded in Wireless Markup Language (WML). They have minimal requirements for memory and processing power. A mobile phone never communicates directly with your Web server; there is always a WAP gateway acting on its behalf (the gateway may alter the content somewhat on its way through).
- ☑ The market for Personal Digital Assistants (PDAs) is split mainly between those running the Palm operating system from both Palm, Inc. and its licensees, and devices based on Microsoft's Pocket PC or Windows CE. One feature of Pocket PCs that's especially relevant to wireless is that most come with an industry-standard expansion slot, either CF or PCMCIA Type II.
- ☑ PDAs come in a wide range of configurations of connectivity, screen size, memory, and processing power.
- ☑ Several manufacturers have begun shipping laptops with built-in wireless LAN (802.11b) cards, with antennas integrated into the casing. These same manufacturers will soon begin offering Bluetooth-equipped laptops. However, with larger screens, keyboards, and more memory and storage, Handheld PCs are beginning to offer a viable alternative to bulky laptops.
- ☑ Also, several devices are available that seek to combine aspects of each category—a mobile phone with an integrated Palm screen, PDAs that can be used as phones, and laptop-size devices without keyboards that you use by writing directly on the screen.

Something Old, Something New

- ☑ TCP/IP has been able to adapt and grow with the increasing demands of the Internet; both the Palm and Pocket PC use the same HTTP to communicate with your content server; and HTML has also proven to be extremely adaptable and long-lasting. Another Web concept that has been maintained in the wireless realm is the browser.
- ☑ WAP provides for a mapping between all layers of HTTP and the corresponding layers of WAP. This translation is performed transparently by the WAP gateway, so as a Webmaster you really don't have to worry too much about it.
- ☑ Microbrowsers installed on mobile phones tend to be proprietary to the handset manufacturer and impossible to change, but in the future it's likely that they will coalesce around a common standard, and be user-changeable.

Moving from a Wired to a Wireless Internet

- ☑ The new wireless medium requires a change in perspective from a large-screen desktop browser to a small mobile device with limited user-interaction mechanisms and, for now, a slow wireless connection.
- ☑ Probably the main adjustment Webmasters will need to make to the wireless Web is to realize that users of mobile devices need quick access to relevant information only.
- ☑ You'll need to test and verify your code on a variety of handsets, through as many carrier gateways as you can. Similarly, Web Clipping applications can look quite different depending on the transcoding proxy server used. On Pocket Internet Explorer, you'll need to test how your content looks with the different view settings and different user preferences.
- ☑ The best way to deal with differing browser capabilities, and build a truly scalable Web site publishing system, is to completely separate content from presentation.

Frequently Asked Questions

The following Frequently Asked Questions, answered by the authors of this book, are designed to both measure your understanding of the concepts presented in this chapter and to assist you with real-life implementation of these concepts. To have your questions about this chapter answered by the author, browse to **www.syngress.com/solutions** and click on the **"Ask the Author"** form.

Q: What are Tri-Band mobile phones?

A: Tri-Band phones are typically available on the GSM system. Two different frequencies are used on the continent. Almost all European phones are Dual-Band, which automatically sense and switch to the appropriate frequency. Tri-Band phones add the capability to work on the totally different GSM frequencies used in the US. Although not widespread yet, GSM is offered by several carriers in the U.S. A Tri-Band phone allows international travelers to use the same phone both in the U.S. and Europe.

Q: Do I need a special WAP server to deliver WML pages?

A: No, the connection to your server is just a standard HTTP request. You can serve this request with any regular Web server—IIS, Apache, and so on. You will have to configure MIME type settings on the server, so that it knows what to do with pages with a .wml extension.

Q: If I code for the Palm Pilot—will the Visor be able to see the same thing?

A: Yes, the Handspring Visor, as well as the Sony Clié and other devices running the Palm OS, should display your pages identically, provided that your markup is error-free.

Q: My Web site is heavy in tables—will it display on PDAs?

A: Palm Web Clipping does not support nested tables. Any <TABLE> tags beyond the first one will be ignored, giving a result that's rarely what you intended. Pocket PC devices can display much more complicated table structures, but remember that the maximum viewable width is 240 pixels, unless you want your visitors to have to scroll both horizontally and vertically.

Q: Why do wireless devices get their transmissions cut off?

A: Wireless devices must be within a certain distance of a base station to pick up a strong enough signal. They can lose this signal if they move outside the coverage area of the base station or if they enter the radio shadow of a large building.

Q: If I program in Web Clippings—will it show up in other PDAs?

A: Yes, because Web Clipping pages are basically HTML 3.2, they will generally display relatively well on other PDAs. However, if you use the Palm-proprietary method of compiling graphics into the Web Clipping Application, these will not show up.

Q: Will I have to learn different programming if i-Mode comes to the U.S.?

A: I-Mode uses a subset of HTML called Compact HTML (cHTML). Anyone familiar with HTML should have no problem learning this. However, there are signs that the industry may move towards XHTML as the preferred markup language for these devices.

Chapter 2

Wireless Architecture

Solutions in this chapter:

- Components of a Wireless Network
- Adjusting the Metaphor for the Wireless Internet
- Accepting the Challenge of WAP-Enabled Devices
- Adopting Wireless Standards
- Noting the Market for Wireless Browsers and Other Applications

☑ Summary

☑ Solutions Fast Track

☑ Frequently Asked Questions

Introduction

Computer systems are in a constant state of evolution. Consider just the aspect of how we have gotten computers to interact with each other. The first large mainframe computers ran software locally and required the operator to be physically present. As computer networks gained popularity, a new client-server type of application emerged; as developers, we were then required to build software that not only communicated with the end user, but another computer system as well. Over time, developers realized that talking to multiple remote computers is only slightly more difficult than talking to just one, and multiple tier architectures were born. It is not uncommon today to see an application that requires the availability of at least two other computers in order to run.

The mobile Internet is about to change the way we think about Internet applications. Not only do all these devices communicate via different markup languages, but they also don't use the underlying protocol of the Internet: TCP/IP. The mobile world introduces a new type of component, the *gateway* that sits between these two disparate networks and enables them to communicate. But they don't just translate information, they help our small, memory-constrained mobile devices participate on the Internet by validating content before it is sent to them and storing information that they do not have enough space to accommodate.

We look at how the mobile world is set up and what you need to learn in order to take advantage of this exciting new medium. We look at the role of a Wireless Application Protocol (WAP) gateway, the requirements of a WAP server, and various client technologies. We also examine some of the competitors to WAP and identify the ways in which they are better or worse at handling mobile data. Our look at wireless architectures would not be complete without an overview of wireless communications standards and how they affect the performance of your data application.

Components of a Wireless Network

The mobile wireless standard with the most momentum behind it is the Wireless Application Protocol. WAP standards are governed by members of the WAP Forum (www.wapforum.org), an organization started by Nokia, Ericsson, Motorola, and Openwave. Membership in the WAP Forum is open to anyone, but device manufacturers and network operators are the only members eligible to nominate and vote on officer appointments. The WAP specification covers all aspects of building a wireless application including WAP server requirements, recommendations for how a WAP client should display markup, what tasks a WAP gateway handles, and all the protocols and markup languages in between. The average wireless application developer uses only a small percentage of these specifications daily, but understanding the entire picture is crucial to developing a compelling application for users.

A typical wireless solution has three pieces: the WAP browser (client), the Web server (WAP site), and the WAP gateway, as illustrated in Figure 2.1. Web developers will recognize the first two. The WAP gateway is used to translate between the new wireless protocols and the existing Web protocols of the Internet. Let's take a look at the role and uses of each of these pieces.

Figure 2.1 The Three Tiers of WAP

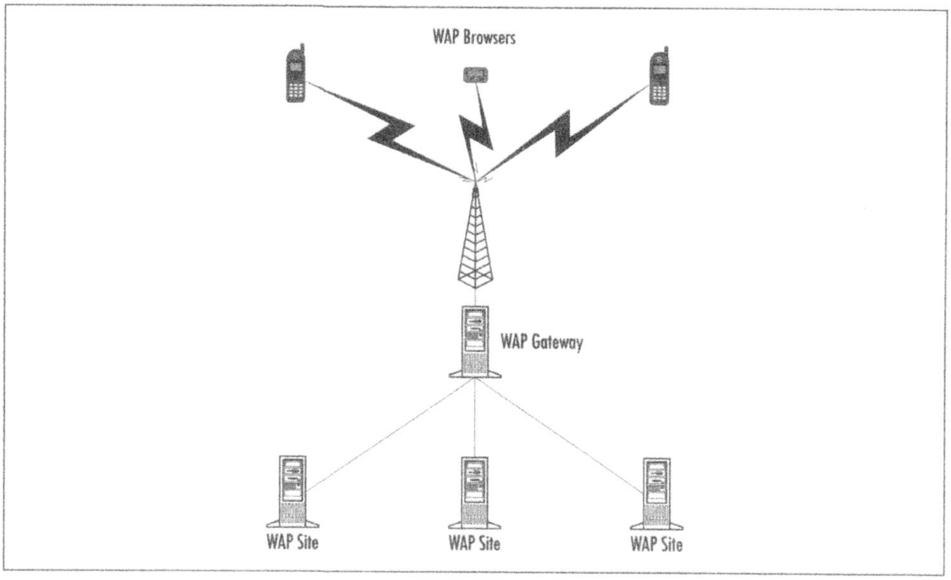

The WAP Browser

The WAP browser is what most people think of when they hear the term *wireless data*. Just like the Web browser is the interface to the Web, the WAP browser is the interface to the wireless Internet. A WAP browser is typically run on a handheld device with limited capabilities (small screen size, limited memory, a slow connection to the Internet) and therefore does not support many of the features of a standard Web browser. You will see in Chapters 3 and 4 that these limitations are counterbalanced by the usefulness of being integrated with a mobile phone.

The WAP Gateway

The WAP gateway is responsible for translating the wireless protocols to standard Internet protocols and vice-versa. This allows the mobile device to communicate with servers on the Internet but use a protocol that is optimized for wireless communication. The WAP gateway also verifies and compiles WML source files to a more compact form that reduces the amount of data that has to be transferred over the slower wireless network.

A variety of WAP gateway products are available on the market today. Commercial versions are available from a variety of companies—Nokia, Openwave, and Ericsson all develop and sell their own gateway solutions. Open source solutions are available also. The most widely known open source WAP gateway project is Kannel (www.kannel.3glab.org). You can try out almost every one of these gateway products because most commercial gateways have a trial license available.

You do not need to install a WAP gateway to make your mobile site publicly available. Most often, it is the network operator that will install and maintain WAP gateways. The gateway is merely the server that translates between the wireless and land-line worlds. Most network operators provide a dial-up service that enables the mobile data user to connect to the Internet via WAP.

Corresponding WAP Protocols

WAP devices use a new set of protocols, created by the WAP Forum, that cater to the strengths and weaknesses of the wireless environment. Table 2.1 shows the Internet/Web protocol and its corresponding WAP protocol.

Table 2.1 Corresponding Internet/Web and WAP Protocols

Internet/Web Protocol	WAP Protocol
HTTP (Hypertext Transfer Protocol)	WSP/WTP (Wireless Session Protocol/Wireless Transport Protocol)
TCP/IP, UDP/IP	WDP (Wireless Data Protocol)
SSL/TLS (Secure Sockets Layer/Transport Layer Security)	WTLS (Wireless Transport Layer Security)
HTML (Hypertext Markup Language)	WML (Wireless Markup Language)
JavaScript/ECMAScript	WMLScript

Understanding Information Flow through the Gateway

WAP devices tend to have slower processors and less memory than most traditional Internet clients. The WAP gateway, on the other hand, is usually a fairly fast server machine with a considerable amount of RAM. The task of browsing is therefore split between the WAP browser and the WAP gateway. Figure 2.2 shows the flow of information between the WAP browser, WAP gateway, and WAP site, which results in the verification and compilation of the WML.

1. The browser requests a URL from the gateway via WTP.
2. The gateway requests the URL from the WAP site via HTTP.
3. The site sends the WML deck indicated by the URL to the gateway via HTTP.
4. The gateway validates the WML deck it receives to ensure that it doesn't contain any syntax errors. If it finds errors, it simply sends a WML deck containing an error message to the browser. If it doesn't find any errors, the gateway sends a compiled version of the WML deck to the browser. (We look at gateways in more detail in Chapter 10.)

Figure 2.2 Information Flow in a WAP System

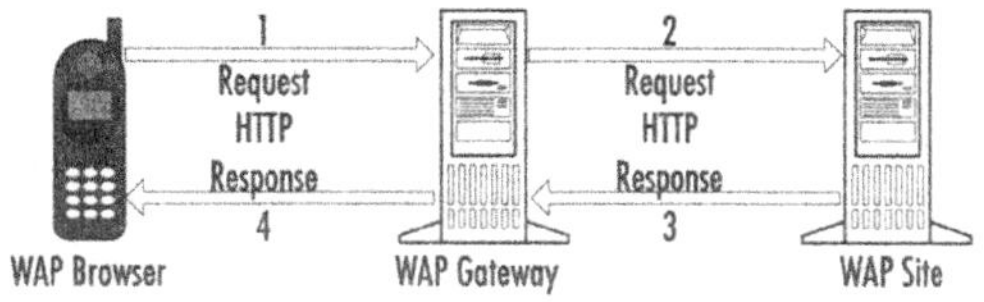

The Web Server

You can use any traditional Web server—such as Apache (www.apache.org), Microsoft SiteServer (www.microsoft.com/siteserver), or iPlanet (www.iplanet.com)—to deliver a WAP site. All you need to do is configure the server to send out the MIME types shown in Table 2.2 when WAP content is requested. Step-by-step details on configuring Apache and Microsoft SiteServer are available in Chapter 8.

Table 2.2 MIME Type Additions for Web Servers

Type of File	MIME Type Your Web Server Should Generate
WML (.wml extension)	text/vnd.wap.wml
Compiled WML (.wmlc extension)	Application/vnd.wap.wmlc
WMLScript (.wmls extension)	text/vnd.wap.wmlscript
Compiled WMLScript (.wmlsc extension)	Application/vnd.wap.wmlscriptc
Wireless Bitmap Image (.wbmp extension)	Image/vnd.wap.wbmp

You can use application servers or CGI scripts to generate WAP content—just make sure that you have the script send out the appropriate MIME type for the content you are sending.

Adjusting the Metaphor for the Wireless Internet

The wireless Internet must not be viewed as a wireless version of the existing Internet and Web. In the early days of the Web, companies built Web sites that were merely versions of their print advertising placed online. As these companies were taught the advantages of the Web, they started using features that were not available to them in print publications, such as daily updates, targeted information, and user feedback. The wireless Internet has many of the same capabilities as the Web but also imposes some new limitations, such as small screen sizes, awkward text entry through the use of a number pad, and slow connection speeds. You must take these limitations and the manner in which the user will be accessing your site into account when building your wireless solution.

Translating your Web offering directly into a WAP solution will usually yield a user experience that is not only less than optimal, but probably quite difficult to use. What content you offer on your mobile site, how the user navigates around, and the amount of feedback the user can be expected to give require a complete re-evaluation of how you are attacking the problem. A mobile user is after a specific piece of information and is not going to browse through a WAP site with the same leisure as he does a Web site. Every moment a WAP user spends online is another minute of access they have to pay for. If you don't provide a quick and easy way to find the information the users are after, they will go to another site that does. You need to be open to new ideas and remember that what works in the Web world won't necessarily work in the mobile Internet world.

Considering the Mobile User

The first thing to consider when building any solution is the user. The mobile user is quite different from the user of your traditional Web site, even if it is the same person! A mobile user is seeking an answer to a question—she wants to receive movie listings, make reservations at a restaurant, or find the nearest gas station. Typically, the mobile user isn't interested in *browsing* your site as much as using it to find a specific piece of information—browsing is done on computer with a 17-inch monitor and a full keyboard.

The mobile user is also in a hurry. Openwave (then Phone.com) has presented the results of a study that found that for every click you require a mobile user to perform, you lose 50 percent of your site's audience. These are impatient people on a slow connection, and you must ensure that you get them the information they are looking for as quickly and effortlessly as possible, or your competitor will end up with your customers.

Complementing Your Web Offering

Just because the wireless Internet is currently limited, it doesn't mean that your complete Internet presence has to be. There are tremendous opportunities in tying your Web site and WAP site together in a way that benefits the user. Reserve the time-consuming tasks for the Web site and the quick access to information for your WAP site. For example, if you require a login to access your site, let the mobile user enter a minimal amount of information when signing up through the WAP site and then require them to enter more detailed information the next time they visit your Web site. Keeping your WAP site simple will keep your customers happy and encourage them to come back.

Accepting the Challenge of WAP-Enabled Devices

The largest difference between the wireless Internet and the wired Internet is in the devices used to access them. A Web developer has a fairly standard set of criteria that they assume their user's computer will fulfill, but a wireless developer has no such luxury. The devices used to access WAP services vary quite substantially, from a small mobile phone, to a palm-size PDA, even (rumor has it) a WAP browser in a television. You can see that you have quite a challenge ahead of you.

The situation is made even more complex when you realize that each device can have different versions of the same browser, and some even allow the user to install a third-party browser! The good news is that there are some assumptions you can make as well as some ways to determine device capabilities.

Determining Device Capabilities

The first difficulty you will encounter when designing for a WAP device is in figuring out the screen size and capabilities you can assume that your end user will have. The official stance is that you shouldn't design your application for specific capabilities, but should instead concern yourself with delivering compelling data and let the browser decide the best way to display the data to the end user. This approach has been tried and rejected many times (Java AWT and early versions of HTML are prime examples), but the limited visual control of current versions of WML coupled with the difficulty of upgrading browsers once they are deployed may allow this attempt to succeed. To give you an idea of just how varied WAP devices are, Figure 2.3 shows popular browsers displaying the same WML deck.

Figure 2.3 Device Variation in Displaying the Same WML Deck

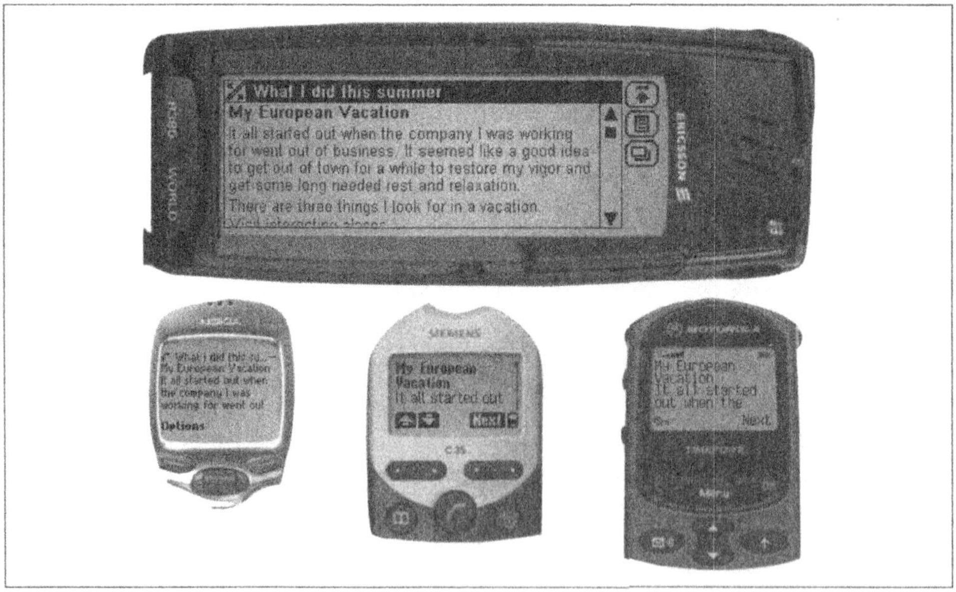

As you can see, there is quite a variation in rendering. The good news is that the WAP specifications do give some general guidelines that you can assume about a device that will be browsing your WAP site. These may not always apply, but they are a good rule of thumb.

- **Display size** Smaller screen size and resolution. A small mobile device such as a phone may only have a few lines of textual display, with each line containing 8 to 12 characters.
- **Input devices** A limited, or special-purpose input device. A phone typically has a numeric keypad and a few additional function-specific keys. A more sophisticated device may have software-programmable buttons but may not have a mouse or other pointing device.
- **Computational resources** Low power CPU and small memory size; often limited by power constraints.
- **Narrowband network connectivity** Low bandwidth and high latency. Devices with 300 bps to 10 Kbps network connections and 5 to 10 second round-trip latency are not uncommon.

Version 1.2 and higher of the WAP specification provide a mechanism for the device to tell the server what capabilities it has, both inherent in the device as well as user preferences, for custom tailoring of content for that device. This specification is called User-Agent Profiling (UAProf) and is currently not adopted by many device manufacturers. This will hopefully change in the future.

Testing Your Application on Various Devices

The old Java joke of "Write Once, Test Everywhere" is now a reality for wireless developers. At least 40 different mobile devices with WAP browsers are on the market, and each one has its peculiarities that must be accounted for. The task of testing wireless applications is complex enough that companies such as Encerca (www.encerca.com) are offering wireless testing services to developers who wish to remain focused on developing their application and let somebody else keep up with the variations in wireless data devices.

Thoroughly testing a mobile application for interoperability is an extremely large task. Testing a traditional Web site could be done by using a Macintosh, Windows, and Linux machine, each with various versions of Netscape Navigator and Microsoft Internet Explorer installed. You then had most of the browsers that would be run by your user base in one place where they could easily be used to test your Web site. WAP browsers, however, vary quite a bit in the way they display data and interact with the user. You would have to purchase each mobile phone and WAP browser to ensure the same level of interoperability.

The most important thing to keep in mind when testing for interoperability is that WAP is not a layout language. The tags are very general and do not give you, as the developer, much control over how content will be laid out on the screen. The WAP specification explicitly says in many places that the actual implementation is left up to the manufacturer. This is kept from getting out of control because although the specification leaves the visual implementation up to the manufacturer, they leave very little confusion as to how the browser should function in any situation. Thus, the display will vary quite a bit, but the action will be performed the same on every browser.

Testing is made even more difficult because the gateway you are going through has an effect on the data the device receives. Some gateways compile WML to smaller files than others, and you may see your application stop functioning on the device merely because you changed the gateway you are using. Also, the current emulators do not behave as the actual devices and thus cannot be used to guarantee that your application works. The only true way to test your application is to try it with every device on every network. You can do this yourself or hire a testing company to do it for you.

Adopting Wireless Standards

Many technologies are competing to become the winning wireless standard, and each of them has their own merits. The unfortunate side effect is that you must learn and use a variety of technologies that are related but not always similar. The good news is that WAP is the most dominant technology at the moment; you can safely use it for the initial version of your mobile site and then roll out other technologies as time permits. For developers targeting the United States market, most devices are using the Openwave browser version 3.*x*, which does not support WML natively. The WAP gateway can translate WML to Openwave's proprietary HDML, but in some situations no equivalent HDML construct exists for a given WML construct.

Choosing what technology to use is a difficult one and must be carefully evaluated by determining the devices used by your target audience. If you are building an application to be deployed on a United States network operator's portal, you will want to build your application in HDML. In fact, many of them will require that you do. Most mobile phone manufacturers and network operators are openly supporting WAP and will eventually migrate to it if they are not using it today.

The safest route is to adopt the open standards that device manufacturers around the world are—WAP. You can build your WAP application in such a way that it will still work on the Openwave 3.*x* browsers using Openwave's gateway translation. This will allow you to have a site that is available on older United States mobile phones that use the Openwave 3.*x* browsers and the next generation of WAP-compliant handsets.

Options in Markup Languages

You have many options for building a wireless site, but many of them will limit you to one or two devices that can be used to view them. The language that will get you the widest audience worldwide is WAP, but you may have a user base that all have devices that support another one of these languages and can therefore use them.

Developing & Deploying…

Introducing XHTML

Not only is the markup language of choice for mobile applications going to change, but also the World Wide Web is evolving to a new format called XHTML. If your application embeds various markup language constructs into your data, you could end up with some incredible difficulties later on.

Store all of your data in a format that does not tie you to your presentation: XML, SQL database with tight restrictions on the content, or any other format you would like. You can then produce whatever presentation markup language you like.

You can do this a few ways. You can use Extensible Stylesheet Language Translations (XSLT) to translate one XML document style into another, allowing you to generate WML from a set of data results that was sent to you in a different XML document. You can use the same tools you use to build HTML Web sites as well—PHP, JSP, and ASP are all quite capable of generating a well-formed XML document.

XHTML is the language being adopted by both Web and WAP browsers, so being prepared to publish XML-formatted data ensures that your system will not be made obsolete by the next generation of markup languages. It is much harder to do and takes a lot more effort up front, but you will be glad you did when the next big technology comes out and you don't have to start over to take advantage of it.

Wireless Markup Language

Wireless Markup Language (WML) is the markup language for WAP implementations. The WAP standard also dictates a scripting language (WMLScript) to complement it. You should use WMLScript if you are trying to reach the general public because it is the most wide-reaching language available on the market today. It is optimized for low-bandwidth connections and small screens.

Compact HTML

Compact HTML (cHTML) is the markup language for the Japanese-based i-mode service. It is a stripped down version of HTML and is served from standard Web servers just like HTML, WML, and others. The inventor of i-mode, NTT DoCoMo, is making the technology available worldwide and trying to make it compete with WAP as the standard of choice for mobile users.

Web Clipping

Palm, Inc.'s Palm VII PDA was the first device to use Web Clipping technology. It uses a simplified version of HTML 3.2 and can be served from any standard Web server. Web Clipping is part of a Palm Query Application (PQA), which is discussed in the next section in more detail (Palm, Inc. is now referring to PQAs as Web Clipping Applications [WCAs]). You can find more information on Palm's Web Clipping in Chapter 6.

Handheld Device Markup Language

Handheld Device Markup Language (HDML) is a predecessor to WML that was created by Openwave. HDML was intended to be an open standard, but Openwave joined the WAP Forum and helped them push WAP as a standard for mobile communication. Therefore, only Openwave browsers can read HDML content. You will find the largest concentration of Openwave browsers installed on mobile phones in the U.S.

Using Wireless Networks and Their Evolving Generations

The network protocols are classified as to their approximate location on the evolutionary path. The first generation was Analog Mobile Phone System (AMPS) and is mostly regarded as obsolete, although many rural areas in the United States continue to only have analog coverage. The second generation (2G) of service (our approximate location on the timeline right now) is digital and only has provisions for accessing data services the same way you do at home, using a modem and a dial-up connection over the particular wireless network you are using. The modem is built into the phone, so you never see it, but it is there. This is often referred to as circuit-switched data because it takes up the entire circuit for your call, even if you don't need it. Examples of 2G networks are Code Division Multiple Access (CDMA), Time Division Multiple Access (TDMA), and Global System for Mobile communication (GSM).

The next logical step would be third generation (3G), correct? Well, not exactly. The infrastructure for 3G is taking longer than expected to build out and companies have made advances in what they can do with the 2G infrastructure to make it more capable of sending and receiving data—thus, two-and-a-half generation (2.5G) technology was born. 2.5G networks are typically higher speed than 2G and are sometimes packet-based allowing an always-on type connection. Packet-based systems behave like a computer network: You can hook up as many people as you would like to the same network, and if the amount of data transferred by everyone is quite low, you will not have a problem. If everyone tries to send or receive a large amount of data at the same time, everyone's connection will be slowed because only a certain amount of data can be sent at once. Global Packet Radio System (GPRS) is a good example of 2.5G technology; it is packet-based and uses the same infrastructure as GSM.

The 3G networks will be rolling out over the next two to three years and promise to provide high-speed, always-on connectivity. There are two competing standards for 3G: Universal Mobility Telephone Service (UMTS) and CDMA2000. Most GSM operators are looking to adopt the UMTS standards in order to continue with the current level of compatibility that GSM users have between various networks today. Ultimately, we may get to a single standard for all mobile devices and be able to travel anywhere in the world while making and receiving calls. Unfortunately, it appears that our near future will still include incompatibilities between networks.

The network operators are not the only important piece in this mobile communications puzzle. Device manufacturers must provide the mobile devices that are capable of taking advantage of these new systems. They are excited about the possibilities are responding to the performance promises of 3G by incorporating color screens and multimedia capabilities into their devices so that we can take advantage of this promised bandwidth when it arrives.

A variety of networks are used around the world, but some generalizations about what technology is adopted where can be made. Europe is mainly GSM, the United States CDMA and TDMA, and Asia is mostly CDMA. The rest of the world uses various networks that depend on the time at which the networks were built and what network operator was interested in building them.

Noting the Market for Wireless Browsers and Other Applications

You can do more than browse the Web on your home computer using your Internet connection: reading e-mail, sending instant messages, and watching real-time entertainment are a few examples of this. Mobile devices are capable of more than just WAP browsing as well—some have POP clients built in for e-mail access or HTML browsers to view the Web. Some of these technologies are just starting to appear and may not be relevant to your wireless development for quite some time, but it's a good idea to be aware of them.

WAP Browsers

A WAP browser is typically installed by the manufacturer of the mobile device and cannot be upgraded by the user. The look and feel of the browser is not dictated by the WAP Forum and usually follows the look and feel of the device it is installed on—navigating between address book entries on your Nokia phone, for example, works the same as moving between pages on a WAP site. This gives the user a consistent experience on a particular device, but not between devices from different manufacturers or even between different models from the same manufacturer.

A WAP browser is responsible for more than just displaying WML decks, it must maintain variables and navigation data such as a history stack. Even when you refer to the basic task of rendering WML decks, the various WAP browsers behave differently—some render all "do" tasks as software-mappable keys on the phone, whereas some always draw graphic buttons on the screen. These variations are all within the rules of the specification and ensure that you will spend many hours testing your WAP application.

The largest market for WAP browsers is mobile phones. The WAP browser is included with the mobile phone software and typically cannot be upgraded or changed aside from bug fixes. This helps the software developer's situation slightly because the WAP browsers that are in use can be identified quite easily, but introduces the much bigger problem that people will have to purchase a new mobile phone in order to get the latest features. The purchase cycle for a mobile phone is quite long, which means that mobile Internet site developers will have to deal with multiple versions of browsers running on various mobile phones for quite some time. This makes the so called "browser wars" between Netscape Navigator and Microsoft Internet Explorer look more like a skirmish.

WAP browsers are also available for a variety of PDAs, and these do not suffer from not being upgradeable like mobile phone WAP browsers do. The extra storage space on a PDA also means that services such as POP-based e-mail can be accessed while you are on the go. Many Web-based e-mail services have provided WAP-based e-mail for their customers as well, so not having a dedicated mail client does not mean that the user will be without e-mail access.

Java2 Micro Edition

"Write Once, Run Anywhere" is the battle cry for Sun and its Java efforts. With Java2 Micro Edition (J2ME), Sun hopes to provide a compelling platform for device manufacturers, application developers, and end users. The device manufacturers will appreciate the low memory and processor requirements, application developers can develop in a language that is quickly becoming universally known, and end users can access the same applications from their Palm Pilot, Nokia phone, Ericsson phone, or any other manufacturer that supports J2ME.

Developing & Deploying...

J2ME

J2ME is fundamentally different from the other technologies listed here. J2ME-enabled devices are able to run applications, called MIDlets, that are stored on the device independent of a network connection. J2ME is a general description of a smaller footprint Java.

J2ME has been further broken down into Configurations and Profiles. The Connected Limited Device Configuration (CLDC) specifies the basic hardware and Java environment requirements for a device to be J2ME compliant under the CLDC specification. (There is also a Connected Device Configuration that doesn't limit processing power and memory as much.) The Mobile Information Device Profile (MIDP) goes into more detail as to what specific Java APIs are available and what the device must support.

The ultimate goal is that a MIDlet written and tested on one Mobile Information Device (MID) will run on any other MID without requiring any modifications. This changes mobile devices from browsers to platforms that can run mobile applications—a much more powerful concept.

i-Mode and cHTML

Just as WAP defines more than just WML, i-mode defines more than just compact-HTML. The i-mode service is packet-based, and the device is always connected to the Internet. This means the user doesn't have to wait for a connection and can use services such as instant messaging to be notified about new e-mail messages or other items of interest. NTT DoCoMo is interested in bringing i-mode services to the rest of the world but has run into some difficulties in trying to do so. The rest of the world will probably never use this technology because the next generation of WAP and 2.5G networks will effectively accomplish the same results.

Palm Query Application

You can probably guess from the name alone that this is a technology unique to PDAs that run the Palm OS. In order to use a Web Clipping site, the user must install a Palm Query Application (PQA) via hot-sync that you, as the site developer, have compiled to include at least the starting page of your application. You can also bundle images and any information that will not change into the PQA so the user will not have to wait on a download over a slow network connection to retrieve these items. The end result is a mobile Internet site that is written in a form of HTML but must be accessed via a special client and must be served up differently than your existing Web site.

Many Palm device users are installing third party WAP browsers on their devices to eliminate this cumbersome burden of preinstalling software for every site they want to visit. PQA capability is not included on all Palm devices. Note, however, that even if you install a WAP browser, you will still be using the Palm.net network to access the Internet. Palm.net uses a paging network and requires coverage by the Palm.net base stations in order for you to access the Internet. Details of how the Palm mobile connectivity works is explained in Chapter 6.

Web Browser

Some device manufacturers are including a Web browser on their wireless devices. You can view normal Web sites using this browser, but it is displayed on your phone or PDA screen. The user experience of these browsers is less than stellar, but users are able to view content that would otherwise be inaccessible.

Microsoft includes Web browsing capabilities in its Mobile Internet Explorer. Including a Web browser is convenient while the mobile Internet is still young because many resources are not yet available as WAP sites. The inclusion of a Web browser allows you to access these sites and get the information you are looking for, even if the content is difficult to read and navigate. Web browsers are a good technology to include while the mobile Internet is just getting started, but they will eventually be replaced by a markup language/browser combination, which will be more suited to these small devices.

Other mobile devices are also gaining connectivity and investigating the best interface to use for their mobile Internet. Palm OS uses a reduced capability Web browser, devices that run the Microsoft PocketPC operating system have Internet Explorer, and SymbianOS has a variety of available Web and WAP browsers. The largest advantage that these types of devices have is the capability to install applications. You can download new types of browsers and decide what you do and don't like.

Short Message Service

The Short Message Service (SMS) allows you to send and receive messages of about 160 characters via your mobile phone using a GSM network. This is a relatively old technology but is still quite popular. Efforts are under way to add multimedia capabilities to SMS and increase the number of bytes that can be sent, effectively removing the "short" from SMS. Many GSM phones allow you to add entries to the address book and send updates to the phone via SMS, making it a much more powerful tool than a simple instant messaging program.

Some other networks allow you to receive text messages, but sending them from your mobile device (called *mobile originate* or MO) is usually not available. This reduces the interest and amount of usage that these services get compared to SMS.

Summary

Although developing for the wireless Internet can seem quite daunting at first because of the variation between devices and technologies, it is not that difficult a task. The designers of WAP wanted any Web developer to feel comfortable building applications using WML and have therefore followed the example set by HTML quite closely. The most difficult transition for Web developers is the strictness of WAP. WAP gateways will not pass your WML deck along to the user if it has any syntax errors. This is a stark contrast to the wired Web world where everything is passed to the browser, and it decides what it can and cannot do. If you say that you have a WML 1.1 file to send to the browser, and you use tags from WML 1.2, the gateway will merely send an error message to your visitor—and you will get no indication on the server.

We have looked at the pieces that fit together to build the wireless Internet, and you should have a good idea of what the roles of each of those pieces are. We will look at each of these technologies in more detail as we progress through the remaining chapters. The most important piece for you to focus on as a wireless developer is the WML markup language and how you can build an engaging WAP site for your customers.

Devices will continue to evolve, and the limitations that we face today may not be around forever. Screen sizes will probably stay about the same (nobody wants a larger mobile phone, after all) but the resolution will increase and we are already seeing color infiltrating the market. As the wireless networks transition to an always-on, high-speed connection, we will be able to take advantage of these increased capabilities in mobile devices.

Many competing technologies are out there, and nobody can guarantee that WAP will ultimately become the only one you need to worry about, but its position in the marketplace looks quite promising.

Solutions Fast Track

Components of a Wireless Network

☑ You can use your existing Web server to provide WAP services with only minor configuration changes.

☑ WAP introduces a gateway between your server and the WAP browser. The gateway helps the limited memory, low bandwidth device browse the Internet by validating WML files and compiling them for quicker transmittal.

Adjusting the Metaphor for the Wireless Internet

☑ Just as the Web required a different approach than print publishing, the wireless Internet requires a different approach than the Web. The capabilities of the mobile device are quite different than that of a desktop computer.

☑ The mobile user is, by definition, on the move and will not tolerate difficult-to-navigate sites or extra fluff that just gets in the way of helping her find what she is looking for.

☑ Your Web site and WAP site should work together to provide an experience that never inconveniences the user. Long signup forms and surveys should be reserved for the Web site, and the WAP site should help the user find the information he is looking for as quickly as possible.

Accepting the Challenge of WAP-Enabled Devices

☑ The form factor and capabilities of WAP devices can vary greatly—ranging from pocket-sized to handheld, and possibly to the size of a large-screen television.

☑ Some components are in place to help you determine device capabilities as they hit your site. These are not pervasive yet, but may be in the near future.

☑ Testing is important. Each device has its own peculiar set of features that make it behave differently from every other browser.

Adopting Wireless Standards

☑ Many wireless standards are out there. Find out what your audience has access to and build your site accordingly.

☑ WAP is the standard that currently has the most momentum, but this could change as companies experiment and roll out other technologies

Noting the Market for Wireless Browsers and Other Applications

- ☑ A variety of applications are available for mobile devices. The one you can almost guarantee will be available is the WAP browser, however.
- ☑ Java2 Micro Edition is poised as an interesting player in the mobile data arena. You can write an application once that can run on any brand of phone and on any network.
- ☑ Old technologies such as SMS are still going strong. Device manufacturers are slowly overcoming the limitations of SMS, and the concept of SMS is being expanded on to include multimedia capabilities.

Frequently Asked Questions

The following Frequently Asked Questions, answered by the authors of this book, are designed to both measure your understanding of the concepts presented in this chapter and to assist you with real-life implementation of these concepts. To have your questions about this chapter answered by the author, browse to **www.syngress.com/solutions** and click on the **"Ask the Author"** form.

Q: Do I need to run my own WAP gateway to let people on mobile devices access my site?

A: You probably do not need to run a WAP gateway. WAP gateways are usually installed by network operators and/or ISPs. You don't need to install a modem pool for people to access your Web site, but some people want the extra privacy that comes along with it. The same holds true for a WAP gateway.

Q: Can I download a browser for my mobile phone?

A: Unlike your home computer, most phones do not let you install software on them. You need extra hardware to support WAP anyway, so downloading a browser wouldn't do you any good. You can, however, download WAP browsers for Palm devices and PocketPC products.

Q: Is it safe to bank on a WAP device?

A: Yes. There is a very finite chance for an attacker to view your data, but he would have to break into your network operator's computer room and then sift through millions of transactions looking for your bank account information before he could do anything with it. The WAP browser will negotiate an encrypted connection using a form of the Transaction Layer Security (TLS) designed specifically for the WAP environment: Wireless TLS (WTLS). You run a larger security risk when you bank by telephone or give your credit card to your waiter to pay for your restaurant bill.

Chapter 3

A New Markup: WML

Solutions in this chapter:

- A Brief History of Wireless Content
- WML Overview
- WML Elements
- Creating WML Content
- WML Editors, WAP SDKs, and Emulators

☑ Summary

☑ Solutions Fast Track

☑ Frequently Asked Questions

Introduction

Telecommunications technology has arrived at the point where we can now access information on the Internet through a mobile cellular device. Wireless Markup Language (WML) is a lightweight markup language specifically created to address the limitations of wireless devices and the rigors placed on the transmission of content over the air through cellular networks. This chapter presents an overview of the core basics necessary to understand the WML markup language. Once you have the basics under your belt, you can go on to take a concise yet thorough examination of the various elements that make up the WML language.

With a thorough understanding of the WML language, you will then take a look at the various approaches you can take to create WML sites that will really shine. The chapter provides an overview of the many software development kits (SDKs), WML editors, and emulators that are available to aid you in the construction of WML sites.

A Brief History of Wireless Content

The *wireless* transmission of data occurred longer ago than one may think. Our ancestors were using sound to transmit primitive coded signals between villages thousands of years ago, transmitting information without any apparent physical connection between source and receiver; and the pioneering work of inventors such as Samuel Morse and Charles Babbage in the 19th and 20th century laid the foundations for the massive worldwide cellular networks we now enjoy.

Similarly, there is more than meets the eye when examining the Wireless Application Protocol (WAP) and specifically, the WML that WAP specifies, because WML has its historical roots in the development of several separate offerings from different vendors.

Developing the Intelligent Terminal Transfer Protocol

The Intelligent Terminal Transfer Protocol (ITTP) was developed by Ericsson in 1995 with the specific aim of allowing network operators to provide enhanced wireless services to their subscribers. ITTP essentially handles the communication between the network-based application and an appropriately equipped mobile phone, however, its limitation is that such services are specific to the network implementing them.

Developing the Handheld Device Markup Language

The Hypertext Markup Language (HTML) necessitates a clear visual and structural reference with which to successfully render content within Web browsers. Much of HTML is unnecessary to users of wireless devices, and with the bandwidth overhead present in current cellular networks, developing wireless content with just HTML doesn't make sense. Much of the HTML would be unnecessary or even useless to the end device. This problem was very much in the minds of Unwired Planet, which in mid-1996 developed the Handheld Device Markup Language (HDML) and made it available to developers.

HDML is a lightweight language designed to allow specially equipped "thin-client" wireless devices to access Internet-based content using the underlying World Wide Web transports and protocols. Unwired Planet submitted their proposal for HDML to the World Wide Web Consortium (W3C) in April 1997. The specification currently stands at version 3.0 and is used extensively in wireless devices in the United States. Although the Extensible Markup Language (XML) had become available around the same time that Unwired Planet submitted HDML to the W3C, at that time the huge potential of XML had yet to be realized, and it was passed over by Unwired Planet as a means of representing wireless content.

Developing the Tagged Text Markup Language

The Tagged Text Markup Language (TTML) was developed by Nokia Corporation as part of its Smart Messaging solution to solve the same problem that Unwired Planet was seeking to address with HDML: accessing Internet-based content from a wireless device.

The Nokia Artus NetGate, (known in the US as the Nokia TTML Gateway) allowed filtered content to be harvested from existing sites and sent to the user's device as a Short Message Service (SMS). The Artus NetGate gateway and an accompanying NetGate compatible phone (the 8110i for enhanced browsing) were announced in March 1997.

Forming the WAP Forum

In 1997, the US network operator Omnipoint Communications asked Nokia and Unwired Planet to apply for the contract to provide wireless content services to Omnipoint. Omnipoint did not want to have to deal with the proprietary solutions that vendors such as Nokia (with Smart Messaging) and Unwired Planet (with HDML) proposed and requested that they work together to provide a single solution. In June 1997, Nokia and Unwired Planet formed the WAP Forum in response to Omnipoint's request, also bringing together Motorola and Ericsson. These initial founders represented over 90 percent of the wireless market. The aim was to develop a protocol that could be built on any platform to allow users to interact with services and information as fast and efficiently as possible. Where HDML dealt with structuring and presenting data to the user, WAP defines a whole series of specifications that deal with every aspect of Internet-based wireless communications, including the language used to describe wireless content. WAP essentially took all that was best from ITTP, HDML, and TTML and combined them in a single series of protocols (with many improvements along the way) to form a single network-independent technology that could be utilized from any appropriately equipped devices.

Combining Languages into the Wireless Markup Language

The WAP Forum examined the various markup languages being offered by the different companies and took the best aspects of each to form the Wireless Markup Language. WML was released by the WAP Forum in 1999 and proved an immediate success—all the handset manufacturers quickly adopted it. Those devices that contained HDML browsers also gained the capability to browse WML content from HDML version 3.1 onwards.

As was noted earlier, when HDML was created, XML was not thought to be a proven technology. However, with the subsequent runaway success of XML, it was obvious that WML would serve developers' needs best if it was formulated as an application of XML.

At first glance, a WML file looks quite similar to an HTML file. WML uses brackets (< and >) to enclose *elements,* and the elements have *attributes* just as HTML does. However, this is where the similarity ends. WML is purely concerned with the structuring of data. It does not specify how the elements should appear on-screen—this is left to the browser, which will render the WML as it sees fit. This was a deliberate move on the part of the WAP Forum, and though sometimes criticized for being too unstructured, it has allowed WML to be used in everything from mobile phones with a tiny two-line display to more sophisticated "Smart Phone" devices such as the Ericsson M280.

WML offers many improvements over HDML, which this chapter covers later when it looks at the specifics of the language. The most important change is that WML, as an application of XML, must abide by the rules that govern the creation of XML documents.

Projecting Future Growth

As with so many Internet standards and technologies, evolution of wireless standards continues at incredible speed. Nippon Telegraph and Telephone (NTT) DoCoMo's i-mode service, a well documented runaway success in Japan, delivers a highly popular service to its subscribers using a subset of the HTML language called compact HTML (cHTML). Roughly equivalent to HTML 3.2 and requiring no extra server software over and above that used for hosting Web sites, developers have been able to supply content without the need to learn complex new protocols.

With such popularity, it might seem safe to say that WAP's days could well be numbered, but this is not so. WAP is a continuously evolving specification and (in line with the continuing development of HTML) is set to embrace XHTML Basic and Cascading Style Sheets (CSS), though WML will continue to be supported. NTT DoCoMo also has indicated it is likely to support XHTML in the future and will thus fall in line with the WAP Forum in ensuring that future developments are as interoperable as possible and will provide a firm mutual base to expand upon.

Commenting on the invention of the telephone in 1876, Western Union said "This 'telephone' has too many shortcomings to be seriously considered as a means of communication." Who could have predicted that the humble telephone would throw off its wire shackles and empower people to receive personal calls from across the globe?

WML Overview

When HTML was first conceived, it was primarily meant to be a way of structuring data so that its creator, Tim Berners-Lee, could more easily find the content he needed. As HTML progressed from version to version, the limitations of a structural markup language became so frustrating that the now near-legendary Netscape and Microsoft HTML extensions were added, allowing the HTML authors to specify what sort of fonts were to be used, in what color, and so on. HTML, together with Cascading Style Sheets (CSS), companion scripting languages, and a whole plethora of XML-based languages is now a very different beast. However, its development into the mature form it takes today has much to do with a return to using HTML for what it was meant to do—structure content. Similarly, WML seeks to provide structure (and therefore meaning) to content. As mentioned earlier, the use of tags and attributes shows a similarity with HTML, but this is a language that was developed from the ground up for use on *wireless* devices, an environment which has many limitations concerning what content can be easily viewed. WML has no corresponding CSS style sheet to tell a device how the content should be formatted—that is left up to the device. This was intentional, because many types of different devices would be making use of WML, from personal communicators to appliances. The biggest difference between WML and HTML is that WML is also an application of XML, bringing new considerations that we examine in the following sections.

The most important issues that affect how you will approach the creation of WML documents is that WML as an application of XML is a strictly interpreted language. A document is a WML document if it is both *well-formed* and *valid.* Additionally, WML must meet certain further constraints, which we examine later in the chapter.

Creating Well-Formed Documents

A WML document contains *elements* that have a *start element* and an *end element.* If the element isn't a container for data, then the element must be self-closing. This may seem somewhat confusing, so let's take a look at an example partial document (don't worry about what everything means, we take a look at that later).

```
<wml>
      <card>
            <p>I like Ice-cream.<br/>Do you?</p>
      <card>
</wml>
```

As you can see, the code has four elements: <wml>, <card>, <p>, and <br>. The <wml>, <card>, and <p> elements are container elements and as such have corresponding closing tags. The <br> element, however, is empty—it doesn't contain any data, and thus is self-closing, which is indicated by the backslash.

Nesting

WML documents must be *well-formed.* This intimidating statement simply means that a document's elements must match. WML is constructed hierarchically, as shown in the example in the preceding section. The opening element that occupies the same position in the hierarchy must correspond to the closing element at the same level. The following example shows an example of a document that is not well-formed:

```
<wml>
    <card>
        <p>I like Ice-cream.<br/>Do you?<card>
    </p>
</wml>
```

Here, the <card> element has been closed before the <p> element. This is an example of *invalid nesting*. In addition to being properly nested, the elements must be closed, as detailed in the specification. Consider the following example:

```
<wml>
    <card>
        <p>I like Ice-cream.<br/>Do you?
    <card>
</wml>
```

The closing element for the <p> element has been left out, which would result in the document not being well-formed. With the code nested and all elements closed, we have a well-formed piece of WML:

```
<wml>
    <card>
        <p>I like Ice-cream.<br/>Do you?</p>
    <card>
</wml>
```

Nesting of elements should come easily to all those who have been practicing good HTML. However, due to the very forgiving nature of HTML, a lot of developers could be in for a big surprise, so it will stand you in good stead to get into the habit of nesting and closing elements properly, not only in WML but in HTML as well.

Creating Valid Documents

In addition to being well-formed, a WML document must be *valid*. Validity is achieved by the inclusion of a Document Type Definition (DTD). The DTD describes the elements that may legally exist within the WML document and ensures that for the document to display, the WML document contains only those elements allowed by the DTD.

To make our previous well-formed example valid we must add the appropriate XML declaration and the reference to the DTD:

```
<?xml version="1.0"?>
<!DOCTYPE wml PUBLIC "//WAPFORUM//DTD_WML_1.1//EN"
http://www.wapforum.org/DTD/wml_1.1.xml>
<wml>
      <card>
            <p>I like Ice-cream.<br/>Do you?</p>
      </card>
</wml>
```

This example is both well-formed and valid. The following document, although it is well-formed, is *not* valid:

```
<?xml version="1.0"?>
<!DOCTYPE wml PUBLIC "//WAPFORUM//DTD_WML_1.1//EN"
http://www.wapforum.org/DTD/wml_1.1.xml>
<wml>
      <card>
            <para>I like Ice-cream.<br/>Do you?</para>
      </card>
</wml>
```

WARNING

Although the various SDK emulators are excellent for providing in-depth information on the interactions that take place during the loading and execution of WML content, the actual end-device will very likely react differently upon encountering an error; it will also almost certainly provide precious little (if any) information on what went wrong. Do not rely 100 percent on emulators to test your content.

At first glance, everything may look all right, but <para> is an element that is not defined in the DTD; therefore, the WML is not valid and will cause an error on any device that tries to display it. Figure 3.1 shows how well-formed and valid WML displays; Figure 3.2 shows how incorrectly formed WML will generate an error.

Figure 3.1 Well-Formed and Valid WML

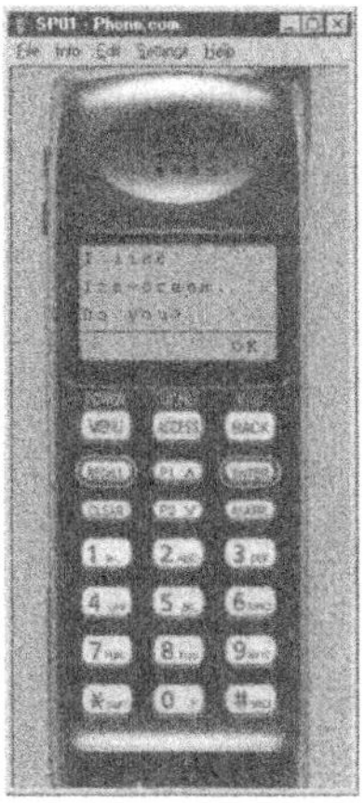

Figure 3.2 The SDK Catches an Error

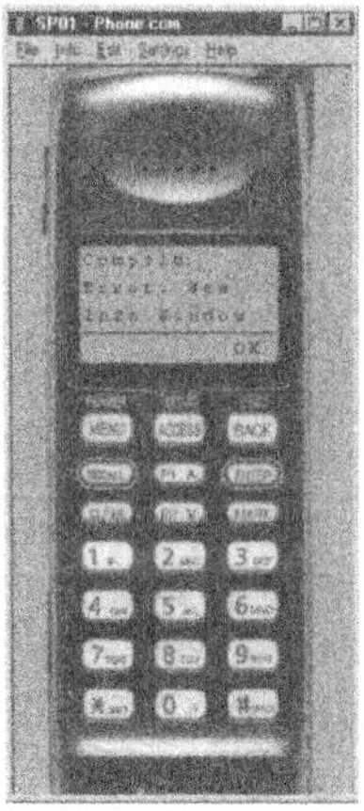

This example was created using the Openwave UP.SDK emulator, which includes a handy screen that provides more information in the event of an error. By referring to the information screen we can see exactly where we went wrong.

Figure 3.3 shows that the SDK has picked up that the closing element for <card> did not match the closing element for <p>, which causes an error.

Figure 3.3 The Error in Detail

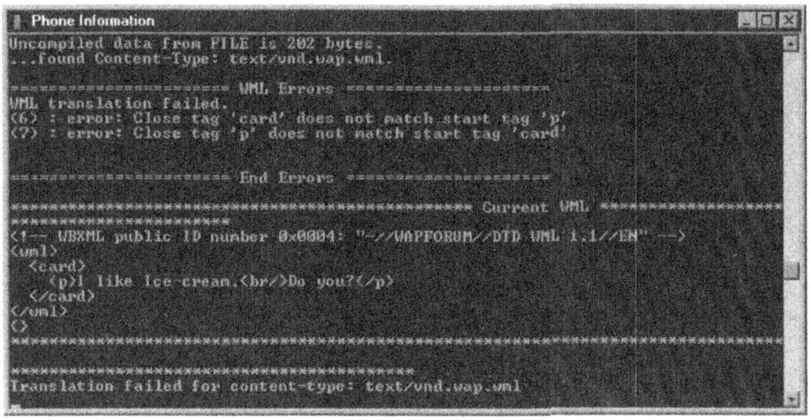

DTDs are essentially a set of rules that say what elements can exist and in what form they can appear. Thus, it determines whether the element contains content or not, what attributes it has, and where it can appear in the document. In the following example, taken from the WML DTD, you can see how the head element should appear (we added line numbers for reference):

```
1 <!ELEMENT head ( access | meta )+>
2 <!ATTLIST head
3 %coreattrs;
4 >
```

Getting to know how to interpret DTDs can be worthwhile because they often provide a definitive guide to what can and cannot be used in the language they define. Although appearing complex at first, the DTD is written according to a convention known as Backus Naur Form (BNF). BNF is a notation that describes the syntax a language must use. Knowing how BNF works will allow you to "read" the specification with ease. Our preceding example reads as follows:

- In Line 1, !ELEMENT specifies the name of the element (<head>) and what other elements it may contain. For the <head> element, this can be <access> or <meta>.

- In line 2, !ATTLIST specifies which attributes the <head> element can contain. In this case, the <head> element can contain only those defined as *core attributes* elsewhere in the DTD; the attribute *%coreattrs;* is a reference to another part of the DTD where the core attributes are specified in a similar fashion to the head.

The various WML elements are covered in the later section "WML Elements."

NOTE

You can find out more about DTDs and XML at www.xml.com.

Using WML Syntax

As mentioned earlier, WML is XML-based, which means that every WML file is an XML file and must contain a reference to the DTD. Therefore, the following *must* be included at the beginning of every WML file:

```
<?xml version="1.0"?>
<!DOCTYPE wml PUBLIC "//WAPFORUM//DTD_WML_1.1//EN"
http://www.wapforum.org/DTD/wml_1.1.xml>
```

This code tells the device interpreting the file that this file is an XML document (in this case, conforming to XML version 1.1) and that the DTD is located at www.wapforum.org/DTD/wml_1.1.xml.

WARNING

Unlike HTML, the XML declaration *must* be on the first line. Even a single space before the XML declaration will cause an error—the browser cannot interpret white space until it knows the file is an XML file and to which DTD it should be referring. In HTML, white space at the beginning of a file is highly prevalent because pages are frequently constructed dynamically from a database, which results in files with expanses of white space where the server-side code was stripped out (this can of course be avoided by sensibly constructing the server-side code).

Following Syntax Rules

WML can consist of a mixture of entities, elements, attributes, comments, and variables. Many of the syntax rules in WML are directly inherited from XML:

- All WML documents must contain the root element WML that contains any other WML elements.
- All elements must be lowercase (with the exception of keywords such as DOCTYPE and ENTITY, which are in uppercase).
- All element attribute values must be quoted.
- All elements must have corresponding endings.
- Elements which are empty elements (that is, have no content) must use /> to signify closure of the element.
- All white space is treated as significant.
- Elements must not overlap, though they may be nested (as with HTML).
- Element names are case-sensitive: name and Name are not the same.

Replacing Entities

Either numeric or named, *entities* are specific characters within the document character set that require escaping in WML or that may not be supported for entry within editors (due to their using a different character set, for example). All WML entities have the following form:

```
&entityreference;
```

Thus, the commonly used ampersand (**&**) becomes:

```
&amp;
```

In WML, certain characters are used to denote special situations, such as the start and end of an element (< and >). Simply placing the character (<) in the content would thus generate an error. Entities are used to reference content by placing the entity on the content as a placeholder. Thus, to show a code snippet, relevant entities would be replaced as follows (Figure 3.4 shows the result when viewed on a device or emulator):

```
<p>The  &lt;p&gt; element</p>
```

Figure 3.4 WML Entities

As you can see in Figure 3.4, the *<* and *>* entities as output on a device show how you can insert content into WML that would not otherwise be possible.

Closing Elements

Elements are similar to HTML elements (or *tags*) in that they specify the markup and structure of a WML file. However, due to the use of XML, WML elements do not seek to provide formatting information. This is left to the end device to work out.

Elements can be found in one of two forms:

```
<element>Content</element>
```

or:

```
<element/>
```

Although the first example, with its opening and ending tag, will be familiar to anyone who has used HTML, notice the backslash on the second example. WML is far less forgiving than HTML, and if an element is not a container for content, you must use the backslash as shown to explicitly close it. If the element does not contain any content but has a corresponding closing element, you must still include the closing element, for example:

```
<element> </element>
```

Characterizing the Element with Attributes

Although an element can provide information, such as identifying enclosed content as a paragraph (as in the <p> element), further information about the element's characteristics is provided by adding attributes to the element, as necessary. Thus, if you want to right-align a paragraph, the attribute would read as follows:

```
<p align="right">Right-aligned text</p>
```

All attributes must be enclosed in quotation marks (either single or double)—this is strictly required by WML. Failure to enclose all attributes in quotes generate an error, and the content will fail to load in the device.

NOTE

No attribute may be named more than once in any element that contains it.

You can find more information about which attributes are applicable to which elements in the later "WML Elements" section.

Case Sensitivity

In addition to enclosing all element attributes in quotes, WML—unlike HTML—is case-sensitive. All elements and attributes must be in lowercase.

Handling White Space

White space within text is handled by WML in the same manner as XML default white space handling. White space before or after elements is ignored completely, and in fact, sequences of white space (such as tabs and spaces) will be collapsed into a single space, the treatment of which will depend on the locale. Thus, you cannot space words within text by using multiple spaces or tabs. The handling of white space within elements and attributes is dependent on the rules defined in the XML specification referenced within the XML declaration at the beginning of the WML deck.

Collapsing Carriage Returns

The numerous examples in this chapter make use of carriage returns and tabs to format the content, making it easier to follow. You can continue this practice through to actual WML files to make code easier to read when editing. In WML, the user-agent (or the WAP Gateway) will take carriage returns, tabs, new lines, and multiple spaces, and collapse them to a single space as part of the process of minimizing the file size.

Commenting

WML comments are much like their HTML counterparts, though they must not extend across more than one line. Thus, the following is valid:

```
<!-- A comment -->
```

This, however, is invalid:

```
<!-- A Comment...
     ... and another -->
```

Using Variables

A variable is a temporary parameter, commonly stored on the user-agent into which a value can be inserted for future access during the session. A variable within WML has a very exact syntax.

Where white space can be expected to signify the end of a variable, the following is acceptable:

```
$identifier
```

If this is not the case, the variable must be enclosed in parentheses:

```
$(identifier)
```

Variables are covered in more detail in Chapter 4.

Formatting Text

Now for the bad news: Whereas HTML contains much to help you format your content, such as font tags and Cascading Style Sheets, the WML specification leaves that pretty much up to the receiving device. This behavior was intentional, given the huge range of possible wireless devices that are bound to be created, and means that if you rely on some kind of formatting to get across a key part of your application functionality, you could be heading for problems. This is compounded by the haphazard implementation of what little formatting control is allowable in WML by the currently available devices.

The formatting that is available addresses the bare minimum necessary and includes the following:

- Elements for bold and strong emphasis (<b> or <strong>)
- Elements for italic and emphasized text (<I> or <em>)
- Elements for underlined text (<u>)
- Elements to manipulate font size (<small> and <big>)

Displaying Fonts

You have very little influence over the fonts used in a device. They will almost certainly be nonproportional in nature, which rules out fun ASCII text of the type sometimes used to create basic pictures because these require proportional fonts. Take a look at the differences in the interpretation of markup containing formatting instructions in the comparison between Nokia and Phone.com devices in Figures 3.5 and 3.6. Both emulators are displaying the same WML content, but the Nokia device fails to display the bold text as intended. In fact, the actual Nokia 7110 does not display formatting such as emphasized, bold, or underlining.

Figure 3.5 Use of <b> on a Phone.com Browser

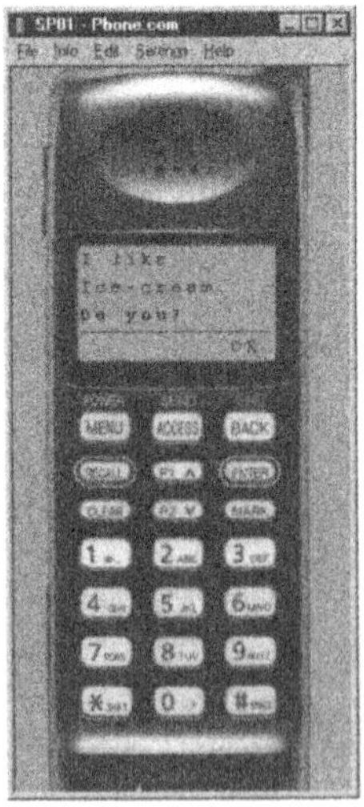

Figure 3.6 Use of <b> on a Nokia Browser

Both emulators will interpret the WML, which is well-formed and valid, but the Nokia browser doesn't have the capacity to render bold text, so the <b> element is simply ignored, and the text is displayed in the normal default font.

NOTE

Figures 3.5 and 3.6 are for guidance only. Although sophisticated, emulators do not necessarily exactly reflect what your WML will look like on an actual live device. Always remember to check your WML on a real device to prevent any unwelcome surprises. You can learn more about emulators later in this chapter in the section called "WML Editors, WAP SDKs, and Emulators."

Reserved Characters

WML uses a number of special characters to denote characters that may not be present within the current document encoding. The characters have the following syntax:

```
& entity reference ;
```

The entity reference can be numerical, named, or hexadecimal, for example:

```
&#32;
&lt;
&#x20;
```

These will all cause the < character to be displayed on the device screen.

It is vitally important to include the ampersand and semicolon because missing either of these will generate an error. You need to consider seven important entities within WML, as shown in Table 3.1.

Table 3.1 Character Entity Reference Table

Entity Name	Entity	Entity Description
quot	*"*	Quotation mark
amp	*&*	Ampersand
apos	*&#39*	Apostrophe
lt	*<*	Less-than
gt	*>*	Greater-than
nbsp	* *	Nonbreaking space
shy	**	Soft hyphen

Displaying Tables

Tables in WML are fairly simple in comparison to HTML tables, reflecting the limitations of the display generally available. You cannot nest tables, nor can you set explicit widths, although you must specify the number of columns within a row set.

WARNING

Only the more advanced devices, such as the Ericsson R320, are likely to be capable of displaying data marked up using tables. You must carefully inspect the target device to ensure that the device is capable of handling the display of tables and that the contents of the table will display as intended.

Meta Information

Meta information is information designed for use by the browser or gateway and is not displayed to the user. Meta information is included within the head of the document, the precise range of which is generally left to the device manufacturer to specify.

Controlling Caching

Whenever a request is made for a WML page, the device will cache the received file, allowing it to be called up from the cache instead of having to download the whole file again. This can considerably speed up browsing . The current devices do not have large caches; when dealing with dynamic data that may have the same URL but different contents each time the URL is accessed, you may want to disable caching.

You can control caching in a number of ways. Caching is a somewhat complicated issue to address because many devices cache differently than others and also differ in what instructions can be given to them to control caching. The following meta information is intended to cater to as many devices as possible:

```
<meta http-equiv="Cache-Control" forua="true" content="no-cache,
    max-age=0,must-revalidate, proxy-revalidate, s-maxage=0"/>
```

NOTE

As you can see from the examples in this section, you can specify from a number of headers to cater for as many eventualities as possible. Whenever caching is a concern, make sure you do the appropriate background research and testing to target the device on which you will be deploying your solution.

Additionally, making use of the *Expires* header is an ideal way to control browser caching. It works very well on many different devices. If the document is set to expire in the future, the browser will always re-request the content, thus ensuring the document is never reloaded from the cache. You can include this in server-side script, such as ASP:

```
<%
Response.Expires = -1
```

```
Response.AddHeader "Cache-Control", "no-cache, must-revalidate"
Response.AddHeader "Pragma", "no-cache"
%>
```

NOTE

In addition to checking how the individual device handles caching, be aware that WAP gateways may employ caching technology as well, which can be harder to identify.

Bookmarking

Bookmarking works much in the same way as Web browsing, allowing a user to mark a page of interest so that they can return directly to the page at a later date. Sometimes you may not want a user to bookmark your page (such as when the URL also contains information specific to that particular session). You can control bookmarking on the Openwave platform with the following meta information:

```
<meta name="vnd.up.markable" forua="true" content="false"/>
```

Understanding the Deck of Cards Paradigm

A WML file uses a "deck of cards" paradigm to structure content. Think of each file as a deck, within which are any number of cards. Each card is a single page that can be displayed on the device. A simple WML file containing two cards within the deck would look like the following:

```
<?xml version="1.0"?>
<!DOCTYPE wml PUBLIC "//WAPFORUM//DTD_WML_1.1//EN"
http://www.wapforum.org/DTD/wml_1.1.xml>
<!-- Start of the deck -->
<wml>
      <!-- Card 1 -->
      <card>

      </card>
      <!-- Card 2 -->
```

```
    <card>

    </card>
<!-- End of the deck -->
</wml>
```

Decks are extremely handy for sending the user groups of pages that they are likely to access, meaning that the user has to make only one connection to download several separate cards.

WML Elements

The previous example introduced the concepts of *decks* and *cards*.You may have noticed that the structure of the deck looked a lot like HTML. In fact,WML is quite similar to HTML in its use of elements and attributes to describe the content within each file.The <wml> and <card> elements in the example are just two examples of the elements you'll find in the WML language.

Adding Attributes

Most WML elements have at least one attribute that you can use to define parameters that specify how the device should handle the element.The element's attribute(s) are placed in the opening element and an attributes' values are enclosed in either single quotes (') or double quotes ("). Here is an example of how an element containing two attributes would appear:

```
<element attribute1="value1" attribute2="value2">text</element>
```

WARNING

As you can see in the example in this section, there is a space between each attribute. This is required in the WML specification; failure to separate each element with a space will cause the WML to fail to load.

You will see that most of the elements in the WML Elements section of this book contain several different attributes that you can set to specify how the element will be used.

The *id* and *class* Attributes

The *id* and *class* attributes respectively allow specific elements or groups of elements to be individually identified and manipulated. An *id* may be assigned only once within a particular deck and is thus unique in that instance, whereas a *class* may be assigned to many different elements within the deck and is thus useful for grouping similar elements. You can have multiple *class* names within the *class* attribute, but these should be separated by white space. A *class* is case-sensitive, so **class1** and **Class2** are two separate entities.

NOTE

For each WML element detailed in the sections following this one, a table shows the various attributes that each element can contain. Because *id* and *class* are core attributes that can be applied to *any* WML element, for the sake of repetition, they will not be shown within each individual element attribute table.

The <a> Element

The <a> element is an abbreviated form of the <anchor> element. Text within the <a> element forms a hyperlink to another card or deck. It is preferable to use <a> instead of <anchor> wherever possible. You cannot nest the <a> element, and it may only contain either a <br> or <img> element. The following is an example of the syntax for the <a> element:

```
<a href="deck2.wml">A Link to Deck 2</a>
```

The *href* attribute is required. All other attributes are optional. See Table 3.2 for a list of attributes for the <a> element.

Table 3.2 Attributes for the <a> Element

Attribute Name	Description
href	The target location for the link
title	A short string of text that identifies the element
xml:lang	The natural or formal language of the element

The <access> Element

The <access> element allows the author to control how the deck is accessed from other areas. You should consider the use of an <access> element when the privacy and security of the information being accessed is important. The use of variables within WML (a situation that does not exist within HTML) could theoretically allow malicious manipulation of information. By restricting access at the deck level, the user's information can be kept private.

The <access> element works by specifying which particular domains and/or paths are allowed to access the deck. When the deck is accessed, the user agent checks to see whether the requested destination is allowed access from the current deck. If the domain and/or path do not match those specified, access is not allowed.

Domains are evaluated according to suffix order. Thus, *www.thedomain.com* is a match for *thedomain.com*, but *domain.com* will not match. Similarly, paths are matched according to prefix. Thus, */path/path/* will match *path/path* but */pathpath* will not. The default for the *domain* attribute is the domain where the current deck is located, and the *path* attribute defaults to "/". A deck may contain only one <access> element. See Table 3.3 for a list of attributes for the <access> element.

Table 3.3 Attributes for the <access> Element

Attribute Name	Description
domain	The particular domain that may access the deck
path	The particular path that may access the deck

The following is an example of the syntax for the <access> element:

```
<access domain="domain.com" path="/path"/>
```

In this example, the referring Uniform Resource Identifier (URI) would be allowed access to the deck: http://domain.com/path/deck.wml.

The <anchor> Element

The behavior of the <anchor> element is specified by the task it contains. A *task* can be thought of as an action that must be performed as a result of the user selecting the element. In the case of the <anchor> element, this can be either <go>, <prev>, or <refresh>, but must consist of one task only. <Anchor> elements cannot be nested. See Table 3.4 for a list of attributes for the <anchor> element.

Table 3.4 Attributes for the <anchor> Element

Attribute Name	Description
accesskey	Signifies the access key that is assigned to the element
title	A short string of text that identifies the element

The following is an example of the syntax for the <anchor> element:

```
<anchor>
     A link to Deck 2
     <go href="deck2.wml">
</anchor>
```

As you can see, this example uses a <go> task to perform the same task as the example given for the <a> element.

NOTE

For both the <a> and <anchor> elements, the URI can be relative or absolute. Additionally, URL fragments are identified in the same way as anchors in HTML by using the # identifier.

The <b> Element

The <b> element signifies that the text contained within should be rendered by the user-agent as a bold font. Note that many WML microbrowsers do not render text marked up as bold with a bold font, so if you are relying on conveying meaning with bold, check with the target device for conformity.

It is perhaps a better idea (and is suggested within the WML specification) that text should use <strong> or <em> elements instead, resorting to using <b> only where specific control of the text is required. This will be familiar to anyone who has studied the use of <bold> versus <strong> within HTML. Table 3.5 lists the attribute for the <b> element.

Table 3.5 Attribute for the <b> Element

Attribute Name	Description
xml:lang	The natural or formal language of the element

The following is an example of the syntax for the <b> element:

```
This text is normal text, but <b>this text is bold text!</b>
```

The <big> Element

The <big> element indicates that the user-agent should render the text in a larger font size than the base font size for the device. Table 3.6 lists the attribute for the <big> element.

Table 3.6 Attribute for the <big> Element

Attribute Name	Description
xml:lang	The natural or formal language of the element

The following is an example of the syntax for the <big> element:

```
This text is a normal size... <big>but this text is bigger!</big>
```

The
 Element

The <br/> element forces a line break wherever it is placed within the text. Table 3.7 lists the attribute for the <br/> element.

Table 3.7 Attribute for the
 Element

Attribute Name	Description
xml:lang	The natural or formal language of the element

The following is an example of the syntax for the <br/> element:

```
This is on one line.<br/>This is on the next line.
```

The <card> Element

Each WML deck can contain one or more cards. The <card> element acts as a container for text and other elements that together form discrete units for display in a device. The *id* of a card can be used as the target for a fragment identifier within any navigation element. See Table 3.8 for a list of attributes for the <card> element.

Table 3.8 Attributes for the <card> Element

Attribute Name	Description
newcontext	This can be true or false and specifies if the user-agent should reinitialize upon entry. The default value is false.
onenterbackward	This is an event that is fired upon entry to the card as a result of a <prev> task.
onenterforward	This is an event that is fired upon entry to the card as a result of <go> task.
ontimer	This is an event that fires when a timer expires.
ordered	This can be true or false and specifies whether the content of the card should be displayed in an ordered fashion. The default value is true.
title	Specifies the title of the card. This is typically displayed by the user-agent to provide meaning to the user for the purpose of the card and should be kept short and descriptive.
xml:lang	The natural or formal language of the element.

The following is an example of the syntax for the <card> element:

```
<card title="A New Card" newcontext="true">
     This is a card.
</card>
```

All attributes of the card element are implied—that is, they are not absolutely necessary:

```
<card>
     This is a card.
</card>
```

This code is just as valid as the prior example. However, you should at least include a title in all of your cards if only to give users some sort of indication what the card is about.

The <do> Element

In certain situations, you may want to interact with the user in some way. The <do> element provides an interface to initiate actions from your users at the deck or card level. If the <do> element is present at the deck level, it can be contained within a template element to provide the same functionality to all cards within the deck. A <do> within a card will override a <do> within the parent deck if they share the same name.

Exactly how the interface is rendered to the user is entirely dependent of the device, and the <do> may take the appearance of a soft button, a link, or choice through the menu system. You can use the *type* attribute to provide some indication to the user-agent as to the intended use of the <do> element. See Table 3.9 for a list of attributes for the <do> element.

Table 3.9 Attributes for the <do> Element

Attribute Name	Description
label	A text label that identifies the element.
name	The name of the event binding.
optional	This can be either true or false. If true, this element may be ignored by the user-agent.
type	The intended function for which the element is intended.
xml:lang	The natural or formal language of the element.

NOTE

The *type* attribute is required and must be specified at all times. Note that the <do> element may not be rendered where it is placed within the text of the card. In fact, the only safe assumption you can make is that the user-agent will map the element to a specific user interface. This can cause problems because the <do> element can appear at the top of the rendered card, at the bottom, in the middle—in fact just about anywhere—so you must carefully consider the use of the <do> element with respect to the target device.

The following is an example of the syntax for the <do> element:

```
<do type="accept" label="Next Card">
    <go href="#nextcard"/>
</do>
```

The <em> Element

The <em> element specifies that the text should be rendered by the user-agent with emphasis. Table 3.10 lists the attribute for the <em> element.

Table 3.10 Attribute for the <em> Element

Attribute Name	Description
xml:lang	The natural or formal language of the element

The following is an example of the syntax for the <em> element:

```
This text is normal but <em>this text is emphasized</em>.
```

The <fieldset> Element

The <fieldset> element is useful for grouping similar fields and text together to allow better representation of the contents on the target device. You can nest further <fieldset> elements to provide more information on how the fields and text relate to each other. See Table 3.11 for a list of attributes for the <fieldset> element.

Table 3.11 Attributes for the <fieldset> Element

Attribute Name	Description
title	The title of the fieldset, which is typically used to describe the contents of the fieldset, and may also be rendered by the user-agent to provide information on the content to the user.
xml:lang	The natural or formal language of the element.

The following is an example of the syntax for the <fieldset> element:

```
<fieldset title="Ice-Creams">
      Strawberry<br/>
      Vanilla<br/>
      Chocolate
</fieldset>
```

The <go> Element

The <go> element is a task that specifies navigation to a URI. The *href* attribute is required. See Table 3.12 for a list of attributes for the <go> element.

Table 3.12 Attributes for the <go> Element

Attribute Name	Description
accept-charset	Used to specify the character set the server should accept. The default is to use the character set the deck was sent in.
cache-control	If cache-control is set to no-cache, the URL must be reloaded from the server. This allows new values to be set and sent to the server in the case of submissions sending data pairs.
enctype	Used when the method is set to post, *enctype* specifies the content type that the submission should be sent as. The default value is *application/x-www-form-urlencoded*.
href	The destination that should be navigated to.
method	Either **post** or **get**. The **go** method is exactly the same as the **submission** method used in HTTP.
sendreferer	This is either true or false, and if true, the user-agent must send the URI of the deck that contains the<go> element to the server. This allows access controls to be exercised.

The following is an example of the syntax for the <go> element:

```
<go href="card1.wml"/>
```

You can find further examples of navigating using the <go> element later in this chapter in the section called "Creating WML Content."

The <head> Element

The <head> element contains data relating to the deck as a whole. The following is an example of the syntax for the <head> element:

```
<head>
     <access domain="domain.com"/>
</head>
```

The <i> Element

The <i> element signifies that the text contained within should be rendered by the user-agent in an italic font. However, <em> is the recommended use to signify emphasis. Table 3.13 lists the attribute for the <i> element.

Table 3.13 Attribute for the <i> element

Attribute Name	Description
xml:lang	The natural or formal language of the element

The following is an example of the syntax for the <i> element:

```
This is normal text but <i>this is italic text</i>.
```

The <img> Element

The <img> element allows a wireless bitmap (WBMP) image to be included. See Table 3.14 for a list of attributes for the <img> element.

Table 3.14 Attributes for the <img> Element

Attribute Name	Description
align	Specifies how the image should be aligned with reference to the text flow it appears within. Possible options are one of top, middle, or bottom.
alt	Alternate text that can be displayed when the image is unavailable.
height	The height of the image in pixels.
hspace	The amount of padding that should be applied to the image horizontally.
localsrc	An image, contained internally within the device, that can be displayed as an alternative.
src	The URI where the image to be displayed resides.
vspace	The amount of padding that should be applied to the image vertically.
width	The width of the image in pixels.
xml:lang	The natural or formal language of the element.

The following is an example of the syntax for the <img> element:

```
<img src="logo.wbmp" alt="Company Logo" height="30" width="60"/>
```

The <input> Element

The <input> element allows data to be entered by the user; it features some useful methods of constraining the input via the *format* attribute, which can mask the content to ensure that only the input you want is sent to the server. See Table 3.15 for a list of attributes for the <input> element.

Table 3.15 Attributes for the <input> Element

Attribute Name	Description
emptyok	This is either true or false, and if set to true, the element will allow the input value to be empty.
format	The format attribute allows conditions to be set that must be met before the data entry will be accepted. All other entries will be ignored. These options are available: *A* Only uppercase, non-numeric characters *a* Only lowercase, non-numeric characters *N* Only numeric characters *X* Any uppercase character *x* Any lowercase character *M* Any character (the default value) *m* Any character but assumed to be lowercase **f* Appearing at the end of the format string, this allows any number of characters and must be preceded by one of the above characters *nf* A number of characters (*n*) may be entered where *f* is one of the above formatting characters (other than **f*) \c Displays the next character (c) in the text field. Useful for formatting phone numbers and so on
maxlength	The maximum number of characters that can be entered into the input field by the user.
name	The name of the variable that will be set for the input element.
size	The width of the input field in characters.
tabindex	The position in tabbing order.
title	A short string of text that identifies the element.

Continued

Table 3.15 Continued

Attribute Name	Description
type	This can be either text or password. When password is specified as the attribute, input is masked. This helps to keep private data private from casual onlookers.
value	A default value for the input element.
xml:lang	The natural or formal language of the element.

The following is an example of the syntax for the <input> element:

```
<input name="Name" type="text" value="Richard"/>

<card>
    <p>
    Name: <input name="Name" type="text" value="Richard"/><br/>
    Favorite Ice-cream: <input name="Ice-cream" type="text">
    </p>
</card>
```

NOTE

The *name* attribute is required at all times and the *emptyok* attribute defaults to false if not set to true. Do not rely on the *size* attribute to aid layout because not all devices support this.

The <meta> Element

The <meta> element provides meta information in the head of a WML deck as a name and value pair. The <meta> element cannot appear anywhere in the deck other than in the head. See Table 3.16 for a list of attributes for the <meta> element.

Table 3.16 Attributes for the <meta> Element

Attribute Name	Description
content	The value of the property.
forua	This is either true or false, and if false, the meta information must be removed before the content is sent to the user. Conversely, if true, the header information must be sent to the user.
http-equiv	This allows an HTTP header to be set as per RFC2068.
name	The name of the property.
scheme	A structure or form that can be used to interpret the property value.

The following is an example of the syntax for the <meta> element:

```
<head>
     <meta content="charset" value="character-set=ISO-10646-UCS-2"/>
</head>
```

The <noop> Element

The <noop> element specifies that no operation should be carried out by the user-agent. Table 3.17 lists the attribute for the <noop> element.

Table 3.17 Attribute for the <noop> Element

Attribute Name	Description
xml:lang	The natural or formal language of the element

The following is an example of the syntax for the <noop> element:

```
<noop>Nothing to be done here</noop>
```

The <onevent> Element

The <onevent> element binds an event to an enclosed task. Table 3.18 lists the attribute for the <onevent> element.

Table 3.18 Attribute for the <onevent> Element

Attribute Name	Description
type	The intended use of the element. This attribute is required.

The following is an example of the syntax for the <onevent> element:

```
<onevent type="onenterbackward">
     <go href="deck.wml"/>
</onevent>
```

The <optgroup> Element

The <optgroup> element allows the grouping of options hierarchically to provide an indication to the user-agent of how the content should be grouped and rendered. See Table 3.19 for a list of attributes for the <optgroup> element.

Table 3.19 Attributes for the <optgroup> Element

Attribute Name	Description
title	A short text string that is used to identify the group and which may be displayed.
xml:lang	The natural or formal language of the element.

The following is an example of the syntax for the <optgroup> element:

```
<optgroup title="Ice-Creams">
     <option value="Strawberry"/>
     <option value="Vanilla"/>
     <option value="Chocolate"/>
</optgroup>
```

The <option> Element

The <option> element defines an option in a list and occurs within a <select> element. See Table 3.20 for a list of attributes for the <option> element.

Table 3.20 Attributes for the <option> Element

Attribute Name	Description
onpick	The URI to navigate to upon selection by the user
title	A short text string that is used to identify the option
value	The value of the option
xml:lang	The natural or formal language of the element

The following is an example of the syntax for the <option> element:

```
<option title="Strawberry" value="Strawberry"/>
```

NOTE

See the <select> element for further examples of option lists.

The <p> Element

Text that appears within the <p> element is designated as a paragraph. See Table 3.21 for a list of attributes for the <p> element.

Table 3.21 Attributes for the <p> Element

Attribute Name	Description
align	This can be either left (the default), right, or center—though support for this is varied.
mode	This can be either wrap or nowrap and specifies whether the text within the paragraph should wrap where it is too long to fit on the display screen.

The following is an example of the syntax for the <p> element:

```
<p>
    This is a paragraph of text that will wrap on reaching the edge of
    the screen and is left aligned by default.
</p>
```

The <postfield> Element

The <postfield> element specifies a name and value pair that will be sent to the server as part of a URL request. You can use the <postfield> element with the <go> element (described previously) to provide a variety of options for transmitting the information. See Table 3.22 for a list of attributes for the <postfield> element.

Table 3.22 Attributes for the <postfield> Element

Attribute Name	Description
name	The name of the field
value	The value of the field

The following is an example of the syntax for the <postfield> element:

```
<postfield name="Ice-cream" value="Chocolate"/>
```

The <prev> Element

The task element <prev> specifies that navigation should take the user one step back in the history stack. The following is an example of the syntax for the <prev> element:

```
<anchor>
      <prev/>Back
</anchor>
```

The <refresh> Element

The <refresh> element specifies a contextual task to be performed by the user-agent. See the <setvar> element for more information on using <refresh>.

The <select> Element

The <select> element allows the user to make a selection from a list of options (see the <option> element described earlier). Table 3.23 lists the attributes for the <select> element.

Table 3.23 Attributes for the <select> Element

Attribute Name	Description
Iname	The name of the variable that will be set with the option value.
ivalue	The default selection value.
multiple	This is either true or false and signifies whether multiple options may be selected. The default is false.
name	The name of the variable to be set.
tabindex	This is used to set the tabbing position of the current element.
title	The title of the selection list that may be used to aid identification of the purpose of the list.
value	The value that will be applied to a variable when the option is selected.
xml:lang	The natural or formal language of the element.

The following is an example of the syntax for the <select> element:

```
<select name="Ice-cream" value="Chocolate" title="Ice-cream:">
     <option value="Strawberry">Strawberry</option>
     <option value="Vanilla">Vanilla</option>
     <option value="Chocolate">Chocolate</option>
</select>
```

The <setvar> Element

The <setvar> element is used to set a variable within the user-agent after a task is executed. See Table 3.24 for a list of attributes for the <setvar> element.

Table 3.24 Attributes for the <setvar> Element

Attribute Name	Description
name	The name of the variable
value	The value of the variable

The following is an example of the syntax for the <setvar> element:

```
<setvar name="variable1" value="one"/>
<setvar name="variable2" value="two"/>
```

The <small> Element

The <small> element indicates that the user-agent should render the text in a smaller font size than the base font size for the device. Table 3.25 lists the attribute for the <small> element.

Table 3.25 Attribute for the <small> Element

Attribute Name	Description
xml:lang	The natural or formal language of the element

The following is an example of the syntax for the <small> element:

```
This text is a normal size... <small>but this text is smaller!</small>
```

The <strong> Element

The <strong> element indicates that the contained text should be rendered with strong emphasis. Table 3.26 lists the attribute for the <strong> element.

Table 3.26 Attribute for the <strong> Element

Attribute Name	Description
xml:lang	The natural or formal language of the element

The following is an example of the syntax for the <strong> element:

```
This text is normal but <strong>this text is strongly
emphasized</strong>.
```

The <table> Element

The <table> element, along with the <tr> and <td> elements, is used to create columns and rows of text and/or images within a card. See Table 3.27 for a list of attributes for the <table> element.

Table 3.27 Attributes for the <table> Element

Attribute Name	Description
align	Specifies how the content should be laid out; Allowable values are *L* (left), *C* (center), and *R* (right).
columns	The number of columns for the row set.
title	The title of the selection list that may be used to aid identification of the purpose of the list.

The following is an example of the syntax for the <table> element:

```
<table align="left" columns="1" title="Ice-creams">
     ...
</table>
```

The <tr> Element

The <tr> element signifies a table row. The following is an example of the syntax for the <tr> element:

```
<table align="left" columns="1" title="Ice-creams">
     <tr>
          ...
     </tr>
</table>
```

The <td> Element

The <td> element signifies a cell that contains the text or image. Table 3.28 lists the attribute for the <td> element.

Table 3.28 Attribute for the <td> Element

Attribute Name	Description
xml:lang	The natural or formal language of the element

The following is an example of the syntax for the <td> element:

```
<table align="left" columns="1" title="Ice-creams">
```

```
    <tr>
        <td>Ice-creams</td>
        <td>Strawberry</td>
        <td>Vanilla</td>
        <td>Chocolate</td>
    </tr>
</table>
```

The <template> Element

A <template> element describes features that are common to all the cards within the deck. Thus, all cards within a deck where a template element is present will include the elements specified within the template. See Table 3.29 for a list of attributes for the <template> element.

Table 3.29 Attributes for the <template> Element

Attribute Name	Description
onenterbackward	This event is fired when the card is entered from a <prev> task.
onenterforward	This event is fired when the card is entered from a <go> task.
ontimer	This event is fired when a timer expires.

The following is an example of the syntax for the <template> element:

```
<template ontimer="#card2">
    ...
</template>
```

The <timer> Element

The <timer> element is fired upon entry to the card and counts down in one-tenth of one second intervals. The countdown is terminated if the card is exited from prematurely. See Table 3.30 for a list of attributes for the <timer> element.

Table 3.30 Attributes for the <timer> Element

Attribute Name	Description
name	The name of the bound event
value	The timer value

The following is an example of the syntax for the <timer> element:

```
<template ontimer="#card2">
     <timer name="countdown" value="30"/>
</template>
```

The <u> Element

The <u> element indicates that the contained text should be underlined. Because anchors are generally underlined to indicate that they are a hyperlink, you should use underlining judiciously to avoid creating confusion.

The following is an example of the syntax for the <u> element:

```
This text is normal <u>but this text is underlined</u>.
```

The <wml> Element

The <wml> element signifies a deck and encloses all the elements that make up the deck, including card elements. Table 3.31 lists the attribute for the <wml> element.

Table 3.31 Attribute for the <wml> Element

Attribute Name	Description
xml:lang	The natural or formal language of the element

The following is an example of the syntax for the <wml> element:

```
<wml>
     <card>
     ...
     </card>
     <card>
     ...
```

```
        </card>
</wml>
```

Creating WML Content

The "WML Overview" section of this chapter touched briefly on the structure of a WML deck. We now take a closer look at constructing WML decks that can be displayed on emulators, or even on an actual device.

Let's take a look at a simple card, using what you learned earlier:

```
<?xml version="1.0"?>
<!DOCTYPE wml PUBLIC "//WAPFORUM//DTD_WML_1.1//EN"
http://www.wapforum.org/DTD/wml_1.1.xml>
<wml>
        <card>
        <p>I like Ice-cream.<br/>Do you?</p>
        </card>
</wml>
```

This card is all very well but a better option would be to allow the visitor to answer the question and form a reply in response. For that, you will need a few more cards and will need to be able to navigate from one to the other.

Navigating within the Deck

By using the ability of WML to store multiple cards within the deck, you can ask a question and give an answer without the user having to make another round trip to the server:

```
<?xml version="1.0"?>
<!DOCTYPE wml PUBLIC "-//WAPFORUM//DTD WML 1.1//EN"
"http://www.wapforum.org/DTD/wml_1.1.xml">
<wml>
        <card id="start" title="Ice-cream">
        <p>
                I like Ice-cream, do you?<br/>
                <a href="#yes">Yes</a><br/>
                <a href="#no">No</a>
        </p>
```

```
        </card>
        <card id="yes" title="Ice-cream Lover">
              <p>
                    I'm glad you like ice-cream!<br/>
                    <a href="#start">Back</a>
              </p>
        </card>
        <card id="no" title="Ice-cream Hater">
              <p>
                    I'm sad you don't like ice-cream.<br/>
                    <a href="#start">Back</a>
              </p>
        </card>
</wml>
```

This example, using the <a> element, works well for static content, but when dealing with content where the results of the selection must be sent back to the server, you need to assign a task.

Getting Information from the User

The <select> and <go> elements allow you to carry out more complex navigational tasks than is possible using the previous example. In the following example, you'll combine a number of elements to allow the user to select and view a choice.

First of all, make your XML declaration and specify the DTD:

```
<?xml version="1.0"?>
<!DOCTYPE wml PUBLIC "-//WAPFORUM//DTD WML 1.1//EN"
"http://www.wapforum.org/DTD/wml_1.1.xml">

'Now we start the document proper.

<wml>
```

The first card uses a simple link to find out if the user likes ice-cream (after all, why ask them which flavor they prefer if they don't even like ice cream):

```
<card id="start" title="Ice-cream">
      <p>
```

```
            I like Ice-cream, do you?<br/>
            <a href="#yes">Yes</a><br/>
            <a href="#no">No</a>
        </p>
</card>
```

Great! The user likes ice cream. Now use the <select> element to present the choices to the user. Exactly how the device will render the options varies, but you can be sure that the user will be able to choose a flavor:

```
<card id="yes" title="Choose an Ice-cream">
      <p>
      What is your favorite Ice-cream?<br/>
      <select name="icecream">
            <option value="Strawberry">Strawberry</option>
            <option value="Vanilla">Vanilla</option>
            <option value="Chocolate">Chocolate</option>
      </select>
</p>
<do type="accept">
      <go href="#showchoice"/>
</do>
</card>
```

You want the user to know how glad you are with their choice. You can use a variable substitution to show the user their choice:

```
<card id="showchoice">
      <p>
            You like $icecream. So do I!
      </p>
<do type="accept" label="back">
      <go href="#start"/>
</do>
</card>
```

There's no accounting for taste!

```
<card id="no" title="Ice-cream Hater">
```

```
        <p>
                I'm sad you don't like ice-cream.<br/>
                <a href="#start">Back</a>
        </p>
</card>
</wml>
```

So far this is static, but what if we wanted to store the user's choices or build the list from another source? Server-side dynamic applications using scripting are the answer.

Using Server-Side Programs to Create Dynamic WML

Dynamic applications are applications that build content "on the fly" in response to requests made. Thus, a single template file filled with dynamically-served content can replace hundreds, even thousands of similar HTML pages.

To add the capability of serving WML from your Web server, you need to first add the following MIME entries to the Web server's configuration table (see Table 3.32).

Table 3.32 Web Server MIME Configurations

Extension	MIME Type
Wml	text/vnd.wap.wml
Wmlc	application/vnd.wap.wmlc
Wmlsc	application/vnd.wap.wmlscriptc
wmlscript	text/vnd.wap.wmlscript
ws	text/vnd.wap.wmlscript
wsc	application/vnd.wap.wmlscriptc
wmls	text/vnd.wap.wmlscript
wbmp	image/vnd.wap.wbmp

In Apache, one of the most popular Web servers, you would need to edit the AddType section in the srm.conf to include whatever MIME types you require, such as the following:

```
# WAP MIME Types
AddType text/vnd.wap.wml .wml
```

```
AddType image/vnd.wap.wbmp .wbmp
AddType application/vnd.wap.wmlc .wmlc
AddType text/vnd.wap.wmlscript .wmls
AddType application/vnd.wap.wmlscriptc .wmlsc
```

The server will accept these new MIME types once restarted. You may find that you do not have access to the Web server to carry out configuration changes. If you are using a scripting language to construct the WML content, you can add the MIME type into your script. If you are using Perl, print the HTTP response header string before printing a WML deck:

```
print "Content-type: text/vnd.wap.wml\n\n";
print $WML;
```

If you are using Microsoft Active Server Pages (ASP), set the MIME type response at the beginning of your script:

```
<%Response.ContentType = "text/vnd.wap.wml"%>
```

In Perl, make sure that the header information is separated from the WML content by a blank line (two CRLFs). In ASP, place the **<@** declaration immediately after the Response.Contentype—otherwise, a blank line will be inserted into the rendered page before your XML declaration, invalidating the page and generating an error.

Returning to our previous example, you may have decided that you want to build a list of ice creams from a database and also store each individual user's preference so that you can see at a glance at some later stage everybody who likes chocolate ice cream.

In ASP, open a database connection and use a bit of server-side scripting to populate the options in the select element. Don't worry if you are unfamiliar with ASP scripting, we are more interested in demonstrating just the concept here:

```
<%
' First we set up our database connection
Dim oConn, sConn
Set oConn = Server.CreateObject("ADODB.Connection")
sConn = "DRIVER={Microsoft Access Driver (*.mdb)};" & _
    "DBQ=" & Server.MapPath("icecream.mdb") & ";"
oConn.Open(sConn)
```

```
'next we grab all the flavors from the database

Dim SQL, oRS
SQL = "SELECT flavors FROM icecreams"

Set oRS = oConn.Execute(SQL)
%>
<%Response.ContentType = "text/vnd.wap.wml"%><?xml version="1.0"?>
<!DOCTYPE wml PUBLIC "-//WAPFORUM//DTD WML 1.1//EN"
"http://www.wapforum.org/DTD/wml_1.1.xml">
<wml>
      <card id="start" title="Ice-cream">
      <p>
            I like Ice-cream, do you?<br/>
            <a href="#yes">Yes</a><br/>
            <a href="#no">No</a>
      </p>
      </card>
      <card id="yes" title="Choose an Ice-cream">
            <p>
            What is your favorite Ice-cream?<br/>
            <select name="icecream"><%
' we're now able to loop through the results of our selection
' and build up the list

Do While Not oRS.EOF
%>
                  <option value="<%= oRS.Fields("flavors")%>"><%=
                   oRS.Fields("flavors")%></option><%
' adding the <% to the end of the line above instead of a new line
' stops a line break being inserted into the WML output
' keeping the WML source tidy.

oRS.MoveNext
```

```
Loop
%>
            </select>
      </p>
      <do type="accept">
            <go href="#showchoice"/>
      </do>
      </card>
      <card id="no" title="Ice-cream Hater">
            <p>
                  I'm sad you don't like ice-cream.<br/>
                  <a href="#start">Back</a>
            </p>
      </card>
      <card id="showchoice">
             <p>
                  You like $icecream. So do I!
            </p>
      <do type="accept" label="back">
            <go href="#start"/>
      </do>
      </card>
</wml>
```

This capability to mix server-side scripting with WML is a powerful way to add functionality and interaction to your application.

Using Openwave Extensions

Early incarnations of Web browsers sought to push the boundaries of what was capable by introducing extensions to HTML. In much the same spirit, Openwave Systems Inc. has been keen to push the boundaries of what is capable with a wireless device.

Openwave (formerly Unwired Planet, and then later known as Phone.com prior to their merging with Software.com in 2000) has sought to combine the rich features of both the Openwave UP.Browser (the microbrowser contained in many wireless devices) and the UP.Link gateway (the WAP gateway through which requests are translated) through extensions to WML. Openwave has provided developers with features that allow the development of contextual services, that is, services that allow different possibilities to be enacted depending on the context within which the events take place.

Opinion is divided on how useful the Openwave extensions to WML are. A pessimistic viewpoint says that unless your application will definitely be used exclusively on a device featuring an Openwave microbrowser, accessing content through an Openwave gateway (as could well be the case in corporate settings), the extensions should not be used at all. An optimistic viewpoint argues that the application can easily feature conditional branching to divert Openwave devices to specific Openwave WML decks and non-Openwave devices to a more basic WML deck. This is a relatively trivial task to programmers but can become a headache when the number of devices to be catered for spirals upwards.

The reality is that compromises will almost certainly have to be introduced in the meantime. Whether or not an application features Openwave extensions is a judgment call: Are they are actually needed, and how many users utilizing Openwave technology will access the live application?

Take care to ensure also that the capabilities of different versions of the UP.Browser are taken into consideration. There are several different versions of the Phone.com browser. See Table 3.33 for an overview of the differences between these browsers.

Navigating Parent/Child Relationships Using Extensions

As noted earlier, WML is structured hierarchically. This allows your applications to be built with a "top-down" philosophy, breaking down the tasks that must be performed into ever more discrete portions the deeper into the hierarchy you go. The concept of "parent/child relationships" describes how the individual parts relate to and interact with each other. We've used the parent/child convention throughout this chapter. You can see in the following example that *element 1* is contained within *parent 1* making *element 1* the *child* of *parent 1*. The same situation exists for *parent 2* and *element 2*. However, *element 1* has no relationship to *parent 2*.

Table 3.33 The Various Microbrowsers and Their Capabilities

Browser	Browser Version	HDML 3.0 Support	WML 1.1 Support	WML1.1 with Openwave Extensions	WMLScript 1.1 Support
Openwave Mobile Browser*	4.*x*	Yes, via Mobile Access Gateway** translation service	Yes	Yes Recommended	Yes Recommended
Openwave Mobile Browser*	3.1	Yes Recommended	Yes, via Mobile Access Gateway** translation service	No	No
Openwave Mobile Browser*	3.0	Yes Recommended	No	No	No
Other	Any	No	Yes Recommended	No	Yes Recommended

** formerly UP.Browser ** formerly UP.Link (Source: Openwave)*

```
<parent 1>
      <element 1>
      </element 1>
</parent 2>
<parent 2>
      <element 2>
      </element 2>
</parent 2>
```

The Openwave extensions take this concept a stage further. By dividing the tasks you wish to carry out into a hierarchical series and applying *context* to the specific children, it becomes much easier to handle such things as the user interface, the use of variables, and the exchanging of information between contexts.

Navigation within the current context is possible in WML using the <go> and <prev> elements. However, using the Openwave extensions, we can carry on further to provide contextual navigation. Because the Openwave extensions are not covered by the current WML specification, remember to reference their DTD instead at the beginning of the WML document as follows:

```
<?xml version="1.0"?>
<!DOCTYPE wml PUBLIC "-//PHONE.COM//DTD WML 1.1//EN"
"http://www.phone.com/dtd/wml11.dtd" >
```

Using the <spawn> and <catch> Extensions

The <spawn> element allows navigation from a parent to a child in a similar way to a <go> task. However, using the <spawn> element *spawns* a new nested context. When this context is exited, the user is returned to the parent context. This may seem somewhat trivial, but the use of <spawn> allows users to browse a number of possible cards within this context while returning to the parent context in one move (as opposed to <go>/<prev> where all viewed cards would have to be navigated through to reach the parent card). This can be a powerful way to manage how the user navigates by condensing many frustrating clicks into one click.

```
<spawn href="url.wml">
</spawn>
```

The <spawn> tag can contain the <catch> element to trap any errors:

```
<spawn href="url.wml">
<catch/>
</spawn>
```

Using the <exit> and <throw> Extensions

In addition to the <prev> task, the <exit> and <throw> extensions allow navigation back to the parent context. As noted previously, <throw> allows exceptions to be trapped and handled accordingly using <catch>. The <exit> element is used to cater for a specific eventuality, returning the user to the parent context where the spawn attribute <onexit> is used to specify what should happen:

```
...
<do type="options" label="Return">
      <exit/>
</do>
<do type="options" label="Exit">
      <throw name="abort"/>
</do>
...
```

Using the <catch> Extension

The <catch> element provides a series of mechanisms to trap errors. This very useful element allows different situations to be dealt with accordingly. For example, if the user cancels a request, you may want to handle what happens as a result differently than, say, the user encountering an error from the server:

```
<card>
<do type="accept" label="Choice">
      <spawn href="submit.wml" onexit="#success">
            <catch name="error" onthrow="#error1"/>
            <catch name="cancel" onthrow="#error2"/>
</do>
</card>
```

Using the <send> and <receive> Extensions

When the user returns to the parent context, you may want to bring back some information with them as the result of a task that was carried out. The <send> and <receive> elements allow data to be sent from the nested child context and received in by the parent context. The following is an example of using <send>:

```
<card>
...
     <send value="x"/>
     <send value="y"/>
...
</card>
```

The following is an example of using <receive>:

```
<card>
...
<receive name="value1"/>
<receive name="value2"/>
...
</card>
```

NOTE

The ordering of the names and values is important. In the preceding examples, the receiving deck will assume that the value for *value1* will be *x* and that the value for *value2* will be *y*. If *y* appeared before *x*, the value of *value1* would be *y*.

Preloading URLs

The <link> element is used to preload a URL into the device, and you should use it only when you know that the user will probably want to follow this link. A common use may be to preload the next page in a news item. The link element is placed within the head of the document:

```
<head>
     <link href="next_url.wml" rel="next"/>
</head>
```

WML Editors, WAP SDKs, and Emulators

A whole plethora of tools are available to the aspiring wireless developer. They range from freeware and shareware items to full-blown SDKs from phone manufacturers such as Nokia and Openwave. Those with a degree of experience using HTML editors will be pleased to know that most of the popular HTML editors support editing WML.

WML Editors

If you are comfortable with hand-coding WML, Allaire's Homesite is a great editor that comes with the ability to work with WML. Although not immediately apparent, you can enter WML and use the context-sensitive menus to access all the various attributes, as shown in Figure 3.7. Homesite is inherently extensible, so if you don't like how it does things, you can always rewrite it.

Figure 3.7 Allaire Homesite

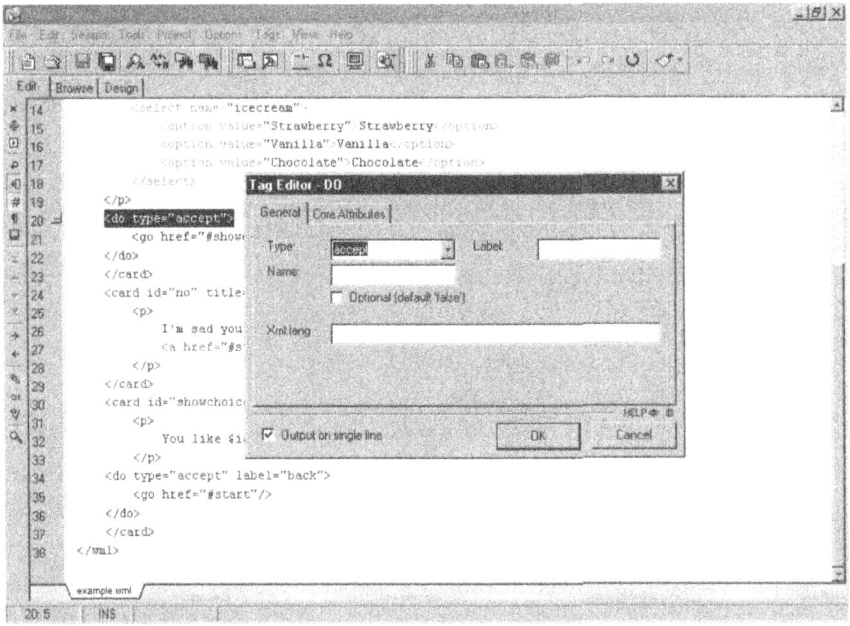

If you aren't quite ready to work with raw WML code, the Macromedia WML Studio extension may interest you. Developed by Nokia, the WML Studio allows the creation of WML pages from within Macromedia's popular editor Dreamweaver.

The Nokia WML Studio for Dreamweaver is an extension to Dreamweaver that you can download from the Macromedia Web site. It allows the creation of WML content within Dreamweaver's what you see is what you get (WYSIWYG) environment, as shown in Figure 3.8.

Figure 3.8 Macromedia Dreamweaver Together with the WML Studio Extension from Nokia

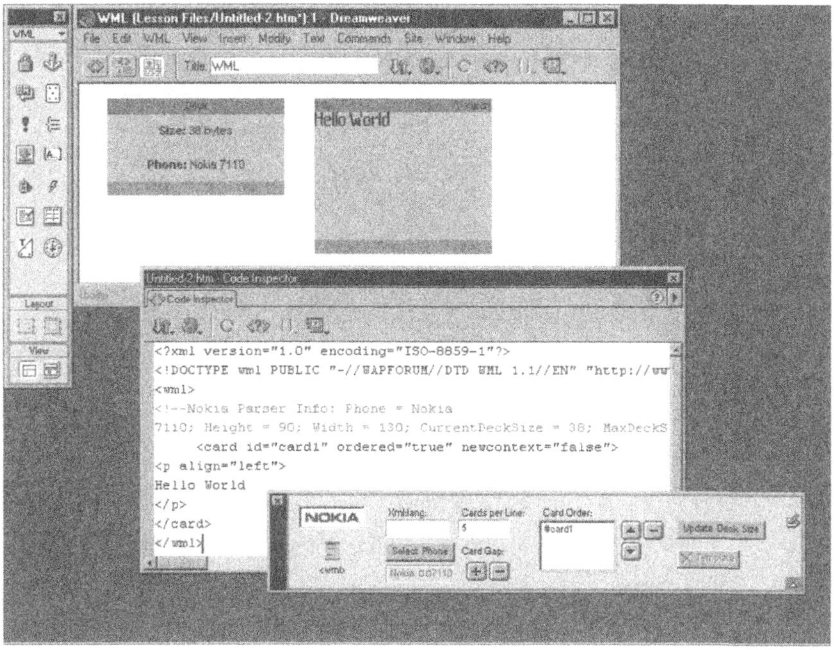

The extension includes a WML 1.1 parser, error notification, plus the ability to show previews of the WML content.

NOTE

At the time of this writing, the WML Studio was not compatible with Macromedia UltraDev 1 or UltraDev 4 and is unfortunately not available to Apple Macintosh users.

EasyPad WAPtor (shown in Figure 3.9) is a simpler WML editor available for Windows users. It allows the easy creation of WAP pages and in fact is specifically designed to ease WML creation. WAPtor features syntax highlighting to allow the WML to be more easily navigated and also has a content preview pane so you can see how you are doing at any time. The preview is limited, however (for example, there is no provision for handling WMLScript), but it can be helpful when getting started.

Figure 3.9 EasyPad WAPtor

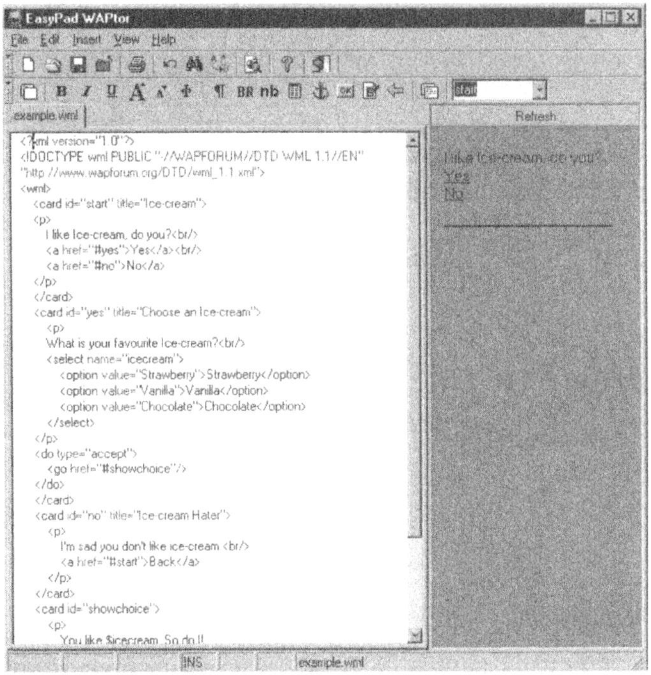

Supporting WML 1.1, WAPPage 2.1 allows the easy creation and maintenance of WML content without users necessarily needing to know too much about WML. WAPPage shows the content in an emulated WAP handset, and you can navigate the WML content by using the built-in tree view. The compiler allows you to quickly locate errors and projects help you group files together. As with many other editors, it features syntax highlighting but also features drag-and-drop WML editing.

Other Editors

Many other editors are available, some freeware, some shareware, and others full-blown retail products, so you should easily be able to find the editor that suits your style of working. The following list covers some of the more well-known editors:

- **Card One** offers a simple point-and-click interface to WML creation and is available from www.peso.de/wap_en/index.htm.
- **DotWAP** is a basic but popular editor for creating WML files and is available from www.inetis.com/freeware.asp.
- **Santana Builder** is a WML editor for the more advanced developer that can connect to databases for complex interactive site creation and is available from www.inetis.com/santanabuilder.asp.
- **WAPPage** is a WML editor with drag-and-drop functionality, visual editing, and helpful syntax highlighting together with a number of ways of previewing WML. WAPPage is available from www.zyglobe.com/products.html.
- **Wap Pro 2.0** features extensive support for the WML standard and also allows code created for dynamic applications using ASP, PHP3, and Cold Fusion among others and is available from www.wapemperor.com.
- **WBuilder Espresso** is a template-based editor that features WYSIWYG editing, WML site previews, and site publishing. **WBuilder Pro** is also available and offers workflow solutions. You can find both at www.3tl.com/products/espresso/index.htm or www.3tl.com/products/pro/index.htm.
- **WML Writer** is a simple WML creation editor reminiscent of Microsoft's WordPad but features syntax highlighting and the creation of full WML files. WML Writer is available from http://inin-wap.avalon.hr/zdravko/index.htm.
- **XML Spy** is a full-featured XML editing tool for those who want maximum control. You can use XML Spy to create WML files. For the more experienced user at home with the various WML elements, XML Spy provides XML validation, custom schema, DTD editing and creation, and more. XML Spy is available at www.xmlspy.com.

WAP SDKs

WAP SDKs offer a number of tools to developers to speed the creation of WAP sites. They generally contain at least a WML editor and an emulator to view content in. Some even go as far as to include a dedicated WAP gateway to simulate live requests and other tools such as WBMP creation and manipulation tools. The following sections outline the features of several WAP SDKs.

Ericsson WapIDE SDK

Available through registration at the Ericsson Developers' Zone (www.ericsson.com/developerszone), the WapIDE SDK enables the development and testing of WAP applications for Ericsson phones.

The SDK simulates the R320s, R380s, and R520m Ericsson phones and includes an application designer facilitating the creation and testing of WML applications. Additionally, the inclusion of a push initiator allows push messages to be sent to the WapIDE browser or real device.

The SDK will run on Microsoft Windows NT 4.0, Windows 98, or Windows 2000 and requires Java 2 Platform, version 1.3.0 or later.

Motorola Mobile ADK

The Motorola Mobile ADK is available to individual developers who register at the Motorola Applications Global Network (MAGNET). It allows the developer to create and simulate WML applications targeted towards Motorola devices. You can find additional information at www.motorola.com/developers/wireless.

Nokia WAP Toolkit

Nokia WAP Toolkit 2.1 includes WML, WMLScript, WBMP, and multi-part editors plus simulators for various Nokia phones. It also includes debugging tools, a push simulator, and sample applications.

The SDK is available to registered users and will run on Microsoft Windows NT 4.0, Windows 98, or Windows 2000 and requires Java 2 Platform, version 1.3.0 or later. A minimum 300MHz Pentium with 128Mb of RAM is recommended. You can find additional information at http://forum.nokia.com.

Openwave UP.SDK

The UP.SDK allows applications to be developed targeting devices that utilize Openwave technologies. The SDK contains an UP.Simulator, UP.Browser phone simulator for Windows and relevant developer documentation, UP.Link notification library and tools, plus sample application source code. For additional information, visit http://developer.openwave.com.

WAPObjects

The WAPObjects framework tightly integrates with Apple's popular WebObjects framework. Featuring drag-and-drop integration with WebObjects builder and support for databases and Enterprise Resource Planning (ERP) systems, WAPObjects allows rapid application development targeted at wireless users. Additional information is available at www.wapobjects.com/wapobjects/en.

WML Emulators

WML emulators add the facility to view your WML decks in an emulation of a phone device. These emulators vary wildly in how they render content and how closely this compares to actual real-life deployment of a finished application. Although emulators are useful, there is no substitute for real-world testing using actual devices over live public networks. For emulators specific to the phone manufacturers, check the previous WAP SDK listing.

- **M3Gate (www.m3gate.com/m3gate)** M3Gate allows you to surf WAP sites from the comfort of your PC and is launched when you encounter a WAP address in your browser. It can be custom-designed according to your needs for corporate applications.
- **Virtual WAPJag (www.wapjag.com/news/virtual.php)** Link to the Virtual WAPJag to launch a browser window displaying the WAP site's content.
- **WAPAka (www.wapaka.com)** A free WAP microbrowser written in WAP that can be used within Web browsers or Palm, Windows CE, and Linux operating systems.
- **YOSPACE SmartPhone Emulator (www.yospace.com)** A well-known WAP emulator that can be placed on a Web site with a huge variety of skins and sizes to choose from.
- **WinWAP PRO (www.wap-shareware.com/directory/wapemulators/winwappro.shtml)** A microbrowser available for a number of devices. The Palm OS and Windows versions are publicly available.

Summary

Although wireless markup languages have been around for some four years or so now, they are still very much a "work in progress." Forthcoming WAP specifications will doubtless add to the equation as wireless devices evolve and mature. However, WML has borrowed much from the past, and we can imagine this will continue to be the case for the foreseeable future as the language is developed further. Thus, there is still much to be learned from an appreciation of WML in its present commercially available form.

The single most important point concerning WML is that it is an application of XML and is thus subject to all the rules this entails. Although it may appear a complex issue when dealing with white space restrictions, proper nesting of elements, and representation of elements, these are common-sense points that have the added benefit of prompting better coding standards, making the resultant WML more readable by others. In an ideal world, it also guarantees platform interoperability, though individual browser interpretations of the WML standard will doubtless have their own say on how the markup is represented.

Due to the huge range of devices that will be capable of interpreting WML, you should take care in diverting from the specification produced by the WAP Forum. For some applications, such as use within a corporate intranet where you know which devices will be in use, extensions can provide much added capability; however, for someone attempting to access the same service available over the Internet on a device that does *not* support the extensions, their use could also spell disaster.

The WML language provides enough capabilities to get your content out in front of what could be the single biggest audience for any distribution medium since radio or television. For a young technology, there is already heavy backing from the biggest players in the industry. The inclusion of WML editing in the most popular HTML editors and the availability of specialized WAP SDKs are sure signs that support for WML and the creation of applications destined for viewing on mobile devices will be ongoing and extensive.

Solutions Fast Track

A Brief History of Wireless Content

☑ The Intelligent Terminal Transfer Protocol (ITTP) was developed by Ericsson in 1995. Unwired Planet developed the Handheld Device Markup Language (HDML) in mid-1996 and made it available to developers. The Tagged Text Markup Language (TTML), developed by Nokia Corporation, and the Extensible Markup Language (XML) had become available around the same time.

☑ In June 1997, Nokia and Unwired Planet formed The WAP Forum, also bringing together Motorola and Ericsson. These initial founders represented over 90 percent of the wireless market. The WAP Forum's primary goal was to develop a protocol that could be built on any platform to allow users to interact with services and information as fast and efficiently as possible and to promote product interoperability.

☑ The WAP Forum examined the various markup languages being offered by the different companies and took the best aspects of each to form the Wireless Markup Language (WML), which was released in 1999.

☑ Those devices that contained HDML browsers gained the ability to browse WML content from HDML version 3.1 onwards.

WML Overview

☑ WML is an application of XML.

☑ A WML document contains *elements* that have a *start tag* and an *end tag*. If the element isn't a container for data, the element must be self-closing (indicated by a backslash).

☑ WML files consist of a deck containing one or more cards. Each file can be thought of as a deck, within which can be any number of cards. Each card is a single page that can be displayed on the device.

☑ WML is constructed hierarchically. Files must be well-formed and valid XML documents. Validity is achieved by the inclusion of a Document Type Definition (DTD).

WML Elements

- ☑ WML elements specify the structure of the content.
- ☑ WML is quite similar to HTML in its use of elements and attributes to describe the content within each file. There are relatively few elements in comparison to HTML.

Creating WML Content

- ☑ Dynamic applications are applications that build content "on the fly" in response to requests made. A single template file filled with dynamically served content can replace hundreds of similar HTML pages.
- ☑ Openwave extensions to WML allow further context and better error handling to be introduced to your WML application.
- ☑ WML provides a number of navigation aids that are more flexible than those available in HTML.
- ☑ Tasks allow the user to perform actions dependent on the situation encountered.

WML Editors, WAP SDKs, and Emulators

- ☑ WAP editors allow the quick and easy creation of WML files. Most of the popular HTML editors support editing WML.
- ☑ WAP editors can also sometimes contain a built-in emulator to preview work.
- ☑ You should always check WML content on the target device wherever possible.

Frequently Asked Questions

The following Frequently Asked Questions, answered by the authors of this book, are designed to both measure your understanding of the concepts presented in this chapter and to assist you with real-life implementation of these concepts. To have your questions about this chapter answered by the author, browse to **www.syngress.com/solutions** and click on the **"Ask the Author"** form.

Q: I created formatted content that doesn't show up on my Nokia 7110. What's wrong?

A: Not all WAP devices are created equal. Because the WAP specification is quite loose in what is absolutely required and what is absolutely not, the device manufacturers make a judgment call as to which features are available and which are not. This has led to vast differences between how different devices handle WML, such as the Nokia 7110 compared to an Ericsson R380.

Q: How do I display characters such as a dollar sign? Is there an entity similar to *&* for an ampersand?

A: To display a dollar sign, enter it twice as follows: **$$**. The dollar sign will now display correctly.

Q: Which scripting language should I use to develop dynamic WML?

A: You can use whatever scripting language you are most comfortable with. The example in this chapter is in ASP, but you could use PERL, PHP3, or Java Server Pages to equal effect.

Q: My content does not display on a phone but works fine on an emulator. What's wrong?

A: Although many emulators are very close to the actual device, there is no substitute for real-world testing. Check that the syntax of your WML is correct and the DTD is referenced properly. If you are using nonstandard extensions, don't forget to change the DTD reference accordingly.

Q: Can I use sound or video in my WML application?

A: The use of multimedia within WAP devices is not possible at present, though this looks set to change with the introduction of new standards for third-generation (3G) services.

Chapter 4

Enhancing Client-Side Functionality with WMLScript

Solutions in this chapter:

- What Is WMLScript?
- Understanding Basic Elements of WMLScript
- Learning to Interpret WMLScript
- Performing Mathematical Operations Using WMLScript
- Using WMLScript for Input Validation
- Credit Card Validation
- Using WMLScript and Microsoft ASP: A Case Study

☑ Summary

☑ Solutions Fast Track

☑ Frequently Asked Questions

Introduction

Besides using HTML for Web page rendering, Web developers also commonly use a scripting language like VBScript or JavaScript to perform simple client-side tasks such as user input validation. Such a task might be to validate that the user has entered a valid date and to inform them if it isn't. Although tasks like validation could be done on the server side, it is far more productive and efficient to perform the checking on the client side. Besides saving a round-trip to the server for the inputs to be validated, it allows your application to be more responsive to the user.

As it is for developing Wireless Application Protocol (WAP) applications, the counterpart for Wireless Markup Language (WML) is the WMLScript language. The WMLScript language has similar objectives to those of JavaScript and VBScript. In this chapter, we will look at how WMLScript can be used in your application for client-side processing. We will first present an overview of the language, followed by its syntax, operators, and control structure. We will then illustrate the various features of the WMLScript language by walking through several examples. Each example will then be dissected. The approach to this chapter is learning by example. This chapter discusses WMLScript version 1.1.

What Is WMLScript?

WMLScript is a language that provides scripting capabilities to the WAP architecture. It complements the Wireless Markup Language. WMLScript is to WML what JavaScript is to HTML. In the context of WAP, WMLScript performs useful functions like user input validations and user prompts so as to reduce the round-trip delays to the origin server. WMLScript is loosely based on the ECMAScript (ECMA262). It is similar in syntax to scripting languages like JavaScript and JScript.

Not All Phones Support WMLScript

Before you dive into WMLScript programming, be aware that not all WAP phones support WMLScript. However, phones from the following vendors do support WMLScript:

- Ericsson
- Nokia

In addition, phones utilizing the UP.Browser from Openwave support WMLScript (e.g., Siemens and some models from Ericsson). For this chapter, we will be making use of the Nokia WAP Toolkit as well as the UP.Simulator (which contains the UP.Browser) for testing our WMLScript programs. Developers targeting their applications at the UP.Browser market have to be aware of the browser version currently installed in most of the phones in the U.S. Table 4.1 shows the different versions of the UP.Browser and their support for the Handheld Device Markup Language (HDML), WML, and WMLScript.

Table 4.1 UP.Browser Language Support

Browser Version	Supported Languages
UP.Browser 4.*x*	HDML (through translation at the gateway), WML1.1, WMLScript1.1
UP.Browser 3.1	HDML, WML1.1 (through translation at the gateway), no support for WMLScript
UP.Browser 3.0	HDML, no support for WML and WMLScript

As you can see, WMLScript is not supported by phones running the UP.Browser version 3.*x*. Therefore it is important for you to know the browser version of your targeted user when developing your application. One solution might be to customize your application such that during runtime, a check is made to ensure that the user can support WMLScript.

NOTE

Devices using the UP.Browser 3.1 rely on the gateway to translate WML codes into HDML so that they can execute WAP applications.

Using a server-side technology like Microsoft Active Server Pages (ASP), you can have the code shown in Figure 4.1.

Figure 4.1 Code Snippet for Detecting the Kind of Devices Accessing the Deck

```
<%
  if InStr(Request.ServerVariables("HTTP_USER_AGENT"), "Mozilla") then
    // user is using a Web browser
    // place codes for handling web browser here
```

Continued

Figure 4.1 Continued

```
   else
      // assumes the user is using a WAP device
      // place WAP-related codes here
      if InStr(Request.ServerVariables("HTTP_USER_AGENT"), "3.1") then
         // we can further examine the browser version using
         // the HTTP_USER_AGENT variable
      end if
   end if
%>
```

The code snippets in Figure 4.1 illustrate how you can detect the kind of devices accessing your page. Basically, when a device accesses a document from a Web server, it will send information about itself to the Web server. This information is stored in special variables on the Web server, known as Environment Variables. HTTP_USER_AGENT is one such variable. It stores information about the device type, such as browser version and brand. In the case of the UP.Browser 4.1, it will set the following string in the variable:

```
OWG1 UP/4.1.20a UP.Browser/4.1.20a-XXXX UP.Link/4.1.HTTP-DIRECT
```

Based on this information, developers can then decide if the target device is able to support WMLScript, and send the appropriate content to the device.

WMLScript Compilation

Before the WMLScript is sent to the WAP device for execution, it has to be compiled (either by the WAP gateway or through explicit compilation) into a binary format known as WMLScript bytecode. The WMLScript bytecode is then sent to the device to be interpreted by the WMLScript interpreter (located on the WAP device).

This compiled bytecode, together with the compiled WAP binary, will have to fit into the memory of the target device. Hence, the rule for minimizing the size of the WMLScript programs and WML decks still holds.

How WMLScript Interacts with WML

For a WML deck to interact with WMLScript, it has to call functions in a WMLScript program defined with the *extern* keyword (see Figure 4.2). The

WMLScript program is stored in another file ending with the wmls extension. Unlike JavaScript, it cannot be embedded within the calling program—WML in this case.

Figure 4.2 How WML Interacts with WMLScript

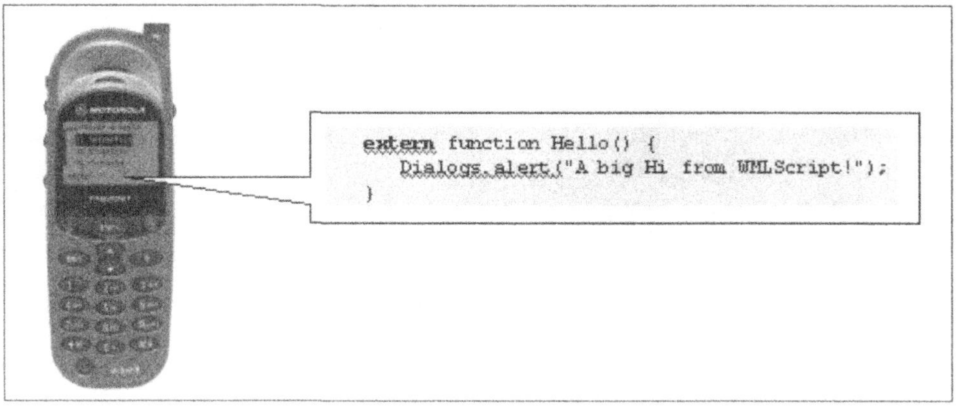

For WMLScript to interact with a WML deck, the WMLBrowser library is used (more on this in later examples). Note that in order to use WMLScript, you need to set the MIME type for WMLScript in your Web server. The MIME type for the .wmls extension is text/vnd.wap.wmlscript.

Understanding the Basic Elements of WMLScript

We will illustrate the WMLScript language in this chapter by examining several examples. For a complete reference to the language syntax, please refer to the WMLScript reference and documentation that come with the UP.Simulator. The UP.Simulator can be downloaded from Openwave at http://developer.openwave.com/download/license_41.html.

Examining WMLScript Syntax

WMLScript is a case-sensitive language. That is, proper capitalization of keywords and function names from libraries is required. It ignores white space, new lines and tabs. Each statement in a WMLScript program is terminated by a semicolon (;), for example:

```
result *= i;
```

Comments are either encapsulated within a pair of "/*" and "*/" or are preceded with the "//" combination, like this:

```
/* This is a block of
comments that spans multiple lines
*/
// This is a single line of comment
// This is another line of comment
```

WMLScript 1.1 also reserves a set of keywords that have special meaning to the compiler. They are shown in Table 4.2.

Table 4.2 Keywords in WMLScript

access	extern	path
agent	for	return
break	function	typeof
continue	header	url
div	http	use
div=	if	user
Domain	isvalid	var
else	meta	while
equiv	name	

Examining WMLScript Data Types

WMLScript supports five built-in data types:

- Integer
- Floating Point
- String
- Boolean
- Invalid

To declare a variable, use the *var* keyword. There is no need to explicitly declare the data types; WMLScript will handle them internally. The following illustrates how WMLScript automatically converts the variable to the appropriate data type:

```
var month=12;
var price=5.95;
var msg="Hello World!";
var printName=true;
var except=Invalid;
```

The *Invalid* type is used to differentiate itself from the other data types, for example:

```
if (5/0=Invalid) {
   // codes here
}
```

Examining WMLScript Operators

Similar to most programming languages, WMLScript supports the sets of operators shown in Tables 4.3, 4.4, 4.5, 4.6, and 4.7.

Table 4.3 Assignment Operators

Operator	Description
=	Assignment
+=	Add and then assign; for example, x += y is equivalent to x = x + y
-=	Subtract and then assign; for example, x -= y is equivalent to x = x – y
*=	Multiply and then assign; for example, x *= y is equivalent to x = x * y
/=	Divide and then assign; for example, x /= y is equivalent to x = x / y
div=	Divide (integer division) and then assign; for example, x div= y is equivalent to x = x div y
%=	Remainder (the sign of the result is the same as the sign of the dividend) and then assign; for example, x %= y is equivalent to x = x % y
<<=	Bitwise left shift and then assign; for example, x <<= y is equivalent to x = x << y
>>=	Bitwise right shift with sign and then assign; for example, x >>= y is equivalent to x = x >> y

Continued

Table 4.3 Continued

Operator	Description
>>>=	Bitwise right shift zero file and then assign; for example, x >>>= y is equivalent to x = x >>> y
&=	Bitwise AND and then assign; for example, x &= y is equivalent to x = x & y
^=	Bitwise XOR and then assign; for example, x ^= y is equivalent to x = x ^ y
|=	Bitwise OR and then assign; for example, x |= y is equivalent to x = x | y

Table 4.4 Binary Arithmetic Operators

Operator	Description
+	Addition (for number) or concatenation (for strings)
-	Subtraction
*	Multiplication
/	Division
div	Integer division
%	Remainder, the sign of the result is the same as the sign of the dividend
<<	Bitwise left shift
>>	Bitwise right shift and sign
>>>	Bitwise shift right with zero fill
&	Bitwise AND
|	Bitwise OR
^	Bitwise XOR

Table 4.5 Unary Arithmetic Operators

Operator	Description
+	Plus
-	Minus
--	Pre/post decrement

Continued

Table 4.5 Continued

Operator	Description
++	Pre/post increment
~	Bitwise NOT

Table 4.6 Logical Operators

<table>
<tr><th>Operator</th><th>Description</th></tr>
<tr><td>&&</td><td>Logical AND</td></tr>
<tr><td>||</td><td>Logical OR</td></tr>
<tr><td>!</td><td>Logical NOT (unary)</td></tr>
</table>

Table 4.7 Comparison Operators

Operator	Description
<	Less than
<=	Less than or equal
==	Equal
>=	Greater than or equal
>	Greater than
	Inequality

WMLScript also supports the conditional operators. For example, the following if-else statement:

```
if (x==0) {
   x = 1;
}
else {
   x=10;
}
```

can be rewritten as:

```
x = 0 ? 1 : 10
```

Examining WMLScript Control Structures

WMLScript supports the *if* construct for making decisions and the *while* and *for* loops for repetitive execution.

Using the If Statement

The *if* statements allows decisions to be made based on the result of a condition. For example, the following code snippet will calculate the average if the total is more than zero; otherwise it will assign the average to be zero:

```
if (total>0) {
   average = sum / total;
} else {
   average = 0;
}
```

Using the While Loop

The *while* loop executes a block of instruction repeatedly as long as the condition is true. For example, the following sums up all the integers from 1 to 5:

```
var num = 5;
var sum = 0;
while (num>=1) {
   sum += num–;
}
```

Using the For Loop

The *for* loop executes a block of instruction repeatedly for a finite number of times. For example:

```
   var result = 1;
   for (var i=1; i<=num; i++)  // loop counter i starts at 1, ends when
      result *= i;              // i is less than or equal to num. i is
                                  // incremented by 1 in each loop
```

Using the Break Keyword

The *break* keyword interrupts the loop within a *while* or *for* loop. For example:

```
while (num>1) {
   sum += num--;    // add up num and decrement num by 1
   if (sum>20)       // if the sum is more than 20,
      break;         // break out of the loop
}
```

Using the Continue Keyword

The *continue* keyword allows execution of either a *for* or *while* loop to continue, thereby skipping the rest of the block. For example:

```
  var num = 20;
   for (var i=1; i<=num; i++) {
    if (i%2==0)    // if no remainder (meaning it is an even number),
      continue;    // continue the loop
     Console.print(i)  // else print out the odd number   }
```

Using WMLScript Libraries

The WMLScript specification contains the following libraries:

- **Lang Library** Contains functions that relate to the language core.
- **Float Library** Contains functions that perform floating point operations.
- **String Library** Contains functions that perform string operations.
- **URL Library** Contains a set of functions for handling absolute URLs and relative URLs.
- **WMLBrowser Library** Contains functions by which WMLScript can access the associated WML context.
- **Dialogs Library** Contains a set of typical user-interface functions.

Libraries are named collections of functions that belong logically together. To call these functions, simply specify the library name followed by a dot (.) separator and the function name with the appropriate parameters. We will take a look at some of the examples in the following sections.

The library collection can be extended by emulator vendors for debugging purposes. For example, the UP.Simulator contains the Console library to help developers in debugging.

Functions in the Class Libraries

Within the libraries there are functions. Table 4.8 shows the functions within the various libraries described in the previous section. We will be making use of some of these functions in the examples that follow.

Learning to Interpret WMLScript

Let's look at our first example on how WML interacts with WMLScript. In this example, we will look at how a WML deck (see Figure 4.3) calls a WMLScript program (Figure 4.4) using the <go> element. The WMLScript program in this example contains one function defined with the *extern* keyword. It also illustrates the use of functions located in the libraries.

Figure 4.3 Example1.wml—WML Deck Calling a WMLScript Program

```
<?xml version="1.0"?>
<!DOCTYPE wml PUBLIC "-//WAPFORUM//DTD WML 1.1//EN"
"http://www.wapforum.org/DTD/wml_1.1.xml">
<wml>
    <card id="card1" title="Card 1">
        <p>
            Say hello to WMLScript!
            <do type="accept" label="Hello">
                <go href="Example1.wmls#Hello" />
            </do>
        </p>
    </card>
</wml>
```

Figure 4.4 Example1.wmls—WMLScript Program Displaying an Alert

```
extern function Hello() {
    Dialogs.alert("A big Hi from WMLScript!");
}
```

Table 4.8 Functions of the Various Class Libraries

Lang	Float	String	URL	WMLBrowser	Dialogs
abort	ceil	charAt	escapeString	getCurrentCard	alert
abs	floor	compare	getBase	getVar	confirm
characterSet	int	elementAt	getFragment	go	prompt
exit	maxFloat	elements	getHost	newContext	
float	minFloat	find	getParameters	prev	
isFloat	pow	format	getPath	refresh	
isInt	round	insertAt	getPort	setVar	
max	sqrt	isEmpty	getQuery		
maxInt		length	getReferer		
min		removeAt	getScheme		
minInt		replace	isValid		
parseFloat		replaceAt	loadString		
parseInt		squeeze	resolve		
random		subString	unescapeString		
seed		toString			
		trim			

Dissecting the Code

The WML deck (shown in Figure 4.3) contains a <go> element, which points to a WMLScript file:

```
<go href="Example1.wmls#Hello" />
```

To link a WML deck to the WMLScript file, specify the filename of the WMLScript file in the *href* attribute of the <go> element. The name following the # symbol is the function name in the WMLScript.

Within the WMLScript file (see Figure 4.4), we have a function named **Hello()** defined with the *extern* keyword:

```
extern function Hello() {
    ...
}
```

Only functions in WMLScript with the *extern* keyword preceding the function name may be called by a WML deck. In this case, the function named **Hello()** accepts no input parameters.

```
Dialogs.alert("A big Hi from WMLScript!");
```

This line simply tries to display an alert on the user's screen. In this case, we use the **alert()** function from the **Dialogs** library. Using the Nokia WAP Toolkit, you should see the screens shown in Figure 4.5.

Figure 4.5 Linking a WML Deck to a WMLScript File

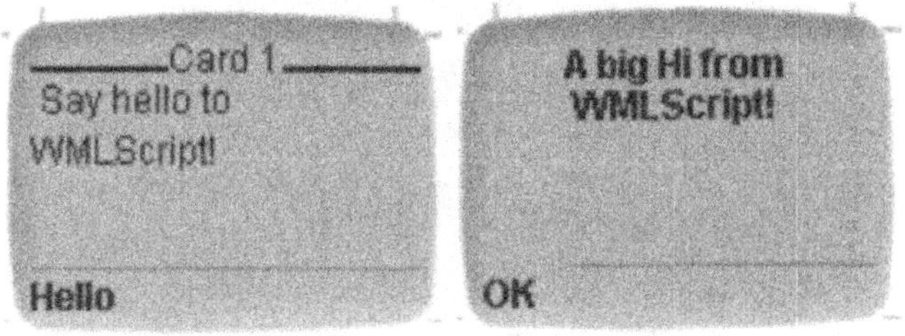

NOTE

WMLScript statements end with a semicolon (;). Readers familiar with JavaScript should feel right at home!

Performing Mathematical Operations Using WMLScript

The next example that we will illustrate is performing mathematical operations, using WMLScript to calculate the factorial of a number. This example uses a WML deck to prompt the user to enter a number (see Figure 4.6). The number is then passed to the WMLScript program for calculation (see Figure 4.7). This example illustrates looping construct in WMLScript as well as setting variable values in WMLScript and how it is passed back to the WML deck.

Figure 4.6 Example2.wml—WML Deck to Prompt the User to Enter a Number

```
<?xml version="1.0"?>
<!DOCTYPE wml PUBLIC "-//WAPFORUM//DTD WML 1.1//EN"
"http://www.wapforum.org/DTD/wml_1.1.xml">
<wml>
   <card id="card1" title="Card 1">
      <p>
         Factorial machine: <br/>
         Enter a number:
         <input type="text" name="num" />
         <do type="accept" label="Calculate!">
            <go href="Example2.wmls#Calculate($(num))" />
         </do>
      </p>
   </card>
   <card id="card2" title="Card 2">
      <p>
         $num ! is $(result)
      </p>
   </card>
</wml>
```

Figure 4.7 Example2.wmls—WMLScript Program to Calculate the Factorial of a Number

```
extern function Calculate(num){
    var result = 1;
    for (var i=1; i<=num; i++)
        result *= i;
    WMLBrowser.setVar("result", result);
    WMLBrowser.go("Example2.wml#card2");
}
```

Dissecting the Code

In this example, we want the WMLScript (see Figure 4.7) to calculate the factorial of a number and display the result in a card. This example illustrates several different features of the WMLScript language.

Let's take a closer look at the WML deck (see Figure 4.6):

```
<input type="text" name="num" />
```

The user enters a number through the use of the **<input>** element.

```
<go href="Example2.wmls#Calculate($(num))" />
```

The **Calculate()** function within the Example2.wmls file is called. The number entered by the user (**num**) is passed to the function.

```
<card id="card2" title="Card 2">
    <p>
        $num ! is $(result)
    </p>
</card>
```

Card2 will display the result of the operation performed by the WMLScript. The value of *result* is set by the WMLScript function.

Within the WMLScript function, we have the function declaration of **Calculate()**:

```
extern function Calculate(num){
    var result = 1;
```

A new variable *result* is defined with the *var* keyword and set to a value of 1.

```
for (var i=1; i<=num; i++)
   result *= i;
```

The *for* loop repeatedly executes a set of instructions. In this case, it multiplies all the numbers from 1 to num.

```
WMLBrowser.setVar("result", result);
```

The result is stored into the WML variable *result* using the **setVar()** function from the WMLBrowser library. Notice that a pair of double quotes encloses the WML variable *result.*

```
   WMLBrowser.go("Example2.wml#card2");
}
```

Once the result is stored, #card2 from the WML deck is loaded using the **go()** function from the WMLBrowser library. Figure 4.8 displays the resulting screens on the WAP Toolkit.

Figure 4.8 Performing Mathematical Operations Using WMLScript

Using WMLScript for Input Validation

The next example illustrates a very common usage of WMLScript—input validation. Input validation is a very common task performed by Web applications. Imagine asking the user for his or her birth date. If the user enters 13 for month, the error could be detected early by client-side input validation, rather than posting the input to the server and causing a round-trip delay only to realize that the input is erroneous. This is especially important for WAP application, as the connection is inherently slow and therefore there is a necessity to reduce the number of connections to the server.

In this application, we have a user registering using a WAP browser. The user keys in his or her userID and enters a password twice for confirmation. The WMLScript will compare the two passwords to ensure that they are identical before proceeding to register the user. (The WML deck is shown in Figure 4.9 and the WMLScript is shown in Figure 4.10.)

Figure 4.9 Example3.wml—WML Deck to Prompt Users to Enter a UserID and Password

```
<?xml version="1.0"?>
<!DOCTYPE wml PUBLIC "-//WAPFORUM//DTD WML 1.1//EN"
"http://www.wapforum.org/DTD/wml_1.1.xml">
<wml>
   <card id="card1" title="Registration" newcontext="true">
      <p>
      UserID : <input type="text" name="userID"/>
      Password: <input type="password" name="password1"/>
      Confirm Password: <input type="password" name="password2"/>
      <do type="accept" label="Register!">
          <go href="Example3.wmls#verifyPassword('$password1',
                '$password2')"/>
       </do>
      </p>
   </card>
</wml>
```

Figure 4.10 Example3.wmls—WMLScript Program to Perform Input Validation

```
extern function verifyPassword (Password1, Password2)
{
  var URL;
  if (String.compare(Password1, Password2) == 0) {
    URL = "register.asp?userID=" + WMLBrowser.getVar("userID") +
         "&password=" + Password1;
  WMLBrowser.go(URL);
  }
```

Continued

Figure 4.10 Continued

```
  else {
     DisplayMessage("Passwords do not match! Please retry...");
     WMLBrowser.go("Example3.wml");
   }
}

function DisplayMessage(message) {
  Dialogs.alert(message);
  return ;
}
```

Dissecting the Code

Again, let's start with the WML deck shown in Figure 4.9:

```
UserID : <input type="text" name="userID"/>
Password: <input type="password" name="password1"/>
```

User enters a userID and password

```
Confirm Password: <input type="password" name="password2"/>
```

The user re-enters the password:

```
<go href="Example3.wmls#verifyPassword('$password1', '$password2')"/>
```

The **verifyPassword()** function in Example3.wmls is called. The two passwords are passed to this function. Notice the pair of double quotes surrounding the two input parameters.

At the WMLScript end, shown in Figure 4.10, is:

```
extern function verifyPassword (Password1, Password2)
```

The first function in this file, **verifyPassword()**, has two input parameters: Password1 and Password2.

```
var URL;

if (String.compare(Password1, Password2) == 0) {
```

The **compare()** function in the String library is used to compare the two strings. If they are identical, the function will return a value of 0. If the two passwords were identical, an ASP file would be called.

```
URL = "register.asp?userID=" + WMLBrowser.getVar("userID") +
    "&password=" + Password1;
```

The URL for the ASP file is created with the query string containing the userID and password.

```
WMLBrowser.go(URL);
```

The browser is then redirected to the ASP file:

```
else {
    DisplayMessage("Passwords do not match! Please retry...");
```

If the two passwords are not identical, the **DisplayMessage()** function is then called. This function takes in a single input parameter:

```
WMLBrowser.go("Example3.wml");
```

Once the message is displayed, we reload the Example3.wml deck:

```
function DisplayMessage(message) {
    Dialogs.alert(message);
    return ;
}
```

Notice that the **DisplayMessage()** function does not have the *extern* keyword. This function can be used only within the WMLScript file and is not callable from a WML deck directly. The output of Example3.wml and Example3.wmls are shown in Figure 4.11.

Figure 4.11 Comparing User Inputs Using WMLScript

NOTE

Functions that only are used internally do not require the *extern* keyword.

Credit Card Validation

Another common use for WMLScript is in validating credit card numbers. This example illustrates several WMLScript language constructs by checking the validity of a credit card number.

The Credit Card Validating Algorithm

Depending on the credit card type, most credit card numbers are encoded with a check digit. By running the credit number through some algorithms, a check digit is often appended to the end of the credit card number. To validate that the number is a valid credit card number, the numbers are applied the same algorithm in the reverse manner. The following illustrates the LUHN Formula (Mod 10) for validating a credit card number.

1. Multiply the value of alternate digits by 2, starting from the second rightmost digit.
2. Add all the *individual* digits derived from step 1.
3. If the sum of all the digits is divisible by 10, the card number is valid; otherwise it is invalid.

Let us demonstrate this algorithm's use with an example. In this example we will attempt to validate a credit card with the number 123467890123456.

1. First, multiply the value of the alternate digits by 2 starting from the second rightmost digit as described previously.

Digit	1	2	3	4	5	6	7	8	9	0	1	2	3	4	5	6
Multipler	x2		x2		x2		x2		x2		x2		x2		x2	
Result	2		6		10		14		18		2		6		10	

2. Next, add the individual digits derived from the previous step.

```
2 + 2 + 6 + 4 + ( 1 + 0 ) + 6 + ( 1 + 4 ) + 8 + ( 1 + 8 ) +
0 + 2 + 2 + 6 + 4 + ( 1 + 0 ) + 6 = 64
```

3. Finally, attempt to divide the resultant sum from step 2 by a value of 10.

```
Sum=64
```

Sixty-four is not divisible by 10; therefore the card number is invalid! Our implementation of this algorithm using WMLScript is shown in Figure 4.12 and Figure 4.13.

Figure 4.12 Example4.wml—WML Deck to Prompt the User to Enter a Credit Card Number

```
<?xml version="1.0"?>
<!DOCTYPE wml PUBLIC "-//WAPFORUM//DTD WML 1.1//EN"
"http://www.wapforum.org/DTD/wml_1.1.xml">
<wml>
<template>
   <do type="options" label="Main">
      <go href="#card1"/>
   </do>
</template>
   <card id="card1" title="Card 1">
      <p>
         Please enter credit card number:
         <input type="text" format="*N" name="num"/>
         <do type="accept" label="Validate!">
            <go href="Example4.wmls#Validate('$(num)')" />
         </do>
      </p>
   </card>
   <card id="card2" title="Invalid">
      <p>
         Credit number not correct.
      </p>
   </card>
   <card id="card3" title="Valid">
      <p>
         Credit number correct.
```

Continued

Figure 4.12 Continued

```
        </p>
    </card>
</wml>
```

Figure 4.13 Example4.wmls—WMLScript Program to Validate the Authenticity of a Credit Card Number

```
extern function Validate(num) {
var sum = 0;
var temp, length;

    length = String.length(num);
    for (var i=length-1; i>=0; —i) {             //start with rightmost
digit
        if (i % 2 == 0) {
           temp = Lang.parseInt(String.charAt(num,i)) * 2; //multiply the
                                                           //number by 2
           sum += Lang.parseInt(String.charAt(temp,0));   //sum up the
                                                          // first digit
           if (String.length(temp) > 1)                   //if more than 1
                                                          //digit...
              sum += Lang.parseInt(String.charAt(temp,1));//    sum up the
                                                          //    second digit
        } else {
           sum += Lang.parseInt(String.charAt(num,i));   // simply sum up
                                                         // the number
        }
    }
    if (sum % 10 != 0)                                  // if not divisible
                                                         // by 10
        WMLBrowser.go("#card2");                       //    card number
                                                         //    not valid
    else                                                 // else
```

Continued

Figure 4.13 Continued

```
        WMLBrowser.go("#card3");                    //   card number
                                                    //   is valid
}
```

Dissecting the Code

We start with the <template> element of the WML deck shown in Figure 4.12:

```
<template>
    <do type="options" label="Main">
        <go href="#card1"/>
    </do>
</template>
```

The <template> element defines deck-level event binding. In this case, the <do> element is applicable to all the cards in the deck.

Because WMLScript does not support the use of array, we have to improvise the use of array using a string. Since a string supports element indexing, we can manipulate the digits as though we are using an array (this can be seen in Figure 4.13). For example, if we have 1234567890123456, we can manipulate it as a string (see Figure 4.14).

Figure 4.14 Manipulating a String Much Like an Array

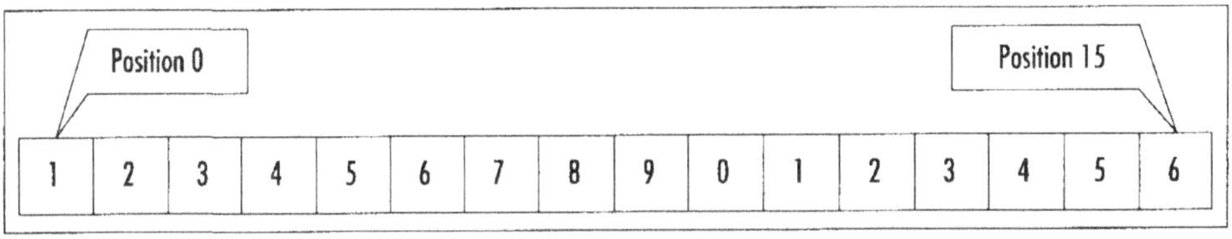

Given the following statement:

```
length = String.length(num);
```

We will first want to know the length of the number:

```
for (var i=length-1; i>=0; –i) {        //start with rightmost digit
```

We will then use a *for* loop to cycle through all the digits in the number:

```
if (i % 2 == 0) {
    temp = Lang.parseInt(String.charAt(num,i)) * 2; //multiply the
                                                    //number by 2
```

If the position is an even number (the % is the modulus operator), multiply the digit at that position by 2:

```
sum += Lang.parseInt(String.charAt(temp,0));  //sum up the first digit
```

and sum up the result *digit-by-digit.*

```
if (String.length(temp) > 1)                  //if more than 1
                                               //digit...
  sum += Lang.parseInt(String.charAt(temp,1));//  sum up the
                                               //   second digit
```

If the result contains more than a digit, sum up the second digit.

```
} else {
 sum += Lang.parseInt(String.charAt(num,i)); //simply sum up the number
}
```

If the position number is not an even number, simply sum up the number.

```
if (sum % 10 != 0)                          //if not divisible by 10
   WMLBrowser.go("#card2");                 //card number not valid
else                                         //else
   WMLBrowser.go("#card3");                 //card number is valid
```

Finally, take the result and perform a modulus 10 operation. If there is no remainder the card is valid; otherwise it is invalid. Figure 4.15 shows the resulting screens on the WAP Toolkit.

Figure 4.15 Validating Credit Card Numbers Using WMLScript

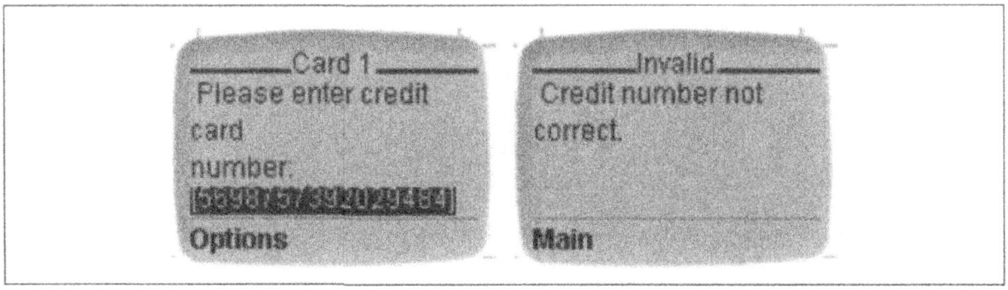

Using WMLScript and Microsoft Active Server Pages (ASP): Case Study

We have seen how WMLScript can be used to perform client-side validation and to complement WML applications that run on a WAP device. One particular application that is very popular is a currency converter. However, the conventional currency converter usually hardcodes the exchange rate in the WMLScript program. Once the WMLScript is downloaded onto the device, it is cached and any changes to the currency conversion rate would not be reflected in the application.

In this case study, we will illustrate how you can use ASP to create a truly dynamic WMLScript program using the currency converter application as a case study. Our currency converter is able to reflect the daily changes in the exchange rates.

Designing the Application

A currency converter application often is used to illustrate the use of WMLScript. For this example, we will use the UP.Simulator provided by Openwave. Figure 4.16 and Figure 4.17 illustrate the desired outcome of our application.

Figure 4.16 Selecting the USD Option to Convert from, and Keying the Amount to Convert

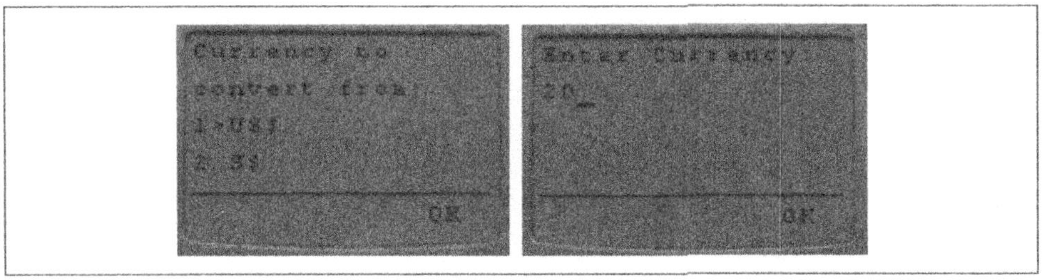

Figure 4.17 Selecting the SIN Option to Convert to, and Viewing the Result of the Conversion

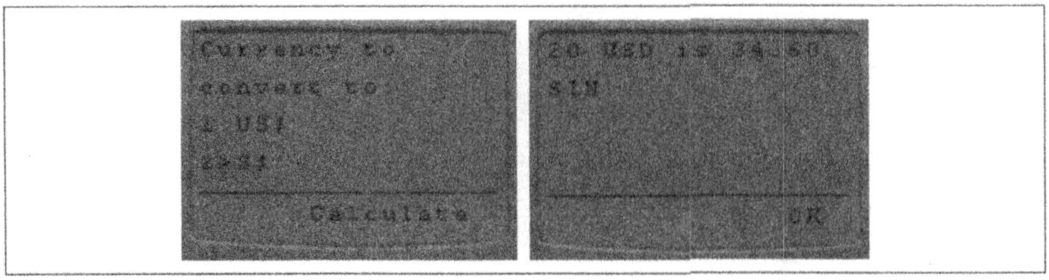

The user simply chooses the currency to convert from, keys in the amount to be converted, and selects the target currency. The converted currency would then be displayed.

Creating the Database

Our application makes use of a database containing a single table named **Conversion**. The database table can be seen in Figure 4.18.

Figure 4.18 Our Database Contains One Table Named Conversion

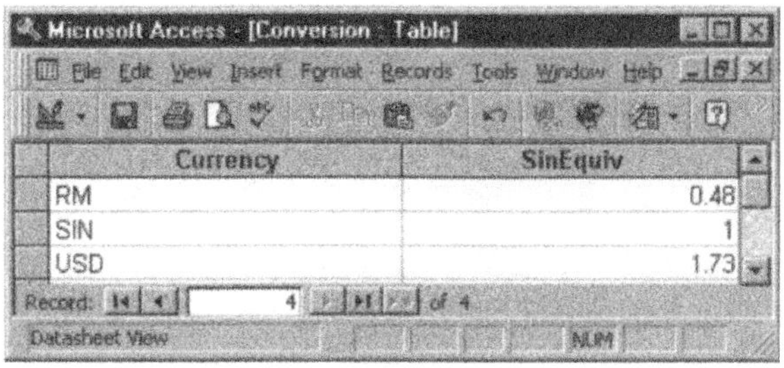

This table simply contains the exchange rate of currencies. The exchange rate is tagged to a fixed currency, the Singapore dollar in this case. For example:

1 USD (US Dollar) = 1.73 SIN (Singapore Dollar)

1 RM (Malaysian Ringgit)= 0.48 SIN

Converting from one currency to another is a two-step process. For example:

1. To convert 15 USD to RM, first convert the USD to SIN:

   15 * 1.73 = 25.95 SIN

2. Then convert the SIN to RM:

   25.95 / 0.48 = **54.0625 RM**

The Conversion table contains two fields: Currency and SinEquiv. The Currency field contains the currency name and the SinEquiv field contains the equivalent amount of the currency in Singapore dollar.

The WML Deck

Let's take a look at the WML deck that loads the application. The code can be seen in Figure 4.19.

Figure 4.19 Currency.wml

```
<?xml version="1.0"?>
<!DOCTYPE wml PUBLIC "-//WAPFORUM//DTD WML 1.1//EN"
"http://www.wapforum.org/DTD/wml_1.1.xml">
<wml>
   <card id="card1" title="Currency">
      <p>
         Currency to convert from:
         <select name="fromCurrency">
            <option value="USD">US$$</option>
            <option value="SIN">S$$</option>
            <option value="RM">RM</option>
         </select>
         Enter Currency: <input type="text" name="amount" format="*N"/>
         Currency to convert to:
         <select name="toCurrency">
            <option value="USD">US$$</option>
            <option value="SIN">S$$</option>
            <option value="RM">RM</option>
         </select>
         <do type="accept" label="Calculate">
            <go href="Calculate.asp#Convert($(amount))"/>
         </do>
      </p>
   </card>
   <card id="card2" title="Note">
      <p>
         Please select a different currency.
      </p>
   </card>
</wml>
```

There are two cards within the deck. The first card takes care of user input, and once the user is done with it, links to the WMLScript:

```
<go href="Calculate.asp#Convert($(amount))"/>
```

Notice that we did not link to a WMLScript file with the .wmls file extension. Instead, we have pointed the deck to an ASP file. We are going to use Microsoft Active Server Pages to dynamically generate the WMLScript program. The amount to be converted is also passed as an input parameter to the function named **Convert()**.

Generating the WMLScript Program from ASP

In the early days of the Web, most of the pages were static—content remains the same unless it was changed by a webmaster or a Web designer. However, with the explosive growth of the Internet (and the World Wide Web), people have realized the importance and necessity of dynamic content. And very soon after, different technologies were developed to enable Web sites to publish content that was dynamic, through the use of server-side technologies. A good example would be CGI scripts that return stock pages when requested. These pages often contain information stored in a database. Some of the other server-side technologies/products include:

- Microsoft Active Server Pages (ASP)
- Java Server Pages (JSP)
- ColdFusion Application Server
- PHP Hypertext Preprocessor (PHP)

In this example, we will illustrate server-side processing using Microsoft ASP. Readers who are not familiar with ASP could refer to the following sources for learning ASP:

- www.w3schools.com/asp/default.asp
- www.learnasp.com

The listing in Figure 4.20 shows the ASP document generating the WMLScript program.

Figure 4.20 Calculate.asp

```
<!-#INCLUDE file="adovbs.inc" ->
<%
      Response.ContentType="text/vnd.wap.wmlscript"
      if hour(time())>=0 AND minute(time())>=00 AND hour(time())<8 AND
minute(time())<=59 then
```

Continued

Figure 4.20 Continued

```
            Response.ExpiresAbsolute = MonthName( month(date()) , true) &
" " & day(date()) & " 8:00:00"
        else
            Response.ExpiresAbsolute = MonthName( month(date()+1) , true)
& " " & day(date() + 1) & " 8:00:00"
        end if
%>
extern function Convert(amount){
    var origAmt=amount;
    var fromCurrency = WMLBrowser.getVar("fromCurrency");
    var toCurrency = WMLBrowser.getVar("toCurrency");
    if (String.compare(fromCurrency,toCurrency)==0) {
        WMLBrowser.go("currency.wml#card2");
        return;
    }
     <%
     Dim rs
     Set rs = Server.CreateObject("ADODB.Recordset")
     connStr = "DRIVER={Microsoft Access Driver (*.mdb)};DBQ=" &
Server.MapPath("currency.mdb") & ";"
     rs.Open "Conversion", connStr, adOpenKeySet, adLockOptimistic
     %>
     var USD =<% rs.Find "Currency = 'USD'"
                 response.write rs("SinEquiv")
             %>;
     var SIN =<% rs.MoveFirst
                 rs.Find "Currency = 'SIN'"
                 response.write rs("SinEquiv")
             %>;
     var RM = <% rs.MoveFirst
                 rs.Find "Currency = 'RM'"
                 response.write rs("SinEquiv")
             %>;
    if (fromCurrency=="USD") {
```

Continued

Figure 4.20 Continued

```
        amount = USD * amount;
    } else if (fromCurrency=="RM") {
        amount = RM * amount;
    }
    if (toCurrency=="USD") {
        amount = amount / USD;
    } else if (toCurrency=="RM") {
        amount = amount / RM;
    }
    amount *=1.0;
    var str = origAmt + " " + fromCurrency + " is " ;
    Dialogs.alert(str + String.format("%.2f",amount) + " " +
toCurrency);
}
```

We use ASP to dynamically generate the WMLScript program. The reason for this is that we want to load the currency exchange rate from a database so that it is always current. By doing that, the user is always using the latest exchange rate for conversion.

However, there is a little problem is doing this. As database access is required, it could be a time-consuming affair if we generate the WMLScript program every time someone needs to use the application. In a Web environment where concurrency is an important factor in determining the success of your site, this problem is going to drastically slow down your server.

Fortunately, the nature of this application does not require that the user require up-to-the-minute exchange rates. It would be reasonable if the exchange rates were updated once a day.

To solve this problem, we make use of the caching property of WMLScript on the device. What we could do is to set the expiration date of the WMLScript to every morning at 8:00 A.M. When a user accesses the application after 8:00 A.M., or loads the application for the first time, the WMLScript is fetched from the server and cached for later use. Subsequent usage would then be loaded from the cache.

Let's now take a closer look at our WMLScript file:

```
<!-#INCLUDE file="adovbs.inc" ->
```

Since we are using ActiveX Data Objects (ADO) for database access, we need to include the adovbs.inc file containing all the ADO constants used by VBScript.

```
<%
    Response.ContentType="text/vnd.wap.wmlscript"
```

Remember that since we are generating the WMLScript file dynamically, we need to explicitly set the MIME type in the ASP document using the Response.ContentType property. Note that a pair of <% %> tags encloses the ASP codes (VBScript in this case).

```
if hour(time())>=0 AND minute(time())>=00 AND hour(time())<8 AND minute
(time())<=59 then
   Response.ExpiresAbsolute = MonthName( month(date()) , true) & " " &
day(date()) & " 8:00:00"
else
   Response.ExpiresAbsolute = MonthName( month(date()+1) , true) & " "
& day(date() + 1) & " 8:00:00"
end if
```

The next portion of the code determines the expiration date of the WMLScript. The checking is simple: if the user loads the ASP document after 12 midnight, the expiration date would be set to 8:00 A.M.. the same day. If the ASP document is loaded after 8:00 A.M., the expiration date would then be set to 8:00 A.M. the next day. To set the expiration date, use the Response.ExpiresAbsolute property. The date format looks like this: "Oct 21 8:00:00".

```
function Convert(amount){
   var origAmt=amount;
   var fromCurrency = WMLBrowser.getVar("fromCurrency");
   var toCurrency = WMLBrowser.getVar("toCurrency");
```

Next we have the **Convert()** function. For a WMLScript function to be callable from WML, it needs to have the *extern* keyword. Within the function we defined three variables using the *var* keyword. The first variable is used to store the original amount to be converted, and the next two variables retrieve the two currencies involved in the conversion. In order for WMLScript to interact with WML, you can use the WMLBrowser library. There are a number of functions within the library that allow you to communicate with the WML deck. The **getVar()** function retrieves the values of WML variables.

Before we start the conversion, we want to make sure that the two currencies involved are not identical. For string comparisons, use the **compare()** function from the String library. If they are identical, load the second card in the WML deck and exit the WMLScript function using the *return* keyword.

```
if (String.compare(fromCurrency,toCurrency)==0) {
   WMLBrowser.go("currency.wml#card2");
   return;
}
```

Because we are getting the conversion rates from a database, we need to use ADO for data access.

```
<%
Dim rs
Set rs = Server.CreateObject("ADODB.Recordset")
connStr = "DRIVER={Microsoft Access Driver (*.mdb)};DBQ=" &
Server.MapPath("currency.mdb") & ";"
rs.Open "Conversion", connStr, adOpenKeySet, adLockOptimistic
%>
```

Once the records in the database are retrieved, we proceed to assign the individual rate to the respective variables.

```
var USD =<% rs.Find "Currency = 'USD'"
            response.write rs("SinEquiv")
        %>;
var SIN =<% rs.MoveFirst
            rs.Find "Currency = 'SIN'"
            response.write rs("SinEquiv")
        %>;
var RM = <% rs.MoveFirst
            rs.Find "Currency = 'RM'"
            response.write rs("SinEquiv")
        %>;
```

The **Find()** method of the *Recordset* object is used to locate the correct record to assign to the variables. Note that after the first variable is assigned, you need to perform a **MoveFirst()** operation so as to ensure that the search always begin from the first record. Also, recall earlier that we opened the recordset using the *adOpenKeyset* cursor:

```
rs.Open "Conversion", connStr, adOpenKeySet, adLockOptimistic
```

This is important because using the default cursor (adOpenForwardOnly) will cause the **MoveFirst()** method to fail. Finally, we perform the conversion:

```
if (fromCurrency=="USD") {
    amount = USD * amount;
} else if (fromCurrency=="RM") {
    amount = RM * amount;
}
if (toCurrency=="USD") {
    amount = amount / USD;
} else if (toCurrency=="RM") {
    amount = amount / RM;
}
```

The result is then displayed using the **alert()** function from the Dialogs library.

```
amount *= 1.0;
var str = origAmt + " " + fromCurrency + " is " ;
Dialogs.alert(str + String.format("%.2f",amount) + " " + toCurrency);
}
```

The **format()** function from the String library formats the result to two decimal places.

Debugging the WMLScript

One of the difficulties that we found when coding this application is deciding how to troubleshoot your WMLScript when you are faced with problems. Since we are using the UP.Simulator for this application, we naturally turn to the Phone Information window for help when it comes to debugging.

Apart from some of the syntax errors that would quite often emerge, another tricky problem is with caching. You need to ensure that the WMLScript file is cached and used at the right time.

Let's discuss the first problem, syntax error. Syntax error can be detected easily using the Phone Information window. For example, assume we have the following error in our WMLScript program:

```
var USD =<% rs.Find "Currency = 'USD'"
            response.write rs("SinEquiv")
        %>  // missing ";"
```

This error will generate an error in the compilation process, and the deck shown in Figure 4.21 would be displayed.

Figure 4.21 The UP.Simulator Displaying an Error Message

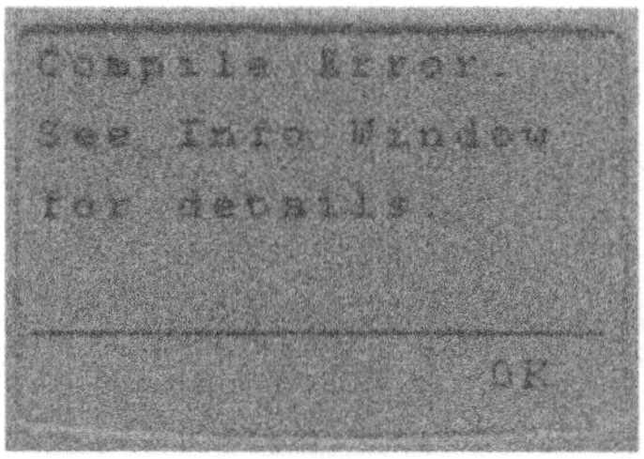

Looking into the Phone Information window (see Figure 4.22) reveals the following source of error.

```
(25) : error: syntax error at "var" missing ;
```

Figure 4.22 Looking into the Phone Information Window for Sources of Error

The second problem is trickier. You want to know whether you have set the expiration date of the WMLScript correctly. For instance, when you load the application for the first time at 7:30 A.M., the WMLScript should expire in 30 minutes. To check that, the UP.Simulator provides an option for you to display the cache information of the browser. To display the cache information, press the F6 function key or click on **Info->Cache** (this can be seen in Figure 4.23). The cache information would then be displayed in the Phone Information window displayed in Figure 4.24.

Figure 4.23 The UP.Simulator Allows Cache Information to Be Examined

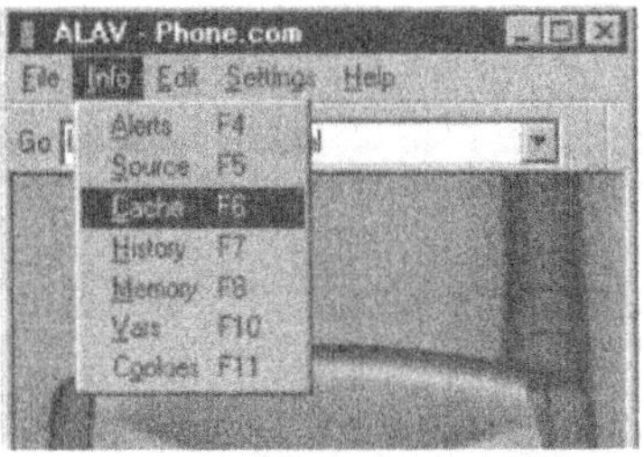

Figure 4.24 Viewing the Cache Information in the Phone Information Window

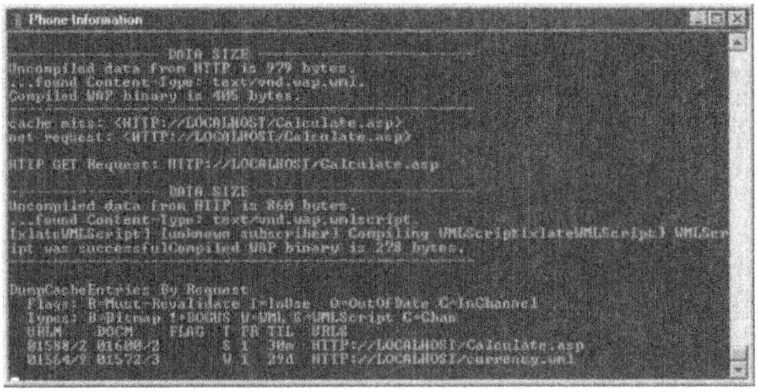

Notice that the Calculate.asp document (generating the WMLScript file) has a Time-To-Live (TTL) of 30 minutes. This indicates that the WMLScript will expire in 30 minutes (since loading time is 7:30 A.M.).

```
DumpCacheEntries By Request
  Flags: R=Must-Revalidate I=InUse  O=OutOfDate C=InChannel
  Types: B=Bitmap !=BOGUS W=WML S=WMLScript C=Chan
```

```
URLM     DOCM     FLAG  T  PR TTL  URLS
01588/2 01600/2         S  1  30m  HTTP://LOCALHOST/Calculate.asp
01564/9 01572/3         W  1  29d  HTTP://LOCALHOST/currency.wml
```

Once the application is loaded, the WMLScript in the cache would be used if the application is accessed anytime from 7:30 A.M. to 8:00 A.M. This is reflected in the Phone Information when the application is run again:

```
cache hit: <HTTP://LOCALHOST/Calculate.asp>
```

When the same application is accessed after 8:00 A.M., the WMLScript would then have expired, and a reload is necessary. To be certain that the WMLScript is reloaded, check the Phone Information window to see that the WMLScript is recompiled:

```
HTTP GET Request: HTTP://LOCALHOST/Calculate.asp

----------------- DATA SIZE ------------------------
Uncompiled data from HTTP is 860 bytes.
...found Content-Type: text/vnd.wap.wmlscript.
[xlateWMLScript] [unknown subscriber] Compiling
WMLScript[xlateWMLScript] WMLScr
ipt was successfulCompiled WAP binary is 278 bytes.
---------------------------------------------------
```

During the debugging stage you might be tempted to forward your system clock to see the expiration effect of the WMLScript. However, this does not work. For example, if you load the application at 7:45 A.M., the TTL of the WMLScript file would be 15 minutes. If you now adjust your time to 8:00 A.M., the WMLScript would still be loaded from cache. This is because the expiration of the WMLScript works based on the "count-down" effect. The correct way to do this is to set the clock to 7:58 A.M. and load the application. After that, wait for about five minutes before loading the application again. This time round, the WMLScript would expire!

Lessons Learned

What was originally thought of as a simple project turns out to be quite an experience for us. Let us share what we have learned with you.

Caching Problems

We have tested the application on three emulators:

- UP.Simulator 4.0
- Nokia WAP Toolkit version 1.3 beta and 2.0
- Ericsson WapIDE 2.1

The Nokia WAP Toolkit 2.0 and the UP.Simulator have no problem with caching. However, the Ericsson WapIDE performs caching regardless of setting the HTTP header to expire the cache at a certain time. The Ericsson emulator will work correctly only if the cache is disabled. This results in the ASP document being executed every time the application is loaded, which causes a significant increase in load time, both on the client and server sides.

Debugging the Emulators

Recall that we have this line in the last part of our WMLScript:

```
amount *= 1.0;
```

This seemingly redundant line resolves a bug in the UP.Simulator's implementation of the **format()** function in the String library.

```
String.format("%.2f",amount)
```

The problem with this function is that if the *amount* is an integer, it will not format the string correctly. When used together with the **alert()** function from the Dialogs library, the screen simply remains unchanged even when the user presses the **Calculate** soft key.

This problem was irritating, as it was hard to pinpoint at the beginning of the project. The other emulators like Nokia WAP Toolkit and the Ericsson WapIDE do not have problems with this issue.

Emulators Are Relatively Unstable!

When it comes to running WMLScripts, emulators are still pretty unstable. We spent a good portion of our time trying to run the application on the different emulators. Sometimes it worked, sometimes it didn't. So far, the UP.Simulator has been pretty stable, except for the bug noted previously.

Summary

In this chapter, we have taken a quick look at how WAP applications can make use of WMLScript to perform client-side tasks such as input validation. We have demonstrated the various features of the language by examining several examples.

The syntax of WMLScript is similar to that of JavaScript. In this chapter we have seen the various language features like data types, looping constructs, keywords, and operators. Since not all WAP browsers support WMLScript, special care must be taken to ensure that the target device is able to execute the WMLScript program before sending them one.

The WMLScript language itself comes with a set of libraries providing most of the commonly used functions to help the developers. However, note that some vendors may provide additional libraries that will work only on their particular platform.

To get you started on WMLScript, we have demonstrated four scenarios in which we can make use of WMLScript. These examples illustrated the various language features such as linking a WML deck with a WMLScript program, looping, improvisation of arrays using strings, and so on. And finally, we put together a WAP application using WML, WMLScript, and Microsoft ASP to illustrate a practical use of WMLScript.

Solutions Fast Track

What Is WMLScript?

- ☑ WMLScript is loosely based on the ECMAScript (ECMA262).
- ☑ Most devices in the market support WMLScript.
- ☑ WMLScript programs are compiled into bytecode by WAP gateways.
- ☑ WMLScript is activated by WML decks.

Understanding Basic Elements of WMLScript

- ☑ WMLScript contains libraries.
- ☑ Within each library are functions that provide most commonly needed functionality.

Learning to Interpret WMLScript

☑ WMLScript functions that are preceded by the *extern* keyword are callable by WML decks.

Performing Mathematical Operations Using WMLScript

☑ Variables are declared in WMLScript using the *var* keyword.

☑ WMLScript handles data type internally.

☑ WMLScript supports looping using the for construct.

Using WMLScript for Input Validation

☑ The **compare()** function in the String library compares two strings.

Credit Card Validation

☑ WMLScript does not support arrays.

☑ Use a string to improvise an array if needed.

Using WMLScript and Microsoft ASP: A Case Study

☑ A server-side technology like ASP can be used to generate dynamic WMLScript programs.

☑ WMLScript programs are cached on the client-side.

☑ Use the HTTP directives to control caching behavior on the client-side.

Frequently Asked Questions

The following Frequently Asked Questions, answered by the authors of this book, are designed to both measure your understanding of the concepts presented in this chapter and to assist you with real-life implementation of these concepts. To have your questions about this chapter answered by the author, browse to **www.syngress.com/solutions** and click on the **"Ask the Author"** form.

Q: Why is it that on certain emulators my WMLScript program would fail to execute?

A: Some emulators do not execute WMLScript properly. A good idea is to try out different emulators during the development phase.

Q: Why is input validation important for mobile devices?

A: Input validation is especially important for mobile application because the connection to the back-end server is inherently slow. Input validation reduces the round-trip delay caused by server-side validation since the validation is done on the client-side.

Q: What are the similarities and differences between WMLS and JS as it applies in this realm?

A: WMLScript and JavaScript both perform client-side operations. However, unlike JavaScript, WMLScript programs are compiled before they are sent to the client side. Also, WMLScript programs are saved in separate files, unlike JavaScript, which has the option to embed within the HTML document.

Q: What kind of setup is required of me if I want to run the ASP example?

A: You need to have a Web server (Microsoft Personal Web Server or Internet Information Server will do). If you are not using Microsoft Windows Operating System, you may need additional setup for your Web server (e.g., Apache, etc.).

Q: Where can I learn more about the WMLScript language? What is the latest version of WMLScript?

A: We strongly recommend that you check out WAPForum's Web site for the latest release of WMLScript and its specifications. The WAPForum's Web site is at www.wapforum.org.

Chapter 5

Wireless Development Kits

Solutions in this chapter:

- The Openwave UP.SDK 4.1
- The Nokia WAP Toolkit 2.1
- The Motorola Mobile Application Development Kit 2.0
- The Ericsson Mobile Internet WapIDE 3.1
- The Yospace SmartPhone Emulator 2.0

☑ Summary

☑ Solutions Fast Track

☑ Frequently Asked Questions

Introduction

When you start developing Wireless Application Protocol (WAP) applications, you will probably find that continuously testing your application using your WAP-enabled mobile phone is both difficult and expensive. The good news is that emulators and software development kits (SDKs) are available to help you during the design, development, and testing phases of creating your mobile application. These tools not only make testing the application easier than using your mobile phone, but they also provide more detailed feedback, including information such as line numbers where the errors occurred and the size of the compiled Wireless Markup Language (WML) deck.

Each SDK has different features, advantages, and disadvantages. Developers also have quite a variation in their preferences. The information in this chapter should help you choose an SDK that is best suited to your needs and work style. We look at the following SDKs in this chapter:

- The Openwave UP.SDK 4.1
- The Nokia WAP Toolkit 2.1
- The Motorola Mobile Application Development Kit 2.0
- The Ericsson WAP-Integrated Development Environment 3.1
- The Yospace SmartPhone Emulator 2.0

We go step-by-step through the process of downloading, installing, and using each SDK with simple examples. This chapter should give you a good feel for each one and help you decide which one you would like to use during your development process.

The Openwave UP.SDK 4.1

A large percentage of mobile phones sold in the United States use Openwave System's WAP browser. Openwave provides an SDK to help you develop applications and test them on the UP.Browser. The software is available free of charge, and you can use it to test applications on your local file system or on remote servers. The UP.SDK can, through the use of *skins,* emulate a variety of mobile phones on the market to make testing your application on multiple devices easier. The UP.SDK includes a variety of tools and documentation, including the following:

- The UP.Simulator for WML
- Libraries for Common Gateway Interface (CGI) programs that make generating WML easier (Perl and C)
- C++ (Solaris) and COM (Windows) notification, digest, and fax libraries and tools
- Tools for requesting and installing SSL certificates
- Sample WML and WMLScript files
- Developer documentation in Hypertext Markup Language (HTML) format

You can use the Openwave UP.SDK to simulate phones that use the UP.Browser version 4.*x*. You can develop WAP applications and applications that use the Openwave extensions to WML using the UP.SDK. The sample application we develop does not use these extensions. You will need a separate program for editing your WML and WMLScript files because an editor is not included in the UP.SDK.

Installing Openwave UP.SDK

The UP.SDK is written for the Win32 platform—this includes Windows 9*x*, Windows NT, and Windows 2000. We look at the specific requirements for your system, how to obtain the software, and how to install it on your computer.

System Requirements for the Openwave UP.SDK

Openwave gives the following requirements for running the UP.SDK:

- To run the UP.Simulator, you need a computer with an Intel (or compatible) processor running Windows 95, Windows 98, or Windows NT 4.0 (Service Pack 5).
- To test WML services available on the Internet (such as the example services provided by Openwave), your computer must have an Internet connection.
- To test your own WML services, you need a Hypertext Transfer Protocol (HTTP)-compliant Web server.

Openwave does not explicitly state support for Windows Me or Windows 2000, although we have run the UP.SDK on both platforms without any problems.

Openwave does not claim any memory requirements either, but we have found that you should have *at least* 64MB of memory.

Obtaining the Openwave UP.SDK

You can download the UP.SDK from the Openwave Developer Program Web site at http://developer.openwave.com in the **Downloads** section. You are not required to register in order to download the UP.SDK, but you are required to register if you wish to test through the UP.Link gateway that they provide on the Internet. Also on the Web site are directions for signing up and provisioning the UP.Link gateway for testing.

You can download various emulator skins to simulate testing on multiple devices. The term *skins* is a bit misleading, actually, because the browser will not only inherit the look of the device but also the behavior. This is useful for checking the navigation and appearance of your application on multiple devices in a rapid manner. The skins are downloadable from the same location as the UP.SDK.

Installing the Openwave UP.SDK

When you download the UP.SDK from the Openwave Web site, you will download a file called upsdkW41e.exe. Run this application, and you will be greeted with the initial install screen shown in Figure 5.1.

Figure 5.1 The UP.SDK Initial Install Screen

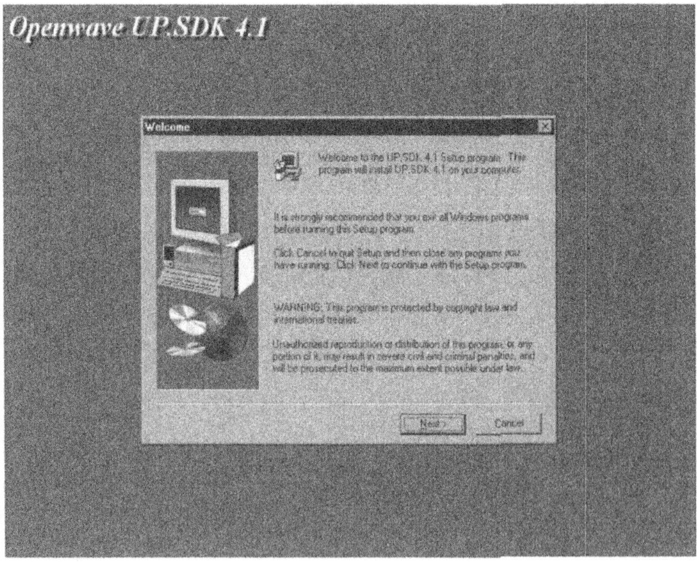

Click **Next** to continue. You will have to click **Yes** to agree to the Software License Agreement as well as the Screenshots and Image Use Agreement. You will also have to verify that you are not residing in a country that the United States currently has an export embargo against (a peculiar requirement for a WapIDE!).

The installation program then asks you where you would like to install the UP.SDK on your computer and what program group you would like to set up for your Start menu. You can accept the defaults for this or specify another location. The installer then copies the software to your system, and the final install screen gives you the option of viewing the ReadMe file and starting the UP.Simulator. Choose the option to start the UP.Simulator and click **Finish**.

Working with the Openwave UP.SDK

When you first launch the UP.Simulator, you will see two screens, as shown in Figure 5.2.

Figure 5.2 The UP.Simulator

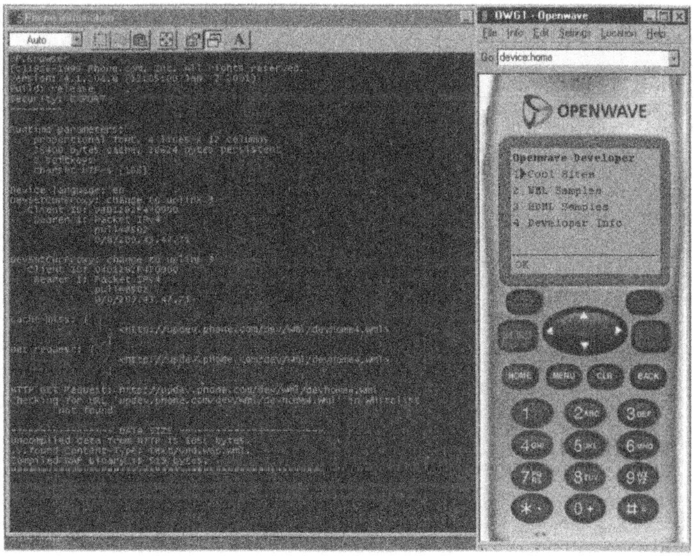

The Phone Information screen provides you with details about what the UP.Simulator is doing. Shown here are the URLs that you are trying to access as well as information about the currently loaded WML Deck. This is information that is usually not critical to your application, but useful to know if, for example, you are debugging a problem or curious about the compiled size of your WML. You may want to work with the Phone Information window minimized so that you look at it only when you run into problems.

The emulator window shows a picture of the selected device and will be the window you use to interact with the application.

Accessing and Editing Local Files

This version of the UP.SDK requires you to type in every WML deck you would like to access in the address bar located at the top of the emulator window. To access local files, use the syntax file://c:\wap\hello.wml and normal HTTP URLs to access decks on a Web server such as http://127.0.0.1/hello.wml. Let's save the following WML file as a simple Hello World page called hello.wml in the c:\wap directory:

```
<?xml version="1.0"?>
<!DOCTYPE wml PUBLIC "-//WAPFORUM//DTD WML 1.3//EN"
                       "http://www.wapforum.org/DTD/wml13.dtd">
<wml>
  <card id="hello" title="Hello World">
    <p>Hello World!</p>
  </card>
</wml>
```

The emulator window with our example file is shown in Figure 5.3.

In most cases, you can use the keyboard to enter information into the emulator instead of using the graphical keypad. However, use the keypad to verify that input formatting restrictions and other GUI features work as you expect.

NOTE

The UP.SDK does not provide a mechanism for editing files. You must use an editor such as TextPad or Emacs to create and change your WML files. The advantage of Openwave's approach is that you do not have to learn a new editor just to write WML applications. The disadvantage is that your favorite editor may not have the WML-specific editing features that make developing WAP applications easier.

Figure 5.3 The UP.Simulator

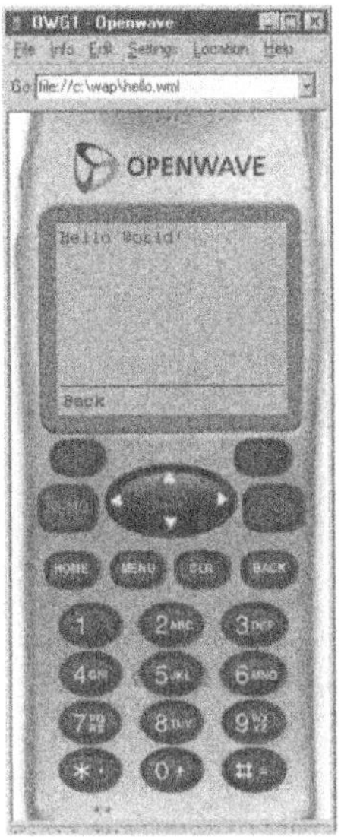

The Phone Information window will show you the uncompiled and compiled size of the WML file you access. The Phone Information window also shows you caching information; because wireless networks are low bandwidth, every effort to cache files is made. This may become a problem when you are developing an application that is constantly updating with new information, such as a game. WAP provides mechanisms for telling gateways and browsers how long to cache information, but it may not behave as expected in all cases. This is a good way to ensure that your page is caching only your page for the duration you specify. Figure 5.4 shows the Phone Information window after we have loaded our example page.

Figure 5.4 Information About the Current WML Deck

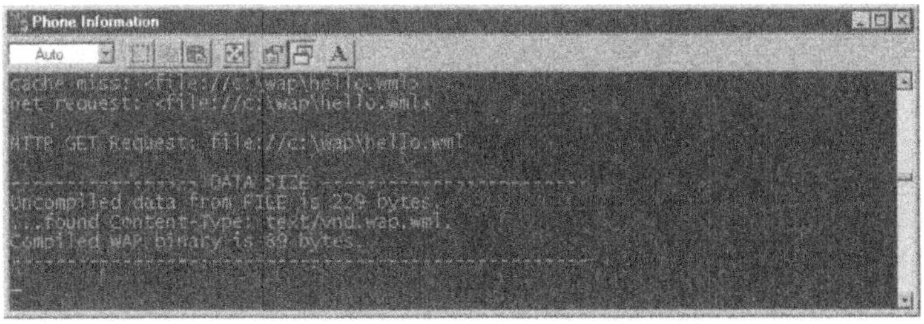

Accessing Files through a Gateway

Openwave provides access to a UP.Link gateway free of charge for developers. You are required to sign up for the Openwave Developer Program in order to access this service. You can sign up at the Openwave Developer Program Web site by clicking the **WAP Gateway** button along the top navigation bar or the **UP.Link Provisioning** link along the left navigation bar. You will be prompted to sign up if you are not a member. Once you log in, you can add, delete, or edit users that are allowed to access the UP.Link gateway. Follow the directions on the Openwave Web site to manage your users and gain access to the UP.Link gateway.

You need to change the settings in your UP.Simulator to use the UP.Link you have just set up. From the emulator window, select **Settings | UP.Link Settings** from the menu bar. You will then be able to select either a direct HTTP connection, or to use one of the gateways specified. The gateways are all prefilled with the names of the Openwave gateway servers, so all you have to do is click the radio button as shown in Figure 5.5 and click **OK** to start using the gateway.

Figure 5.5 UP.Simulator Gateway Setup Screen

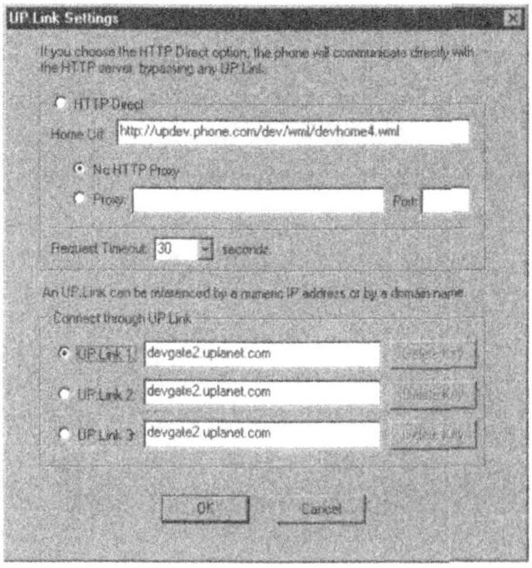

Once you are using the gateway, you cannot access local files anymore; the simulator will attempt to contact the gateway first and have it deliver the file. You can access only servers that are not blocked by firewalls. You must run a Web server that is accessible by the outside world to test your WAP application using a gateway. Other than that, the simulator acts as it did before, but it proxies all of its requests through the UP.Link gateway.

Debugging Techniques

As described earlier, the UP.SDK provides a Phone Information console window that provides great information for the developer of a WAP application. This window gives you information that helps you track down the source of any problem. Figure 5.6 illustrates this with our hello.wml file from which we have removed the close paragraph tag (</p>).

Figure 5.6 The Phone Information Window after Loading an Invalid WML File

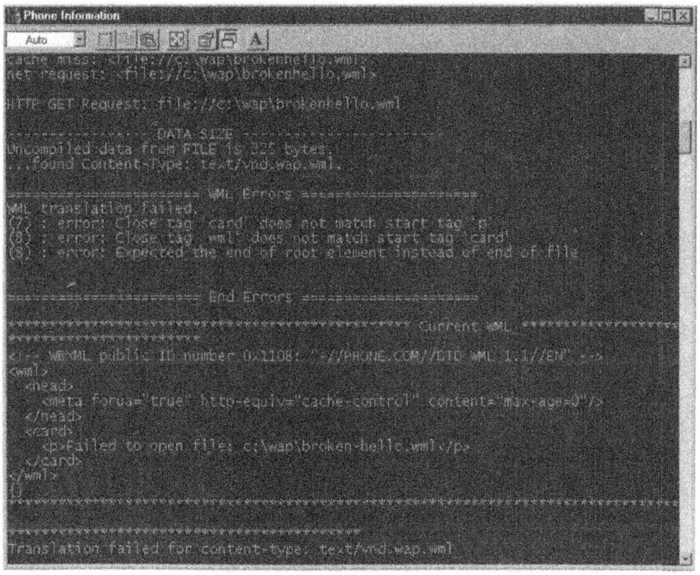

Unfortunately, the error message isn't as descriptive as "No close tag for <p> tag opened on line 6," but it does help you find the problem. The phone emulator window simply tells you to look in the Phone Information window because a compilation error occurred. You will also notice in Figure 5.6 that the file was not found in the cache. We had a compilation error, so the UP.Simulator will look for the file on the disk again, but if we load the hello.wml file from the previous example again, we notice that it finds the file in the cache. This is indicated by the text "cache hit: file://c:\wap\hello.wml" in the Phone Information window.

The UP.SDK will not reload the WML deck from the server unless you first clear the cache by selecting **Edit | Clear Cache** from the emulator window menu bar. You can now reload the hello.wml file and get the compiled size and other information from the Phone Information window.

The Info menu allows you to view information about the status of the UP.Simulator. You can find out what cookies have been set, what documents are in the cache, the source of the current WML deck, and other information.

WARNING

The use of cookies is not always supported in WAP browsers, and even if it is supported, it may not always be available. The UP.Browser, for instance, relies on a UP.Gateway being used for cookie support. You may want to investigate, using URL rewriting to insert user information into links or some other technique for tracking users on your mobile site to avoid these incompatibilities.

The Nokia WAP Toolkit 2.1

Nokia is the largest mobile handset manufacturer in the world, so a large percentage of your WAP site visitors will be using Nokia phones. The Nokia WAP Toolkit can simulate WAP-enabled Nokia phones as well as a prototype phone that implements features not yet available on consumer handsets. The Nokia WAP Toolkit is an environment for developing, viewing, and testing WAP applications. It includes many features that will make your mobile development easier, such as the following:

- Editing, validating, and viewing WML decks
- Editing and debugging WMLScript files
- Viewing and changing WML variables inside the WAP browser
- Examining debug messages from the WAP browser
- Creating and editing WBMP images

The Nokia WAP Toolkit is a complete development environment, but you can use any editor of your choice and merely use the Toolkit to view and debug your applications. You can use the Nokia WAP Toolkit to simulate Nokia phone models 6210 and 7110 after you download additional modules from the Forum Web site. You can only develop WAP 1.2 applications using the Nokia Blueprint phone, a concept phone that comes with the toolkit. WAP 1.3 is not supported at this time. The SDK includes an editor for WML, WMLScript, and Wireless Bitmap (WBMP) image files.

Developing & Deploying...

Supporting Multiple Versions of WML

The browser in a mobile phone cannot be easily upgraded, and sometimes it cannot be upgraded at all. Because of this, your WAP site will most likely need to support multiple versions of the WML standard. The advantage to you is the ability to determine what browsers people will be using based on the devices that are most prominent in the marketplace. The disadvantage is that you cannot tell your users to upgrade to the latest browser in order to view your site—they are stuck with that browser until they purchase a new mobile phone.

Requiring a certain version of WML will cause your site to be unviewable by users with devices that do not support that particular version. By doing so, you will lose customers before ever getting a chance to make a first impression.

Installing Nokia's WAP Toolkit

The Nokia WAP Toolkit is written in Java for the Win32 platform—this includes Windows 9*x*, Windows NT, and Windows 2000. The installation may require you to install additional software from Sun Microsystems if you do not have an appropriate Java Virtual Machine (JVM) already installed on your computer. In the following sections, we cover the specific requirements for your system, how to obtain the software, and how to install the Nokia WAP Toolkit on your computer.

System Requirements for the Nokia WAP Toolkit

Nokia gives the following requirements for running the WAP Toolkit:

- Java Runtime Environment (JRE) version 1.3. If you do not have the JRE installed, the setup program will install it for you automatically.
- Adobe Acrobat Reader for Online Help and User Documentation.
- A Pentium II 266 MHz (or faster), 128MB RAM (256MB recommended), Windows NT 4.0 with SP3 or Windows 98 or Windows 2000, 16-bit color, 1024x768 resolution, 20MB of hard disk space.

Nokia does not state support for Windows Me, but we have installed and run the toolkit successfully on Windows Me. The memory requirements might seem high, especially coming from an embedded device manufacturer, but the WAP Toolkit's performance is noticeably better with more memory.

Obtaining the Nokia WAP Toolkit

You can download the Nokia WAP Toolkit from the Forum Nokia Web site at http://forum.nokia.com. You have to register to download the WAP Toolkit, but registering allows you to download the SDK free of charge.

You can download a variety of other tools for WAP and other technologies from the Forum Nokia Web site. The Nokia Activ Server is a WAP gateway/Web server that you can use to develop, test, and deploy WAP applications. You also gain access to developer discussions and documentation on Nokia products.

Installing the Nokia WAP Toolkit

The file you download from Forum Nokia is called NokiaToolkit2_1.zip. It contains the setup.exe program as well as the license agreement and release notes. You must unzip this file to run the setup program. You can use any program that can handle zip archives, such as Aladdin Expander (www.aladdinsys.com/expander) or WinZip (www.winzip.com).

Once you unpack the zip archive, run the setup.exe program. You will be greeted with the initial install screen shown in Figure 5.7.

Figure 5.7 The Nokia WAP Toolkit Initial Install Screen

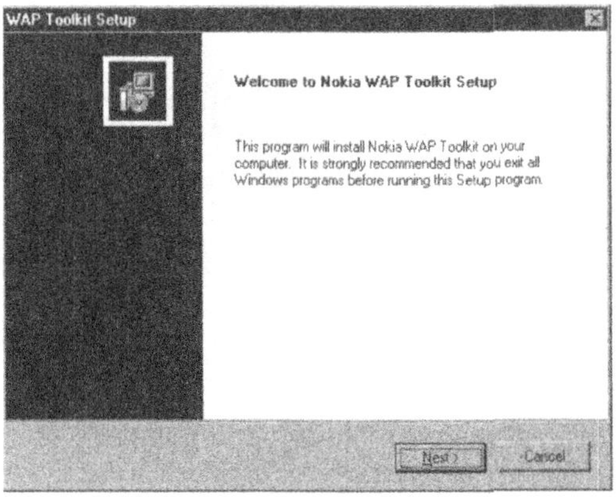

Click **Next** to continue with the installation.You then have to accept the terms of the license agreement by clicking **Yes**.You are now presented with the choice of where to install the program; it is safe to accept the default location. The next screen, shown in Figure 5.8, lets you choose what components of the Nokia WAP Toolkit you want to install.

Figure 5.8 Nokia WAP Toolkit Install Options

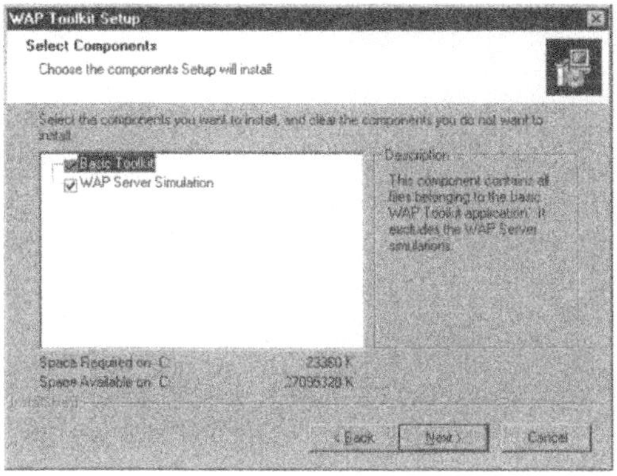

The Basic Toolkit is required; you cannot uncheck it.The second component is the WAP Server Simulation, which allows you to test applications locally when you do not have access to a WAP gateway. If you do not install this component, you must have access to a WAP gateway in order to use the toolkit. Unless you are extremely cramped for disk space, do install the WAP Server Simulation because it makes prototyping and development much easier.

Choose what Program Group to install the Toolkit into and confirm all your decisions.The setup program will finish the installation, and you can then use the Nokia WAP Toolkit.

Working with the Nokia WAP Toolkit

If you installed using the defaults, you can launch the Nokia WAP Toolkit by selecting **Programs | Nokia WAP Toolkit | WAP Toolkit** from the Start menu.You will see a splash screen while the application loads and then the initial window, shown in Figure 5.9, will appear.

The window on the left is where you will do most of your work—it includes the WBMP editor,WML and WMLScript source editors, and various debugging facilities.The window on the right is the phone emulator where you will view your application and enter information using the phone interface.

Figure 5.9 Nokia WAP Toolkit

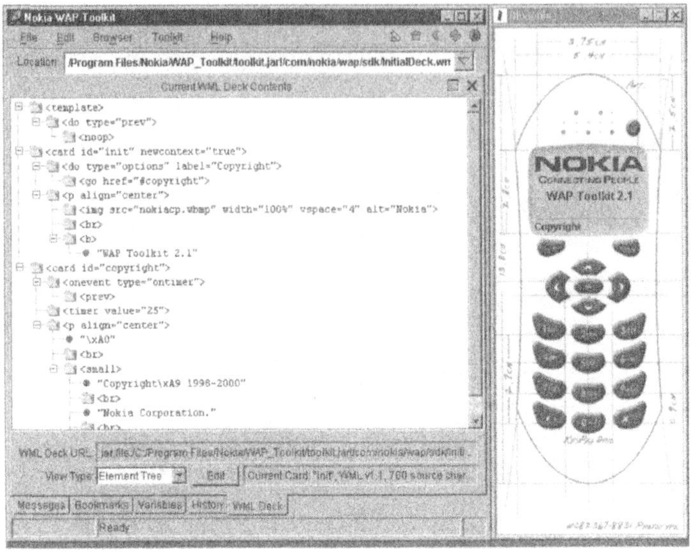

Accessing and Editing Local Files

You can use the Nokia WAP Toolkit to create, edit, and view files stored locally on your computer. Let's create a simple WML file called hello.wml and save it in the c:\wap directory. First, select **File | New | WML Deck** from the menu bar, or press **Ctrl+N** on your keyboard. A new WML deck will appear in the editor with a large amount of skeleton code already filled in. This is great for the first couple of files that you write, but you will quickly find yourself deleting large portions of the skeleton files every time you create a new WML deck. Let's use the template and customize it to mimic our other examples.

The WML deck defaults to WML 1.1, but has version 1.2 and 1.3 declarations commented out in the default file. You can use one of the other declarations if your application requires features not available in version 1.1 of WML. For our example, version 1.1 suffices, so we can delete the other declarations. We do not need a head element in our deck, so we can delete that comment. The default template provides a Back button for every card. The Nokia browser does not provide backwards navigation by default, so if you do not place this functionality in the template section or in every card, users on Nokia phones will not be able to navigate to previous cards when viewing your application.

The first card contains a quite a few comments that guide you through building your own card. The first thing we need to do is change the title. Let's make the attribute read **title="Hello"** instead of the default "Card #1." We aren't going to add anything new to the card, but we can see where we would have to add elements such as <onevent>, <do>, and <timer> from the comments. We can remove these comments to make our final code cleaner. The default <do> tag has a type attribute of *unknown*. We want this to be the default action, so let's change this so that it reads **type="accept"** and leave the rest as it is.

We have a paragraph in card1 that has the text *First Card* in bold. Let's change the text to be "**Hello World!**" and leave it bolded. We can leave the rest of the deck as it is. Our final example file now looks like this:

```
<?xml version="1.0"?>
<!DOCTYPE wml PUBLIC "-//WAPFORUM//DTD WML 1.1//EN"
    "http://www.wapforum.org/DTD/wml_1.1.xml">
<wml>
  <template>
    <do type="prev"><prev/></do>
  </template>

  <card id="card1" title="Hello" newcontext="true">
    <do type="accept" label="Next">
      <go href="#card2"/>
    </do>

    <p align="center">
      <big><b>Hello World!</b></big>
    </p>
  </card>

  <card id="card2" title="Card #2">
    <onevent type="ontimer">
      <prev/>
    </onevent>

    <timer value="25"/>
```

```
    <p align="center">
      <big><b>Second Card</b></big>
    </p>
  </card>
</wml>
```

You need to save your file before the Toolkit can compile it, but let's make our lives easier by clicking the **Compile** button and letting the Toolkit prompt us to save the file. Save the file in c:\wap as nokia.wml and then you should see that it compiles with no errors. You need to compile your file before viewing with the Nokia Blueprint phone in order to see the latest version. If you do not compile it, you will be viewing the last version that was compiled and your changes will not be shown. You can now click the **Show** button, and your sample file will appear in the Blueprint phone as shown in Figure 5.10.

Figure 5.10 Blueprint Phone with Our WML Deck

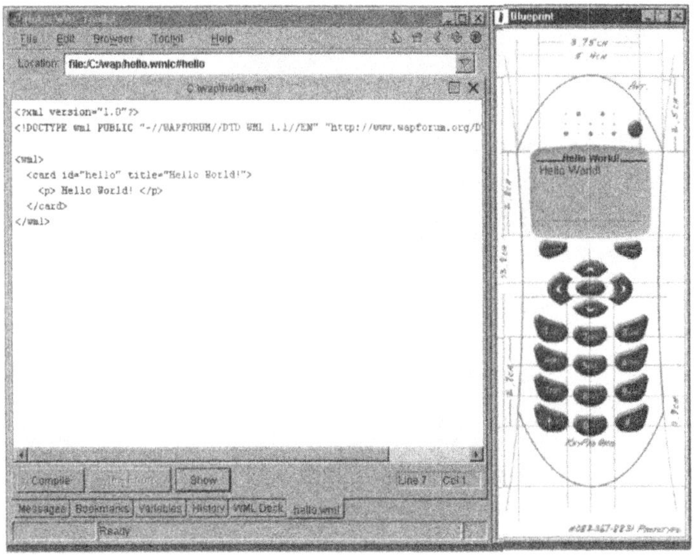

The Nokia WAP Toolkit provides a substantial amount of information about the WML file you are currently viewing. If you select the **WML Deck** tab along the bottom of the Toolkit window, you will see the WML Deck that is currently loaded into the emulator in an Element Tree view—a tree representation of the WML file. You can choose from a variety of views including:

- **Original Source** This is only available if you are viewing an uncompiled WML file in the emulator. If you compile your file before viewing it or you are retrieving it through a gateway, this option will not appear.
- **Decoded WML** The WML source represented by the Compiled Wireless Markup Language (WMLC) file the emulator received. This will not have any of the comments and will more than likely be indented differently than the original file, but the functionality should be the same. This is handy when your source files are heavily commented for maintenance reasons and you just want to see the actual WML code.
- **Bytecode** The compiled version of the WML file. This is what the actual WAP devices will receive on the network. This is of little value except to determine the compiled size of the WML deck. If you are developing WAP tools such as a gateway or WMLC decompiler, this is a useful view to have.
- **Element Tree** A tree representation of the WML file. A quick and easy way to see the overall structure of your WML deck.

The Nokia WAP Toolkit provides a large number of features that developers of all types of WAP applications will find useful. Not all of them may seem relevant at first, but chances are you will use each one of them during some point in your development cycle.

Accessing Files through a Gateway

Nokia does not provide access to a WAP gateway through their developer program. You will have to download and install the Nokia Activ Server to access files through a Nokia gateway. Interoperability is a large issue in the WAP world, so testing various WAP browser and gateway combinations is recommended. Let's use the Ericsson public gateway and the Nokia WAP Toolkit together.

To change the WAP gateway, select **Toolkit | Device Settings** from the menu bar. The Blueprint Device Settings dialog box will appear. Check the radio button labeled **Use WAP Gateway Connection** and enter the IP address of **195.58.110.201** in the WAP Gateway Address text box. The Nokia WAP Toolkit with these settings is shown in Figure 5.11.

The Nokia WAP Toolkit will not use the WAP gateway to access WML decks on your local file system. Only WML decks loaded from URLs will be retrieved through the gateway. You can continue to develop and test local files without setting the Toolkit back to HTTP Direct mode.

Figure 5.11 The Nokia WAP Toolkit Gateway Settings

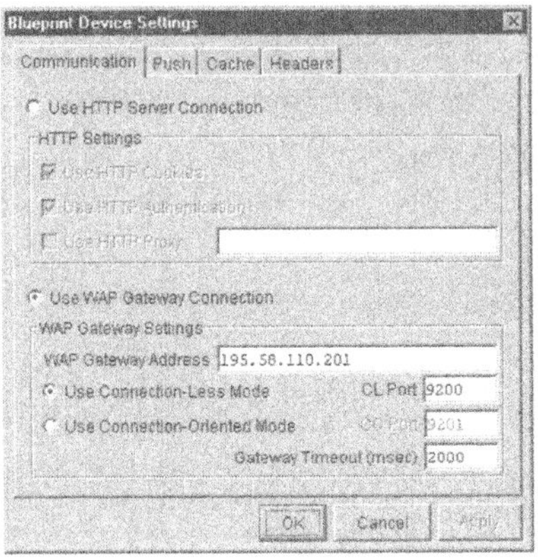

Debugging Techniques

The Nokia WAP Toolkit has many advanced debugging features. Let's start off by looking at how it handles invalid WML. Let's remove the closing big element (</big>) from the first card in our nokia.wml file, so that the paragraph looks like this:

```
<p align="center">
  <big><b>Hello World!</b>
</p>
```

Click **Compile** in the Toolkit window, and a dialog box pops up telling us that the source file contains two errors. Click **OK** and use the error message box that appears in the source editing window to review the errors, as shown in Figure 5.12.

When you double-click on an error message, the cursor is placed on that location in the source file. The first error message says "Error: 3077,line:15, column:8 XML:name within end tag does not match with the start tag." Line 15, column 8 is in the middle of our </p> element. The error message isn't very explicit about what it was expecting, but it does tell us that it was expecting something other than a paragraph element to be closed. We know it is the big element, and if we put the </big> element back into the source file, everything works as expected.

Figure 5.12 Invalid WML Error Message in the Nokia WAP Toolkit

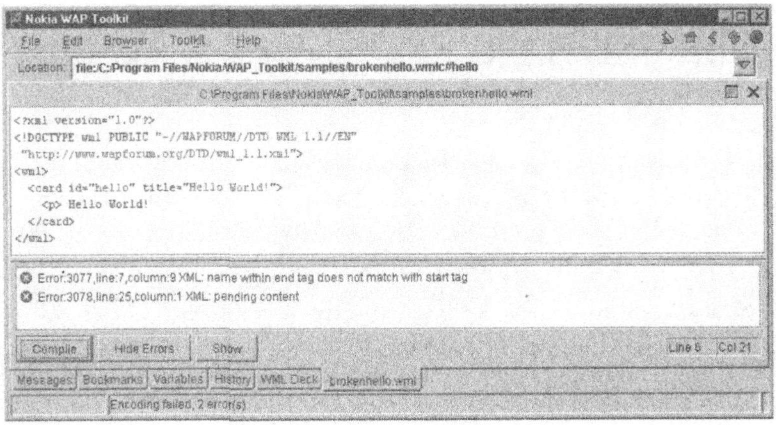

WARNING

The final error: "Error:3078,line:44,column:1 XML: pending content" of our example in this section does not make much sense. Our source file is only 29 lines long. This type of error message was common in C compilers and generally means that a close tag is missing somewhere in the file. First, look into the error messages that point to actual line numbers, then recompile your deck—you will often find that the other errors were actually side effects of the more explicit errors.

We need a more complex WML file to see the advanced features. This WML deck isn't very useful on a real WAP device, but it is useful for illustrating the debugging features of the Nokia WAP Toolkit.

```
<?xml version="1.0"?>
<!DOCTYPE wml PUBLIC "-//WAPFORUM//DTD WML 1.1//EN"
 "http://www.wapforum.org/DTD/wml_1.1.xml">
<wml>
  <card id="home" title="Toolkit demo" ontimer="#home">
    <timer value="300"/>
    <p> Hello $name. Welcome. </p>
  </card>
</wml>
```

When you open the file and show it in the Blueprint phone, you will notice that the status bar along the bottom of the Toolkit window counts down to the next timer event. Figure 5.13 shows it along the bottom as well. Debugging a timer is much easier when you see it counting down. Otherwise, you just wait for a while and wonder if something is wrong with your code or if your computer is just slow!

Our deck does not set the *name* variable. We can do this through the toolkit and see the results on the Blueprint phone. Select the **Variables** tab along the bottom of the Toolkit window to bring up the variable editing screen. We can add variables to the browser environment by entering the name and value and clicking **Set** at the bottom-right of the window. Let's set up our variable by setting Name to **name** and Value to **phyllis** as shown in Figure 5.13.

Figure 5.13 Advanced Debugging Features of the Nokia WAP Toolkit

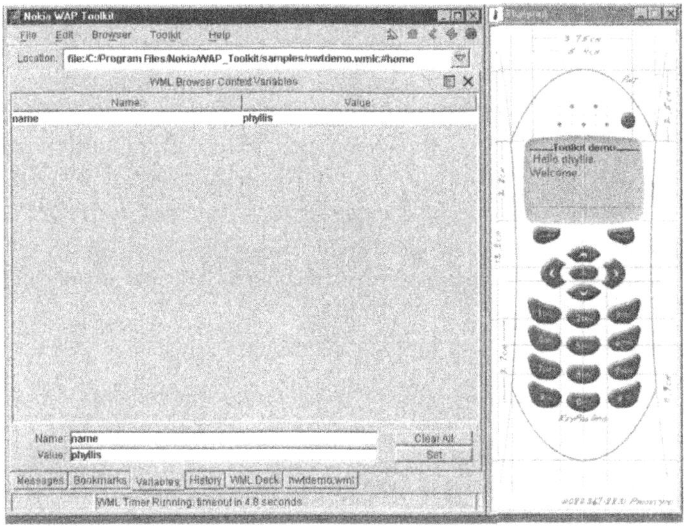

Once you click the **Set** button, you will notice that the deck is updated in the Blueprint phone. Let's change the value to **darrell** and click **Set** again. You'll notice that the Toolkit automatically updates your application when you change variables. You can alter variables and debug your application without going through the tedium of actually reloading the deck every time using the Nokia WAP Toolkit.

The Motorola Mobile Application Development Kit 2.0

The Motorola Mobile Application Development Kit (Mobile ADK) supports the widest variety of mobile standards of any of the SDKs we have covered here. The Mobile ADK supports the following mobile technologies:

- WML and WMLScript via an IDE and WAP Emulator for a variety of Motorola phones
- VoxML and VoiceXML for developing voice response systems
- Microsoft ASP-generated XML, WML, VoxML, and VoiceXML

The Mobile ADK relies on the Motorola Wireless IDE for many of its features. The two packages provide a complete development environment with project management, source control integration, and error tracking.

Installing the Motorola Mobile ADK

The Mobile ADK is written in Java for the Win32 platform—this includes Windows 9*x*, Windows NT, and Windows 2000. The installation may require you to install additional software from Microsoft if you do not have the appropriate Java Virtual Machine already installed on your computer. We cover the specific requirements for your system, how to obtain the software, and how to install the Mobile ADK on your computer.

The Mobile ADK requires that the Motorola IDE be installed before you can use it. You can use both applications separately from each other, but they must both be installed for the Mobile ADK to work.

System Requirements for the Motorola Mobile ADK

Motorola gives the following requirements for running the Mobile ADK:

- Windows 95, Windows 98, Windows 2000, or Windows NT 4.0
- Microsoft JVM version 5.00.3186 or later (Microsoft JVM version 5.00.3234 or later for Windows 2000)
- Microsoft Internet Explorer 5.0 (or later)
- Service Pack 3 or later (required for Windows NT 4.0)
- A Pentium II 266 MHz (or faster)

- 80MB of free disk space
- 64MB of RAM (128MB or more required for running voice applications)
- A video card that supports 1024x768 resolution and 16-bit color mode
- A Windows-compatible sound card (required for running voice applications)
- A compatible set of speakers and microphone (required for running voice applications)

Windows Me was not listed as a compatible platform, but we have successfully installed and used it on that platform. The Java requirements are quite strict. You cannot use the JDK from Sun to run the application. Motorola requires the Microsoft JVM to function correctly.

Developing & Deploying...

Microsoft Java Virtual Machine

You probably already have the Microsoft JVM installed on your machine. Open Internet Explorer and select **View | Java Console** from the menu bar. If you do not have that option, you need to enable the Java console by opening up your **Control Panel** and running the **Internet Options** applet. Select the **Advanced** tab and scroll down the options until you find the **Java Console Enabled** option. Check that box and restart your machine. You should now be able to pull up the Java console by selecting **View | Java Console** and figure out what version of the JVM you are running.

Upgrading your JVM is easy through Windows Update. Select **Start | Windows Update** from the **Start** menu and then choose **Product Updates** from the resulting Web page. The Microsoft Java Virtual Machine should be one of the packages available for you to download. You can also download the latest version at www.microsoft.com/java if you do not want to use Windows Update.

Obtaining the Motorola Mobile ADK

You can download the Mobile ADK from the Motorola Applications Global Network (MAGNET) Web site at www.motorola.com/developers/wireless in the Tools & Downloads section. You have to register with Motorola before you can access the Mobile ADK. Once you have registered and logged in to the site, click on the **Tools & Downloads** section and then click on the link to the **Mobile Application Development Kit** on the next page. Once you get to the page that actually lets you download the Mobile ADK, you will also find a link to the Wireless IDE. You must download and install this before you install the Mobile ADK. This is the largest SDK we look at, and it is unfortunate that the way Motorola initiates downloads is incompatible with many download managers that let you recover from a dropped connection.

Download the Mobile ADK 2.0 after you have downloaded the Wireless IDE. The Wireless IDE filename is FlexIde_Ver_2_1_0_83_rel.exe and the Mobile ADK filename is MobileADK2_0.exe. Motorola will also e-mail you a license key that you will have to enter during installation. We walk through installing both of these applications next.

Installing the Motorola Mobile ADK

Run the **FlexIde_Ver_2_1_0_83_rel.exe** first. You will be greeted with the installation screen shown in Figure 5.14. Click **Next** to go to the next screen that asks you where you would like to unpack the setup program. You can accept the defaults and click **Next** to continue with the installation.

Figure 5.14 Initial Install Screen for the Motorola Wireless IDE

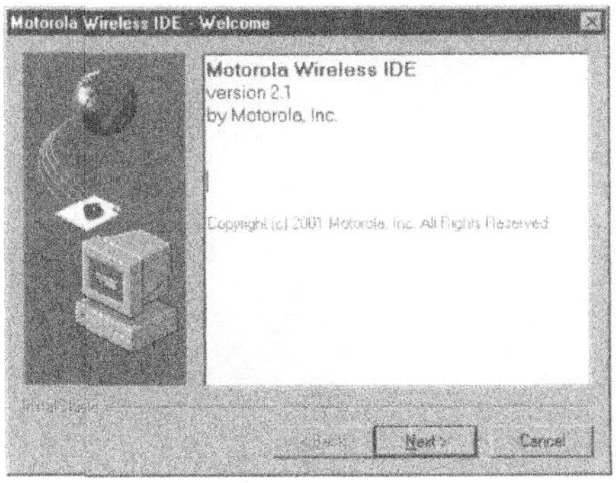

The setup program will be unpacked and then run. The Motorola logo will appear on your screen for a moment and then a dialog box welcoming you to the install will appear. Click **Next** to begin the installation. You will have to accept the License Agreement by clicking **Yes** on the next screen. The install program will then ask for your name and organization; enter them and click **Next** to continue. Choose the defaults for the installation directory and Program Group, and then the installer will copy the software to your machine.

You cannot launch the Wireless IDE yet because you have to install a target device for it to work with. In our case, this is the Mobile ADK and its related devices. Run the **MobileADK2_0.exe** installation program and a dialog box telling you this is the MADK 2.0 SDK installer will appear. Click **Next** to bring up the screen that asks you where to unpack the setup files. Accept the default location and click **Continue** to unpack the setup program and run it. The Motorola logo will appear on the screen for a moment, and then the setup program will show the initial screen shown in Figure 5.15.

Figure 5.15 Initial Motorola Mobile ADK Installation Screen

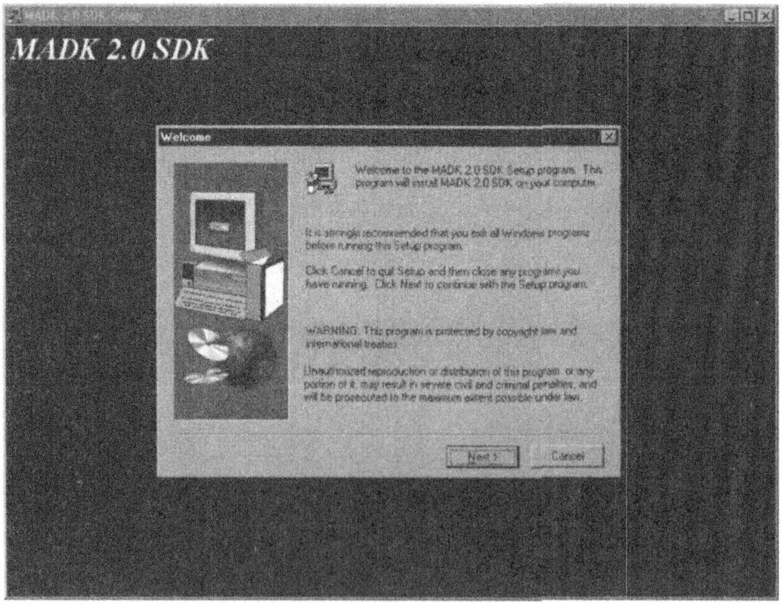

Click **Next** to start the installation. You will be told to ensure that the Wireless IDE is already installed and that you are installing the Mobile ADK to the same location as you did the Wireless IDE on the next screen. We have

installed the Wireless IDE and will be installing the Mobile ADK to the same location, so click **Next** to continue. The License Agreement is then shown. If you agree to the terms, click **Yes** to continue with the installation. The next screen asks you for your name, your company's name, and your serial number as shown in Figure 5.16.

Figure 5.16 Serial Number Verification Screen for the Motorola Mobile ADK

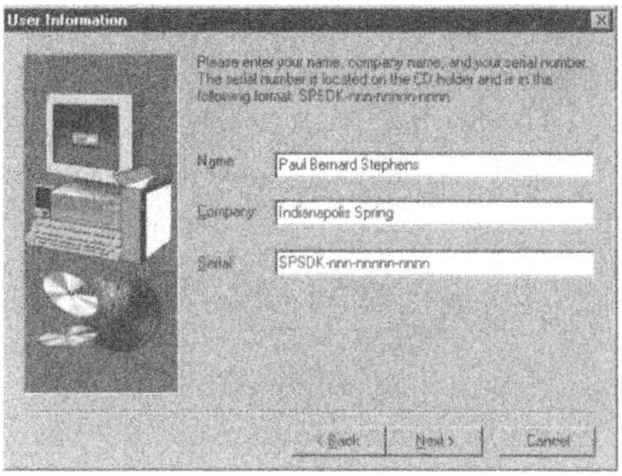

Motorola e-mails the serial number to you. If you did *not* get your license key e-mailed to you, contact Motorola through their Web site. The e-mail you receive should include some additional instructions that may be relevant to your installation. Enter the license key, which is in the form: SPSDK-*nnn-nnnnn-nnnn*, then click **Next**. You can choose the default locations for the installation directory and Program Groups by clicking **Next** on the following two screens. Depending on what software you already have installed, you may have to go through the setup programs for Microsoft Agent and Speech Recognition software. This will include agreeing to some license agreements and choosing some options. The Speech Recognition software will bring up the dialog box shown in Figure 5.17.

This begins the process of ensuring that your microphone and speakers are correctly hooked up. If you do not wish to work with VoiceXML, you can skip this step by clicking **Cancel**. You can always adjust the microphone settings later through the **Speech** applet in the Control Panel. A final screen is shown indicating that all the software was installed correctly. Click **Finish** to complete the installation process.

Figure 5.17 Microsoft Speech Recognition Setup Screen

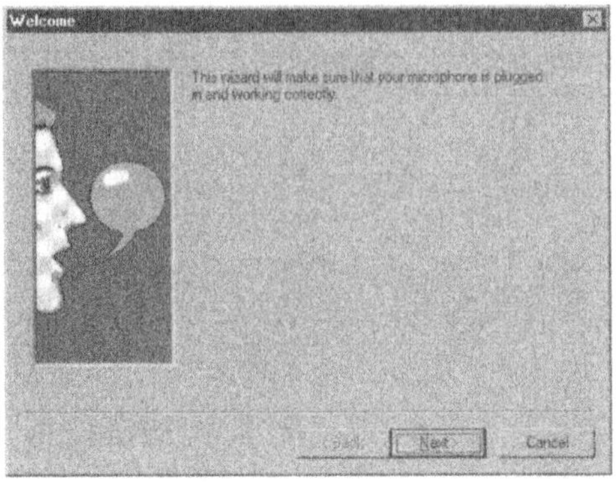

Using the Mobile ADK

The Mobile ADK is project based. You will have to start a new project to begin using the software. Select **Programs | Motorola Wireless IDE | Wireless IDE** from the Start menu to launch the application. The initial dialog box will ask you if you wish to open a new or existing project. We want to start a new project because this is the first time we've used the Mobile ADK. Select **Open a new Wireless IDE Project**. You will then be asked to fill in the name of the project, where the source files are located, and from what directory the project will be run. Let's name our project **mobileADK**, make our source directory **c:\wml\madk**, and our run directory **c:\wml\madk\run** (as shown in Figure 5.18); click **Next** to continue.

The next dialog box asks us to select a predefined application as a starting point for your code. The available options are shown and explained in Table 5.1.

Table 5.1 Explanation of Wireless IDE Predefined Application Types

Predefined Application Name	Project	Description
MADK2_0.asp	Microsoft ASP project	ASP can be used to generate a variety of other markup languages including VoxML, VoiceXML, WML, and HTML.

Continued

Table 5.1 Continued

Predefined Application Name	Project	Description
MADK2_0.vml	VoxML project	VoxML is Motorola's proprietary voice markup language. Motorola is moving towards VoiceXML, and this support is mostly for legacy applications.
MADK2_0.vxml	VoiceXML project	VoiceXML is a joint effort by IBM, AT&T, Lucent, and Motorola to combine various proprietary voice markup languages into one standard. The World Wide Web Consortium Voice Browser Working Group used VoiceXML as a model for its Dialog ML specification.
MADK2_0.wml	WML application	This provides a basic WML deck as a starting point for your application.

Figure 5.18 Creating a New Project in the Motorola Wireless IDE

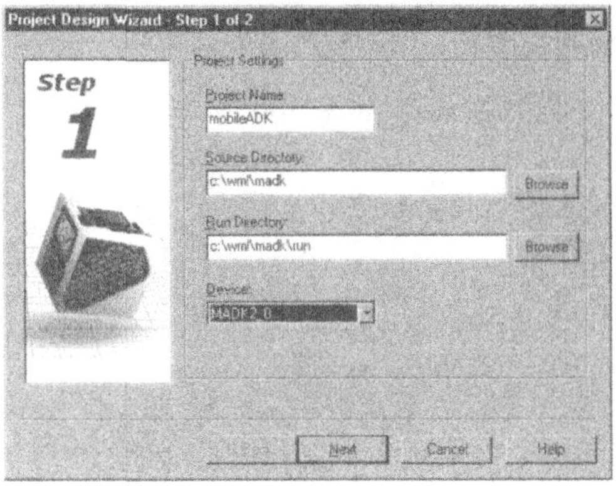

We want a WML application, so let's choose **MADK2_0.wml** as our starting point and click **Finish** to start working with the Wireless IDE.

Accessing and Editing Local Files

The Wireless IDE automatically creates a file called mobileADK.wml for you. Let's insert our "Hello World!" contents into this file:

```
<?xml version="1.0"?>
<!DOCTYPE wml PUBLIC "-//WAPFORUM//DTD WML 1.2//EN"
 "http://www.wapforum.org/DTD/wml12.dtd">
<wml>
  <card id="hello" title="Hello World">
    <p>Hello World!</p>
  </card>
</wml>
```

Let's validate the file to make sure it will work correctly. Select **File | Save** from the menu bar to save the file. Then select **Project | Compile File** to compile it. You should see a new pane appear underneath your source window that says no errors were found. Your Wireless IDE should now look like the one shown in Figure 5.19.

Figure 5.19 The Motorola Wireless IDE with No Errors

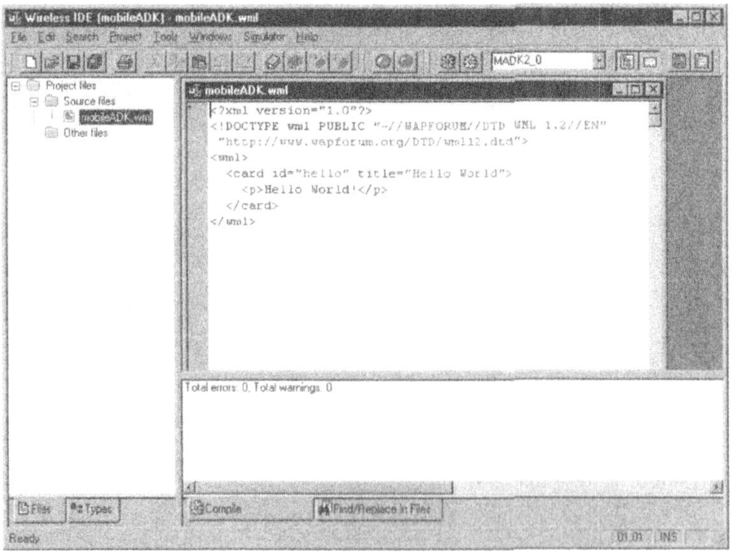

We have no errors, so we should be able to look at it in the simulator now. You can launch the current file in the simulator by selecting the **Simulator | Run** menu option in the Wireless IDE. A new simulator window will appear with our WML deck loaded.

Accessing Files through a Gateway

Motorola produces and sells a WAP gateway, but they do not provide one for developer use on the Internet. You can find out more about the Developer Version of the Motorola WAP Gateway at www.motorola.com/wap. Ericsson realizes the value a public gateway provides to developers and has one available for developer use. We'll connect to their gateway. Make sure the simulator is running or you won't be able to access the **Simulator | Mobile Settings** menu. If that option is grayed out, select **Simulator | Run** from the menu bar to start the simulator. Once you select the **Simulator | Mobile Settings** menu option, a dialog box with various options will appear. At the bottom in the WML Settings section, select the option that says **Connect through WAP Gateway**. A new section will appear at the bottom of the dialog box, as shown in Figure 5.20.

Figure 5.20 Gateway Settings in the Motorola Mobile ADK

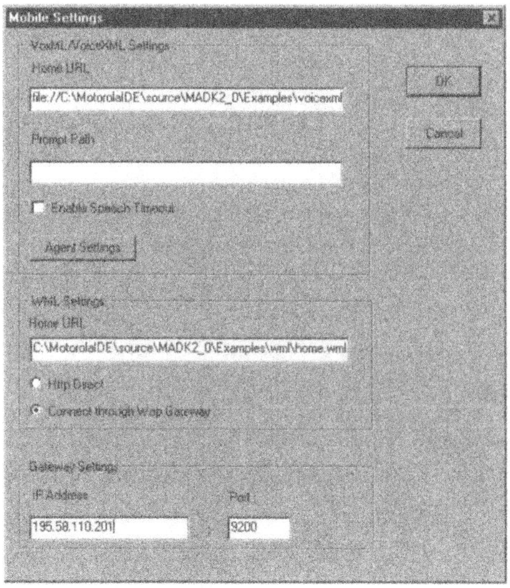

Enter the IP address of **195.58.110.201** and port **9200**, for connectionless mode to the WAP gateway. You can now access any server that is visible on the

Internet just as you would when using HTTP direct mode, but the request will be proxied through the Ericsson WAP gateway first. The Mobile ADK has trouble testing local files while you have the WAP gateway set, so you will want to switch back to HTTP Direct mode for development and testing. This will probably be fixed before the final product is released.

Debugging Techniques

The Wireless IDE works like a programming language IDE. If you change the files in the project, you must compile the files again before running them in the simulator. If you do not, you will see the old version of the source, not the updated one. The Wireless IDE will warn you if files have been changed but not recompiled, but it is still easy to mistakenly test an old version of your WML file without realizing it. The safe way to use the Wireless IDE is to always compile the project before running the simulator.

Let's remove the close paragraph tag from our mobileADK.wml file so that it now contains the following markup:

```
<?xml version="1.0"?>
<!DOCTYPE wml PUBLIC "-//WAPFORUM//DTD WML 1.2//EN"
 "http://www.wapforum.org/DTD/wml12.dtd">
<wml>
  <card id="hello" title="Hello World">
    <p>Hello World!
  </card>
</wml>
```

We can now select **Project | Compile Project** from the Wireless IDE menu to compile our file; the Wireless IDE will automatically save our changes before compilation. The pane where we saw a report that no errors were found now contains some error information. The error message is "c:\wml\mobileADK.wml(8): Error: syntax error." This doesn't help us debug our application very easily. The number in parentheses is the line number, which in our case is the end of the file. A syntax error is very general and could be anything from a misspelled tag to, in our case, a missing close tag. Luckily, we know where the error is, and we can insert the close paragraph tag to make the WML deck compile correctly again.

You can open the invalid WML file in the simulator, but it will simply respond with an error message of "Syntax error in source. Open the file in the

IDE and compile to find more information." The Mobile ADK, despite its large download size, provides the least useful information during debugging compared to the others. This is unfortunate because the Wireless IDE is a very useful tool for creating, editing, and managing projects.

The Ericsson Mobile Internet WapIDE 3.1

Ericsson has developed a software development kit that emulates their most popular WAP-enabled phones. This SDK is supported and complemented by the Developer Zone Web site (www.ericsson.com/developerzone) and a multitude of developers from around the world who use it on a daily basis. The Ericsson WapIDE helps you build and test WAP applications. The WapIDE includes the following components:

- **Browser** Simulates various Ericsson mobile phones with WAP services for testing. You can use it to demo WAP applications as well.
- **Application Designer** Makes building and testing a WAP application easier by integrating a WML and WMLScript editor with an Ericsson mobile phone simulator.
- **Push Initiator** Can send push messages to the simulator or an actual WAP terminal.

This version of the WapIDE can simulate the Ericsson R320s, R380s, and R520m. You can develop WAP applications that use WAP 1.1 (R320s and R380s) and WAP 1.2 (R520m).

Installing the Ericsson Mobile WapIDE

The WapIDE is written in Java for the Win32 platform—this includes Windows 9*x*, Windows NT, and Windows 2000. The installation may require you to install additional software from Sun Microsystems if you do not have an appropriate Java Virtual Machine already installed on your computer. In the following sections, we cover the specific requirements for your system, how to obtain the software, and how to install the WapIDE on your computer.

System Requirements for the Ericsson Mobile WapIDE

Ericsson gives the following requirements for running the WapIDE:

- Microsoft Windows 98, Windows NT 4.0, or Windows 2000
- Java2 Platform, version 1.3.0 or later.
- Microsoft Internet Explorer 5, or later, is required to access local files and use the application designer.
- 20MB of free disk space
- Intel Pentium II 266 MHz (or faster) with 128MB of RAM (or better recommended for performance reasons)

Ericsson does not explicitly state support for Windows Me, but we have successfully installed it and used it on that platform with no problems.

Obtaining the Ericsson Mobile WapIDE

You can download the Ericsson WapIDE from the Ericsson Developer Zone Web site at www.ericsson.com/developerzone. You are required to register before downloading the WapIDE. You can download other simulators from the Developer Zone Web site, including a dedicated R380 simulator and older versions of the WapIDE.

Installing the Ericsson Mobile WapIDE

The file you download from Ericsson will be called WapIDE_31.exe. Run this application and you will be greeted with the initial install screen shown in Figure 5.21.

Figure 5.21 Initial Install Screen for the Ericsson WapIDE

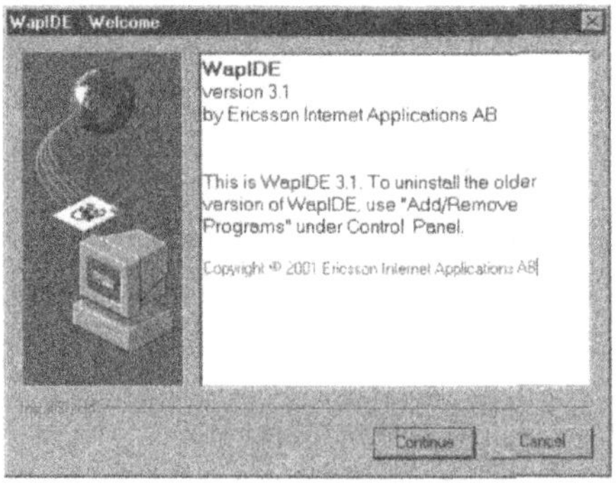

Click **Continue** to begin installing the WapIDE. You will have to accept the License Agreement, view a ReadMe file, and then choose where you want the SDK installed. We chose the default installation location for simplicity. You can choose what Program Group to install the WapIDE into on the next screen. The final screen asks you to confirm your choices, and then the WapIDE is installed on your computer.

Working with the Ericsson Mobile WapIDE

We look at the Application Designer during these exercises because it integrates the browser into a development environment. If you installed the WapIDE in the default location, you can start the application from the Start menu by choosing **Programs | Ericsson WapIDE 3.1 | Application Designer**. The initial window may take some time to appear, this is normal. The initial window is shown in Figure 5.22.

Figure 5.22 Initial Ericsson WapIDE Window

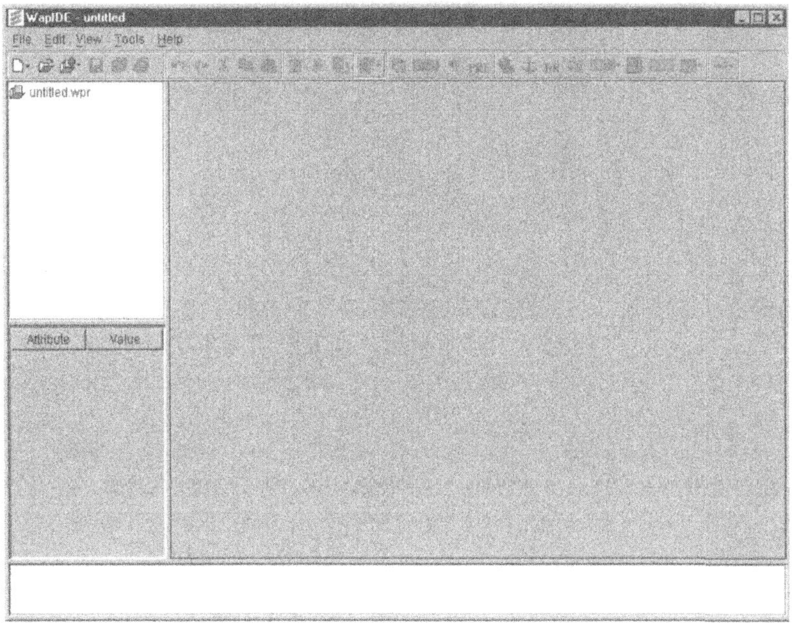

The WapIDE is a project-based environment. This means that you can group files together in a project and can reload them all at once into the WapIDE at a later time, saving yourself the effort of loading each file individually. The top-left pane shows the current project files and lets you navigate through various elements of the WML deck you are currently working with. The bottom-left pane shows information about the current element you have selected: card titles, the WML version of the deck, and so on. The right pane shows the source of the current WML deck. Finally, the bottom pane shows you status messages about the WapIDE, such as validation errors in WML decks.

Accessing and Editing Local Files

Let's create a new project and add our hello.wml file. From the main window, choose the **File | New | New Project** menu item. You will be asked if you want to save the changes to the current project; unless you have already been working on a project that you wish to save, click **No**. You will then be prompted with the dialog box to fill in information about your project. We set ours up as shown in Figure 5.23.

Figure 5.23 Creating a New Project in the Ericsson WapIDE

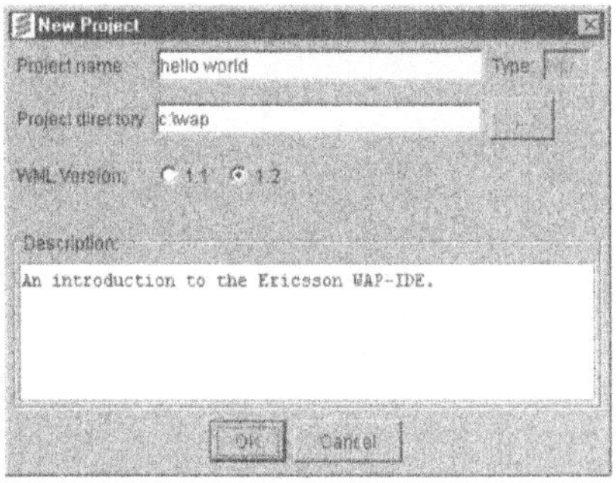

You can use three different methods to accomplish most tasks in the WapIDE: menu choices, the toolbar, and keyboard shortcuts. Let's focus on the menu choices, and you can explore the other two options on your own. To add a new WML file to the project, select **File | New | New WML Deck** from the menu bar. Now, you can edit the WML deck to contain the text you want. You can edit the file in the right pane. Go to the spot after the open <p> element and insert the text "Hello World!" into the file. Also add the ID and title attributes to the card so that the hello.wml file looks like this:

```
<?xml version="1.0"?>
<!DOCTYPE wml PUBLIC "-//WAPFORUM//DTD WML 1.2//EN"
 "http://www.wapforum.org/DTD/wml12.dtd">
```

```
<wml>
  <card id="hello" title="Hello World">
    <p>Hello World!
    </p>
  </card>
</wml>
```

The editor will not show you updated information about the WML deck until you validate it. You can validate the file by selecting the **Tools | Validate "hello.wml"** menu option. Once you validate your document, the left panes will be updated with the information you just typed in, as shown in Figure 5.24.

Figure 5.24 Updated WML Deck Information in the Ericsson WapIDE

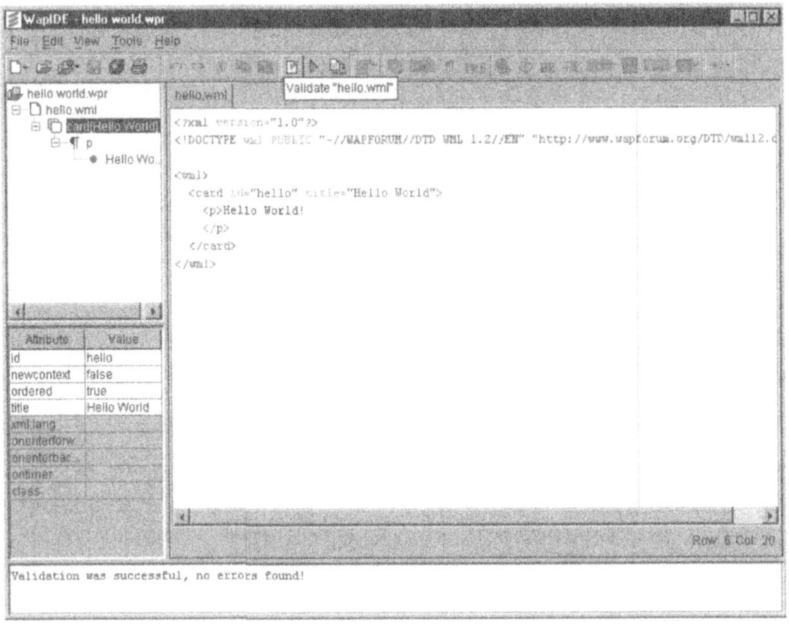

We can now view the document in a WAP device by selecting the **Tools | Test "hello.wml"** menu option This will launch the WapIDE browser in a new window with the hello.wml file we just created. Figure 5.25 shows the R520m with our new deck in it.

Figure 5.25 Ericsson R520 Emulator Viewing hello.wml

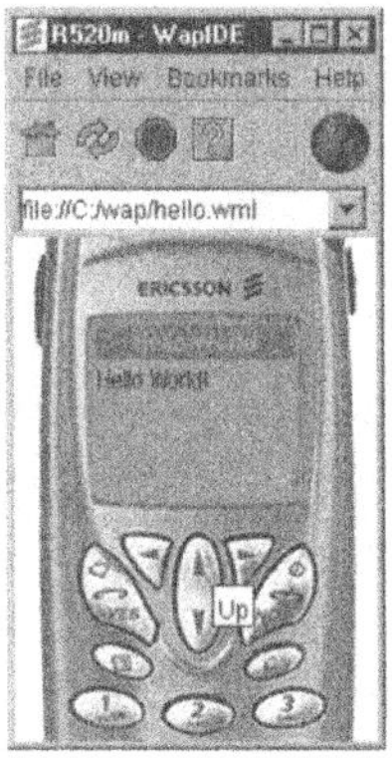

Notice that a **Back** button is not included by default. Ericsson browsers require you to explicitly put in WML to perform backward navigation if you want it to be available to the user. Each card from which the user can navigate backwards requires the following piece of code:

```
<do label="Back" type="prev"><prev/></do>
```

Not all browsers require this, but be careful not to omit it because you could end up with areas of your WAP site that users cannot get out of. If the browser provides a **Back** button by default, it will simply ignore this portion of WML code.

Accessing Files through a Gateway

The browser component can retrieve files locally on your file system or on the network through a gateway. The default behavior is to use the public gateway Ericsson has set up for Developer Zone members, but you can use any gateway you have access to. Ericsson provides information on their Web site for downloading and installing their gateway on your local machine. We add the Ericsson gateway to our configuration even though it is included by default, just to run you through the steps required.

Select the **View | Settings** menu option from your browser window. You will see a configuration dialog box with multiple tabs across the top. Select the **Gateway** tab then click **Add** to create a new gateway entry. Fill out the name as **DevZone** and enter the IP address **195.58.110.201**. The gateway that Ericsson provides does not require a username or password, so leave those fields empty. When you click **OK**, you will be taken back to the gateway selection screen.

From the pull-down list, select the **DevZone** entry and then click **OK** at the bottom of the dialog box to save your changes. Now, whenever you request a document from a network address using HTTP, it will request the file from the gateway, and the gateway will actually retrieve the document before sending it back to you.

Debugging Techniques

The WapIDE provides good error messages that help you debug your application. Let's take our simple WML file and remove the </p> element, so that our paragraph line looks like this:

```
<p>Hello World!
```

When we validate this file, we get some error messages in the bottom pane, as shown in Figure 5.26.

Figure 5.26 Ericsson WapIDE with Error Messages

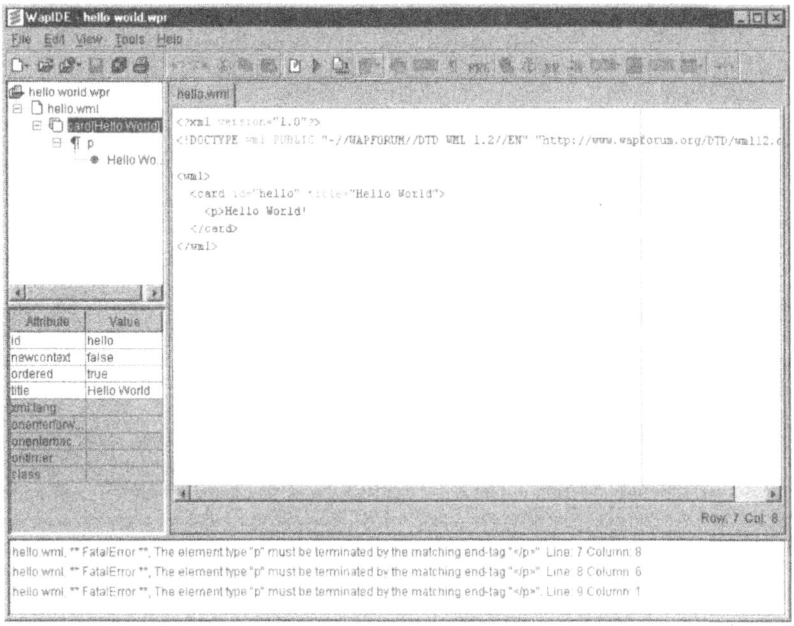

This is pretty good information. We know that we opened a paragraph element and did not close it. The line numbers and columns that are reported match up with the next tag it encountered, but the message is clear and points outs the problem quite well—even if it does miss the location a bit. If we correct the problem and revalidate, we get a comforting message indicating that no errors were found.

The WapIDE does not provide information such as cache status, variable values, or compiled WML size. This is unfortunate because the rest of the environment is nice for building and testing applications. You can open the Trace window to view information about the current status of the emulator, which can be helpful when you are trying to track down a network problem.

The WapIDE allows you to clear the device cache or disable caching altogether. This is handy during repetitive testing, but be sure to test your application with caching on once you believe it is working. You can reach the cache setup by selecting **View | Settings** from the browser window and going to the **Cache** tab, as shown in Figure 5.27.

Figure 5.27 Cache Settings for the WAP Browser in the Ericsson WapIDE

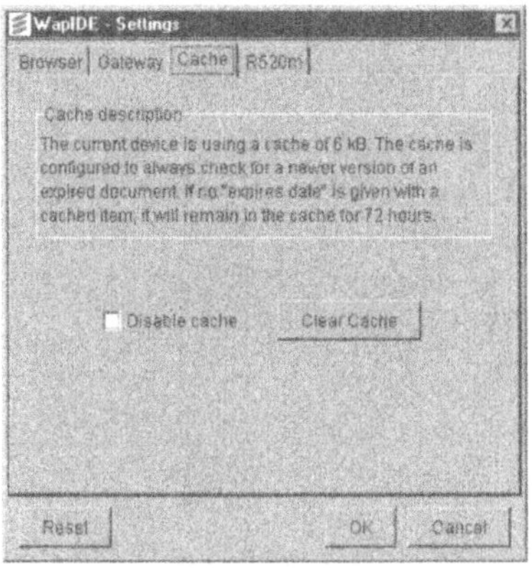

The Yospace SmartPhone Emulator 2.0

The Yospace SmartPhone Emulator Developer Edition is the only SDK in our lineup that isn't developed by a browser manufacturer. This Yospace SmartPhone Emulator is designed to emulate browsers from multiple vendors simultaneously, thus speeding up your development. The SmartPhone Emulator is written entirely in Java; you can run it on any platform that has a Java 1.1.8 compatible VM installed (this includes Java2 VMs). This is the only SDK we've looked at that is truly cross-platform. Linux, Apple MacOS, Sun Solaris, and Microsoft Windows are all known to work well with the SmartPhone Emulator.

Installing the Yospace SmartPhone Emulator

Many versions of the SmartPhone Emulator are available from Yospace. The Developer Edition is for use on your local machine to access files both remotely or on your local file system and is the one that we installed. The Web Site Edition allows you to demo your WAP application to people who visit your site with a regular Web browser. You can use the JavaBean Edition to build your own application that can access WAP services by emulating popular handsets.

We cover only installing the Windows version of the SmartPhone Emulator Developer Edition. The instructions for other platforms are documented on the Yospace Web site at www.yospace.com. We go step-by-step through the system requirements, downloading the SmartPhone Emulator, and installing it on your computer.

System Requirements for the Yospace SmartPhone Emulator

The Yospace SmartPhone Emulator is written entirely in Java and can therefore be run on any computer system that has a Java 1.1.8 or compatible VM installed. As mentioned earlier, Yospace has packaged the SmartPhone Emulator in installation programs for Microsoft Windows, Apple MacOS, Solaris, and Linux/other UNIX platforms. If you download the Windows or MacOS version, you can choose to download it without the JVM if you already have one installed on your system. Yospace gives no specific processor or memory requirements because the software can run on such a wide variety of machines. If you find the program doesn't run fast enough perhaps you should get a faster processor or add more memory. With that said, the Windows install program that we used is a Win32 application, so you must have Windows 9*x*, Me, NT, or 2000 to install the software.

Obtaining the Yospace SmartPhone Emulator

You can download the SmartPhone Emulator from the Yospace Web site at www.yospace.com in the Products section. Yospace requires you to register in order to download the software. Once you download the software, Yospace will e-mail you a license that is good for five days. After this license expires, you will need to purchase a license from Yospace to continue using the software.

Installing the Yospace SmartPhone Emulator

You will download a file called **SPEDE2_0.zip**, which contains one file, from the Yospace Web site. Unzip it with a zip extractor such as WinZip (www.winzip.com) or Aladdin StuffIt Expander (www.aladdinsys.com). Run the **spede2_0.exe** application (which is the file that you extract) and, after some initial splash screens, you will be greeted with a dialog box requiring you to accept the license agreement for the SmartPhone Emulator. If you agree with the terms of the license, click **Yes** and then click **Next** to continue the installation process. You can accept the default installation location on the next screen and then click **Install** to start the actual copying of files to your computer. The software will be installed while a dialog box like the one shown in Figure 5.28 updates you on the status of the installation. Once the installation completes, click **Done**, and the software is installed.

Figure 5.28 The Yospace Installation Screen

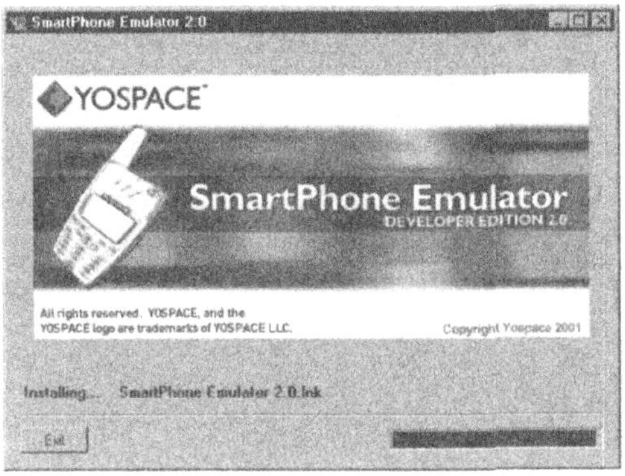

Developing with the Yospace SmartPhone Emulator

You can now start the SmartPhone Emulator by choosing **Programs | SmartPhone Emulator | SmartPhone Emulator 2.0** from the Start menu. The first dialog box you see will ask you for your name, e-mail address, and license key. These must match the registration info you gave to Yospace. You will only be asked for this information when you first run the program or the license expires. The license screen is shown in Figure 5.29.

You can choose what mode you would like to run the program in from this screen: Development Mode or Display Mode. Display Mode shows just one emulator in its own window so that you can demo your WAP application without having a complete development environment cluttering the screen. Development Mode is where we spend most of our time. It allows you to view multiple emulators at the same time, load a file or location into multiple emulators with one command, and view variable names and values and other status information.

Figure 5.29 Yospace SmartPhone Emulator License Screen

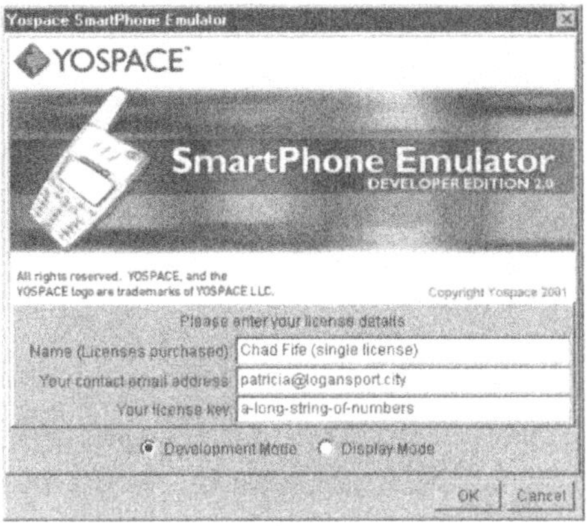

The initial window may seem intimidating at first, but figuring it out is quite easy. Figure 5.30 shows the default workspace when you start in Development Mode.

Figure 5.30 Default Development Mode Workspace

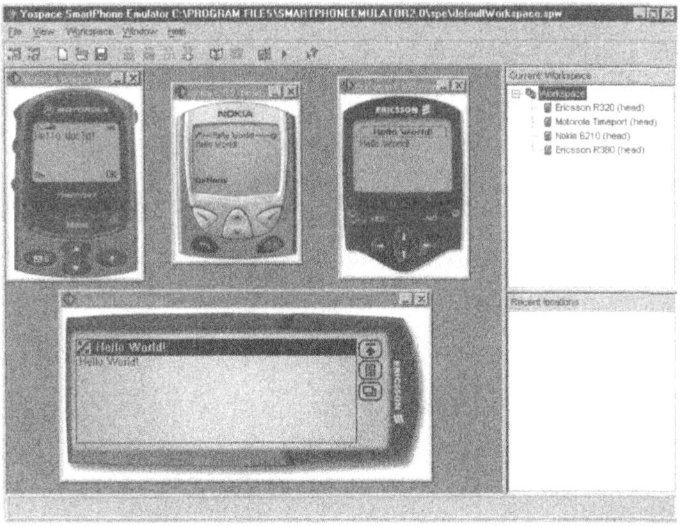

The windows in the main part of the screen are emulators for various mobile phones. The SmartPhone Emulator allows you to create and save groups of emulators as workspaces. You can have one workspace per manufacturer, per browser type (UP.Browser, Nokia Browser, and so on), or any other scheme you can come up with. You can save these workspaces and recall them later when you need to test the same combination of devices again.

The default workspace includes an Ericsson R380, Ericsson R320, Nokia 6210, and Motorola Timeport. Because it includes multiple devices, you must tell the SmartPhone Emulator which emulator you want to work with. You can select the emulator window or its corresponding name from the list in the top-right pane. If you select the Workspace, everything you do will apply to all the emulators. Select the **Workspace** as shown in Figure 5.30 before we start loading files in the next section.

Accessing and Editing Local Files

You will have to use a separate text editor to create WML and WMLScript files. The Yospace SmartPhone Emulator does not include text-editing capabilities. We use the same file we created in other examples and saved as **c:\wap\hello.wml**. If you haven't already created it, save the following WML deck to that location:

```
<?xml version="1.0"?>
<!DOCTYPE wml PUBLIC "-//WAPFORUM//DTD WML 1.1//EN"
 "http://www.wapforum.org/DTD/wml_1.1.xml">
<wml>
  <card id="hello" title="Hello World!">
    <p> Hello World! </p>
  </card>
</wml>
```

Load this file into all the emulators at once by selecting the **File | Open File** menu option. This will bring up a dialog box asking what file to load. Find and select our file (c:\wap\hello.wml) and click **Open** to load the file in all the emulators. You can see how easily you can view your WAP application on multiple devices with the SmartPhone Emulator.

Accessing Files through a Gateway

The Yospace SmartPhone Emulator does not allow you to change the gateway used to access WAP content. The gateway functionality is encapsulated in the emulators. This is unfortunate because testing through multiple gateways is a good way to find many problems.

Debugging Techniques

The Yospace SmartPhone Emulator provides very precise debugging information. Let's break the hello.wml file so that it does not close the paragraph element. The resulting file looks like this:

```
<?xml version="1.0"?>
<!DOCTYPE wml PUBLIC "-//WAPFORUM//DTD WML 1.1//EN"
 "http://www.wapforum.org/DTD/wml_1.1.xml">
<wml>
  <card id="hello" title="Hello World!">
    <p> Hello World!
  </card>
</wml>
```

We have to empty the cache before we reload the file by selecting the **Workspace | Empty Cache** menu option. Then we can load our file the same way we did before. This time, every emulator will give you an error message. These error messages are exactly what each individual phone would show you if you were holding it in your hand—not very informative. However, a new message appears in the status bar along the bottom of the window: "! Last Error: 502." Click on this message and a dialog box (shown in Figure 5.31) will appear giving you more detailed information about the problem.

Figure 5.31 Yospace SmartPhone Emulator Invalid WML Error Dialog Box

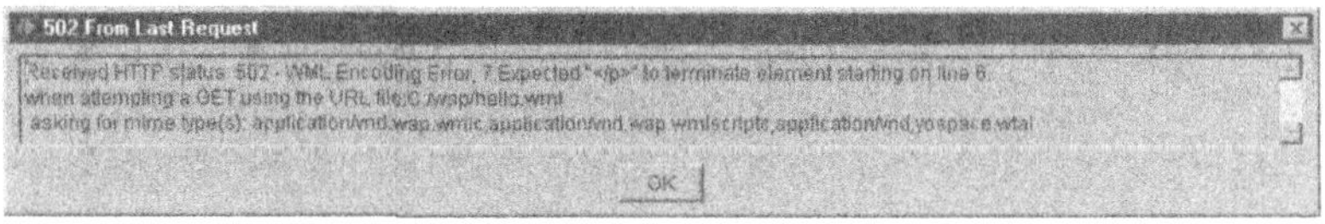

The error message tells us that the paragraph tag on line 6 does not have a corresponding close tag. This is the most descriptive error message from any of the SDKs we've looked at. Although the error message is clear, it is somewhat difficult to find inside the variety of HTTP status messages. This is especially confusing because we were loading a local file. The extraneous error messages are a result of how the SmartPhone Emulator is actually viewing each file internally, and the messages should probably be ignored.

The SmartPhone Emulator also has variable debugging capabilities. Let's create a more complex WML deck and see how variables are handled. Save this as **c:\wap\vartest.wml**:

```
<?xml version="1.0"?>
<!DOCTYPE wml PUBLIC "-//WAPFORUM//DTD WML 1.1//EN"
 "http://www.wapforum.org/DTD/wml_1.1.xml">
<wml>
  <card id="home" title="SmartPhone Emulator demo">
    <p>
      Name: <input type="text" name="name"/>
    </p>
    <do type="accept">
      <go href="#showname"/>
    </do>
  </card>

  <card id="showname" title="My name is...">
    <p> Hello $name. Welcome.</p>
  </card>
</wml>
```

Let's look at this in the Ericsson R380. Select it from the workspace pane on the top left, then load the file via the menu bar. The Ericsson R380 is a touch-screen device, so click your mouse between the angle brackets (< >) to bring up the text entry screen. Type in **consuelo** and then click on the arrow icon in the bottom-right corner of the emulator display. You will be taken back to the first page, but *consuelo* will appear between the angle brackets now. Click **Accept**, and the resulting screen simply repeats the entered name along with a message. Now we can pull up the variable window. Select the **View | View Variables** menu option, and a new window will appear (see Figure 5.32).

You can keep this window open to track the status of your variables as you browse with the emulator. This window also shows your browse history and status messages from the browser.

Figure 5.32 Yospace SmartPhone Emulator Variable Window

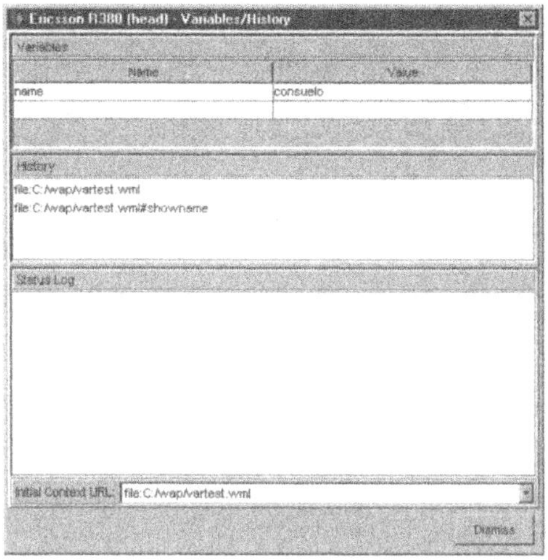

Summary

You can choose from many available WAP SDKs. Finding the right one can be an extremely difficult and time-consuming task. Each SDK has its strengths and weaknesses, but you can use this to your advantage. You may find yourself using one SDK for your normal development, and each of the other ones at different times when it proves advantageous.

Users of operating systems besides Microsoft Windows variants have one choice: the Yospace SmartPhone Emulator. The good news is the SmartPhone Emulator does many of the tasks that other SDKs do, and it reports errors better than the rest. The bad news is that it is the only one that costs money! The Nokia WAP Toolkit provides great error feedback and editing of WML, WMLScript, WBMP image files as well as variable viewing editing and timer status in the running browser. The downside is that it requires separate downloads for each real-world device you want to emulate. The Openwave UP.SDK is very simple, but it provides a large amount of feedback and is a native Windows application, which gives it a performance edge over the Java-based emulators. The Ericsson WapIDE provides project management features that allow you to quickly open and edit groups of WML and WMLScript files. The Motorola Mobile ADK provides a completely integrated environment that integrates with source control software and supports other mobile technologies such as VoiceXML.

Whatever SDK you choose, you will be pleased with the amount of time and work you save over developing and testing applications using your mobile handset, and the ease of developing and testing WAP applications on your home computer.

Solutions Fast Track

The Openwave UP.SDK 4.1

☑ The UP.SDK provides emulation for a variety of mobile devices. You can use it to test your application on a variety of phones from multiple device manufacturers as long as they use the UP.Browser in their phones.

☑ You can download the UP.SDK from the Openwave Developer Program Web site (http://developer.openwave.com) in the Downloads section.

- ☑ The UP.SDK does not provide any text editing or IDE-style capabilities. It is useful for testing applications only, and you must have a separate program to create and edit your WAP files.
- ☑ The error messages reported by the UP.SDK are fairly helpful in finding syntactical problems. They will point you in the correct direction but are not explicit enough to make finding errors a simple task.

The Nokia WAP Toolkit 2.1

- ☑ The WAP Toolkit provides a prototype-like mobile phone for development.
- ☑ You can download modules that emulate actual Nokia phones from the Forum Nokia Web site (http://forum.nokia.com).
- ☑ The WAP Toolkit is a full-featured IDE. You can create and edit WML and WMLScript files as well as WBMP images using the built-in tools.
- ☑ The error messages reported by the WAP Toolkit are geared more towards machines than humans, but the line numbers they report are usually very close to the source of the problem.

The Motorola Mobile Application Development Kit 2.0

- ☑ The Mobile ADK includes support for a large variety of Motorola mobile phones. The Mobile ADK is the only SDK we looked at that also supports voice applications through VoxML and VoiceXML as well as Microsoft ASP support.
- ☑ You can download the Mobile ADK from the Motorola Applications Global Network (MAGNET) Web site at www.motorola.com/developers/wireless in the Tools & Downloads section.
- ☑ The Mobile ADK and Wireless IDE provide a complete development environment for your mobile needs. You can integrate with source control products and develop for a variety of environments using the same IDE.

- ☑ The error reporting in the Mobile ADK is entirely subpar when compared to the other SDKs. The only thing you will find out is that an error occurred with your file. You will have to do all the work of figuring out where the error actually is.

The Ericsson Mobile Internet WapIDE 3.1

- ☑ The WapIDE includes support for three Ericsson mobile phones. You can use the emulator independent of the environment for building and debugging applications, which provides a good mechanism to demo your WAP applications.
- ☑ You can download the Ericsson WapIDE from the Ericsson Developer Zone Web site at www.ericsson.com/developerzone.
- ☑ The WapIDE includes an Application Designer that helps you build WML decks that are syntactically correct as well as compile and debug the ones that aren't.
- ☑ The error reporting is quite descriptive although the line numbers don't tend to match up that well. Also, it displays a lot of error messages for one error (three in our case), which makes tracking down problems a little more difficult.

The Yospace SmartPhone Emulator 2.0

- ☑ The SmartPhone Emulator can emulate a variety of mobile devices from a large variety of manufacturers. Viewing source files in multiple emulators—either individually or at the same time—is quite easy with the layout of the SmartPhone Emulator. It is also written entirely in Java, making it the only emulator that you can use on operating systems other than Microsoft Windows.
- ☑ You can download the SmartPhone Emulator from the Yospace Web site (www.yospace.com) in the Products section.
- ☑ The SmartPhone Emulator includes no editing capabilities, but it does provide good debugging facilities for viewing variables, history stacks, and other portions of the running WAP browsers.

- ☑ The error reporting is the most accurate of the group. It pinpoints the cause of the problem rather than the effect. The error messages are cluttered with a lot of information pertaining to the internal implementation of the SmartPhone Emulator, which makes finding the actual error message a little difficult. Once you do find it however, it points you directly to the error.

Frequently Asked Questions

The following Frequently Asked Questions, answered by the authors of this book, are designed to both measure your understanding of the concepts presented in this chapter and to assist you with real-life implementation of these concepts. To have your questions about this chapter answered by the author, browse to **www.syngress.com/solutions** and click on the **"Ask the Author"** form.

Q: I've tested my application in all the SDKs and it works—but I can't get it to work on my phone. What's wrong?

A: The SDK provides emulation of the actual phone, but it is not perfect. Remember from Chapter 2 that the gateway sits in the middle and can cause incompatibilities to show up in your WML code. The WAP gateway that your network provider is using could be causing the problem. Unfortunately, you are basically left with trial-and-error to figure out what the problem is. You can hire a WAP testing company to figure it out for you if you'd like.

Q: Every SDK but the UP.SDK is written in Java, so why is the Yospace SmartPhone Emulator the only one I can run on my Linux machine?

A: You can find directions on the Internet for getting an older version of the Nokia WAP Toolkit to run under Linux, but you will lose a considerable amount of performance. Many of the slower operations have been written in native code to make the SDK performance better. Unfortunately, you will have to convince the other manufacturers to release a pure Java version to get it running under Linux.

Chapter 6

Web Clipping

Solutions in this chapter:

- What Is Web Clipping?
- What Types of Hardware Support Web Clipping
- Working with the Palm OS Emulator
- Creating a Web Clipping Project with the Web Clipping Application Builder
- Web Clipping Basics and Examples

☑ Summary

☑ Solutions Fast Track

☑ Frequently Asked Questions

Introduction

One of the most interesting and challenging aspects about the evolving wireless Internet is the plethora of devices that are capable of browsing Internet content. These devices range from phones capable of using Wireless Application Protocol (WAP), to pagers capable of sending and receiving e-mails, to handheld Personal Digital Assistants (PDAs) with wireless modems or native connectivity. All of these devices feature different capabilities, interfaces, and usage patterns. They each require a different toolkit with which to craft your Web sites and applications, and each operate under a slightly different set of rules in regards to usability.

In this chapter, we will focus on the tools and methods used to deliver content to the last category of devices mentioned, the PDA. In particular, we will discuss the proprietary Web clipping network that allows Palm-compatible handheld devices to access Internet content. These devices do not necessarily have to be manufactured by Palm, but Web clipping, by definition, is restricted to Palm-compatible devices such as the Handspring Visor, Sony Clie, Qualcomm PDQ, or the Kyocera smart phone. There are slight differences between these devices, but in this case, fortunately, the differences are minimal, and have more to do with the network that the device uses to connect to the Internet than the device itself.

This chapter is not intended to be a comprehensive reference on all of the intricacies all of the aspects of developing Web clipping applications (WCAs), nor is it a guide to programming native Palm OS applications. Rather, it is written as an introduction to the technology, and will provide information useful to Webmasters interested in deploying WCAs. The skills used to develop a WCA are skills that you most likely already have, namely, understanding of HTML and some experience with server-side scripting. If you are interested in a more in-depth coverage of this topic, you may want to read the Palm OS Web Application Developer's Guide, available from Syngress Publishing at www.syngress.com.

First, we will provide a definition and an overview of Web clipping, including the various components that must interact in order for content to be retrieved from a server. We will then cover the devices that can support Web clipping and the additional connection hardware and networks that are used to connect a handheld device to the Internet.

Once we've explained the basics of what Web clipping is and the variety of ways you can connect a Palm-compatible organizer to the Internet, we will move into the development environment and discuss how to install the Palm Operating System Emulator (POSE) on your desktop computer. This program will allow you to test your application and its interaction with your Web server without owning or having access to an actual Palm-powered handheld. We will then discuss how to install the Web Clipping Application Builder provided by Palm and walk you through the creation of your first WCA using this development tool and the POSE.

We will then examine what aspects of HTML are and are not supported within the context of Web clipping. Specifically, we will examine the subset of HTML that can be used to build Web clippings, and the differences between the ways that your code will look and act on a handheld device versus a desktop computer. We will also cover some handy device-specific functions that are unique to Web clipping.

Later in the chapter, we will cover several examples that illustrate what you can do within a WCA, and how these capabilities contrast with how you may be accustomed to programming for the Web. We'll demonstrate how you can implement some familiar features in a new environment, and provide examples of how to send data to and retrieve content from a Web server on the Internet using a WCA.

What Is Web Clipping?

First things first: Web clipping is not Web browsing. Forget the metaphor of "surfing the Web" as you know it from the desktop computing world. That being said, what *is* Web clipping?

Web clipping refers to a proprietary system that allows handheld devices running the Palm Operating System (version 3.5 or higher) to access the Internet using compiled content that resides on the device. This content is first authored in Hypertext Markup Language (HTML) and then converted to a special type of file called a Web clipping application (WCA) that can be installed on the device. WCAs can contain most of the common elements of the earlier versions of Web sites, such as links, forms, and images. The HTML markup used to create a WCA is a subset of HTML 3.2, containing only the elements suited to an environment with little processing power and memory. This subset of HTML is called Compact HTML (cHTML).

A Web clipping application provides a means for your users to access your site or a Web application from their handheld device. There are pros and cons to this situation. An advantage is that you can distribute several HTML pages that can send data to your Web server from the field. On the other hand, you must put some extra effort into making sure that you include the relevant elements for your users *before* deploying your Web application. Once a WCA is installed on the user's device, the only way to change it is to have the user download the latest version of the WCA.

NOTE

You can find over 250 WCAs available for download at wireless.palm.net/apps. Many applications have already been built to solve common features that are requested by Palm.net users (e-mail, messaging, news, shopping, etc.). You can also post your own WCAs for distribution to users. One of the best ways to learn how to build an effective Web clipping application is to see what others have done successfully, and, perhaps more importantly, to see what others have done unsuccessfully!

The WCA is viewed using the Web Clipping Application Viewer, or Clipper browser, which resides on the device. The Web Clipping Application Viewer can send data to (and receive properly formatted HTML from) a Web server located on the Internet through a network of base stations and Palm.net proxy servers. In addition, a WCA can launch, and, vice versa, be launched by, local applications on the device.

NOTE

It helps to think of WCAs as miniature Web sites stored on the handheld device, and to think of Clipper as a Web browser, but remember that these concepts are not directly analogous. In actuality, a WCA is a Palm Database Format record set that is installed on the device. Its content is static and cannot be updated until a user installs a new version of the application. Likewise, Clipper itself is not a Web browser, per se, but rather a unique application that can render HTML stored in a WCA.

Web clipping applications were formerly called Palm Query Applications (PQAs). The files created by the Web Clipping Application Builder are saved with an extension of .pqa, a vestige of their former nomenclature. In this chapter, we will use the term *Web clipping application* or WCA to refer to what we are building. When we refer to Web clipping we will be referring to the entire process, not just an individual part of it

The Components of Web Clipping

Since we are most interested in the wireless Internet, we will focus primarily on the client-server aspects of Web clipping and on the overall architecture of a typical transaction. The basic architecture of Web clipping includes several elements. The basic flow is shown in Figure 6.1: the device communicates with a Palm.net Proxy Server via a wireless network (made up of base stations run by Cingular Wireless), and the Proxy Server communicates with a Web server via the Internet. Any traffic must flow through the Palm.net Proxy Server network in order to be sent to the device.

Figure 6.1 Web Clipping Architecture

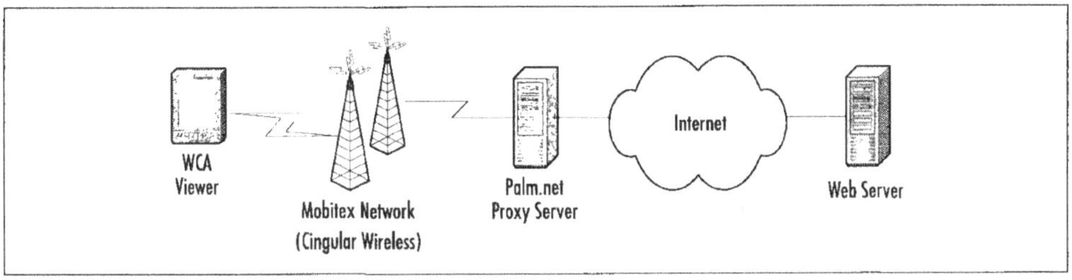

Client-Side Components

The client-side components of Web clipping are the Palm handheld device, the Web clipping application, and the Web Clipping Application Viewer. Another necessary component is a piece of hardware that is used to provide connectivity.

The Wireless Device

The handheld device is the actual hardware that runs the Palm Operating System (OS 3.5 or later). It will typically contain a processor, some memory, a screen, and an input device (usually a stylus, but sometimes a miniature keyboard). Palm currently licenses their OS to a wide variety of vendors, including Handera, Handspring, and Sony.

The Web Clipping Application

This is, technically, a Palm Database Format record set that contains HTML and images. It is the application that you will build and make available for your users to install on their devices. You can create Web clipping applications using the WCA Builder. To create a WCA, you will need to create your HTML and images and import them into the WCA Builder. The WCA Builder will then scan your

HTML and convert your code into a format readable by the Web Clipping Application Viewer.

The Web Clipping Application Viewer

This is the program on the device that is capable of viewing Web clipping applications. It will render the contents of the WCA through a browser-like interface. It is capable of interacting with servers on the Internet as well as device-resident applications on a Palm-powered handheld.

The Connection Hardware

This component connects the device to the Internet. This may be an embedded radio antenna, an attachable third party modem, or a user's cellular phone connected to the device via a cable or Infrared (IR) connection.

Server-Side Components

The server-side components of Web clipping are the Mobitex wireless network, the Palm.Net proxy server network, and any individual Web server or server-side program (such as a CGI script) that is accessed over the Internet. The one consistent server-side component is the Palm.net proxy server network. This is the part of the architecture where the HTML from a Web site is converted to CML and sent to the device, and where the requests from the device are communicated to a Web server on the Internet.

Mobitex Base Stations

These radio stations are owned by Cingular Wireless and make up a wireless network capable of transmitting data at a rate of 9.6 kbps. These base stations are capable of relaying the ZIP code of a Palm VII transmitting wireless data.

NOTE

The actual speed of a Web clipping transaction will be slightly slower than 9.6kbps, due to Internet traffic and the processing that is done by the Proxy server.

Palm.net Proxy Server Network

The Palm.net Proxy Server Network is made up of computers that handle the requests initiated by handheld devices. These servers will, in turn, send a request to other servers on the Internet on behalf of the device. They will then relay the response over the air in a format readable by the Web Clipping Application Viewer.

Web Servers

The final server-side component of Web clipping is the Web server that handles the forwarded request from the device and sends back a response in HTML. This request may be for a static file, or a CGI script, or other server-side script to generate dynamic content that may handle the request.

A Typical Web Clipping Transaction

In a typical Web clipping transaction, a user downloads and installs a WCA on their handheld device; the WCA contains a form that allows the user to input stock symbols and retrieve quotes. When the user launches this WCA using the Web Clipping Application Viewer, they fill out the form and Clipper sends a request over the air to a Palm.net proxy server. The proxy server passes this request on to a Web server connected to the Internet.

The Web server then responds by returning HTML that contains the latest quote for the requested stock symbol. This response is handled by the Palm.net proxy server, which encodes it into the appropriate format for Clipper and then sends the clipping over the air to the handheld device. Figure 6.2 illustrates what the user would see within Clipper after installing and launching the WCA.

Figure 6.2 A Typical WCA Response

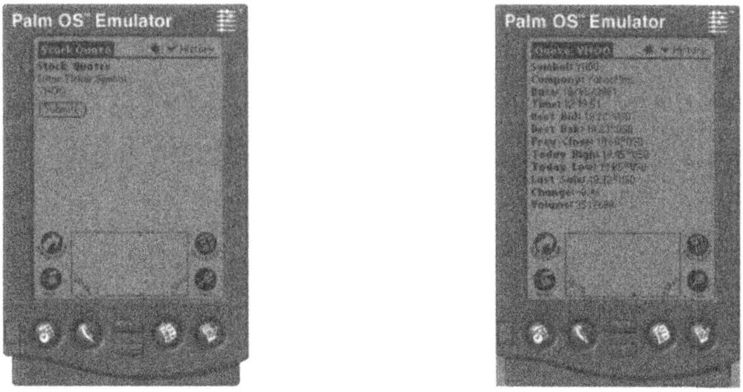

What Types of Hardware Support Web Clipping

There are many different handheld devices that are capable of connecting to the Internet. The actual means of connecting will vary depending on your particular device. For example, the Palm VII/VIIx was designed for Web clipping, and is capable of interacting with the Internet utilizing a radio antenna that is part of the device's hardware. Other Palm models may connect to the Internet via an external modem or cellular phone. Palm-compatible Smart Phones can install and use WCAs.

In this section we will provide an overview of connecting many different handheld devices to the network. In some cases the hardware that handles the physical connection will be included in the device, and in others, the connection will be provided by additional devices. We will first discuss the Palm VII/VIIx, then other handheld devices connected via other networks. Lastly, we will discuss connecting the less costly handheld devices such as the Palm m100, m105, and Palm III series.

NOTE

The RIM 957 (Blackberry) e-mail pager can view the HTML contained in a WCA, but only if the .pqa file is directly accessible from the Internet (www.mysite.com/mypqa.pqa).

A RIM pager does not fully support Web clipping. For example, it is possible for you, in your server response, to reference an image that is embedded in your compiled, device-resident WCA. The RIM will not be able to render the image because it does not store compiled WCAs on the device.

Minimum hardware requirements on any of the handheld devices covered in this section are not an issue. You can take advantage of Web clipping just as easily on a Handspring Visor with a modem and 2MB of RAM as you can on a Palm VIIx with an integrated wireless antenna and 8MB of RAM. The number of WCAs that you can install on your device, however, will be limited to the available memory. The bare requirements for most Palm-compatible devices are version 3.5 or later of the Palm OS, and some method to connect to the Internet.

Regardless of your method of connection, you will need to pay for some type of connection service. All of these various devices are connecting to the Internet via an intermediate wireless layer. This layer can be composed of many different service providers, hardware configurations, and wireless networks, and the solution differs depending on the device you are using.

NOTE

Once your handheld is connected to the Internet via any of the following means, you may also browse WAP content using a third-party browser. The most common browser at this point is the 4thpass.com Kbrowser, available for download at www.4thpass.com. Versions exist for both the Palm VII/VIIx and others, so make sure that you get the appropriate download for your device.

Palm VII/VIIx Connected via Mobitex

The Palm VII/VIIx models contain a radio antenna as part of their hardware configurations. This antenna connects to a network of radio base stations, run by Cingular Wireless. This Mobitex network carries data at a rate of 9.6 kbps, but, as mentioned previously, the actual connection speed may be slower due to delays in Internet traffic and proxy server translation. If you are using a Palm VII/VIIx, you will need to get a subscription to Palm.net in order to connect to this network and use Web clipping applications.

You can activate this service from the device itself. The first time that you raise the wireless antenna, the Activate Setup program starts automatically. You can enter your registration and payment information and be up and running in minutes. There are several different pricing plans available, ranging from about $10 per month to $45 per month. Each plan includes a base volume of transmission plus an additional cost per kilobyte. You can find additional details at http://myaccount.palm.net.

Other Handheld Devices Connected via CDPD

If you are using another Palm handheld device or other Palm-compatible device, such as the Handspring Visor, then it is possible to purchase and install a Minstrel modem that attaches to the unit. This modem operates on the Cellular Digital

Packet Data (CDPD) network, available across most of the U.S. Service may be purchased via AT&T, Verizon, GoAmerica, or Omnisky. Omnisky does not support Palm models below the Palm V/Vx.

Palm-Compatible Handhelds Connected via the Mobile Internet Kit

The Palm Mobile Internet Kit (MIK) allows users of Palm handheld devices other than the Palm VII/VIIx to make use of Web clipping and other Internet-related applications. The Mobile Internet Kit may be used most any Palm handheld, including models that were released several years ago. Included in the purchase of the MIK is a copy of the Palm OS 3.5 upgrade.

The MIK works by allowing your Palm handheld to utilize a modem or a data-capable cellular phone to connect to the Internet, which can be done via a cable or via an Infrared (IR) connection. You may need to purchase a different cable depending on the model of your phone, but the general process is the same. You will not need to pay for Palm.net service, or purchase a monthly flat-rate account from a wireless network carrier. However, any connection time will cut into the minutes available on your cellular phone account.

NOTE

A list of compatible phones can be found at www.palm.com/software/mik/phone.html.

Essentially, the MIK uses the same procedure that some desktop computers use to connect to the Internet. The software of the Palm sends a data signal to the modem, which in turn transmits it to an ISP, which communicates with the Internet. You can use the same ISP as you do with your regular computer (with the exception of proprietary connection and mail protocols). This also eliminates the need for an account with Palm.net.

As you can see, there are a wide variety of handheld devices that are capable of connecting to the Internet, and many ways of connecting these devices to the Internet. It is possible, however, to build and test WCAs without purchasing a device or paying connection fees. There is an emulator available that can run on your desktop computer and mimic a wireless handheld. In the next section, we will discuss the installation and configuration of the Palm Operating System Emulator.

Working with the Palm OS Emulator

Once upon a time, back in the dark ages of 1996 and 1997, a gentleman named Greg Hewgill created an application called Copilot that emulated the software of a Palm Pilot on a desktop computer. In the beginning of 1998, Palm Inc. asked permission to take over the development of the emulator, and have since renamed Copilot to the Palm Operating System Emulator (POSE) and incorporated it into the Palm OS Software Development Kit. The source code remains open and available. The POSE is available for download at www.palmos.com/dev/tech/tools/ and is distributed under the GNU General Public License (GPL). In this section, we will cover the download and installation of the POSE on the Windows and Macintosh platforms.

A UNIX version of this emulator is available in source code format. Source code versions of the emulator are also available for the Windows and Macintosh versions. However, it is not necessary to understand the inner workings of the Palm Operating System, or to understand how to install the emulator from source code in order to build a successful Web clipping application. For our purposes, we will be using the emulator only as it applies to Web clipping.

Downloading and Installing the Emulator

The Palm Operating System Emulator is available for the Windows and Macintosh platforms as a compressed archive (.zip or .sit). You must be running Windows 95, 98, or NT or Macintosh OS 7.5 (or higher) to install the POSE.

To install the POSE on a Windows or Macintosh system, download the archive and extract it to a local folder using your favorite compression utility. Windows users will be familiar with WINZip, and Macintosh users will be familiar with Aladdin StuffIt Expander. A restart of your system is not necessary to install the emulator.

Installing the application is only the first step, however. In order run the emulator, you will need to obtain a Read-Only Memory (ROM) image of the operating system. There are two places to obtain access to a ROM image:

1. Transferring a ROM image from an existing device that you own.
2. Registering with the Palm Developer Program.

Developing & Deploying...

Why Do I Need a ROM Image?

The Palm OS emulator allows you to emulate only the device hardware. To install any applications on the emulator, or even to start it up, you will need to obtain a copy of the Palm OS. It is possible to transfer a ROM image from a device you own (see the next section), but it is recommended that you join the Palm Developer Program (www.palm.com/dev/) to ensure that you know exactly which version of the OS you are installing. You will need to obtain a ROM image of version 3.5 or higher.

Transferring a ROM Image

It is possible to transfer the ROM image of the Palm OS from a handheld device to a desktop computer. This is done by first installing a transfer program onto the device, and then initiating a transfer of the ROM image to the POSE. The application required to perform this transfer, ROM Transfer.prc, is included in the download for the POSE.

To transfer a ROM image from a handheld:

1. Install the Palm OS application named ROMTransfer.prc (included in the emulator download) onto your handheld device.
2. Place the handheld in the HotSync cradle that is connected to the computer that contains the Emulator program.
3. Start your handheld and start the ROM Transfer application (see Figure 6.3). You can also select a port speed here.
4. Start the POSE and select **Download** from the startup screen (see Figure 6.4).
5. Press the **Begin** button on the dialog box containing instructions and port selections (use the same port and speed that connects to your handheld). Once you press **Begin**, the POSE will wait for a response from your handheld (see Figure 6.5).
6. Tap the **Transfer Now** button on your handheld.
7. Be patient while the process completes.

Figure 6.3 Start the ROM Transfer Application on the Handheld Device

Figure 6.4 Download the Image from the POSE

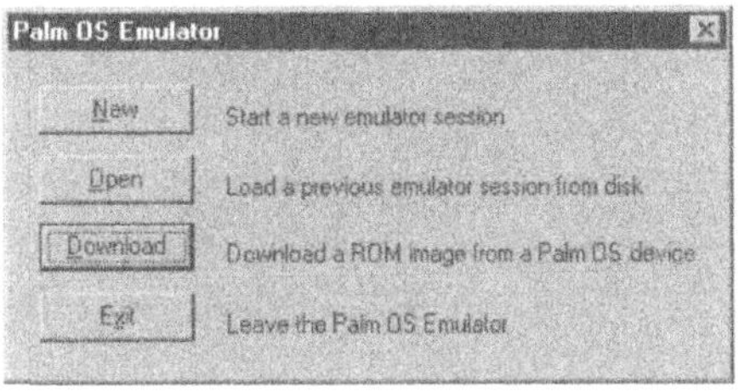

Figure 6.5 Select Port and Speed of Transfer

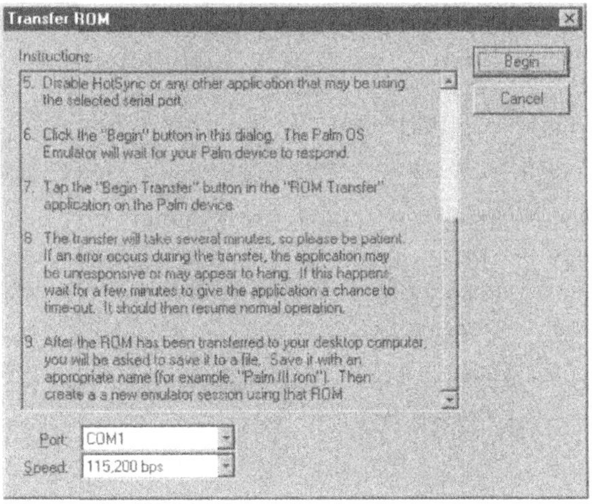

Obtaining ROM Images from Palm

Developers must register with the Palm Alliance Program in order to gain access to ROM images of the Palm OS. Registration is free, and there is no fee to download ROM images. There are several levels of membership with varying degrees of support available. Details on the program, including information on how to join, can be found at www.palmos.com/dev/.

U.S. developers may download ROM images from the ROM Image Clickwrap Area of the Resource Pavilion as soon as their electronic registration is completed. However, developers from outside the United States must send a signed agreement to Palm Inc. in order to gain access to ROM images.

Once you have obtained a ROM image, we suggest that you save it in the same directory as your POSE for ease of installation.

Starting the Emulator

To start the emulator, execute the program named Emulator.exe or Emulator, which will be located where you extracted the downloaded archive. There are several options that allow you to start the emulator with different versions of the Palm Operating system, different Palm hardware models, and different amounts of Random Access Memory (RAM).

Connecting the POSE to the Internet

The Palm VII uses the device's wireless antenna to connect to the Palm.net network via radio waves. Given that the POSE cannot mimic the radio waves emitted and received by the actual device, how do you configure the emulator to connect to Palm.net?

In order for the Palm OS emulator to connect to the Internet, you must configure the software so that it may take advantage of the network interface of your desktop computer to connect to a Palm.net proxy server. This will allow the device to use your desktop's Internet connection to communicate with Palm.net. There are two main steps to setting this up: configuring the device to utilize your Internet connection, and configuring the device to use a Palm.net Proxy Server.

1. Right-click on the emulator window and select **Settings** and then **Properties...** (if you are using the Mac OS, use the **Preferences** item from the **Edit** menu).

2. Check the box **Redirect NetLib calls to host TCP/IP** (this allows applications to use your desktop network interface rather than the handheld's internal library).
3. Reset the emulator.
4. In the emulator, click on the **Prefs** icon and select **Wireless** from the selector in the upper-right corner of the emulator's screen.
5. Make sure the proxy server address is set to either **206.112.114.82** or **206.112.114.83**.

NOTE

The IP addresses of the Palm.net development proxy servers are sometimes changed by Palm. You can always find the latest proxy IP addresses and status at www.palmos.com/dev/tech/webclipping/status.html.

Palm also hosts a read-only mailing list called Web Clipping Announcements. By subscribing to this list, you will receive e-mail updates containing information pertinent to WCA development.

Creating a Web Clipping Project with the WCA Builder

Since Web clipping relies on a subset of HTML 3.2, it is possible to build and test your WCA using tools that will already be familiar to you as a Webmaster: a text editor and a Web browser. Remember that there are some differences between how the browsers handle the HTML that will be covered in detail later in this chapter. It should be fairly easy for you to get your feet wet and begin building WCAs, especially if you typically code your HTML by hand.

The WCA Builder has three main options from the File menu (see Figure 6.6): Open Index, Rescan HTML, and Create PQA. The Open Index function will open up an HTML page and import it into the WCA Builder. When the WCA Builder opens your index file, it will scan your HTML and automatically include any files that you have linked to into the WCA Builder. Likewise, the WCA Builder will automatically include any images that are referenced in your application.

Figure 6.6 WCA Builder Main Options

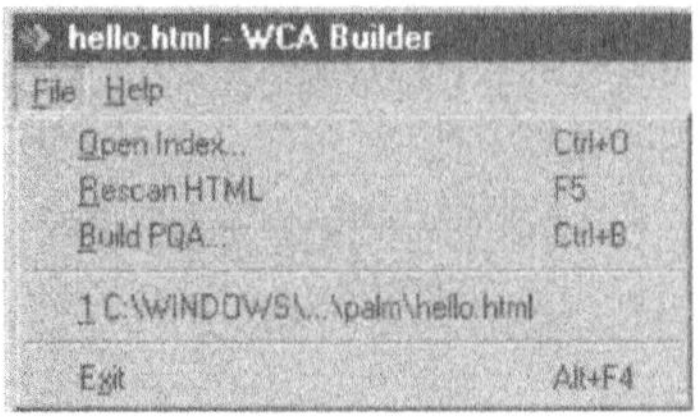

NOTE

The Web Clipping Application Builder (WCA Builder) may be downloaded from www.palmos.com/dev/tech/webclipping/gettingstarted.html. Versions are available for both Windows (.zip) and Macintosh Platforms (.sit). A UNIX version is not available. To install, you will need to extract the contents to a folder on your system and run the file called WCABuild.exe (Windows) or WCA Builder (Macintosh).

Realistically, once you've authored your HTML and saved it to a file, using the WCA Builder is quite simple. All you need to do is drag your index page (containing links to other pages) into the WCA Builder window. The WCA Builder will scan your HTML and will import any pages that you have linked to and add them to your WCA. It will also check your HTML for errors and notify you if there are any bugs in your code. For example, if you omit the *action* element of a form tag, or do not use an absolute reference (www.yoursite.com/cgi-bin/script.cgi), you will be informed of this error when the WCA Builder scans your HTML.

The WCA Builder does not validate your code, however, because CML does not require that all elements be closed, properly nested, or even valid HTML elements. The error-checking done by the WCA Builder is minimal and attempts to ensure that your application will function correctly on the handheld device. It will check your code and alert you if it cannot find an image file specified, or if you have an anchor tag without a filename. It will not, however, detect if your *href* attribute is valid.

It is also important to note that a WCA can contain one and only one file with a given filename. Say, for example, that you build the HTML for your WCA using two subdirectories, each containing an HTML page called index.html. This is a fairly common practice, and intuitively it would seem like you would be able to do this in a WCA. The index page we will use to test this contains the following code:

```
<html>
<head>
        <title>Error Test</title>
</head>

<body>
<a href="one/index.html">Untitled</a>
<a href="two/index.html">Untitled</a>
</body>
</html>
```

When you load this file into the WCA Builder, you will receive the error alert shown in Figure 6.7 if directories one and two exist, and if they both contain a file called index.html. However, in the event that you do not have these directories created, or that the files do not exist, you will not receive an error from the WCA Builder, but your WCA will not function as expected.

Figure 6.7 Error for Duplicating Filenames in a WCA

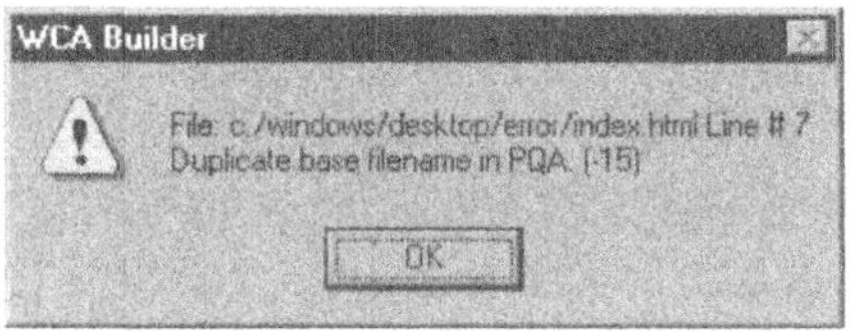

This simple example shows that although the WCA Builder can help to reduce the errors in your code, it cannot eliminate them entirely. It is possible to build a WCA that contains bugs even with the code scanning, so be sure to test all of the links and image references in your application. Chances are you are familiar with automated tools that can validate your links, often within your HTML editor (such as BBEdit for the Macintosh, or HomeSite for the PC). Xenu's link sleuth (http://home.snafu.de/tilman/xenulink.html) is free software that can validate HTML links on local files or Web sites.

While the Application Builder program is running, you can make changes to your index page (or other pages), and simply rescan the HTML by pressing **F5** or selecting **Rescan HTML** from the File menu. Changes on all pages will be implemented into the WCA Builder.

When you are satisfied with your HTML, press **Control-B** or select **Build PQA** from the File menu, and the WCA Builder will create a file (with extension .pqa) that can be transferred to the handheld device and accessed by Clipper.

Now, we will walk through the creation of our first WCA with a Hello, world! program.

Hello, World!

Traditionally, the first program or page built by programmers in any environment is the familiar and trusty "Hello, world!" program. In this section, we will cover the basics of authoring your first Web clipping application (see Figure 6.8). The purpose of this exercise is to make sure that your WCA Builder is installed properly, and that you are able to install your WCA onto the POSE.

Figure 6.8 hello.html

```
<!DOCTYPE HTML PUBLIC "-//POS//DTD WCA HTML 1.1//EN"
        "http://www.palm.com/dev/webclipping-html-dtd-11.dtd">
<html>
<head>
        <title>Hello, world!</title>
</head>
<body>
<h1>Hello, world!</h1>
<p>This web clipping application has been successfully installed!</p>
</body>
</html>
```

Including the Document Type Definition (DTD) at the top of the document is not required, but it is a good idea to validate your HTML code against the DTD in order to ensure that your code is valid. As the Web (both wired and wireless) moves towards a more standardized environment containing well-formed and valid markup such as XHTML (and subsets), best practices dictate that an appropriate DTD be included with every document.

The rest of the code in Figure 6.8 is very straightforward and will generate a page containing a title and a paragraph, shown in a desktop browser in Figure 6.9.

Figure 6.9 hello.html in a Web Browser

Scanning the HTML

To have the WCA Builder scan your code and prepare it for compilation into a .pqa file, drag the icon for your file into the WCA Builder window (or select **Open Index** from the File menu). Figure 6.10 illustrates what hello.html of Figure 6.8 looks like in the WCA Builder. If you make changes to your original HTML file, you can press **F5** to rescan the code and update the changes within the WCA Builder.

Figure 6.10 hello.html in the WCA Builder

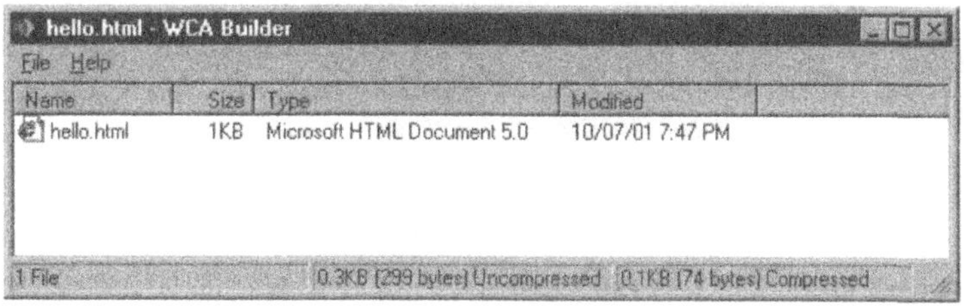

You will notice in that the file sizes of the HTML and of the compressed WCA are displayed in the lower left of the application window. You can tell the size of your application before installing it on the device, a very useful feature.

Creating the .pqa File

To create your Web clipping application that you want installed on the device, press **Control-B** or select **File | Build PQA** from within the WCA Builder. Upon selecting this action, you are presented with a dialog that allows you to save your .pqa file to a directory on your computer (see Figure 6.11).

Figure 6.11 Building the .pqa

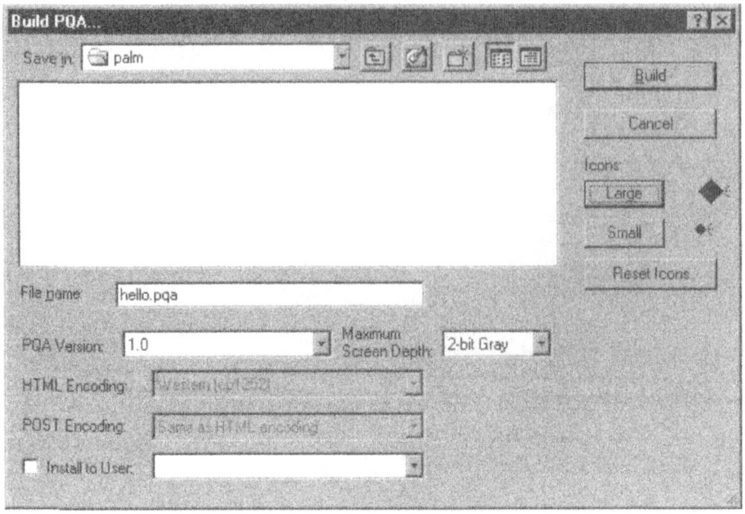

There are several options in the Build PQA dialog box. In addition to **Build** and **Cancel**, you have the option of specifying an icon that will be displayed on the device by clicking the **Large** and **Small** icon buttons. Should you create custom icons for your application, ensure that the small icon is 15 pixels wide and 9 pixels tall, and that the large icon is 32 pixels wide and 22 pixels tall.

You can specify the version of your WCA by changing the value in PQA version. Also, you are able to specify the maximum bit depth that will be used to render the images in your application. The display of images within a WCA is limited by two factors: the display depth of the device, and the bit depth of the images in the application. This feature allows you to ensure consistent presentation of your application on devices with varying display depths by setting the display depth of your application to a lowest common denominator.

Installing and Uninstalling the Web Clipping Application on the POSE

The easiest way to install an application onto the POSE is to drag the icon for the .pqa onto the window of the emulator program. Also, you can select **Install Application or Database** from the File menu on the Macintosh and by right-clicking on the emulator window on a Windows PC.

To install a WCA on a handheld device, use the HotSync utility as follows:

1. Save your WCA to the directory on your desktop that will be used by the HotSync operation.
2. Open the Palm Desktop program on your desktop.
3. Click on **Install** on the Palm Desktop program. The **Install Tool** window will pop up. Locate your WCA and **Add** it. Then click **Done**.
4. Put your device into its cradle and perform the HotSync operation.
5. Your WCA icon should now appear on your handheld.

NOTE

If you have the Palm Desktop software installed on your computer, you can install directly to your device by selecting the **Install to User** option when you build your WCA.

To uninstall a WCA that you no longer wish to use from either the POSE or a handheld device:

1. Choose **Delete** from the App menu.
2. Select your WCA, then select **Delete**.
3. At the confirmation box, select **Yes**.
4. Select **Done** to return to the application launcher and confirm that the application no longer appears.

Viewing the Web Clipping Application

Once your application has been installed on the device, you can view it by clicking on its icon. By default, WCAs are placed within the main launcher window and also are included under the Palm.net screen. Figure 6.12 shows the default icon and title for our first application.

We can launch the application by clicking on it, which starts the Clipper application and displays our HTML code, as shown in Figure 6.13.

Figure 6.12 Launching the WCA

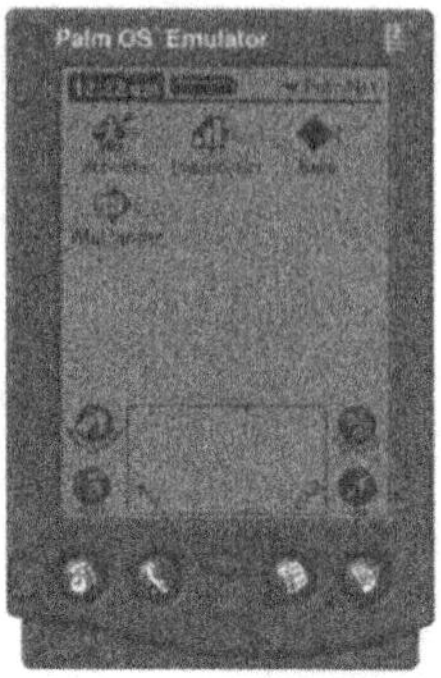

Figure 6.13 Hello, world! in Clipper

Adding Images and Additional Pages to Your WCA

It is possible for your WCA to include multiple pages and images. To add an image to your application, you can use the same image syntax as you do for desktop browsers. For example, to add an image to our Hello, world! application, we can create an image in a graphics program such as Adobe PhotoShop or Paint. We then add the following line of code to our page, just as we would for a desktop browser:

```
<img src="myimage.gif">
```

Figure 6.14 shows what the WCA Builder will look like once we save our changes to hello.html and tell the WCA Builder to rescan the HTML. It is not necessary to drag your images into the WCA Builder to have them included in your WCA. As the HTML of your page is scanned, any images automatically are imported into the WCA Builder.

Figure 6.14 Image Added to the WCA Builder

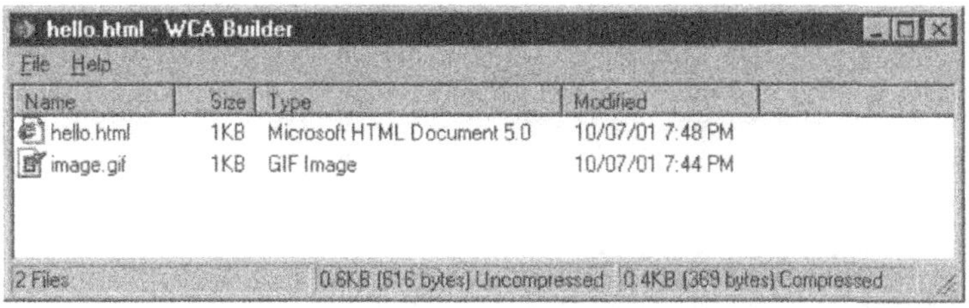

NOTE

You can use images in .gif or .jpg format. The WCA Builder can handle converting either type during the final creation of your WCA. It is not necessary to create images at lower color depths to be able to include them in your application, but there are instances where you may want to optimize the color depth of your images by hand instead of letting the WCA Builder convert them automatically.

Likewise, to add additional pages to your WCA, you simply need to link to them in your index page. For example, if we were to add links to two more pages to our WCA, we simply need to create the pages and add links to them using the anchor tag (<a>):

```
<a href="page2.html">Page 2</a><br>
<a href="page3.html">Page 3</a>
```

Once we save our changes to hello.html and press **F5** in the WCA Builder to rescan our HTML, we will see that the pages have been imported automatically into the WCA Builder, as shown in Figure 6.15.

Figure 6.15 Pages Added to the WCA Builder

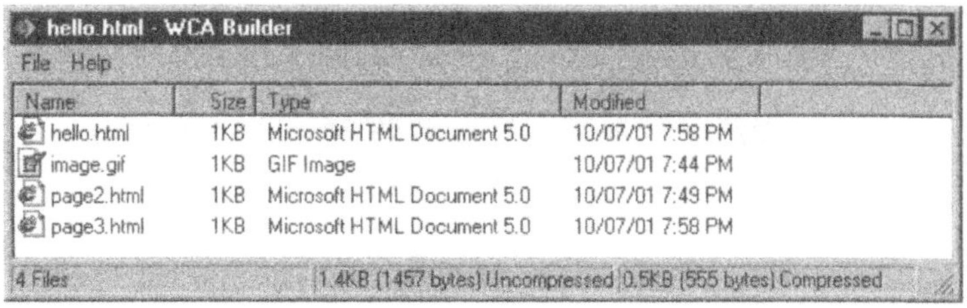

When you build your WCA, all of the elements shown in the WCA Builder window will be included in a single file that you can install on the device. The WCA Builder is a handy, easy-to-use tool that allows you to concentrate on writing your HTML instead of learning another markup language or converting images. The fact that it scans your HTML automatically and includes any elements that you have linked to in your code makes the creation of a WCA simple and straightforward.

In this section, we have covered how to use the WCA Builder to create our first Web clipping application, and how to include images and additional pages into our application. We discussed how to install and run a WCA, and provided instructions on how to uninstall application from your handheld or the POSE. In the next section, we will discuss, in detail, which elements of HTML are or are not supported within Web clipping, as well as items unique to Clipper.

Web Clipping Basics

A Web clipping application, as previously mentioned, is a collection of HTML pages and images that are compiled and installed on a Palm-Compatible handheld device. A Web Clipping Application Viewer renders the content of the WCA on the device.

Although the basic building blocks of a WCA are HTML and images, Clipper does not actually render HTML, per se. Rather, Clipper renders Compact HTML, a subset of HTML 3.2 developed specifically for Web clipping. Don't let that scare you, however, because there is no need to learn another markup language. It is only necessary to know basic HTML to build a WCA.

First, we will discuss HTML features that are not supported by Clipper, and then cover the most common HTML tags and how they behave in a WCA. We will then cover some elements that are unique to Web clipping, and how to implement them in your application. We will then discuss how to interact with a Web server using a WCA, and cover some examples. Finally, we will suggest some general guidelines to make your WCA more user-friendly.

Unsupported Tags and Elements

There are some features of the HTML that are not supported in Web clipping to any degree. The following list consists of elements that you cannot include in your WCA:

- Animated GIFs
- Cascading style sheets (CSS)
- Cookies
- ECMAScript (JavaScript, jscript)
- Frames
- Imagemaps
- Java Applets
- Layers
- Named typefaces
- Nested tables

NOTE

Palm OS version 4.0 does support cookies, although it is unrealistic at this point to assume that your users will have this OS installed.

Simply put, device constraints are responsible for the lack of support for these elements. As time progresses, we can expect that some of these features will become available to handheld devices (although not necessarily under Web clipping). It is up to you as a Webmaster to make effective use of the limited features that are available.

The fortunate thing about Web clipping is that there are several very useful extensions that help to alleviate the constraints of the environment. For example, there is an object called *datepicker* that allows your users to choose a date using a calendar interface and send a string to your server. To gain the same functionality with a desktop browser, you would have to create the calendar object yourself, using a combination of HTML and JavaScript. Also, for some users, you will be able to gain information about their location (ZIP code) and have access to a unique device identifier.

Before we get into the details of these Web clipping-specific extensions to HTML, we will examine the subset of HTML that is utilized by Clipper.

Supported Tags and Elements

As mentioned previously, the markup used to author a WCA is a subset of HTML 3.2, meaning that not all of the elements of the 3.2 specification are available. Furthermore, some of the elements that are supported may not behave exactly as they do on a desktop Web browser. One of the most problematic of these elements is the lack of support for nested tables. If you are in the habit of using tables extensively for layout, you will need to rethink how you apply these features. Form elements are also rendered slightly differently (most notably radio buttons).

In general, if you are comfortable with hand-coding your HTML the jump to Web clipping will give you a new environment in which to apply your skills. When designing and building your application, you will want to take the limitations into consideration and keep your code simple, lean, and optimized for a low bandwidth connection and a small screen size. For the most part, however, you will be able to build WCAs using tools and skills that you already possess.

NOTE

A Document Type Definition (DTD) can be downloaded at www.palm.com/dev/webclipping-html-dtd-11.dtd, and you can specify this DTD at the top of your page using the standard DTD syntax. Once you have done this, you can use the W3C validator at validator.w3.org to ensure that your server-side HTML is error-free without running it through the WCA Builder.

The subset of HTML 3.2 that comprises the markup for Web clipping applications is fairly large, and it is not necessary to run through a laundry list of the entire tag set. We will, however, cover the most common and useful supported tags in this section, as well as their attributes and possible values.

In the event that you can code HTML with your eyes closed (as many of us can), you may already be familiar with the elements and attributes presented here. On the other hand, if you have been using a What-You-See-Is-What-You-Get (WYSIWYG) editor such as FrontPage or DreamWeaver, this section will read as a crash-course in HTML.

Most likely, you have encountered the following tags in your experience as a Webmaster:

- <title>
- <meta>
- <body>
- <table>, <tr>, <td>
- <p>
- <b>, <i>, <u>
- <strong>, <em>
- <ol>, <ul>, <li>
- <h1> – <h6>
- <img>
- <a>
- <form>
- <select>
- <input>

Let's now take a look at how these elements are similar and different from their desktop equivalents, and cover how they behave differently when viewed with the Web Clipping Application Viewer.

Using the <title> Tag

First things first—let's take a look at the <title> tag. In a normal HTML document, the <title> tag is displayed in the top of the browser window, as shown in Figure 6.16.

Figure 6.16 <title> Tag in a Desktop Browser

Likewise, in a WCA, the text within the <title> tag is displayed at the top of the Web Clipping Application Viewer, illustrated in Figure 6.17.

Figure 6.17 <title> Tag within Clipper

One important item to note about this tag is that the length of the title bar in Clipper is slightly less than one-half of the screen width. If your <title> tag is too long, it will be truncated and appended with an ellipsis (...), as illustrated in Figure 6.18.

Figure 6.18 Truncated <title> tag in Clipper

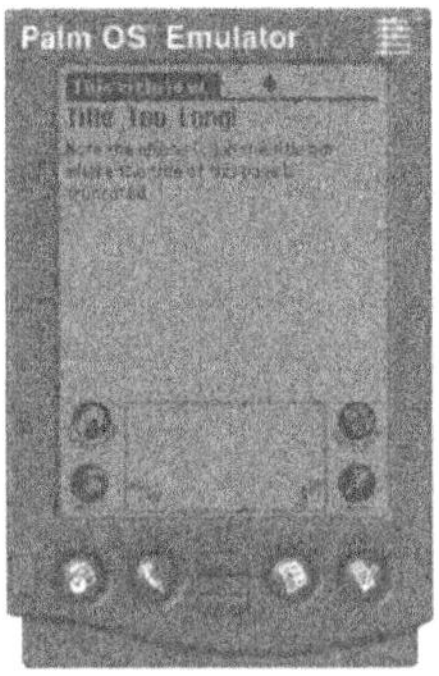

Using the <meta> Tag

The <meta> tag, used to send HTTP header information inline in a document, is less supported by Clipper than it is for standard desktop browsers. Primarily, you will use the <meta> tag to relay information to the Palm.net Proxy Server that your page is built specifically for Web clipping. Palm-specific <meta> tags are discussed later.

Clipper is unable to process HTTP redirects by using a <meta> tag. In the event that you do need to do a redirect, you can do it in a server response by using the Location header. Bear in mind that if you do multiple redirects in the same response, an error will be generated and sent to Clipper. The best guideline is for you to use redirects only when necessary, and ensure that only one redirect is sent in a response.

Using the <body> Tag

The <body> tag attributes of HTML 3.2 are supported in Web clipping. You may specify the background color of the document, as well as text and link colors. However, for the most part, you will be dealing with monochrome or grayscale displays, which greatly reduces your color choices. In fact, there are only four colors supported on all devices that support Web clipping, shown in Table 6.1.

Table 6.1 Colors Supported by All Web Clipping Devices

Hex Value	Display
#000000	Black
#C0C0C0	Silver
#808080	Gray
#FFFFFF	White

NOTE

It is important to avoid selecting low-contrast colors for backgrounds and text. Should you employ the use of colors, be judicious in their use and make sure that your application retains usability on monochrome displays.

Using the <table>, <tr>, and <td> Tags

Tables, when they were first introduced in HTML 2.0, were intended to mark up data displayed in rows and columns. As time progressed (and as many Webmasters can recall), tables were commonly used as a page layout tool to dictate the positioning and display of text and graphics. With the advent of HTML 4.0 and CSS, tables are now being phased out as a design tool, and being used for data once again.

WARNING

The most important item to note is Clipper's lack of support for nested tables. In the event that you include a nested table in your application, Clipper will render the nested table as plain text, which will rarely create the desired effect. You should take this into consideration when designing your WCA.

The <table> tag supports the more common elements of tables used in standard HTML, outlined in Table 6.2.

Table 6.2 Table Elements Supported by the <table> Tag

Attribute	Description	Possible Values	Default Value
Align	The horizontal alignment of the table	Left, center, right	Left
Width	The width of the table, in pixels; percentage values are not supported	Numeric value	Width of contained elements, up to browser width
Cellpadding	The number of pixels between the edge of a cell and its contents	Numeric value	Two pixels
Cellpacing	The number of pixels between rows and columns	Numeric value	Two pixels

NOTE

Tables have a maximum width of 153 pixels under Palm OS 3.5 (due to a lack of horizontal scrolling). It is recommended that you keep the width element unspecified when writing your code. This way, your tables will be rendered by Clipper's table algorithm, which operates similarly to how tables are rendered on a desktop browser. The table will wrap around the elements in the cells, and stretch to the edge of the screen before wrapping cell contents.

The <tr> tag is used to designate the beginning of a row within a <table>. The only valid attribute for the <tr> tag is the *align* attribute, which has possible values of left, center, and right (with a default value of left).

A <tr> tag may contain two elements, <td> (table data cell) or <th> (table header cell). Table 6.3 shows possible attributes for the <td> element, what they specify, as well as the valid and default values for each.

Table 6.3 Table Elements Supported by the <td> Element

Attribute	Description	Possible Values	Default Value
Align	The horizontal alignment of the cell	Left, center, right	Left
Width	The width of the cell, in pixels	Numeric value	Auto
Rowspan	The number of rows that the cell spans within the table	Numeric value	Single row
Colspan	The number of columns that the cell spans within the table	Numeric value	Single column

As in standard HTML, the only difference between the <td> and <th> cells is that the text within a <th> is, by default, bold and centered.

NOTE

If you are sending HTML containing table code back in a server response, you must ensure that you also include the palmcomputingplatform=true header either in the response itself or contained within a <meta> tag. Otherwise, the Palm.net Proxy Server will treat your code as if it originated on a traditional Web site, and your table code will be modified, often with undesirable results!

Using the <p> Tag

The <p> tag denotes a paragraph of text, which supports the *align* attribute. There are several values to specify the alignment of the <p> tag: left, center, and right. The default, as with desktop browsers, is left alignment. Astute readers will note that the rarely used justify value for this attribute is unsupported by Clipper.

Using the <b>, <i>, and <u> Tags

These tags specify the appearance of text within a document as bold, italicized, or underlined, and are functionally equivalent to their HTML counterparts.

Using the <strong> and <em> Tags

These tags logically specify the appearance of text within a document. Clipper will render the <strong> tag as bold text, and the <em> tag as italicized text. In general, there is a current trend to replace display-based markup (<b>, <i>) with logically-based markup.

Using the <ol>, <ul>, and <li> Tags

These tags specify elements of a list. This list may be unordered (<ul>) or ordered (<ol>). These elements behave much as they do on a desktop browser, with an indent from the left side of the browser.

The <ol> element supports the *start* attribute, which specifies the number at which the listing should start. This is often used to split ordered lists between side-by-side table cells. Chances are you will not have the horizontal real estate to implement this within Clipper, however. You can use this to split lists between pages, of course. In addition, the <ol> tag also supports the *type* attribute. You may specify the types shown in Table 6.4 with the effects indicated.

Table 6.4 Type Attribute Effects for an Ordered List

Value	Effect
1 (default)	Incremental numeric listing
A	Ascending uppercase letter listing
a	Ascending lowercase letter listing
I	Ascending uppercase roman numeral listing
i	Ascending lowercase roman numeral listing

The <ul> element specifies an unordered list, and has no optional attributes within Clipper, just like its desktop counterpart. The <li> element specifies a list item. There are several possible values that specify the display of the bullet next to list items in an unordered list. These values are specified with the *type* attribute, and have possible values of circle, disc, and square.

Using the <h1> – <h6> Tags

These elements specify headings within a document, and provide display of bolded text with line breaks before and after the element. They behave similarly to their desktop counterparts, but the size difference is not as great. Also, it is worth mentioning that the <h4>, <h5>, and <h6> elements display rather small within Clipper. When you consider that your users are often on –the go and may not be using your WCA under optimal conditions, it makes sense to keep the headers used within your application at a maximum depth of three levels (<h1> – <h3>).

Using the <img> Tag

The image tag is supported by Clipper, but it behaves somewhat differently than you might expect. As we mentioned earlier, a WCA built using the WCA Builder has the capability of containing one and only one file with a given filename. This means that you cannot have multiple images with the same name within your application, as Clipper will treat them both as the same image. The attributes shown in Table 6.5 are supported for the <img> tag; remember that only the *src* attribute is required.

Table 6.5 Image Attributes Supported by the <img> Tag

Attribute	Description
Src	The location of the image relative to the HTML page
Width	The display width of the image, in pixels
Height	The display height of the image, in pixels
Hspace	Horizontal padding around the image, in pixels
Vspace	Vertical padding around the image, in pixels
Alt	Alternate text for the image, used in place of graphic
Align	Alignment of image: left, center, or right
Border	Specifies a border around the image, in pixels (default is 0)

Developing & Deploying…

The LocalIcon Meta Tag

It is possible to include extra images within a WCA by specifying them as a LocalIcon by using the following syntax:

```
<meta name="LocalIcon" content="myimage.gif">
```

Doing so will instruct the WCA Builder to bundle the image within your .pqa, thus ensuring that the icon exists on the local device (we recommend including all of these references in the index page of your application to keep track of them). You can reference these images later in your server responses with the following syntax:

```
<img src="file:mypqa.pqa/myimage.gif">
```

Clipper will find the image on the local device and display it to the user without them having to download the image from your Web site and send it over the air to the device. This is the preferred method of using images in a server response. It will require some forethought when you initially build your WCA, but it will help to create a faster (and cheaper) user experience!

Using the <a> Tag

The anchor tag is the defining feature of HTML versus other document technologies, and arguably the most important tag in any Webmaster's repertoire. The anchor tag supports three different attributes within Clipper: *href*, *name*, and *button*. The meaning and syntax of these attributes is described in Table 6.6.

Table 6.6 Attributes of the <a> Tag

Attribute	Description	Syntax
Href	Refers to the location of the document being linked to, identical to desktop browser	<a href="">Text</a>
Name	Refers to the anchor itself, identical to desktop browser	<a name="">Text</a>
Button	Displays link as button, unique to Clipper	<a href="" button>Text</a>

The protocols shown in Table 6.7 are valid with an anchor tag in a Web clipping sent to a browser or WCA installed on the device.

Table 6.7 Protocols Valid with the <a> Tag

Protocol	Resource
http://	Uniform Resource Identifier (URI) accessed via HTTP.
https://	Uniform Resource Identifier (URI) accessed via secure HTTP.
mailto:	E-mail address, accessed via the Exchange Manager. The Exchange Manager calls the default e-mail application. This is accomplished via Messaging Application Programming Interface (MAPI), which is the same library that handles this action on a desktop computer.
file:	Location of file on device. You can access individual pages with an installed WCA by using the following syntax: <a href="file:mypqa.pqa/page1.html">.
palm:	Application on device. When linked to, Clipper is closed and the requested location is launched in place of Clipper. For example, <a href="palm:memo.appl"> can be used to launch the Memo Pad.
palmcall:	Application on device. When linked to, the application is launched from Clipper, and Clipper remains in the background until the application is closed.

Whenever Clipper has to send information over the air, it will render three small lines to the left of a link, whether it is a text link or a button. This over-the-air icon informs users that they will be sending and receiving data over the wireless network, and will correspondingly incur charges. Links that point to a page that is located on the device using the protocols will not have this symbol. A secure link will show the image of a small key and the over-the-air icon.

Using the <form> Tag

The <form> tag is a very important aspect of Web clipping, as it enables your WCA to send data to a Web server located on the Internet. Clipper allows you to use both GET and POST methods, and you must specify an *action* attribute, which specifies a Uniform Resource Identifier (URI) for your form to send data to.

Using the <select> Tag

The <select> element allows you to generate a menu that allows your user to make a choice from a variety of options (specified using <option> elements within the <select>), and behaves almost exactly the same as it does in a desktop browser. The select element supports the attributes shown in Table 6.8.

Table 6.8 Attributes of the <select> Tag

Attribute	Contains	Description	Default
Name	String	Name of variable containing selected value to be sent to server	Required – N/A
Size	Number	Number of options to be displayed	1
Multiple	Minimized attribute, no value needed	Allows multiple options to be selected; in order to enable a scrollable list, the minimum value is 2	Off

Using the <input> Tag

The <input> element allows the user to input information that can be sent to a server for processing. It supports a wide variety of formats via the *type* attribute. The <input> element supports the attributes shown in Table 6.9.

Table 6.9 Attributes of the <input> Tag

Attribute	Meaning
Type	The type of input to be rendered: valid values for this include text, password, hidden, radio, checkbox, submit, reset
Name	Name of variable containing value to be sent to server
Value	Predefined value
Checked	Specifies that an input with type *radio* or *checkbox* will be checked
Size	Specifies the length, in character units, of the input (of type *text*) to be rendered
Maxlength	Specifies the maximum number of characters that may be entered in an input of type *text*

NOTE

There are also two Palm OS-specific values that may be specified for the input element: timepicker and datepicker. See the section, "Web Clipping Extensions."

The <input> element behaves quite similarly to its standard HTML counterpart, with the exception of the radio button (type=radio). This type is rendered as a box, which may be selected by the user. In order for this box to display any text, the label must be inserted directly after the input tag, as shown in Figure 6.19 and Figure 6.20.

Figure 6.19 Adding Radio Buttons

```
<html>
<head>
      <title>Radio Button</title>
<meta name="PalmComputingPlatform" content="true">
</head>
<body>
<h1>Radio Button Example</h1>
<form action="http://www.yoursite.com/cgi-bin/script.cgi">
<input type="radio" name="radio" value="Option1">Option1<br>
<input type="radio" name="radio" value="Option2" checked>Option2<br>
<input type="radio" name="radio" value="Option3">Option3<br>
<input type="radio" name="radio" value="Option4">Option4<br>
<input type="radio" name="radio" value="Option5">Option5<br>
</form>
</body>
</html>
```

Figure 6.20 Radio Buttons Added in Clipper

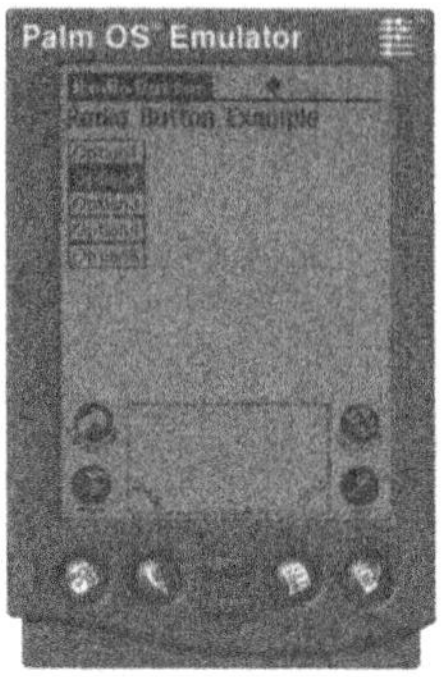

Web Clipping Extensions

There are a few elements unique to Web clipping. These include some <meta> tags that relay information to the Proxy Server, variables that can be used to identify unique devices and their approximate locations, and objects that can gather date and time data from the user.

NOTE

If you have HTML on your existing site that you would like to make available to Web clipping users, you can mark it with the <smallsscreenignore> tag, which tells the proxy server to ignore the code in between.

Palm-Specific <meta> Tags

There are many <meta> tags and header information that are specific only to Web clipping. A full list of these tags is described in Palm Inc.'s Web Clipping Developer's Guide, located at www.palmos.com/dev/tech/docs/webclippings/PalmWebClippingFront.html. Table 6.10 describes the most common and useful tags that you can use to relay information.

Table 6.10 Useful Meta Tags for Web Clipping

Tag Name	Example	Description
Historylisttext	<meta name="historylisttext" content="Hello, World!">	Specifies text to be displayed when users view their history. If omitted, Clipper will display the time the clipping was viewed.
LocalIcon	<meta name="localicon" content="myimage.gif"> This image can later be referenced in clippings sent down from a Web server by using the following syntax: <img src="file:mypqa.pqa/myimage.gif">	Used while building your WCA, this tag specifies the name of an image to be included in a WCA and stored on the device.
PalmComputingPlatform	<meta name="palmcomputingplatform" content="true">	Specifies that a clipping is safe for Clipper and that it should not be modified by the Palm.net Proxy Server. It is strongly encouraged that you include this tag in all of your server responses.

NOTE

Palm OS 4.0 offers a great many more <meta> tags than those listed here, including some caching mechanisms. As time progresses, you may be interested in implementing some of the newer features of Web clipping.

Identifying Users with a Device ID

There is a special variable that you can access on any device that supports Web clipping. It is referenced as such:

```
<input type="hidden" name="id" value="%deviceid">
```

This variable is returned in the format [1, 0, -1].[X].

The content of the first brackets corresponds to the type of device:

- A value of 1 is returned if the proxy server recognizes the device ID as being a Palm VII.
- A value of 0 is returned if the device cannot be determined to be a Palm VII or other device.
- A value of –1 is returned if the proxy server can determine that the device is *not* a Palm VII.

The content of the second set of brackets is a unique string that is created upon device activation. You can use %DEVICEID to identify unique users, but with limited reliability. Depending on the network from which your user is accessing your application (Smart Phones in particular), the value of %DEVICEID may change from session to session, and, in some cases, within a particular session.

NOTE

The actual string format of %DEVICEID may change as time progresses, so it should be treated as a black box when used in a server-side application. That is, do not make any assumptions as to the exact format of the string. Be sure to accommodate this in your application in order to create the best experience for your users.

Developing & Deploying…

Using %DEVICEID to Recognize Individual Users

Given that a Palm.net proxy server processes all Web clipping transactions, you cannot use the user's IP address to identify individual users because all requests will be written to your server logs with the IP of the proxy server. Also, cookies are supported only for Palm OS 4.0, which, at the time of this writing, is not yet prevalent in the market. The %DEVICEID element was implemented as a cookie substitute and was intended to allow developers to identify individual devices.

There are, as previously mentioned, issues with the implementation that severely limit the usage of %DEVICEID for authentication in an environment that deals with sensitive data. However, if no real damage will be caused if the %DEVICEID of a particular user is spoofed, and you make sure to rely only on %DEVICEID for Palm VII users (since it may change midsession for users of other networks), you can use it reliably to identify individual users in a variety of situations.

For example, if you offer downloadable stock quotes, you may provide your users with an option to customize their preferences and select the stocks they want to see. You can develop your application so that when the user initiates a request for stock quotes from their device, they receive quotes for the stocks in which they are interested. This is an effective means of providing a positive user experience while minimizing data sent over the air.

The %DEVICEID element provides Webmasters with something we previously have had to generate ourselves, namely, a unique key that represents an individual user (device). This identifier is unfortunately insecure and not always reliable (depending on the user's connection network), so you must take care in how you use it.

Security Alert

You should not associate any personal information with %DEVICEID. Mobile devices are susceptible to theft, and sensitive information may be compromised if %DEVICEID is the only method of authentication. Furthermore, a determined user can obtain the %DEVICEID from other devices by offering a Trojan Horse PQA. There is not a reliable means of determining the *authenticity* of a request using %DEVICEID, and you should use prudence when using it to identify users.

Estimating User Location by ZIP Code

The %ZIPCODE variable contains the ZIP code of the nearest Web clipping base station to the user. This will provide a rough estimate of where your user is located at the time of access, accurate to within approximately 10 miles.

```
<input type="hidden" name="zip" value="%zipcode">
```

NOTE

This variable may not be always available. Unless your user is connected via the Mobitex network, you will not be able to utilize this feature of Web clipping. In the event that the ZIP code is unavailable, %ZIPCODE returns a value of 000000. You can work around this by building some detection into your server-side application that allows users to enter their locations as opposed to submitting the %ZIPCODE value automatically.

Palm OS 4.0 offers much more information about the user's network, including information regarding the latitude and longitude of the location, as well as county, city, state, and country information. If you are in a situation in which you can reliably know what type of hardware your users have (such as a corporate environment), then you may be able to take advantage of this information before the 4.0 OS becomes prevalent in the general market.

Selecting a Date with the Datepicker Object

A very useful element unique to the Web clipping environment is the datepicker object. You can invoke the datepicker object to generate a string containing a date:

```
<input type="datepicker" name="date" value="MM/DD/YYYY">
```

NOTE

The date attribute is output in YYYY-MM-DD format, but dates are assigned using the MM/DD/YYYY format shown in the preceding code.

If you omit the value attribute, or if the value is not in the expected format, then the current date will be displayed. Figure 6.21 shows how the datepicker object looks in the POSE (in this case, we have specified 01/01/2001 as the date within the HTML code).

Figure 6.21 Datepicker Object with Value Attribute Omitted

When users click on the input field, they are presented with a clickable calendar that allows them to select a date (see Figure 6.22).

Figure 6.22 Selecting a Date

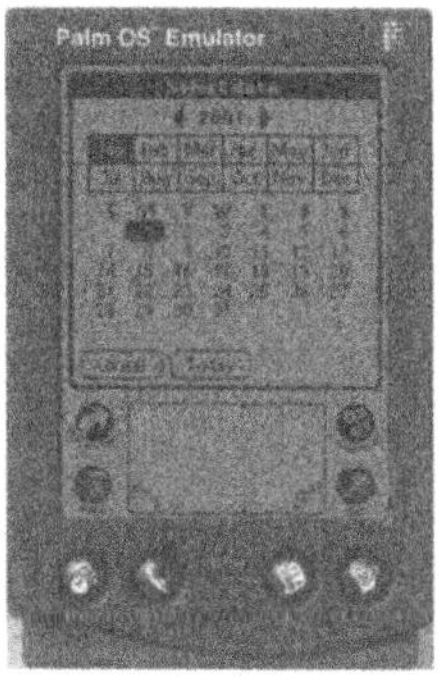

The user is also given the option to select **Today** as the date. This option allows the user to select the current date. Upon pressing the **Today** button, the user is returned to the page containing the datepicker object, as illustrated in Figure 6.23.

Figure 6.23 Selected Date Returns the User to the Datepicker Object

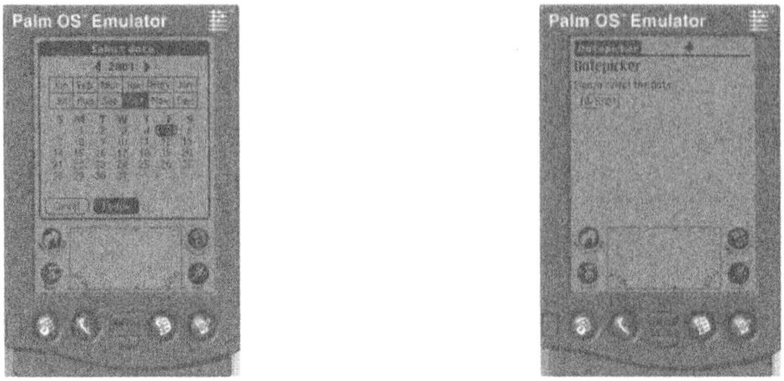

Choosing a Date with the Timepicker Object

The timepicker is another useful element that is unique to the Web clipping environment. The timepicker is invoked using a syntax very similar to the datepicker: Output of this object is always in 24-hour HH:MM format, but the input of this object may be in 12-hour format depending on the user's preferences (accessible via the **Formats** screen under **Prefs**).

The following sets the 24-hour format:

```
<input type="timepicker" name="time" value="hh:mm">
```

The following sets the 12-hour format:

```
<input type="timepicker" name="time" value="hh:mm am/pm">
```

Figure 6.24 illustrates the timepicker object in action. First, the user is presented with a screen containing the specified time (in this case, 11:30 AM), or, if no time is specified, the current time.

Figure 6.24 Timepicker Object with Value Attribute Omitted

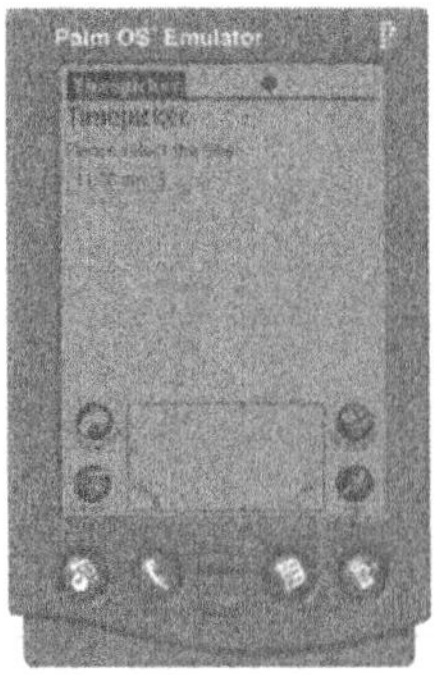

Upon clicking on the input field, the user is presented with a dialog to specify the time. Each field is selected and manipulated with the arrows in the center of the dialog box (see Figure 6.25).

Figure 6.25 Selecting a Time

Once the user selects the new time and presses **OK**, they are returned to the page containing the timepicker object, with the selected time displayed (see Figure 6.26).

Figure 6.26 Selected Time Returns the User to the Timepicker Object

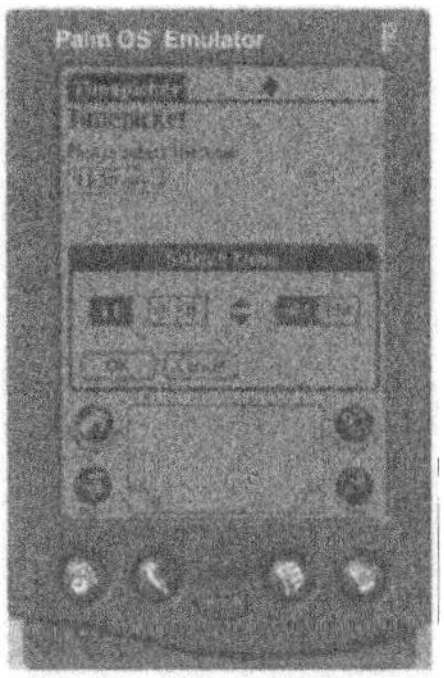

If the value attribute is omitted, or if the value is not in the expected format, the current time will be displayed in the timepicker when the user clicks on it. This being the case, it is not necessary for you to overly concern yourself with the user's preferences. The default preference is 12-hour format, so you may want to keep this in mind as you build your application.

The device-specific extensions to Web clipping are quite useful and convenient, and come in handy both to reduce development time (by eliminating the need to code client-side functionality such as calendars and time inputs), and to increase the quality of the user experience (by providing a consistent interface to input data). In addition, location-based features such as %ZIPCODE (and %LOCATION for Palm OS 4.0) provide an easy route to providing users with information relevant to their location while accessing your server. The %DEVICEID, despite its variability, can be used as a convenient way to recognize individual users when there is not a risk to the user should the authenticity of %DEVICEID become compromised.

Now that we have covered the available code to build a Web clipping application, we can move on to discuss some examples.

Web Clipping in Action: Examples

In this section, we will discuss two examples: one that illustrates how a WCA can pass information to other local applications, and one that illustrates how you can send information to a Web server and return a page that is appropriate for Clipper. For the most part, this will be similar to methods you will already be familiar with from developing HTML for desktop browsers. The first example that we will use is a mailto: link that will be processed using the local e-mail application on the device (iMessenger, in this case). This feature utilizes Messaging Application Protocol Interface (MAPI), a library that allows applications to send parameters to an e-mail program. This is the same feature that allows mailto: links to launch the e-mail program on a desktop computer. The same syntax used to pass parameters to a mailto: link is used to pass parameters to other applications on the device using the palm: or palmcall: URL protocols.

We will then illustrate a form-based example of how you can send an e-mail message using a CGI script installed on your server. Chances are you have used this in one form or another already. In this chapter, we will be using a mailform example using PHP due to its portability across platforms and open-source availability. You can download a free copy of PHP from www.php.net.

Using a mailto: Link with Parameters

This example is fairly straightforward and will illustrate some basic concepts about exchanging information between programs located on a Palm-powered handheld device. We will use an HTML mailto: link to compose an outgoing e-mail using iMessenger, the e-mail application that is included on the Palm VII/VIIx (see Figure 6.27).

Figure 6.27 E-mail Example

```
<html>
<head>
<title>
Email Example
</title>
</head>
<body>
<h1>Email Example</h1>
<p>This example illustrates both how you can use the 'button' attribute
    of the anchor tag to render a link as a button, and how you can
pass
    parameters within a link that will help compose the email.</p>
<a href="mailto:example@syngress.com?subject=From WCA&body=This is a
    message that came from a WCA" button>example@synress.com</a>
</body>
</html>
```

The code in Figure 6.27 should look fairly familiar. It consists of a paragraph of text and a single link with an *href* that uses the mailto: protocol. This is a standard protocol that specifies an e-mail address. It is possible to pass parameters using the mailto: protocol. The only parameters that we can pass here are *subject* and *body*. *Subject* denotes some text that should be used as the subject of the message, and *body* denotes the message text. Figure 6.28 illustrates what this WCA looks like in the POSE, and what users will see once they click on the button.

The same syntax that is used to pass parameters in this example can also be used to pass parameters to other applications called using the palm: or palmcall: protocols. Unfortunately, it is not possible to pass any parameters directly to the native Palm applications such as the Memo Pad or Address Book from a WCA. There is, however, a third-party application called iKnapsack that uses the Palm OS device library to access to these native applications. The iKnapsack application provides an API that allows you to write to the Memo Pad, set contacts in the Address Book, or schedule events in the Date Book using a WCA. You can obtain a copy of iKnapsack (and a WCA that allows you to write memos, set contacts, and schedule events) for free from www.tow.com/software/iknapsack.

Figure 6.28 E-mail Example on the POSE

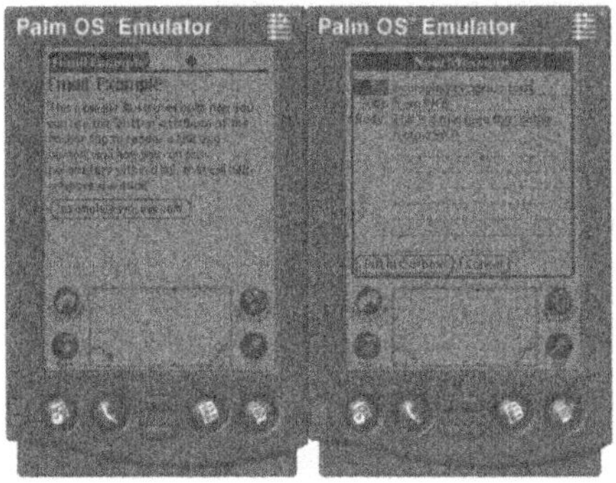

Once users compose their messages, they have the option to put the e-mails in their outboxes. The e-mail will not be sent until the users open the iMessenger application and send/receive their mail. If the information that the users wish to send is time-sensitive, then we may want to deliver the messages via a form submitted to our Web server. This is demonstrated in the following example.

Sending E-mail via a Web Server

In this example, we will use a Web clipping application to send e-mail via a PHP script installed on a Web server. This example is written using PHP, but it is certainly possible to use most any server-side language (such as Perl or ASP) to send e-mail using information submitted from an HTML form. Figure 6.29 contains the HTML that we will use for our WCA.

Figure 6.29 mailform.html

```
<html>
<head>
       <title>Mail Form</title>
</head>
<body>
<form action="http://www.yoursite.com/WCAmailer.php">
<h1>Mail Form</h1>
To:
<input type="text" name="to" size=20><br>
From:
```

Continued

Figure 6.29 Continued

```
<input type="text" name="from" size=20><br>
Subject:
<input type="text" name="subject" size=20><br>
Message:
<textarea name="body"></textarea><br>
<input type="submit" value="Send Message">
</form>
</body>
</html>
```

Once we have scanned this HTML into the WCA builder and created a .pqa file from it, we install it on our POSE and launch it. The WCA as it appears in the POSE is shown in Figure 6.30. In this case, we have filled in the input fields with a simple test message.

Figure 6.30 Mailform.html Launched as .pqa from the POSE

The WCA itself does no good unless we have a script to which we can point it. You can install the PHP script from Figure 6.31 on your Web server and alter the *action* attribute of the <form> tag in Figure 6.29 to point to where you have placed the script. In the event that you do not have PHP available, you can obtain a copy for free from www.php.net.

Figure 6.31 WCAmailer.php

```
<?
header("Content-type: text/html");
header("PalmComputingPlatform: true");

if(empty($to))          error("No recipient specified");
if(empty($from))        error("No from address specified");
if(empty($body))        error("No message text specified");

if( mail($to,$subject,$body,"From:$from\n") ) {

print<<<__THANKS__
<html>
<head>
<title>Success!</title>
<meta name="HistoryListText" content="Success!">
</head>
<h1>Success!</h1>
<p>Your message has been sent!</p>
<b>To:</b> $to<br>
<b>From:</b> $from<br>
<b>Subject:</b> $subject<br>
<b>Message:</b> <br>
$body
</body>
</html>
__THANKS__;
exit();
} else {
error("Message delivery failure!");
}

function error($err) {
print<<<__ERROR__
```

Continued

Figure 6.31 Continued

```
<html>
<head>
<title>ERROR!</title>
<meta name="HistoryListText" content="ERROR!">
</head>
<h1>ERROR!</h1>
<p>Your message cannot be sent for the following reason:</p>
<p><strong>$err</strong></p>
<p>Please go back and try again!</p>
</body>
</html>
__ERROR__;
exit();
}

?>
```

The first element of the header describes the MIME type of the content contained in the response as being composed of HTML text. This header is necessary whenever information is returned to any browser from a server-side script, or else the Web server will return an error.

The second line of the header is optional, but marks the content as valid for display on a handheld device. As mentioned before, the PalmComputingPlatform header informs the Palm.net proxy server that our HTML should not be reformatted for Clipper. It is strongly encouraged that this information be included in any page that is sent to Clipper.

When we are serving out static HTML pages we can specify this information as a <meta> tag within the document. In fact, we could specify this information in a <meta> tag here as well (as we have done with HistoryListText), but instead we are specifying the information directly in the header itself.

This script makes use of the PHP mail() function, which accepts several arguments used to compose an e-mail message. The first argument specifies the e-mail address to which the message should be sent. The second argument contains the subject of the message, and the third argument contains the message body. We can specify additional mail headers (such as cc:, bcc:, or, in this case '-From:'-) in the fourth argument. Any additional headers must be separated by newline characters (\n on UNIX systems, and \r\n on Win32 systems), but in this case, we are submitting only one additional header so this is not necessary. The mail function will return a true value if it is able to successfully send the e-mail, and will return false if it cannot.

We have specified a specific error function that will print an error message to the user's browser if there is a problem with their input or if the mail cannot be delivered. We check to see if the variables have been set by using the empty() function, which will return true if the variable contains a value and false if it does not. In the event that these variables are empty, then the program will print out an error message and stop executing.

NOTE

If we were to implement the Figure 6.31 script into production, we would want to validate the to and from e-mail addresses with a regular expression in the script. There are many examples of e-mail validation that can be found on the php-general mailing list archives at www.php.net.

Once the user submits the form and the mail is successfully sent, the user receives the clipping shown in Figure 6.32. In the event that an error occurs, the user is returned a clipping exemplified in Figure 6.33, with an appropriate error message displayed.

Figure 6.32 Success!

Figure 6.33 ERROR!

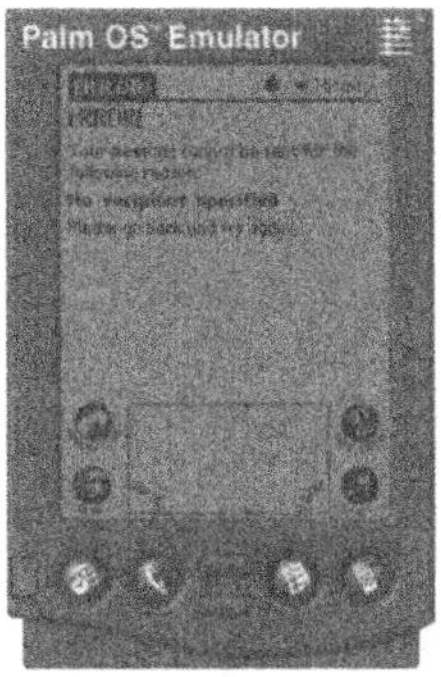

Guidelines for Authoring your Web Clipping Application

As with every application or site you build, you should view any interactive aspect from the user's point of view. It is often best to refrain from thinking about technical architecture until a clear picture of the user's needs is created. Once the user's perception and goals are understood, the application may be built within this framework.

Also, in addition to the needs of your users, you should consider the constraints of the device that will be used to access your application. In this case, your constraints are limited by a slow connection speed, a small (at least in relation to a standard monitor) screen size, and input limited, for the most part, to the use of a stylus.

So, what does this mean for your Web clipping application? We suggest the following guidelines:

- Avoid implementing unnecessary, unwanted, or unused features. For example, let's say that your WCA allows users to browse news headlines, synopses, and full news stories. If you find that 99 percent of your users read only headlines and synopses, you should consider eliminating the option to "read the full story."
- Keep the dominant, or most likely, action highly accessible. For example, if you provide weather information in your WCA, and your users are most interested in a daily forecast, you should use a button instead of a link, and make sure that your users do not have to scroll to find it.

- Design your application so that the minimum content needs to be downloaded over the air in response to a query. For example, if your users are searching a library of books, allow them to narrow their search by as many criteria (title, author, genre, publisher, keyword) as possible before retrieving results from a remote server.
- When you are sending content back to the device from your server, you should link to pages within your WCA instead of sending content over the air whenever possible. Any content that does not change regularly should be stored on the device.
- Keep graphics to a minimum, and store them locally on the device. Palm provides a specific <meta> tag (LocalIcon) for this purpose. Avoid sending images over the air wherever it is possible (dynamically generated images are, of course, an exception). Remember, "A picture is worth a thousand words."

Technically, there is not a display limitation on the length of a Web clipping application page, but realistically, you should endeavor to display your content on one screen in order to limit the amount of scrolling that your users have to do.

There is one limitation in terms of file size. Due to a system memory limitation, no individual WCA page can exceed 63KB. Bear in mind that this page would be very large, as this limitation refers to the compressed version of the page. The limitation on Web clipping application size is determined solely by the amount of memory you have on your handheld device.

Regardless of any technical limitation to the size of your pages, you should keep your HTML markup to a minimum. Every character counts, including markup. You should avoid the use of tables where possible, and refrain from gratuitous use of the <font> tag. You should also keep variable names limited to a minimum of characters. Furthermore, we suggest that the values of <select> lists be an index, as opposed to a text variable. The time that this saves your users will be greatly appreciated. Remember, they are the ones paying for the bandwidth!

Summary

Web clipping allows users of Palm-powered handheld devices to view slimmed-down HTML on their handheld device. They do not use a typical browser, but rather the Web Clipping Application Viewer, also called the Clipper browser, that allows them to view specially compiled device-resident HTML applications on their PDA. These applications are almost like miniature Web sites on the device, but they are, for the most part, static until the user updates them. These applications can be standalone or they can incorporate Web content via HTML links or forms. In addition, these applications have the ability to interact with other applications on the handheld device by passing parameters in a URL.

In this chapter, we have provided an overview of what Web clipping is and how it differs from desktop Web browsing. We have discussed the many devices and networks that may be used to connect a handheld device to the Internet and interact with Web servers. We have covered many of the HTML elements that are supported by the Web Clipping Application Viewer, and discussed the differences between these elements and their desktop counterparts. We also discussed some of the elements that are unique to the Web clipping environment and covered some of the issues that surround the usage of these elements in applications.

We covered the installation and usage of the toolkit that is used to deploy Web clipping applications, including the WCA Builder and the Palm Operating System Emulator. We demonstrated in a few examples how you, the Webmaster, could apply your existing skills to offer content and services to Web clipping users. It's not quite the same as building a Web site, and not quite as different as building WAP content, but it is an interesting step toward true mobile Internet connectivity. As demand for wireless PDAs grows, in the corporate environment in particular, we can expect to see more and more handheld devices with the ability to access the Internet in a manner similar to Web clipping.

Solutions Fast Track

What Is Web Clipping?

☑ Web clipping refers to a proprietary network that allows Palm-compatible handheld devices to connect to the Internet by browsing compressed HTML contained in special files installed on the device. The Web Clipping Application Viewer is also called the Clipper browser.

- ☑ Web clipping differs from Web browsing both in usage patterns and the actual technology used to access the Internet. WCA users are mobile, and deal with limited input mechanisms.
- ☑ A Web clipping application is installed on a device, and cannot be updated until the user installs a new version. This means that extra thought should be put into what interactions are included in a WCA.
- ☑ A subset of HTML 3.2 is used to build Web clipping applications. Not all elements of the specification are supported, but many elements are.

What Types of Hardware Support Web Clipping

- ☑ Devices running the Palm Operating System version 3.5 or higher can take advantage of Web clipping.
- ☑ Many devices can access the Internet via Web clipping, including the Palm VII/VIIx connected via Mobitex and other Palm-compatible handhelds connected via the CDPD Network or Mobile Internet Kit.
- ☑ The RIM 957 (Blackberry) Pager can browse the content of a WCA if it is accessed via a direct link over the Internet. These devices are unable to follow links to, or display images that the WCA expects to be found locally on the device, such as links using the file: protocol.

Working with the Palm OS Emulator

- ☑ The Palm Operating System Emulator (POSE) is freely available from the Palm Web site at www.palm.com/dev/tech/tools/.
- ☑ In order to use the POSE, first you need to install the emulator to emulate the hardware, and then install a ROM image of the OS to start the emulator or run any software.
- ☑ There are two ways to obtain ROM images: transfer one from a device that you own, or download one from the Palm Resource Pavilion. You must register as a Palm developer to obtain ROM images from Palm.
- ☑ It is necessary to configure the emulator to access the Internet via the network interface of the computer upon which it is installed. The emulator must be set to redirect network requests to TCP/IP, and the emulator software must be configured to use a Palm.net Proxy Server.

Creating a Web Clipping Project with the Web Clipping Application Builder

- ☑ The Web Clipping Application (WCA) Builder, like the POSE, can be downloaded from the Palm Web site at www.palm.com/dev/tech/tools/.
- ☑ The WCA Builder is used to compile device-resident Web clipping applications from HTML and images.
- ☑ The WCA Builder automatically will scan HTML from a single index page and automatically include any linked pages or referenced images. It will do some basic error checking, but it is not foolproof, and code should be validated externally.
- ☑ Custom icons may be used for your Web clipping applications. These can be selected in the **Build PQA** dialog box, which is the final step in the application building process.

Web Clipping Basics and Examples

- ☑ Many of the more common tags from the HTML 3.2 specification are available, but many other recent developments are not. Any elements that require client-side processing, such as animated images, imagemaps, and client-side scripting have been eliminated due to device constraints.
- ☑ Some useful features are unique to Web clipping, including variables that relay information about the location of the user and a unique device identifier. Two other elements are available: datepicker and timepicker. These elements help to offset the device constraints of Web clipping.
- ☑ Data transmitted over the air should be minimized as much as possible, and local resources on the device should be leveraged to minimize network traffic. This can be accomplished by linking to local images on the device, and by including content that is not time-sensitive on the device.

Frequently Asked Questions

The following Frequently Asked Questions, answered by the authors of this book, are designed to both measure your understanding of the concepts presented in this chapter and to assist you with real-life implementation of these concepts. To have your questions about this chapter answered by the author, browse to **www.syngress.com/solutions** and click on the **"Ask the Author"** form.

Q: How can I close my WCA and return the user to the Application menu?

A: You can do this by launching the launcher application via a link. Use

```
<a href="palm:launch.appl">Quit</a>.
```

Q: I have added *bgcolor* attributes to my table cells, and they are not working! What is wrong?

A: Clipper supports the *bgcolor* attribute for <table>, but not for <tr>,<td>, or <th>.

Q: Is there any way to get rid of that pesky over-the-air icon?

A: Theoretically you could create an image and use that as your **form submit** button, but the over-the-air icon is useful for the users, as they typically will be paying for any content that they download. It is recommended that you do not implement workarounds for this.

Q: Do I need to test my application on a device, or will the POSE suffice?

A: The POSE will reliably render your HTML, but you should test the usability of your application with an actual device. Using a mouse and keyboard from your desktop to input data is a radically different experience than using a stylus and graffiti for input.

Q: Can I create a custom icon for my WCA?

A: Yes, this can be done in the WCA Builder. You can select your own custom image by clicking the **Large** and **small** buttons in the **Build PQA** dialog. You can author images in .gif, .jpg, or .bmp format using the editor of your choice, and check them using the Palm Image Checker (included in the WCA Builder download). The large icon must be 32x22 pixels, and the small icon must be 15x9 pixels.

Q: Can I use <font> tags in my WCA?

A: Yes, you can make use of the <font> tag, but it will control only the size of your text. Valid values are between 1 and 6, with 3 being the default. It is not possible to use named typefaces within Clipper.

Q: Do I have to rewrite my existing site to be able to view it with Clipper?

A: HTML from standard Web sites can be parsed by the Palm.net Proxy Server and formatted for display within Clipper. If your site is very graphics and JavaScript intensive, it will most likely not translate well. On the other hand, if your site uses logical markup (headers, lists, paragraphs), then it will display better within Clipper. You can use the <smallscreenignore> tag to mark content that should be ignored by the Palm.net proxy server.

Chapter 7

Deck of Cards: Designing Small Viewpoint Content

Solutions in this chapter:

- Thinking In the Hand, not On the Web
- Stacking a Deck of Cards
- Examining Display Differences between Browsers

☑ Summary

☑ Solutions Fast Track

☑ Frequently Asked Questions

Introduction

The wireless Web, although very new, harkens back to the old days of text-only Web browsers. Minimal support for graphics and animations, miserably low bandwidth, tiny screen resolutions, and devices lacking processing power are a few of the commonalities between the wireless Internet and the pre-1994 World Wide Web (WWW).

Due to these differences, developing for the wireless Internet will require different tactics than those to which many Webmasters have become accustomed. Using JavaScript for form validation? Forget it. Applets? Not yet. Graphics? Barely. Tables? As long as you are careful. Images? Yes, but don't expect everyone to see them.

The wireless Internet, and Wireless Markup Language (WML) in particular, has been criticized of late as being ill-designed and hard to use. This is certainly the case in some instances, but it does not have to be. It's up to you, the Webmaster, to design the interface for your content or application in a way that allows the user to form a coherent mental picture of your site and what they can do with it.

We're facing a world much like the early days of the WWW, where designers and Webmasters were attempting to apply print metaphors to the Internet, and failing to reach users in compelling ways. Now, we are facing a situation where Webmasters and applications designers are often expected to re-create the WWW on a handheld device, rather than taking advantages of the Internet in a means most suited to the mobile user of the wireless device. We all need to look at our users in a new way, and to think differently about meeting their needs.

In this chapter, we will first discuss some common mistakes made by Webmasters in terms of information architecture and user interface, and the importance of thinking like a mobile user. We will then cover how to develop your information architecture and interface based on what it means to the wireless user, taking advantage of server-side techniques as well as the *deck of cards* metaphor of the wireless Web. We will also cover display differences between browsers as they apply to usability and cover how to ensure a consistently usable presentation across a variety of devices. We will focus mainly on WML, but remember that many of these principles are applicable to Handheld Device Markup Language (HDML) and, in some cases, Hypertext Markup Language (HTML) displayed on a handheld device.

Thinking In the Hand, not On the Web

Typically, today's Web sites tend to have a somewhat pyramidal structure, one in which the user can browse to various layers of depth within the pyramid. These sites often have a means of moving vertically or horizontally within them. By *vertical* navigation, we are referring to a user being able to move deeper into a specific section of a site. By *horizontal* navigation, we are referring to a user being able to move across pages or subsections within the same section. Figure 7.1 provides a simple example of the pyramid metaphor.

Figure 7.1 The Pyramidal Navigational Structure

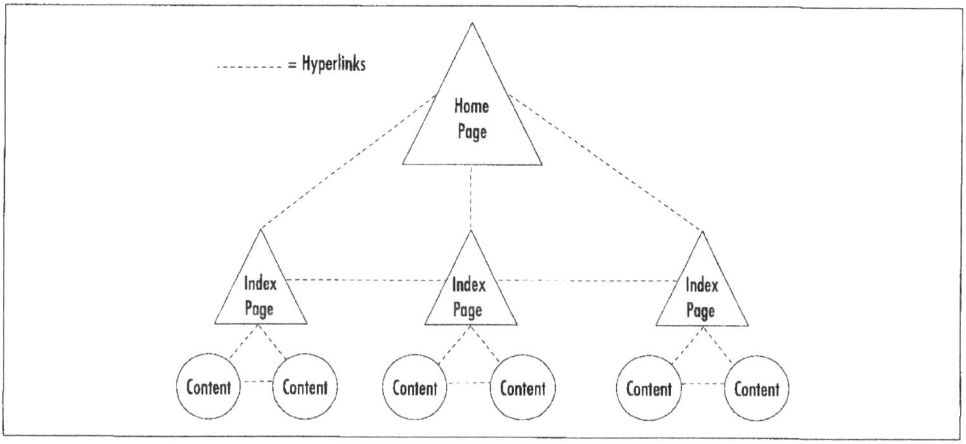

In this structure, the user can browse horizontally through a section, all the while retaining the ability to move up a layer or return to the home page of the site.

A *breadcrumb* is a common element of many Web designs, and an aid to the pyramid metaphor. In case you have not heard the term before, it refers to a list of links that correspond to the main pages of each level of the site hierarchy, which will often mirror the directory structure of the site.

Breadcrumbs are typically found on every page, and allow the user to move between the various layers of the site. A typical example of this is the line at the top of the page on the Open Directory Project site at www.dmoz.org. Many different sites use this element in a variety of ways, but the general theme is fairly consistent: it provides the user with a means of understanding where they are within a site. Figure 7.2 illustrates this element of a site.

Figure 7.2 Use of Breadcrumbs for Pyramidal Navigation

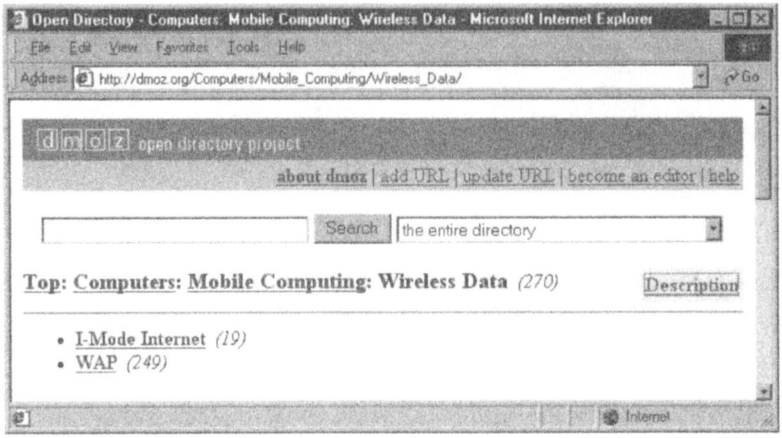

The pyramidal navigational structure and accompanying elements seen across the Web did not suddenly appear overnight: Rather, they were developed as designers and Webmasters began to *understand how users understand the Web.* The end result is a structure that lends itself to the capabilities of the medium, and allows users to make sense of their position within the nonphysical space of the Web. You can see examples of this structure on sites all the way from Amazon to Yahoo!

However, we're barely beginning to understand how users make sense of the *wireless* Internet. It requires a new way of looking at the Internet, and its users have radically different needs and expectations than the users of the WWW.

Users of the wireless Internet do not browse. A contributing factor to this is the *walled gardens* that have been created by many service providers. These sites come up when the user initiates a Web session, and effectively lock users into viewing only the sites that have struck a deal with the service provider. Some carriers do not even offer the opportunity to enter a URL from the browser's start page.

Yet another factor affecting how users interact with the wireless Internet is the difficulty of entering text into the browsers that are currently shipped on mobile phones. Users of Personal Digital Assistants (PDAs) running the Palm OS or Microsoft PocketPC OS have the option of entering data with a stylus or portable keyboard, but it is still a good idea to limit the amount of user input required for your site or application because these tools, although more effective than a numeric keypad, hardly rival their desktop counterparts in terms of input efficiency.

It is important for designers, information architects, Webmasters, and application developers to create intuitive interfaces that allow users to form coherent representations of content and structure by interacting via a wireless device. You should strive to limit user input and help your users make efficient use of your site by providing lean, well thought-out presentation and clear navigation. Omit unnecessary elements, and thoroughly test those that remain with a variety of devices and users.

In this section, we will cover some of the common mistakes that are made by Webmasters and discuss the importance of thinking like a mobile user while building your site. We will recommend some principles that will help to create a mental image of your site for your users, ensuring that they can use your site to quickly get what they need while on the go.

Common Mistakes Made by Webmasters

Some of the more common mistakes made by Webmasters include:

- Wasting bandwidth
- Forgetting task-based design
- Providing too many options or too much information
- Using branded, Web-like terminology instead of plain language

We will cover ways around each of these mistakes in detail, but one theme remains common throughout: The metaphor of the Web is inappropriate to the new medium.

Wasting Bandwidth

In an age where broadband connections to the Internet are becoming fairly commonplace, it is easy to forget the days where a 14.4k connection was considered high-speed. It's rare now to find users that connect at speeds under 56k. This has become the de facto standard of baseline Internet connectivity and the speed for which most Web pages are optimized. The wireless Internet, however, is not subject to this standard. If you are a wireless user in the United States, the fastest connection speed you will see is still below that of a 14.4k modem.

Many Web users these days have a monitor capable of displaying at least 800x600 pixels of resolution and millions of colors. This is very different from the screen of a mobile phone, which will often be capable of displaying between 2 and 5 lines of text, with a resolution of less than 400 pixels square. It's certainly not possible to fully represent a standard Web site on such a small screen.

NOTE

You can save your wireless users some download time (and money) by including all your application's images within your Web Clipping Application (WCA). They can be referenced inside a server response by using the *local icon* element. More details on this can be found in Chapter 6.

Given these strict bandwidth and screen size limitations, how can we maximize the user experience? With simplicity and efficiency is how.

One way to reduce bandwidth is to eliminate the use of graphics altogether. This method does have its advantages in that you will never have to convert any graphics to Wireless Bitmap (WBMP) format for use on a WAP device, but chances are you will still not want to completely give up images in your content or application.

Instead, you should use images only when they are more effective than text. One example that comes to mind is that of a weather report. If you can display an image of a sun to represent "Today it is sunny," you will save your users valuable time in interpreting your content.

In general, images should be eliminated from your content when there is not a direct benefit to the user. Avoid forcing your users to download an image for a splash screen, no matter how much you want users to see your company logo on entry to your site. These splash screens are the functional wireless equivalent of loading a 200k flash movie as the first page of your wired site.

The best advice, should you employ the use of images, is to keep them as small as possible in terms of file size and resolution—squeeze as much value you can out of the bandwidth and screen size you have available. Your users will appreciate it and be more likely to return.

Forgetting Task-Based Design

The concept of browsing is a well-accepted metaphor for how people use the WWW, but it does not make sense to think of mobile users as just browsing the wireless Internet. Mobile users do not have the time or desire to aimlessly surf sites; rather, they have a specific need for information that is relevant to where they are and what they are doing at the time (or what they plan to do later). They are interested in how the wireless Internet can make their lives easier. They want to check their e-mail, view product inventory, check their stocks, or find out what movie is playing tonight.

It's very important, therefore, to provide your user with a clear and efficient path to the task they wish to perform. One common method is to make the browser's Accept key point to the most dominant action, and use the Options key to provide other options for using the site.

While planning your wireless site or application, develop use cases that describe the different tasks that users are expected to perform, and test them. How many steps does it take to perform the most common tasks? Is it clear to the user how to "get in, get it, and get out?" If you find your users are having difficulty finding what they need, then you should make changes to your site accordingly.

Providing Too Many Options or Too Much Information

One need only take a brief look at the front page of www.yahoo.com to see the wealth of information available on the site. There are literally hundreds of links on the front page of this site, which is well known as being fast-loading and easy to use. Yahoo! is one of the oldest Web portals, as well as one of the most successful. The site provides millions of people worldwide with information everyday. Yahoo! also offers free e-mail and personalized home pages that are catered to users' home locations.

One look at the Yahoo! WAP site shows an interface engineered for the mobile user. The site is categorized primarily as a personalized version of the site, including e-mail as the first listed option. Other options in the first few lines include an address book and local information. All told, the Yahoo! WAP site includes two initial pages with a total of approximately 20 links.

The Yahoo! WAP site offers the user great deal of functionality but there is so much information listed that it is hard for the mobile user to quickly know exactly what is available to them. Regular use of the site will generate some familiarity, but it is hard for a new user to tell what is offered. Figure 7.3 illustrates the first page of the Yahoo! WAP site.

In addition to their WAP site, Yahoo! also offers a Palm Web Clipping Application (WCA) for the palmtop user. This application can be downloaded from the Yahoo! Web site and installed on a handheld device running the Palm OS. The Yahoo! WCA is illustrated in Figure 7.4. You can see that they have pared down their site significantly to provide the Palm user with Yahoo! content. The use of well-crafted icons gives Yahoo! WCA user an instantaneous grasp of what is available to them.

Figure 7.3 First Page of the Yahoo! WAP Site

Figure 7.4 Yahoo! Web Clipping Application

The most interesting part of the Palm WCA in comparison to the Yahoo! WAP site is that it actually contains *less* content, despite the availability of more memory and display area on the device. There is no link to the Yahoo! directory, no links to shopping, driving directions, horoscopes, or lottery results. There are many elements that are present in the Yahoo! WAP site that would be of use to the Palm user, but they are curiously absent. We can only speculate as to why these two wireless offerings put forth by Yahoo! are so different.

Using Branded Terminology Instead of Plain Language

Web marketing, in its effort to deliver "eyeballs," has developed a language all its own. Elements of a site are often conceived, developed and labeled with marketing in mind. The result is a medium that is chock-full of language geared towards generating clicks (and advertising impressions). This is in direct opposition to how a wireless site should be built and conveyed to the user.

It's critically important to deliver your information in a clear format. Try to resist the temptation to create new and catchy phrases for your content or application. Don't create new metaphors when you don't have to. Instead, use straightforward, descriptive terms that will inform your users of exactly what to expect when they click on a link.

For example, you may be tempted to think up a catchy name for your application that parses stock quotes. You could call it Market Update, Flash Quote, or Insta-Track. However, you would be best off to simply use "Stock Quotes" to ensure that your users understand exactly what they are getting, and that they do not waste precious seconds figuring out what to do or waiting for content that is not what they are expecting.

Thinking Like a Mobile User

The mistakes mentioned in the previous section have one root cause: *The Webmaster is not thinking like a user.* When you consider building a wireless interface to your application or a new wireless Web site, be sure to ask yourself: "Does my idea make sense for a mobile user?" If the answer is no, you should put down this book and continue to build effective Web sites.

If your idea does provide some utility to the mobile user, then you should engineer it from the ground up as a mobile user-friendly site. Remember what you have learned as a Webmaster, and perhaps more importantly, forget what you have learned when it does not make sense in the mobile environment.

There are three main ways to increase the usability of your small viewpoint content and tailor your application to the mobile user.

First, look at your site and think about how or why someone might use it. What content should be on the site? For example, if you run a local portal site and you know that your users are interested in sports, traffic, and weather, you should make this information available to your mobile users. What tasks are they most likely to perform regularly? If you run a financial information site, you would most likely want to make stock quotes a prominent feature on your mobile site. Which task are users *most* likely to use on a given visit? Prioritize the placement of options on your site according to how they may be used and make it easy for users to get what they need with a minimum of input.

Second, examine your site and remove any elements that do not aid usability. For example, if you have a splash screen that displays your logo and then immediately sends the user to another card, consider reducing the size of the graphic or removing the splash page altogether. Perhaps you've built a card that uses unique icons as the bullets on a list of links. This can be effective, provided that the icons are very clear and easy to understand, but in many cases it will make more sense to remove the icons and use the <OPTION> element or softkeys.

Third, design the navigation of your site with the mobile user and small-viewpoint interface in mind and run through your site with the worst emulator configuration you can find. One with two lines should be sufficient to convince you that it's important to keep your site simple and to the point.

Last, but not least, use DNS wildcards, client detection, and server-side aliases to reduce text input. Typing in http://wap.mysite.com/cgi-bin/applications/weather/weatherfinder.cgi on a mobile phone is much more difficult then entering http://mysite.com/wthr. It may take a little work on the part of your domain administrator, and some forethought on how you structure your site, but it will pay off in the long run.

Segregating Tasks

Task segregation refers to the analysis of the use cases of your site, categorizing the tasks a typical user will perform as actions that occur most often (perhaps on every visit), tasks that occur with lesser frequency (perhaps on every 10th visit), and tasks that occur rarely (perhaps only on the first visit or every 100th visit or so). We will apply this analysis to one of the most common uses of the wireless Web: e-mail.

It is important to look at the different actions that can take place in any e-mail suite. Table 7.1 lists e-mail tasks based on the frequency of the action: high frequency tasks are those that occur on almost every single time your user visits the site, medium frequency tasks are performed periodically by users, and low frequency tasks are rarely performed by the user.

Table 7.1 E-Mail Task Segregation

E-Mail Tasks	Frequency
Account setup	Low
Logging in	High
Retrieving e-mail from the server	High
Composing/Replying/Forwarding	High
Filtering and sorting e-mail into folders	Medium
Deleting e-mail	Medium
Account editing	Low
Logging out	High

If you take care to ensure that the high frequency tasks are always accessible, and that the medium and rare frequency tasks are out of the way yet easy to find when needed, your users will have a better experience using the system.

Optimizing Bandwidth

One of the most difficult bottlenecks to deal with when programming for the wireless Internet is caused by the size of the tiny chunks of data that most wireless devices can receive. This is also frustrating for the mobile user, as they have to wait precious seconds for the trickle of data to download content to their device.

In some instances this is limited by hardware and network connectivity. For example, many handheld WAP devices can accept only a little over 1K of data in any given transaction, due to their limited memory.

There is also the additional concern of the subscription models that are present in the market. In some cases, users will pay a per-minute connect fee, while others may pay on a per-byte basis. Many mobile phone users pay for each minute they are using their microbrowser, and Palm.net users pay by the number of bytes transmitted to their device.

In order to make your users' experiences as smooth as possible, it is up to you to squeeze as much as you can out of every byte. It is even possible to make small refinements in terms of the actual characters used to code the cards that make up your application, which will have a cumulative effect on your deck's the final weight.

Minimize the Use of Images

As we have already seen, the first way to decrease the amount of data sent to your users is to eliminate images from your application. Icons can be used to translate an idea to a user very quickly, however, and you should weigh the usability gained by the icon versus the usability lost by including the icon in the total bytes that make up your deck.

Use Short Variable and Card Naming Conventions

One of the easiest places to trim characters is in the naming of the variables used in your application. For example, *userIdentificationNumber* is a much longer variable name than simply *id*. Furthermore, the shorter variable name is just as easily interpreted by any programmer modifying the code, whether they are coding for the client or the server.

Also, you can save some characters by using shortened ID attributes for the cards in your deck. Consider the size differences between *information* and *info*, or *cat* versus *catalog*. Keeping your card identifiers to three or four characters can save some data without affecting the legibility of the code. In fact, a coherent 3-letter naming convention can make your code *more* legible!

Limit Display-based and Redundant Markup

You can also make your code leaner by minimizing the use of display-based markup within your cards. This does not mean that you should not take care that your application can be interpreted easily, but rather that you should avoid gratuitous use of font tags (such as within table cells in a WCA) or explicitly declaring attributes that are the same as the default value for the element (such as declaring <P ALIGN=LEFT"> when <P> will generate the same effect).

Granted, we do not have intimate knowledge of the proprietary tokenizers (or *compilers*) that run on the WAP gateways, but if you limit the amount of data that you send to the gateway for processing and logically structure your markup to minimize the characters used for the desired display effect, you will save your users time and money.

Index Your <SELECT> Lists

One effective way to generate a smaller WAP binary while maintaining the user experience is by indexing your <SELECT> lists. Figure 7.5 will illustrate how to save characters and reduce the final size of the deck sent to the user. We will construct two different <SELECT> lists that will appear identical to the user, one using indexing, and the other containing a value that matches the description of the <OPTION>. This example is written in PHP, but it is possible to port this simple test page to any server-side scripting language. In the event that you do not have access to a scripting language, you can create two decks: one containing an indexed list, and the other containing descriptive <OPTION> elements.

Figure 7.5 test.php

```
<?php
header("Content-type:text/vnd.wap.wml");
print("<?xml version='1.0'?>");

if(!isset($mode)) {
$mode = "";
```

Continued

Figure 7.5 Continued

```
}

?>
<!DOCTYPE wml PUBLIC "-//WAPFORUM//DTD WML 1.1//EN"
     "http://www.wapforum.org/DTD/wml_1.1.xml">
<wml>
<card>
<p>
Select a Continent:<br />

<?php if( $mode == "index" ) { ?>

        <select name="cn">
        <option value="0">Africa</option>
        <option value="1">Antarctica</option>
        <option value="2">Asia</option>
        <option value="3">Australia</option>
        <option value="4">Europe</option>
        <option value="5">North America</option>
        <option value="6">South America</option>
        </select>

<? } else { ?>

        <select name="Continent">
        <option value="Africa">Africa</option>
        <option value="Antarctica">Antarctica</option>
        <option value="Asia">Asia</option>
        <option value="Australia">Australia</option>
        <option value="Europe">Europe</option>
        <option value="North America">North America</option>
        <option value="South America">South America</option>
        </select>
```

Continued

Figure 7.5 Continued

```
<? } ?>

</p>
</card>
</wml>
```

When we load this page into our browser without specifying the $mode variable (http://localhost/test.php), we can see that the final size of the WAP binary is 187 bytes, as shown in Figure 7.6.

Figure 7.6 Binary Size without Indexing <SELECT> List

However, when we load up the page specifying mode=index within the query string (http://localhost/test.php?mode=index), we see that the final size of the binary is 146 bytes. This is illustrated in Figure 7.7.

You can see from this example that using indexed <SELECT> lists can save significant numbers of characters, even after the code is parsed by the WAP gateway. The end user will notice absolutely no difference between the two different cards, but the indexed card is 22% smaller than the first version. A deck that contains many <SELECT> lists would benefit greatly from this simple method of saving characters.

This implementation should be used with care, however, as a client-side coder can change the order of the list or alter the display value without confirming the meaning of the variable's actual value with the server-side programmer.

Figure 7.7 Binary Size after Indexing <SELECT> List

It is incredibly unlikely that the continents featured in our example will change in our lifetimes and affect our results, so you could store this information as part of a user profile without potential errors resulting in the future. However, if we were using <SELECT> lists to denote information that is somewhat likely to change over time (such as voting districts or area codes), or information that is constantly changing (like current movie listings), we would need to take very special care to ensure that there is a consistent correspondence between the value of the index and the description of the value that is displayed. One way to do this would be to generate the <SELECT> list dynamically with server-side scripting and a database containing the index corresponding to the value.

Designing Coherent Navigation

The pyramidal structure mentioned at the beginning of this chapter has become a well-accepted metaphor for representing information. For now at least, the wireless Internet presents some challenges to this metaphor, primarily because the amount of information that the user can view at any given time is limited. With the limited screen real estate available on a wireless device, you must re-think the mental picture your users form of your site, and make sure that your navigational structure is suited to the reduced view afforded by a handheld device.

It is simply not possible to represent the whole of the pyramidal structure within each card, but it is possible to build a smooth navigational system by using a well-crafted deck. The model that we will discuss here is a menu-driven *hub-and-spoke* metaphor. Most Webmasters should be familiar with the term hub-and-spoke, but if you have not heard of it before, this metaphor was common to the early days of the Web and text-based interfaces, and features a fairly linear and strictly vertical mode of navigation. The user is first presented with a main menu consisting of options. Each item on the main menu points to a sub-menu, each item of which in turn points to the final content. The hub-and-spoke metaphor is illustrated in Figure 7.8.

Figure 7.8 The Hub-and-Spoke Navigational Structure

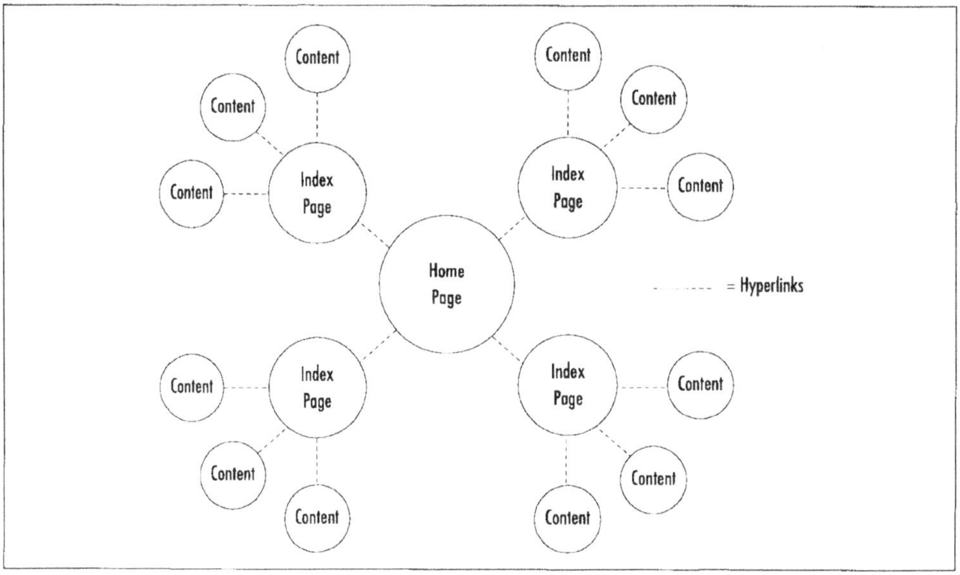

The dashed lines denote links between different cards. You can see that the navigational paths radiate out from a central point, and that a user may navigate from node to node, but only in a vertical direction. In order for a user to get to another card at the same level, they must first hop back to the previous node.

The primary means of navigating within this structure on a mobile phone are the **accept** and the **back** keys that are built into most phones and Web browsers. Users tend to, in a vertical sense, "drill down" and "back up," or in a linear sense, move forward and back throughout the site. The next section will focus on the construction of this navigational system.

Stacking a Deck of Cards

While building Web sites, you have most likely become accustomed to multi-dimensional navigation and sub-navigation structures. You have also become proficient at integrating multimedia content where it is appropriate, and learned how to break up content so that it makes sense for the WWW. You have learned how to provide your users with a means of understanding where they are within your site and how to navigate within your information architecture. These are valuable lessons, but the principles behind them are more important than the specifics.

In this section, we will discuss the methods by which you can provide your users with a coherent small-viewpoint interface to your site, and how to take advantage of these methods to create a smooth and compelling user experience. There are some very important differences between the WWW and the wireless Internet that we must consider here.

While you may be accustomed to sending your users one screen (or page) at a time on the WWW, WML allows you to send your users several pieces of content or navigation (that is, multiple screens or *cards*) at once. A single download consisting of multiple cards is referred to as a *deck*.

The main catch is that the size of the final compiled binary of your content must be under 1397 bytes. Although this is a very small overhead, it is possible to deliver several cards in one deck (usually around 5, depending on the amount of markup and content). An entire application interface can easily fit within a single deck, and in some cases, the entire *application* may fit within a single deck.

NOTE

You can find a list of various WML browsers and their maximum deck sizes at skin.surfnet.nl/mobile/wap/wap-clients.shtml.

We will now cover some examples of parceling your content into decks and how to utilize some of the features of WML to make for a more effective user experience.

Parceling Navigation and Content

In this section, we will discuss the nuts and bolts of dividing your navigation and content into manageable chunks to improve the user experience. The primary focus is on delivering the entire navigational structure of your application in one card, and then allowing the user to download the actual content that they want in a subsequent request. The primary reason for doing this is speed. You don't want to waste your users' time by forcing them to sit through requests while navigating your site.

Let's use the example of a library site. The main functions of the site include general information about the library (hours, location, directions), a catalog (search, browse), and user services (books checked out, late fees due, reservations). We could potentially divide each section of the site into different decks, each containing an index and subsequent files. This would seem a natural approach to the treatment of our content, but it does not make for the most effective wireless user experience.

Instead, we will first send the user a deck containing the navigational structure of the site, and allow the user to initiate a second request to retrieve the actual content.

It is possible to send a user a deck that consists solely of navigation. The first card presented to the user will link to other cards within the first deck. Upon selecting one of the links on the first card, the user is immediately forwarded to that area's menu.

Notice that there is no request sent to the server, and correspondingly no delay in receiving the selected card. This greatly enhances navigation for the user, as they can move back and forth within the navigation deck without sending a request or receiving more content over the air. Figure 7.9 shows the deck that will be sent to the user upon their visit to the site.

Figure 7.9 index.wml

```
<wml>


<card name="home" title="Main Menu">
<p>Library Menu:</p>
<p>
<a href="#info">Information</a><br/>
<a href="#cat">Catalog</a><br/>
<a href="#svc">Services</a><br/>
</p>
</card>


<card name="info" title="Information">
<p>
```

Continued

Figure 7.9 Continued

```
<a href="info.wml#tel">Phone Directory</a><br/>
<a href="info.wml#hrs">Hours of Operation</a><br/>
<a href="info.wml#addy">Address</a><br/>
<a href="info.wml#dirs">Directions</a><br/>
</p>
</card>

<card name="cat" title="Catalog">
<p>
<a href="cat.wml#srch">Search</a><br/>
<a href="cat.wml#brws">Browse</a><br/>
</p>
</card>

<card name="svc" title="Services">
<p>
<a href="svc.wml#out">Books Checked Out</a><br/>
<a href="svc.wml#fee">Late Fees Due</a><br/>
<a href="svc.wml#res">Reservations</a><br/>
</p>
</card>

</wml>
```

Relative links are used extensively in this deck, identified by the hash mark (#). This symbol is used to link to a card contained within the current deck. It may also be used to reference specific cards within other decks by specifying the URI of the deck followed by a hash mark and the name of the desired card.

NOTE

The syntax used in WML to reference cards within decks is the same as the syntax used to reference anchor tags using the <NAME> attribute in HTML.

Figure 7.10 illustrates the relationship between the cards in this deck. The first card, labeled with the *home* id attribute, contains relative links to the other cards in the deck. The other cards in the deck (info, cat, svc) contain links to another deck that contains the content for the section. The svc card, for example, contains links to three cards in the svc.wml deck (out,fee,res). Figure 7.11 illustrates the cards in svc.wml. Note that there are no links between these cards in this deck, and that there is no index to provide navigation. The navigation for this deck is provided by the svc card of the first deck.

Figure 7.10 index.wml Represented Graphically

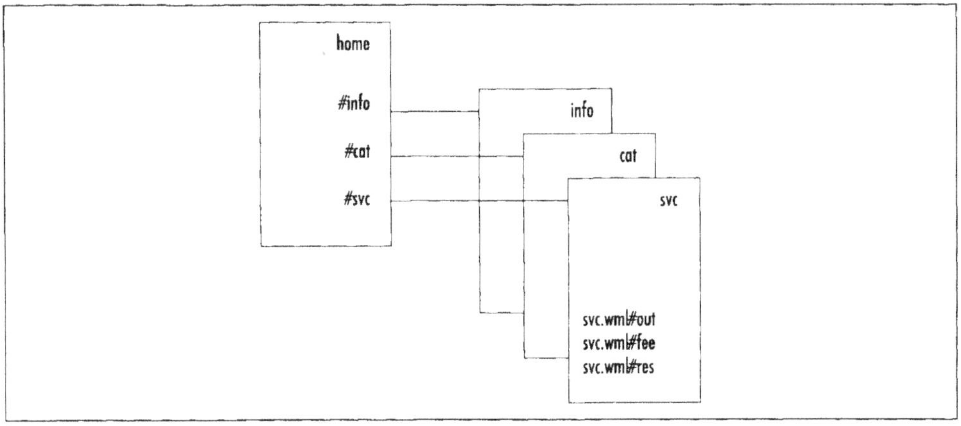

Figure 7.11 svc.wml Represented Graphically

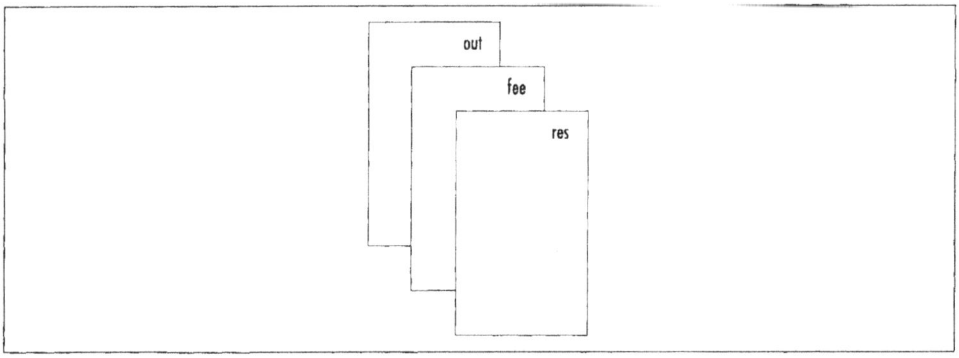

Upon loading up index.wml, the user will see the first card containing links that correspond to each section of the site as follows, in Figure 7.12.

Figure 7.12 index.wml: List of Links

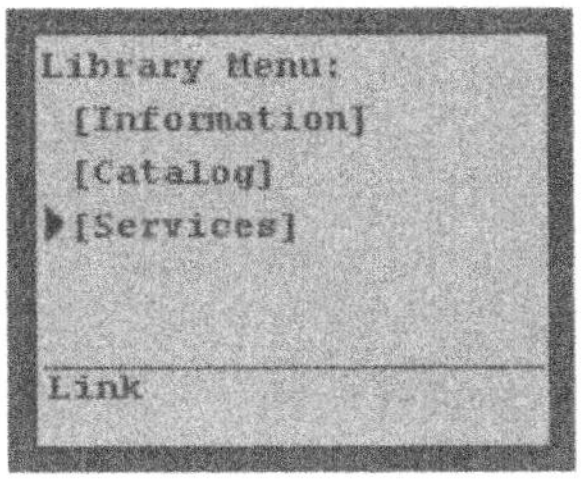

Upon selecting the **services** link, the browser will display the card (svc.wml) containing links to the content within the Services section, shown in Figure 7.13.

Figure 7.13 index.wml: Selecting Services Link

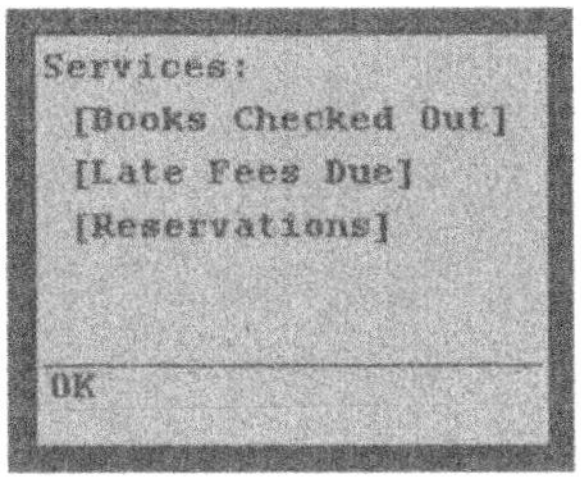

The user of the library WAP site can navigate the entire site using the data downloaded in the first request. Once the user has decided on their final destination however, they must send a request in order to receive the content. The deck that the user receives contains all of the cards for the requested section. The user can then navigate the entire section by using their history stack, as opposed to sending a new request for each page.

In the following example, we will show the path of a user entering the site, browsing to the Information section, and retrieving directions to the library. Figure 7.14 contains the code for the Information section.

Figure 7.14 info.wml

```
<?xml version="1.0"?>
<!DOCTYPE wml PUBLIC "-//WAPFORUM//DTD WML 1.1//EN"
"http://www.wapforum.org/DTD/wml_1.1.xml">

<wml>
```

Continued

Figure 7.14 Continued

```
<card id="tel" title="Phone Directory">
<p>Phone Numbers:</p>
<p>Main: 111-1111</p>
<p>Circulation: 111-1112</p>
<p>Kid's story line: 111-1113</p>
</card>

<card id="hrs" title="Hours of Operation">
<p>The Library is open from 9am-9pm, Monday through Sunday.</p>
</card>

<card id="addy" title="Address">
<p>Mailing address:</p>
<p>Anytown Library<br/>
1 Main Street<br/>
Anytown, USA  00001-0001<br/>
</p>
</card>

<card id="dirs" title="Directions">
<p>The library is located at Main and Center in Anytown.</p>
<p>Directions:<br/>
<a href="#n">From the North</a><br/>
<a href="#e">From the East</a><br/>
<a href="#s">From the West</a><br/>
<a href="#w">From the South</a><br/>
</p>
</card>

<card id="n" title="From North">
<p>Directions from the north:</p>
<p>Follow Spring Highway to Main Street</p>
```

Continued

Figure 7.14 Continued

```
<p>Make a right at Main Street</p>
<p>Follow Main for 3 blocks to center street</p>
<p>Library is on the right</p>
</card>

<card id="e" title="From East">
<p>Directions from the east:</p>
<p>Follow Center street into town</p>
<p>Library is on the left once you pass Main.</p>
</card>

<card id="s" title="From South">
<p>Directions from the South:</p>
<p>Take Exit 9 from Interstate 1</p>
<p>Make a left at Main Street</p>
<p>Follow Main for 2 blocks to Center St.</p>
<p>Library is on the left</p>
</card>

<card id="w" title="From West">
<p>Directions from the West:</p>
<p>Follow River Boulevard to Center St.</p>
<p>Library is on the right before you pass Main.</p>
</card>

</wml>
```

This deck contains all of the cards in the site's Information section. These cards include one containing phone numbers, one containing hours of operation, one containing the library's address, and another card describing the location of the library with links to directions. This may seem like quite a lot of content to send to the user at once, but the size of the final WAP binary (992 bytes) is still under 1K, as shown in Figure 7.15.

Figure 7.15 Phone Information for info.wml

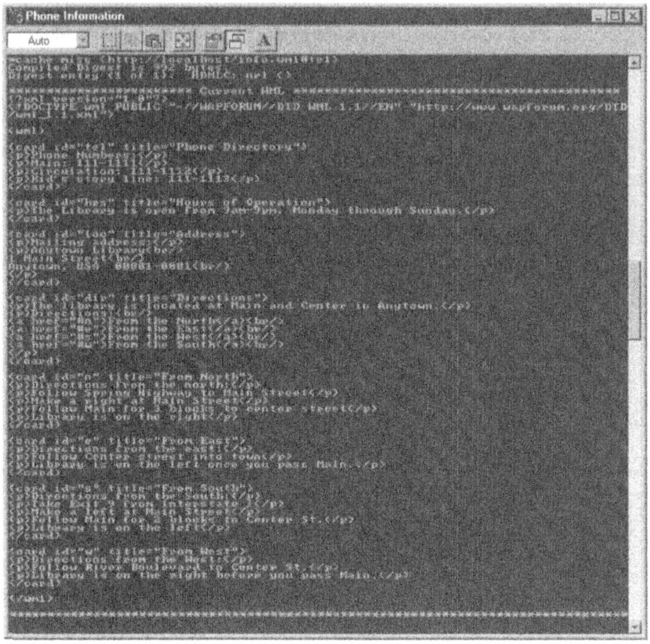

Figure 7.16 shows info.wml, which contains a total of 8 cards, and the relationship between those cards. You will notice that 4 of the cards (n,e,s,w) are linked from the dirs card.

Figure 7.16 info.wml Represented Graphically

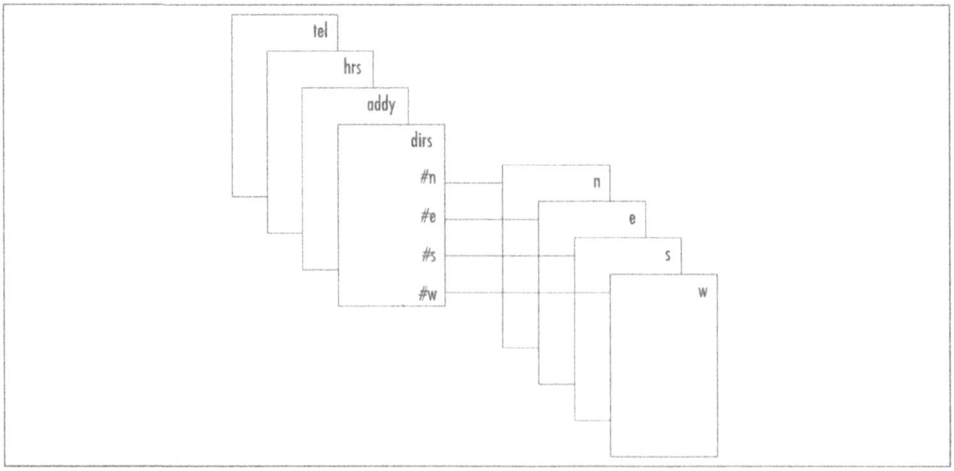

When the user first visits the site, they are shown the first card of index.wml, as shown in Figure 7.17.

Figure 7.17 index.wml

Upon selecting the *Information* link, the user is sent to the Info card, as shown in Figure 7.18.

Figure 7.18 index.wml#info

Upon selecting the *Directions* link, the user will be sent to the dirs card named info.wml. This selection will initiate the second request from the server. The dirs card of info.wml is shown in Figure 7.19.

Figure 7.19 info.wml#dirs

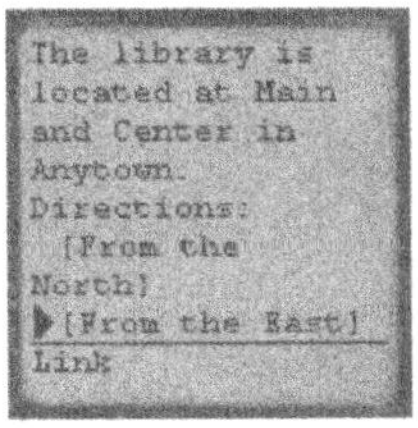

This card describes the location of the library, and also allows the user to choose a link that will give them directions to the library from the 4 compass points. Upon selecting to receive directions from the East, the user is shown the e card of info.wml. This is illustrated in Figure 7.20.

Figure 7.20 info.wml#e

In this example, we have made use of the hub-and-spoke metaphor to deliver the information with a minimum of individual server connections. The user seeking directions in the first request was sent the entire navigation of the site (four cards) in a single deck. On the second request, the user was sent the entire content of the information section (eight cards) in a single deck.

The user only had to connect to the server twice: once to receive the global navigation, and once to receive the content for an entire section. Astute viewers will notice that the content deck has no "index" or "main" page. It merely contains the content, as the navigation deck contains all of the links necessary to navigate the subsection. The user will be able to view the entire Info section without another request to the server.

Since the library's location, phone numbers, and directions are unlikely to change, we may want to specify a header that instructs the browser to keep this deck in the browser cache. This will give the user ready access to this information from their history stack in the future. The syntax for header declarations in WML is identical to that of HTML, as it is part of the HTTP specification.

Utilizing WML Variables

WML has the capability of storing variables on the device, which is a concept unheard of in the stateless world of the WWW. Typically, server-side programmers have had to generate Web sessions or maintain the state of the transaction by printing out variables in hidden form fields to pass their values from transaction to transaction. With the ability to store information on the device, you can gather input from the user in a series of cards instead of gathering information CGI-style by passing variables in hidden fields.

Let's say, for example, that we are building an interface to a company directory. The directory contains the department, title, name, phone number, e-mail, and mailing address of every person in a 45,000 employee company. In order to get the information they need, a wireless user may wish to narrow their search by location, department, or title.

Instead of gathering information from the user in a series of requests, we can gather the desired information by sending one deck to the user. The function of this deck is to generate the parameters necessary to execute a short list of relevant contacts. In the example shown in Figure 7.21, we will allow the user to set parameters, then display the selected parameters. We will be using the UP.Browser SDK to view this deck, but rest assured that it works in both the Nokia and 4thpass Kbrowsers. In the next section, we will explore display differences in detail.

Figure 7.21 directory.wml

```
<?xml version="1.0"?>
<!DOCTYPE wml PUBLIC "-//WAPFORUM//DTD WML 1.1//EN"
"http://www.wapforum.org/DTD/wml_1.1.xml">
<wml>

<template>
<do type="options" label="GO!">
<go href="#search"/>
</do>
</template>

<card id="home" title="Directory">

<onevent type="onenterforward">
        <refresh>
                <setvar name="dept" value=""/>
                <setvar name="loc" value=""/>
                <setvar name="title" value=""/>
        </refresh>
</onevent>

<p>Select your Criteria:</p>
<p>
<a href="#dept">Department</a><br/>
```

Continued

Figure 7.21 Continued

```
<a href="#loc">Location</a><br/>
<a href="#title">Title</a><br/>
</p>
</card>

<card id="dept" title="Department">
<p>Department:</p>
<p>
<select name="dept">
<option value="Any">Any</option>
<option value="Sales">Sales</option>
<option value="Shipping">Shipping</option>
<option value="Operations">Operations</option>
<option value="Marketing">Marketing</option>
<option value="HR">HR</option>
<option value="Accounting">Accounting</option>
</select>
</p>
</card>

<card id="loc" title="Location">
<p>Location:</p>
<p>
<select name="loc">
<option value="Any">Any</option>
<option value="New York">New York</option>
<option value="San Francisco">San Francisco</option>
<option value="Denver">Denver</option>
<option value="Dallas">Dallas</option>
<option value="Washington, DC">Washington, DC</option>
<option value="Phoenix">Phoenix</option>
<option value="Salt Lake City">Salt Lake City</option>
<option value="Chicago">Chicago</option>
```

Continued

Figure 7.21 Continued

```
<option value="Seattle">Seattle</option>
</select>
</p>
</card>

<card id="title" title="Title">
<p>Title:</p>
<p>
<select name="title">
<option value="Any">Any</option>
<option value="Associate">Associate</option>
<option value="Supervisor">Supervisor</option>
<option value="Manager">Manager</option>
<option value="Vice President">Vice President</option>
<option value="President">President</option>
</select>
</p>
</card>

<card id="search" title="Search">
<p>
The following parameters have been set:<br/>
Department: $(dept)<br/>
Location: $(loc)<br/>
Title: $(title)<br/>
</p>
</card>
</wml>
```

You will notice the <TEMPLATE> element at the top of the deck. This element allows us to render the same code on every card within the requested deck. No matter which criteria the user decides to narrow their request by, they will still have the option of viewing the selected parameters by selecting the **Options** key or moving back to the main page with the **Accept** key to further narrow their search.

Debugging...

Persistent Variables

WML variables are persistent throughout time. The example shown in Figure 7.21 will store the selected variables between browser sessions. It is recommended that these variables be set to an empty value using the <SETVAR> command before sending the user to the search application, to avoid using old parameters. It is possible to clear ALL of the variables stored on the phone by using the newcontext="true" attribute, but this can cause problems for the user on other sites, as well as any other stored variable-dependent applications they may be using on your site.

NOTE

In the example shown in Figure 7.21, we are displaying a link to the card with an id of *search* to display the user's parameters. However, this link could very easily point to a CGI script that would execute the search with the selected parameters.

Figure 7.22 illustrates what the user will see when they pull up directory.wml in their browser and select Department.

Figure 7.22 directory.wml: Department Criteria

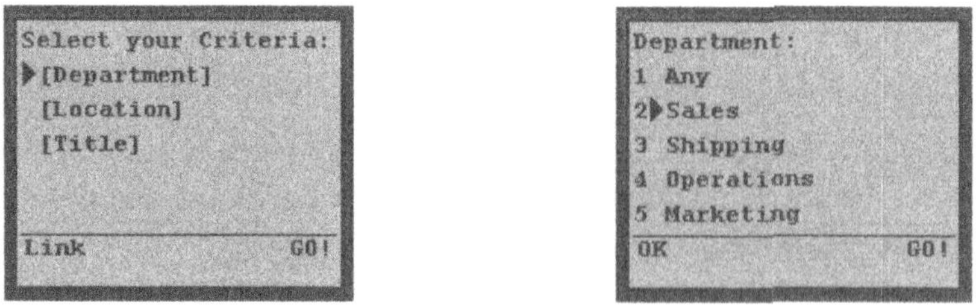

Once the user has selected the Department in which to search by pressing the **accept** key, they are returned to the first card in the deck. They can then narrow their search by Location and Title, as illustrated in Figure 7.23.

Figure 7.23 directory.wml: Location and Title Criteria

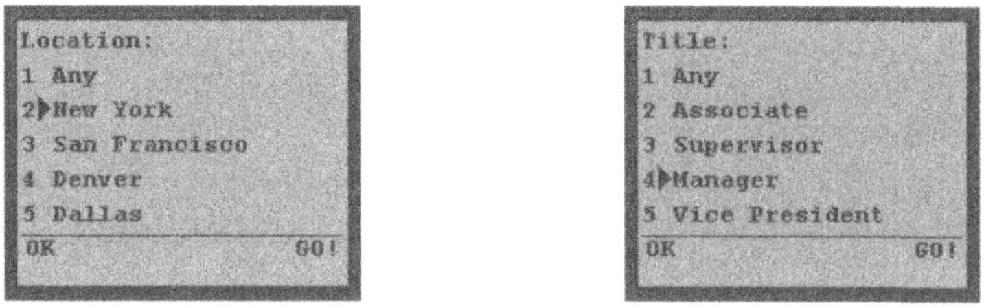

Once the user has selected their criteria, they can select the **Options** key (labeled GO!) to view their parameters, as shown in Figure 7.24.

Figure 7.24 directory.wml: Viewing Parameters

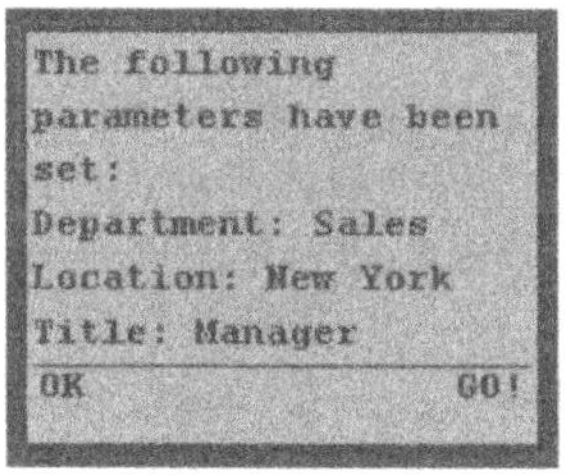

The advantage to this multi-card approach is that the user can quickly enter the information using the first deck, without having to initiate a server request to set each different variable. We could potentially render all of the select lists on one card, although this would result in a very different user experience depending on the browser being used.

For example, the Nokia WAP browser has no problems displaying multiple <SELECT> lists on a single card, so the user can individually select the elements of each <SELECT> list. On the other hand, if the user is using the UP.Browser (version 3.*x* or 4.*x*) from Openwave (formerly Phone.com), then the select lists will automatically be rendered on different cards and the user will be run through the select lists in a linear fashion.

In the next section, we will discuss the most common display differences among browsers. Depending on the markets in which you are deploying your content, you may want to focus on a specific browser or use server-side scripting to branch your code.

Examining Display Differences Between Browsers

Whereas the wired Internet browser wars of the mid 1990s were the result of different companies trying to dominate the market, you should be prepared for the multiplicity of wireless devices and browsers that are available. WML browsers have been developed for many different devices; including mobile phones, e-mail pagers, and PDAs.

When designing for the wireless Internet, you are dealing not only with a browser that may implement features differently, but with different devices that will interact with the features in a different manner. Developing for two browsers on a desktop computer is very different to developing for 10 different browsers on 10 different devices with radically differing input methods.

For example, a mobile phone user will have only keys with which to input data. Usually, one key acts as a positive acknowledgement (accept), and one offers more options (options). Many phones will have a **back** key built into the handset. Alternately, a PDA will often use a stylus as the primary input device, allowing for a somewhat mouse-like interface. Some e-mail pagers (such as the RIM 957 Blackberry) have a miniaturized keyboard and a scrolling wheel for the interface. It is generally accepted, therefore, that user input should be minimized wherever possible.

Fortunately, WML is defined as an application interface, so you will not have to code individually for each device. It is up to the browser programmers and device manufacturers to interpret the feature set of WML and map it to the input mechanisms of the device.

Unfortunately, this world is not perfect, and there are some large differences in how your code will be interpreted on the different devices and browsers.

NOTE

Openwave has published a list of UI guidelines for the UP.Browser. It is available online at http://developer.openwave.com/resources/uiguide.html. In addition, they have published guidelines for markets that serve both the Nokia and Openwave browsers. A full list of Openwave UI white papers may be found at http://developer.openwave.com/support/techlib.html.

In this section, we will examine a few of the differences among the devices and discuss methods of ensuring a consistently usable application. We will focus on the Openwave UP.Browser, the Nokia browser, and the 4thPass Kbrowser. We will also provide an example of submitting a search form that contains both a <SELECT> and an <INPUT> element in order to illustrate the usability differences among these three browsers.

Figure 7.25 contains the same <SELECT> lists as the example in Figure 7.21, but with all of the <SELECT> lists contained in a single card. We are still clearing our variables on entry, but we are not including the <TEMPLATE> element because the user will be directed linearly through each element on the single card in the deck.

Figure 7.25 directory2.wml

```
<?xml version="1.0"?>
<!DOCTYPE wml PUBLIC "-//WAPFORUM//DTD WML 1.1//EN"
"http://www.wapforum.org/DTD/wml_1.1.xml">
<wml>

<card id="home" title="Directory">

<onevent type="onenterforward">
        <refresh>
            <setvar name="dept" value=""/>
            <setvar name="loc" value=""/>
            <setvar name="title" value=""/>
        </refresh>
</onevent>

<p>Select your Department:</p>
<p>
<select name="dept">
<option value="Any">Any</option>
<option value="Sales">Sales</option>
<option value="Shipping">Shipping</option>
<option value="Operations">Operations</option>
```

Continued

Figure 7.25 Continued

```
<option value="Marketing">Marketing</option>
<option value="HR">HR</option>
<option value="Accounting">Accounting</option>
</select>
</p>

<p>Select your Location:</p>
<p>
<select name="loc">
<option value="Any">Any</option>
<option value="New York">New York</option>
<option value="San Francisco">San Francisco</option>
<option value="Denver">Denver</option>
<option value="Dallas">Dallas</option>
<option value="Washington, DC">Washington, DC</option>
<option value="Phoenix">Phoenix</option>
<option value="Salt Lake City">Salt Lake City</option>
<option value="Chicago">Chicago</option>
<option value="Seattle">Seattle</option>
</select>
</p>

<p>Select your Title:</p>
<p>
<select name="title">
<option value="Any">Any</option>
<option value="Associate">Associate</option>
<option value="Supervisor">Supervisor</option>
<option value="Manager">Manager</option>
<option value="Vice President">Vice President</option>
<option value="President">President</option>
</select>
</p>
```

Continued

Figure 7.25 Continued

```
<p>Enter a Keyword:<br/>
<input name="key"/></p>

<p>
The following parameters have been set:<br/>
Department: $(dept)<br/>
Location: $(loc)<br/>
Title: $(title)<br/>
Keyword: $(key)<br/>
</p>
</card>
</wml>
```

UP.Browser Interpretation

In this section we will walk through the above deck (Figure 7.25) using the UP.Browser SDK. We will illustrate how this browser will render multiple <SELECT> and <INPUT> elements in a single deck. In sharp contrast to how a desktop browser would render these individual form elements, the user is stepped through the different elements on the single card as if they were individual cards in the deck and linked in a linear fashion. When the user pulls up this deck in the UP.Browser, they will see only the first <SELECT> list, as illustrated in Figure 7.26.

Figure 7.26 directory2.wml on UP.Browser: Department Criteria

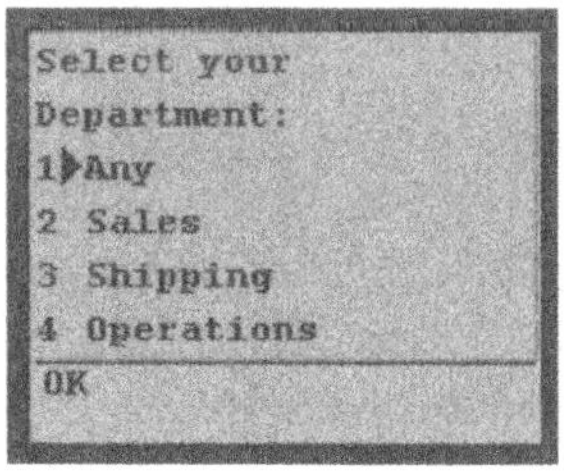

Upon selecting the Department, the user is forwarded to the next <SELECT> list on the card; in this case it is the *Location* selector. This is shown in Figure 7.27.

Figure 7.27 directory2.wml on UP.Browser: Location Criteria

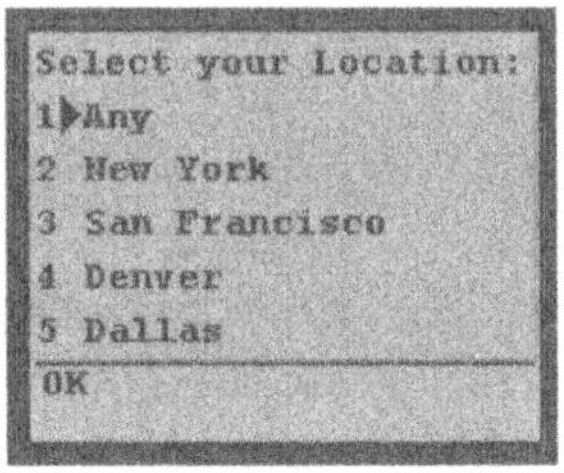

Again, upon selecting an item in this list, the user is forwarded to the next (and final) list on the card, the *Title* selector, shown in Figure 7.28.

Figure 7.28 directory2.wml on UP.Browser: Title Criteria

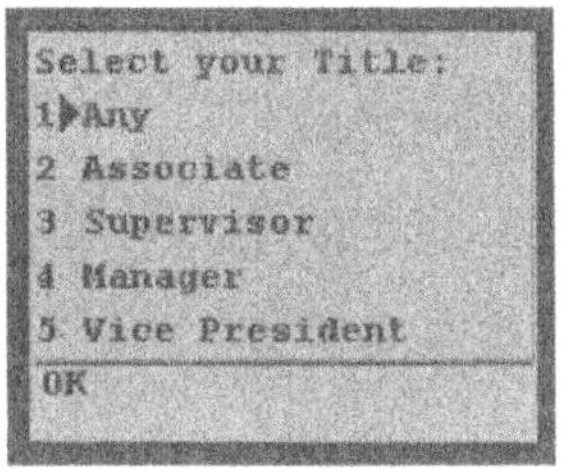

Once the user has selected the criteria by which they would like to search, they are given the option to enter a keyword, shown in Figure 7.29.

Figure 7.29 directory2.wml on UP.Browser: Keyword Option

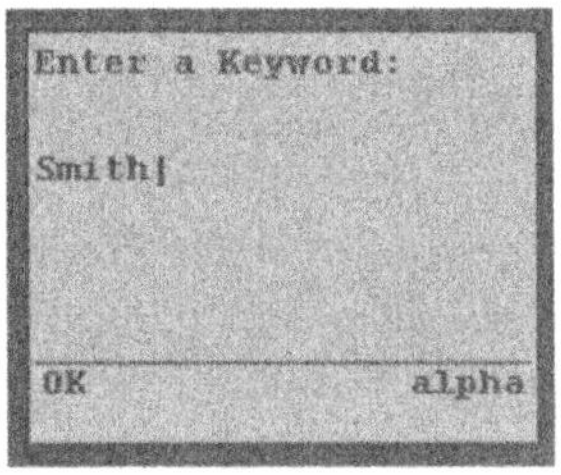

Finally, the user is shown the results of their entry, as illustrated in Figure 7.30.

Figure 7.30 directory2.wml on UP.Browser: Viewing Parameters

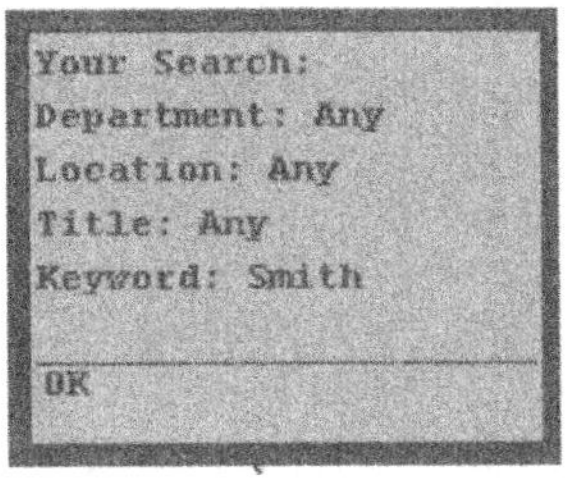

As you can see, the UP.Browser will step the user through individual <SELECT> lists on a single card as if they were individual cards (keeping keystrokes to a minimum). The reason for this has to do with the evolution of the UP.Browser: When it was first introduced, the UP.Browser was strictly capable of rendering Handheld Device Markup Language, and in many cases (especially in the U.S.), the binary that the phone receives is actually HDML that has been transcoded from WML by the WAP Gateway.

This transcoding can pose some strange behavior in your application if you are using 3.1 UP.Browser features on a phone that only supports HDML 3.0. A full discussion of these differences is outside the scope of this chapter, but more details on this can be found on the Openwave Developer Web site at http://developer.openwave.com.

Nokia Interpretation

One of the key differences between the UP.Browser and the Nokia browser is that the Nokia browser renders any <SELECT> list as being mapped to a List option on the **Accept** key. This feature forces the user to list the options before they can select one. Once they have listed the options, they can select one.

Once the user has selected an item and hit **OK**, they are returned to the card containing the <SELECT> list. The usability hindrances imposed by this will become evident when we load up directory2.wml in the Nokia SDK.

When the user first pulls up this deck, they are presented with several screens of text with all of the <SELECT> lists and the <INPUT> element rendered on the same page. In addition, the user can scroll down to see the final paragraph in our card, which displays the state of the variables on the card. Figure 7.31 illustrates what the user will see when loading up this card (note that this browser renders the *title* attribute of the <CARD> element, unlike the UP.Browser).

Figure 7.31 directory2.wml on Nokia SDK: Selector List

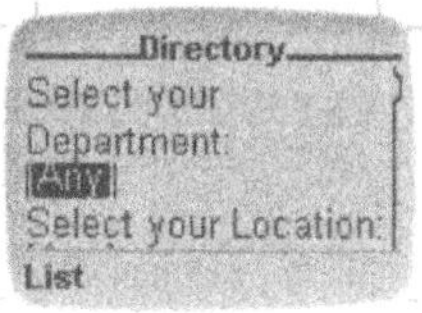

Once the user selects the **List** option while the Department selector is active, they see the following screen (Figure 7.32).

Figure 7.32 directory2.wml on Nokia SDK: Department List Option

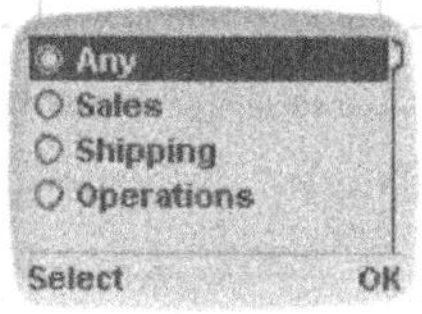

On this screen, the user can use their arrow keys to move up and down the list. Once they have highlighted the desired option, they must hit the **Select** button to change the value, as illustrated in Figure 7.33.

Figure 7.33 directory2.wml on Nokia SDK: Selecting from List

Once they have selected the option, they must then hit the **OK** button to return to the card that contains the <SELECT> list. This process must be repeated for each <SELECT> element on the card.

This feature is similarly implemented with the <INPUT> form element. The user must select the input, then select **Edit** to enter their selection. Figure 7.34 illustrates what this looks like for the user.

First, they must edit the <INPUT> element. Once they select **Edit**, they can enter text to be stored within the variable. When they are done entering their text, they must hit the **OK** button to be returned to the card containing the <INPUT> element.

Figure 7.34 directory2.wml on Nokia SDK: Entering Keyword

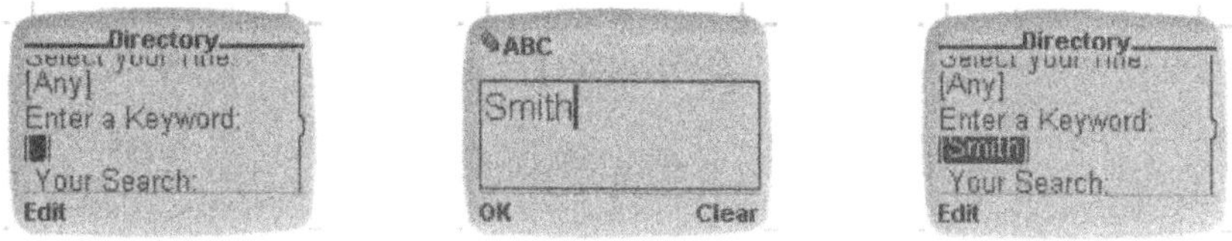

NOTE

It is possible to do some rudimentary input validation by using the *format* attribute of the <INPUT> element. More details on this can be found in Chapter 4. It is also possible to do some complex input validation by using WMLscript. More information on this can be found in Chapter 5.

At the end of this process, the user can scroll down to see the state of the variables that they have entered, as shown in Figure 7.35.

Figure 7.35 directory2.wml on Nokia SDK: Viewing Parameters

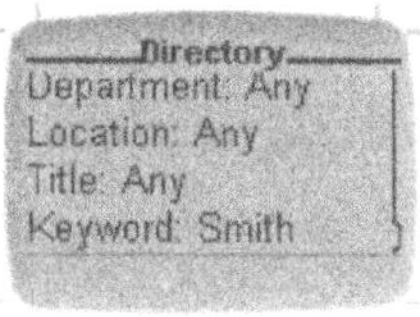

As illustrated here, there are large differences in how the UP.Browser and Nokia browsers will render <SELECT> and <INPUT> elements. The cumbersome way the Nokia browser interacts with these elements is certainly cause for careful attention to be paid as to which browsers are being used to access your WAP site.

4thPass Kbrowser Interpretation

The Kbrowser, available at www.4thpass.com, renders WML significantly differently than either the UP.Browser or the Nokia browser. In order to illustrate these differences, we will compare how this browser renders the first example (with <SELECT> elements on different cards) with how it renders the second example (with the <SELECT> elements on the same card).

Directory.wml Example

Figure 7.36 illustrates how the 4thpass Kbrowser will render directory.wml. One of the first things that we notice is that the <TEMPLATE> element is rendered at the top of the user's screen.

Figure 7.36 directory.wml on Kbrowser: Selector List

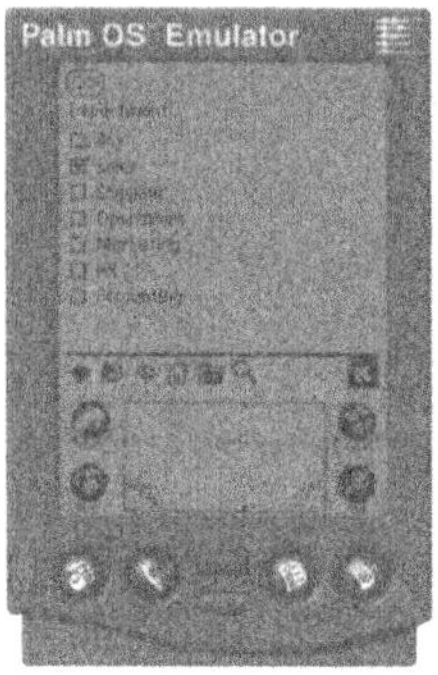

Figure 7.37 illustrates how the Kbrowser renders <SELECT> elements. Their behavior is similar to how a desktop WWW browser renders radio buttons. They are treated as a set of mutually exclusive checkboxes, and the user is not able to select more than one element.

Figure 7.37 directory.wml on Kbrowser: Department Criteria

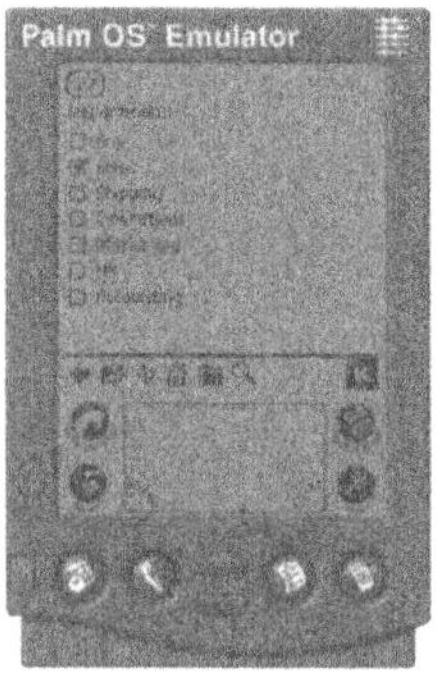

Figure 7.38 illustrates what the final card of this deck looks like. Note the encoded space that is displayed when we show the *Location* variable. This can be eliminated by unescaping the value of the variable by entering:

```
$(loc:unesc) instead of $(loc)
```

Figure 7.38 directory.wml on Kbrowser: Viewing Parameters

NOTE

The 4thPass Kbrowser is will render keys that have been disabled with the <NOOP/> attribute. It is not possible to disable the <PREV/> element with <NOOP/> for this browser. There is a workaround, however, which involves assigning an <ONENTERBACKWARD> event to kick the user one element forward in their history stack.

This example behaves pretty much as expected, assigning values to the variables and allowing the user to see the results of these values. When the <SELECT> elements are on different cards, this browser behaves functionally equivalent to the other browsers, but what happens when we implement the second example?

Directory2.wml Example

When we load up directory2.wml in the 4thpass Kbrowser, all of the elements are displayed on the same page, as shown in Figure 7.39.

However, the state of the page is not updated upon selecting any of the elements on the page, and we cannot refresh the page without resetting the values of the variables. If this application were to be deployed into production, any users browsing the site with the 4thpass Kbrowser would be faced with an unusable application. If you are including this browser in the target browser set for your application, you would be best to branch your code according to the

HTTP_USER_AGENT string, and test it thoroughly on a variety of devices and emulators.

Figure 7.39 directory2.wml on Kbrowser: Selector List

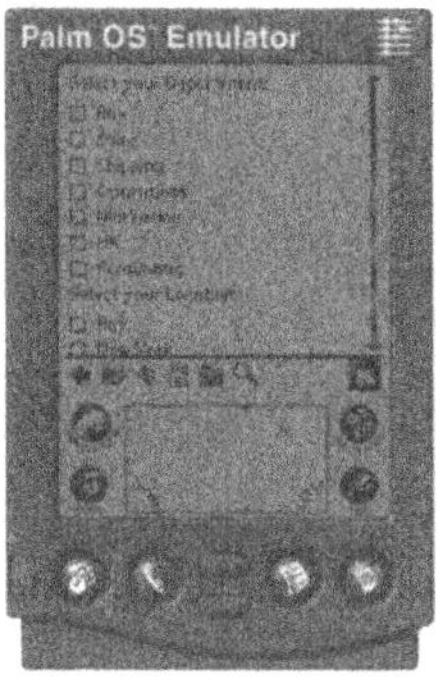

In this section, we've seen that the same WML code may be compiled and rendered on a variety of devices with radically different interfaces resulting from how the browser interprets the code. In some cases, it is possible to write WML that will compile for a wide variety of browsers, but that will not be functionally equivalent among them. The examples presented here should be enough to convince you that it is important to view your code on different devices and branch it accordingly.

Developing & Deploying...

The Importance of Testing

It is extremely critical to test your WML site or application on every single emulator or device you can get your hands on. If your target audience lies within the United States, it is doubly critical to do so, as the binary that is displayed on any given device will not necessarily be the WML that you have written (due to WAP gateway transcoding). Also, some emulators and devices may behave differently.

In addition to the technical concerns, it is critical to test the human factors of your application using real users in real-world scenarios. Try testing your application while on the train, or in a cab, or walking down

Continued

the street. It may be very easy for you to use your site while you are sitting comfortably at your desk, but it may be very hard to use in the field. You will also find that it is much easier to enter input with a desktop keyboard and mouse than it is to do with a stylus or keypad.

You may find that an application that works gracefully in an emulator and a controlled environment is clunky and hard to use in a real world situation. You may also find that regular users will have difficulty interpreting your application because they are unfamiliar with it. By showing a prototype of your application to a novice user, you will gain valuable information on how to make the final version more usable, and by testing on real-world devices you will be subject to the constraints that all users face in the field.

Summary

In this chapter, we have discussed the pyramidal navigational structure that is fairly prevalent on the WWW. We have discussed the many mistakes that are commonly made by Webmasters making the transition to wireless, and how these mistakes are largely the result of an attempt to represent the WWW on a small-viewpoint device.

In order for Webmasters to provide effective, compelling applications, it is necessary for us to work within the constraints of the wireless landscape. This involves accommodations of a technical nature, such as the minimized use of images and extraneous markup; as well as accommodations of a human nature, such as taking mobility into consideration and minimizing the data a user must input to interact with an application.

There are some unique features to WML that allow us to send multiple screens to the user at once, and it is possible to use this feature to our user's advantage by limiting the number of server connections that must be initiated by the handheld device. It's possible to build a swift-feeling application by making use of the hub-and-spoke metaphor and parceling our site into one deck for navigation and several decks of content. In addition, a linear, task-based navigation scheme will result in a more efficient relay of information to the user.

In this chapter, we also examined the display differences among the different browsers, and found that there are significant differences in how the most common WML browsers display content and UI elements. Designing an application and branching your code with these differences in mind will help to ensure the best user experience possible.

It is of critical importance to test your applications on a wide variety of devices, and although we're dealing with a great many devices and input mechanisms, it is possible to apply some thought to the usability of our applications so as to create a more effective user experience.

Last, but certainly not least, it is of utmost importance to test your application with real users in the field. As of yet, there is no emulator that can effectively recreate the experience of entering text into a mobile phone browser on a crowded train at rush hour! With a little forethought and a lot of patience, it is possible to build usable WML applications and debunk the myth that WML is, by nature, a hindrance to usability.

Solutions Fast Track

Thinking *In the Hand*, not *On the Web*

☑ The wireless Internet provides us with a smaller viewpoint for content, and it is not possible to represent the typical pyramidal site structure of the WWW on handheld devices.

☑ It is difficult to provide both horizontal and vertical navigation on a mobile device due to a lack of screen real estate.

☑ The needs of the mobile user necessitate a fairly linear, task-based navigational scheme, with a frequency of access-based segregation of tasks.

☑ Working within the bandwidth and input constraints of the wireless medium can prevent the mistakes that are typically made by many Webmasters.

Stacking a Deck of Cards

☑ It is possible to make many small refinements to your markup that will have a cumulative effect on the final size of your content.

☑ A hub-and-spoke metaphor can be used effectively within the framework of WML. Users have full freedom of vertical navigation, though this metaphor does not use horizontal navigation.

☑ Minimizing the number of server connections can greatly increase a site's usability, and one of the easiest ways to do this for small sites is to send one deck consisting of navigation, and, on request, send decks that contain the sections' content.

☑ WML variables are stored on the device (similar to cookies), and are persistent between decks as well as cards. You should be aware of the state of the user's variables in your application, and clear them as appropriate.

Examining Display Differences Between Browsers

- ☑ One of the most notable differences between the UP.Browser and the Nokia browser is in the rendering of the <SELECT> and <INPUT> elements. On average, the Nokia browser user will need to enter twice as many keystrokes.
- ☑ The 4thpass Kbrowser (for the Palm OS) renders WML differently than either the Nokia or the UP.Browser. If you are supporting this browser in your site, you should take care to branch your code and test your application thoroughly.

Frequently Asked Questions

The following Frequently Asked Questions, answered by the authors of this book, are designed to both measure your understanding of the concepts presented in this chapter and to assist you with real-life implementation of these concepts. To have your questions about this chapter answered by the author, browse to **www.syngress.com/solutions** and click on the **"Ask the Author"** form.

Q: How many devices should I test my application on?

A: You should test your application on as many devices as is possible, because each device manufacturer may interpret your code slightly differently depending on the browser and carrier. Emulators are widely available, but they do not necessarily provide the same real-world experience. Furthermore, once your code is run through a gateway, it may function differently on different devices.

Q: How can I disable the user's Back button?

A: You can use the following code to prevent your users from re-entering your application:

```
<do type="prev">
<noop/>
</do>
```

Q: Where can I learn more about usability?

A: Jakob Nielsen is one of the foremost usability experts. He publishes regular usability reports (mostly pertaining to the Web), and has a comprehensive archive of his articles on his Web site at www.useit.com.

Q: Should I use <SELECT> lists for navigation?

A: It is generally recommended that <SELECT> lists be used for navigation on the UP.Browser, but that a list of links be presented to the Nokia browser. If you do use select list for the Nokia browser, be sure to use the *onpick* attribute to save your users a click.

Chapter 8

Wireless Enabling Your Big Bandwidth Site

Solutions in this chapter:

- Defining WAP MIME Types
- Detecting WAP Devices
- Optimizing Content Distribution
- Delivering Wireless Data
- Implementing Wireless Graphics

☑ Summary

☑ Solutions Fast Track

☑ Frequently Asked Questions

Introduction

So, your supervisor has told you that your company must take advantage of the wireless Internet and that as the Webmaster, you are to convert the company's existing Web site to a wireless version. Seems easy enough, right? You should be able to run a program over the document area of your site and in a day or so your site will be available to any user with a wireless device!

Although the idea is appealing, it certainly is not a reality. Delivering content over the airwaves to mobile devices carries with it several limitations, most notably in terms of device display, bandwidth, and the sheer number of different devices capable of browsing Internet content over a wireless connection. It is of utmost importance that Webmasters be aware of the limitations of wireless devices and devise a new strategy for delivering content to said devices.

In this chapter, we will cover the nuts-and-bolts issues of adding wireless capabilities to your existing site. We will cover server configuration for the two most common Web servers on the market and discuss methods for detecting which users can access wireless content. We will discuss the issues and solutions surrounding the automated conversion of existing Web sites. We will also cover how to make your wireless data applications accessible and how to implement graphics that will be viewable on wireless devices.

This chapter assumes that you already have some experience with server configuration and CGI programming, and that you have a basic knowledge of WML. If you do not have any experience working on the server-side, then this chapter will cover the basics, and you should not have a problem setting up the wireless section of your site.

Defining WAP MIME Types

Setting up your Web server software to dispatch wireless content is the first step to making your Web site available to the wireless Internet. The steps needed to accomplish this will differ according the server software and platform, but the basic process is the same.

As you probably already know, Web browsers recognize and handle content according to information sent in the response header by the server. In any given response, the Web server will send out a file accompanied by a Multipurpose Internet Mail Extension (MIME) type. A MIME type, in relation to an HTTP transaction, is a definition of the type of content contained in a given file being sent to a Web browser.

MIME types are typically associated with file extensions that are mapped in the server configuration and sent out with all files containing that extension. In a server-side programming environment (using PHP or ASP, for example), it is possible to specify the MIME type manually within the response.

Selecting which MIME Types to Add

First off, depending on the market in which you want to provide your wireless content, and the extent to which you use WMLScript, you will need to add some or all of the MIME types and file extensions to your server configuration that are listed in Table 8.1.

Table 8.1 MIME types and file extensions for your server configuration

MIME Type	File Extension
Text/vnd.wap.wml	.wml
application/vnd.wap.wmlc	.wmlc
Text/vnd.wap.wmls	.wmls
application/vnd.wap.wmlscriptc	.wmlsc
image/vnd.wap.wbmp	.wbmp
Text/x-hdml	.hdml

NOTE

If you are already familiar with the basics of WML and with adding MIME types to your server, you may want to add the types from Table 8.1 and skip down to the section titled "Detecting WAP Devices."

If your audience is located in the U.S.., it is important to define the last MIME type listed above and to build support for HDML into your site. The reason for this is that there are many phones in use in the United States that do not support WML, and many of the phones that do support WML do so only via gateway translation. You may be able to get around this by restricting your use of WML to the features that are supported in HDML 3.0, however. More details on this can be found at the developer section of the OpenWave Web site (http://developer.openwave.com).

Adding MIME Types to Your Server Configuration

In this section, we will discuss how to add the requisite wireless MIME types to your site in order to dispatch wireless content. Before we get into the details of adding MIME types to your server configuration, it makes sense to have at least one piece of content to dispatch for testing purposes. The following code, saved as hello.wml, will create your first WML page; Figure 8.1 shows the resulting screen on the UP.Browser.

```
<?xml version="1.0"?>
<!DOCTYPE wml PUBLIC
"-//WAPFORUM//DTD WML 1.1//EN"
"http://www.wapforum.org/DTD/wml_1.1.xml">
<wml>
      <card id="hi" title="Hello!">
            <p>
            <b>Hello, world!</b>
            </p>
      </card>
</wml>
```

Figure 8.1 Our hello.wml File as viewed with the UP.Browser SDK

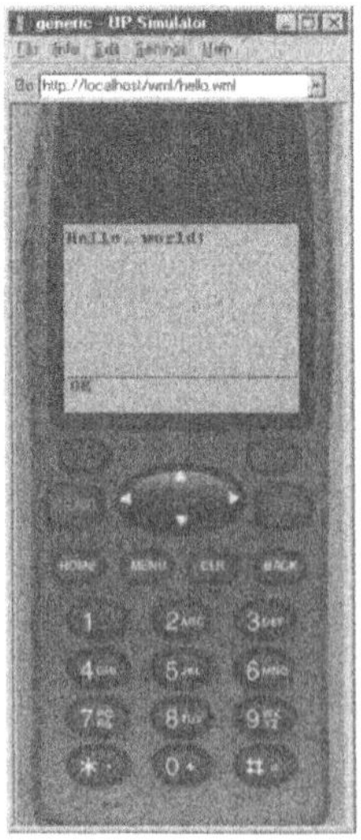

The first two elements of this file are very important. They carry the message that the file is an Extensible Markup Language (XML) document, and that it must be validated against the Document Type Definition (DTD) specified. In this case, our markup needs to comply with the DTD published by the WAP Forum. These lines are a form of guarantee that the document will contain valid markup without any stray, missing, or uncompleted tags. You should place this file in a publicly accessible place in the document area of your site.

If you try to access this file from a WML browser without setting the MIME types in your server configuration, you will receive an error. On most Web servers, text/html is set as the default MIME type, so if you have yet to associate the .wml extension with the text/vnd.wap.wml MIME type your server will not recognize the content of the file as WML or send out the correct MIME type. Correspondingly, the client will not be able to render the content.

Depending on the server software you are running, you will need to perform a different set of steps to add the MIME types. We will cover adding the MIME types to the two most common Web servers on the market: the Apache Web Server (www.apache.org) and Microsoft's Internet Information Server (www.microsoft.com/iis).

Configuring the Apache Web Server

There are many options available to add MIME types to the Apache environment. Where you choose to add the configuration depends largely on the implementation of the server itself. If you want to implement the MIME types in a global manner, simply add a few new lines to the mime.types file. If you are running many individual Web sites (VirtualHosts), you may want to add the MIME types on a site-by-site basis. If you do not have root access to the machine running the Web server, it may make the most sense to use an .htaccess file to add new directives to the server configuration. We will examine these three methodologies in detail.

WARNING

Before making any changes to a server configuration file, it is generally good practice to make a backup of the file you are editing. That way, in the event that you make a mistake while editing, you can be assured to have a working version of your configuration file.

Adding to the mime.types File

To add wireless MIME types to this Apache configuration file, you first need to locate mime.types. On a Linux/UNIX system, the file will typically be located in /usr/local/apache/conf. On a win32 system, the default Apache Web server installation will place the file in C:\Apache\conf.

Open the file using a text editor (such as vi or Notepad), and add the following lines:

```
text/vnd.wap.wml .wml
application/vnd.wap.wmlc .wmlc
text/vnd.wap.wmls .wmls
application/vnd.wap.wmlscriptc .wmlsc
image/vnd.wap.wbmp .wbmp
text/x-hdml .hdml
```

Save your changes, and then restart the Web server. You should now be able to see your "hello, world" WML document when you request http://your.site.com/wap/helloworld.wml using a WML browser.

Adding to the httpd.conf File

The configuration file httpd.conf is used to configure many (or in some cases, all) of the options available within the server environment. Adding the MIME types to this file allows us more flexibility as far as defining the MIME types for any individual VirtualHost running on our server.

You must add the types using the AddType directive according to the following syntax:

```
AddType text/vnd.wap.wml .wml
AddType application/vnd.wap.wmlc .wmlc
AddType text/vnd.wap.wmls .wmls
AddType application/vnd.wap.wmlscriptc .wmlsc
AddType image/vnd.wap.wbmp .wbmp
AddType text/x-hdml .hdml
```

The AddType directive can be added to any Directory or VirtualHost defined in httpd.conf. Appending the entries to httpd.conf accomplishes the same effect as adding them to mime.types. Save your changes, and then restart the Web server. You should now be able to see your WML document when you request http://your.site.com/wap/helloworld.wml using a WML browser.

Using the .htaccess File

In the event that you do not have root access to the Web server (as is often the case in shared hosting environments), you can define the MIME types in an .htaccess file residing in the directory in which you will be placing your content. As above, the MIME types are defined using the AddType directive and syntax. An .htaccess file containing only the AddType definitions would contain the following:

```
AddType text/vnd.wap.wml .wml
AddType application/vnd.wap.wmlc .wmlc
AddType text/vnd.wap.wmls .wmls
AddType application/vnd.wap.wmlscriptc .wmlsc
AddType image/vnd.wap.wbmp .wbmp
AddType text/x-hdml .hdml
```

You should now be able to see your WML document when you request http://your.site.com/wap/helloworld.wml using a WML browser.

Adding MIME Types to Microsoft IIS

MIME types can be registered in IIS 4.0 and 5.0 using the **Internet Service Manager** console. Adding the MIME types to Microsoft's Internet Information Server (IIS) can be done via the following steps:

1. Select **Default Web Site** (or whatever Web site you wish to enable for wireless content) and bring up the **Properties** dialog box.
2. Select the **HTTP Headers** tab.
3. Under **MIME Map**, click the **File Types** tab and select **New Type**.
4. Type **.wml** in the **Extension** field and **text/vnd.wap.wml** in the **Content Type** field, and then click **OK**.
5. Repeat the previous steps for each of the MIME types and extensions mentioned earlier in this chapter for each site running on your machine.

In addition, Under IIS 5.0, you have the option to add MIME types for all sites running on the same server by doing the following:

1. Select **Internet Information Services** and bring up the **Properties** dialog box.
2. Under **Computer MIME Map**, click the **Edit** button and select **New Type**.

3. Type **.wml** in the **Extension** field and **text/vnd.wap.wml** in the **Content Type** field, and then click **OK**.

You should now be able to see your WML document when you request http://your.site.com/wap/helloworld.wml using a WML browser.

Detecting WAP Devices

Thus far in this chapter, we have covered the MIME types that you need to add to your server configuration in order to serve content to wireless devices, and we have discussed how to add those MIME types to your server configuration. At this point, your Web server should be running and happily sending out the appropriate MIME types for your content. Now, we will shift our attention to the client and discuss how to detect the types of content that a user can accept according to the information sent in their request.

There are, at present, many different devices capable of accepting WML content. These range from mobile phones with 2 lines of visible text, to Personal Digital Assistants (PDAs) with screens capable of displaying much more, to desktop WAP emulators capable of rendering WML. It is very important for the Wireless Webmaster to understand the unique ways in which their services will be rendered on these differing devices, and to have a solid means of determining the attributes of the browser that is being used to access the content at any given time.

In this section, we will provide a simple example of detecting and redirecting WAP devices to the correct content according to the information sent in the request header. We will provide an example of how to detect the language that the device can accept and how to detect which type of device is requesting your content. Examples will be provided in PHP and Perl, but it will be possible for you to adapt these examples to any server-side scripting language, such as ASP, Java, or Python (to name a few). The means of parsing header information are language-specific, but the information is common to any HTTP transaction, and any server-side programming or scripting language will do.

Parsing Header Information

As you are probably already aware, all browsers using the Hyper Text Transfer Protocol (HTTP) send certain information along with any request. This information is sent within the request header, and tells the Web server about the browser making the request. These environmental variables include text strings that describe the computing environment of the Web server. Some of these strings describe aspects of the Web server, such as the software that the server is running, or the email address of the server administrator. Other variables contain information about the client, such as the different types of content the device can accept or the URL of the referring document.

You may have used the HTTP_USER_AGENT header to discern which browser your user is using, in order to deliver appropriate Cascading Style Sheets (CSS), or perhaps you have parsed the HTTP_ACCEPT header to figure out if your user can accept a Macromedia Flash Movie. These are the same variables used in order to detect wireless devices. We will briefly discuss these variables before moving on to an example of how to redirect users based on their device.

NOTE

You will not be able to detect wireless devices with a client-side scripting language such as JavaScript. The request must be handled at the server level in order to deliver the appropriate MIME type with your content.

HTTP_USER_AGENT

The HTTP_USER_AGENT variable contains a text string identifying the browser that is sending the request. It will most commonly contain an abbreviated name and the version number of the browser. The Nokia browser will report the model of the phone in this string, and any phone using the UP.Browser (also known as the Phone.com browser) will report the version of UP.Browser that the device is using. Ericsson phone browsers identify themselves by name as well.

NOTE

A comprehensive list of device specifications and WAP User Agents can be found at www.allnetdevices.com.

To read the value contained in HTTP_USER_AGENT using PHP, you will use the **getenv()** function, requesting the name of the variable. The function will return the value of the variable requested. While using Perl, you will obtain the value of the HTTP_USER_AGENT by accessing a special data structure (a hash, for those familiar with Perl data types) called **%ENV**. For example, to get the value of HTTP_USER_AGENT, you would use the following fragment in a PHP page:

```
<?
$useragent = getenv( "HTTP_USER_AGENT" );
print $useragent;
?>
```

or the following fragment in a Perl program:

```
$useragent = $ENV{ HTTP_USER_AGENT };
print $useragent;
```

or the following fragment in an ASP page:

```
<%
useragent = Request.ServerVariables("HTTP_USER_AGENT")
Response.Write(accept)
%>
```

It certainly does not provide much value if we just print out the variable to the user! In order to make some use of the variable, we must evaluate it and make a decision on what to do.

One of the most pragmatic uses of this variable is to differentiate phones, and pagers with very limited displays, from PDAs with larger displays. Remember that any user browsing your site through a phone will be largely dependent upon a text interface, while a user browsing your content with a PDA will be able to interpret the content in a more visual manner.

In the following example, we will cover how you can use HTTP_USER _AGENT header to redirect your users to appropriate content based on which browser they are using. We will differentiate the two major phone browsers from the major PDA browsers and redirect our users appropriately.

First off, we will need some means of storing our device profiles. For our expository purposes here, we will be using a text file that lists a few strings that will be contained in the HTTP_USER_AGENT header and associates each string with a device type (Figure 8.2). Note that this is a simplified implementation of this concept. It is also possible to create elaborate device profiles using XML or Databases.

Figure 8.2 Contents of ualist.txt

```
4thpass.com KBrowser 1.0:PDA
UP.Browser/3.1-UPG1 UP.Link/3.2:Phone
Nokia-WAP-Toolkit/2.1:Phone
```

Next, we will need a program to retrieve the HTTP_USER_AGENT header and compare it to the entries in the file (Figure 8.3).

Figure 8.3 Contents of device.cgi

```
#!/usr/bin/perl
use strict;

my $test = $ENV{ HTTP_USER_AGENT };
my $type;

open(DB,'<ualist.txt');
while(<DB>) {
        my($ua,$dev) = split(/:/,$_);
        if ($test eq $ua) {
        $type = $dev;
        }
}
close(DB);

print STDOUT "Content-type:text/vnd.wap.wml\n\n";
print STDOUT<<_CARD;
<?xml version="1.0"?>
<!DOCTYPE wml PUBLIC
"-//WAPFORUM//DTD WML 1.1//EN"
"http://www.wapforum.org/DTD/wml_1.1.xml">
<wml>
      <card id="ua" title="HTTP_USER_AGENT">
            <p>
            <b>HTTP_USER_AGENT:<br/>$test<br/><br/>
```

Continued

Figure 8.3 Continued

```
                        Device Type:<br/>$type</b>
            </p>
        </card>
</wml>
_CARD

exit;
```

As you can see from Figures 8.4 and 8.5, this file successfully detects a pre-typed HTTP_USER_AGENT string and returns the type of device back to the browser.

Figure 8.4 Output of type.cgi in UP.Browser 3.2

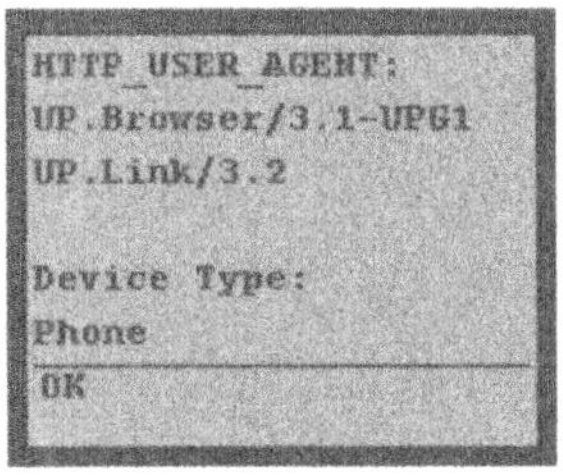

Figure 8.5 Output of type.cgi in 4thpass Kbrowser

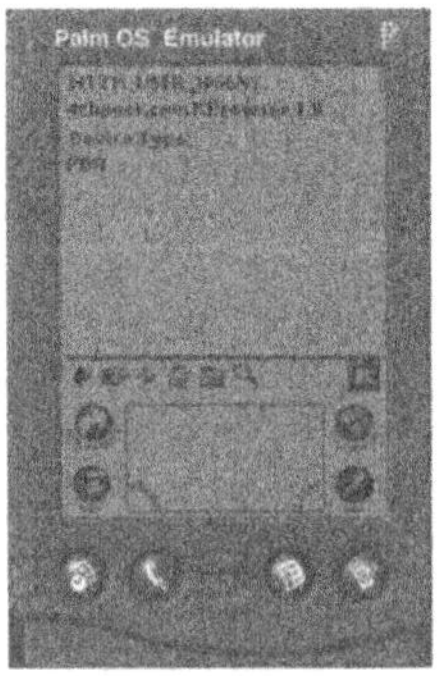

HTTP_ACCEPT

The HTTP_ACCEPT variable contains a semicolon-delimited text string listing the MIME types that the device can accept (text/vnd.wap.wml, for example). A pattern match can be executed against this string to make sure that the device can accept the content that you wish to send to it.

You will access the value of this variable using the same syntax as HTTP _USER_AGENT. You will use the following in PHP:

```
<?
$accept = getenv( "HTTP_ACCEPT" );
?>
```

and the following in a Perl program:

```
$accept = $ENV{ HTTP_ACCEPT };
```

and the following in an ASP page:

```
<%
accept = Request.ServerVariables("HTTP_ACCEPT ")
%>
```

Just as with HTTP_USER_AGENT, we will need to do some additional processing in order to do anything meaningful with the variable. In this case, what is called for is a pattern match against the string to isolate the MIME types for the client to accept. We will search the HTTP_ACCEPT variable and look for the types of wireless markup languages in which our content is coded. For example, to find out if our client can accept WML content, we need to look for the following string:

```
text/vnd.wap.wml
```

To do this in PHP, we will use the `ereg()` function, which executes a regular expression search for a pattern in a string. The pattern and the string are passed as arguments to the function. It is commonly used in a true/false context:

```
if ( ereg("text/vnd\.wap\.wml",$accept) ) {
//do something here
} else {
//do something else
}
```

To accomplish the same in Perl, we will use the ~ (tilde) operator, which is used to determine whether the expression on the left contains the text delimited within the slashes on the right. In this case, we are using the tilde operator to determine whether the environmental variable HTTP_ACCEPT contains the string "vnd.wap.wml".

```
if ( $ENV{HTTP_ACCEPT} =~ /text\/vnd\.wap\.wml/ ) {
#do something here
} else {
#do something else
}
```

There is certainly more to these functions that what we are doing here, but neither an extensive discussion on regular expressions nor a serious foray into the intricacies of programming is necessary here to deliver wireless content to your users. The main thing that you should get from this section is the means to access environmental variables using PHP and/or Perl, and gain some knowledge on how to use these variables within the context of your site.

The next section will describe a program that will allow you to see all of the environmental variables for any browser that queries it. You can install this script on your site and take a peek under the hood of the browser that you use.

Reading Other Environmental Variables

There are many variables that are of use in the server environment besides the ones mentioned in this section. Some devices will report their screen size or the number of buttons that are on the device as environmental variables. You can print out a list of all of the environmental variables to a browser by installing the following Perl program on your server:

```
#!/usr/bin/perl
# this program will print out the environmental variables
# to the client in WML, HDML, or HTML depending on the browser

# this routine will detect whether the device
# accepts WML, HDML, or HTML

sub detect_accept {
```

```
# variable in which we will store the results
    my $result;

    # first, test for wml
       if ( $ENV{'HTTP_ACCEPT'} =~ m%text/vnd\.wap\.wml% ) {
            # assign result
            $result = "wml";

    # next, test for HDML
        } elsif ( $ENV{'HTTP_ACCEPT'} =~ m%text/x-hdml% ) {
             # assign result
             $result = "hdml";

    #if neither HDML or WML, then send HTML
    } else {
             $result = "html";
    }

    # finally, send back string containing result
    return $result;
}

# now, we test the result of this routine and print out
# our environmental variables

if(&detect_accept eq "html") {
#print HTML header and print out results
    print "Content-type:text/html\n\n";
    map { print "$_ : $ENV{$_}<br/>" } keys %ENV;

} elsif (&detect_accept eq "hdml" ) {
#print HDML header and print out results
    print "Content-type:text/x-hdml\n\n";
    print "<HDML VERSION='3.0'><DISPLAY>";
```

```
    map { print "$_ : $ENV{$_}<br>" } keys %ENV;
    print "</DISPLAY></HDML>";

} elsif (&detect_accept eq "wml") {
#print WML header and print out results
print "Content-type:text/vnd.wap.wml\n\n";
print<<HEAD;
<?xml version="1.0"?>
<!DOCTYPE wml PUBLIC
"-//WAPFORUM//DTD WML 1.1//EN"
        "http://www.wapforum.org/DTD/wml_1.1.xml">
HEAD
print "<wml><card id='first' title='printenv'><p>";
map { print "$_ : $ENV{$_}<br/>" } keys %ENV;
print "</p></card></wml>";
}
```

To install the program, save the above text as printenv.cgi, and put it in your cgi-bin. If you are using a UNIX system, you will need to make sure that the file is executable and that the first line of the file corresponds to the location of your Perl installation.

You can request the file (http://your.site.com/cgi-bin/printenv.cgi) with most any browser and view the complete list of environmental variables. There is no flow control in this script, so bear in mind that when you send the content to an actual device you may find that the deck is too large for the device to handle. However, the emulators that are available for both the UP.Browser and the Nokia WAP Toolkit do not suffer from the limitations imposed by WAP gateways. They will deliver the deck contents even if they are too large for an actual device.

Redirecting Your Users to Static Content

Now that your Web server is up and running and you know where to look to find out what types of content your users can accept, you can use this knowledge to give your users what they want: content. In this section we will cover how to redirect your users to separate static pages based on their browser. If you implement this on your site, it will allow you to send all of your users to the same URL (http://your.site.com), regardless of the device that they are using. When the user queries your URL, they will execute the redirection script (index.cgi) and be directed to an appropriate index page coded in either HTML, WML, or HDML.

We will provide examples in PHP and Perl in the following sections, and also provide code samples of pages to make sure that the redirection example is working correctly. The first code sample should look very familiar. It's a small HTML page that informs you (the user) that your script is correctly installed. The last two code samples are written in WML and HDML, respectively, and will display the same message as the first example.

Redirecting Users in PHP

PHP stands for "PHP Hypertext Preprocessor" . It is a server-side scripting language that allows you to embed control structures within your markup. It has recently grown in popularity due largely to its portability, flexibility, and ease of use.

```
<?
$accept = getenv("HTTP_ACCEPT");
if ( eregi("vnd\.wap\.wml",$accept) ) {
    header("Location:/wml/index.wml");
} elseif ( eregi("text/x-hdml",$accept) ) {
    header("Location:/hdml/index.hdml");
} else {
    header("Location:/html/index.html");
}
?>
```

Redirecting Users in Perl

Practical Extraction and Reporting Language (Perl) has long been a favorite language of many Webmasters due to its utility and interpretive syntax. Perl can be used from the UNIX shell or implemented as a Web-accessible CGI program. In this subsection, we will provide a Perl program that will redirect users to a page, depending on the browser that they use to request the page.

```
#!/usr/bin/perl
$accept = $ENV{HTTP_ACCEPT};
if ( $accept =~ m%text/vnd.wap.wml%i ) {
```

```
    print "Location:index.wml\n\n";
} elsif ( $accept =~ m%text/x-hdml%i ) {
    print "Location:index.hdml\n\n";
} else {
    print "Location:index.html\n\n";
}
exit;
```

Code for index.html:

```
<html>
<head>
     <title>Congratulations!</title>
</head>
<body>
<h1>Congratulations!</h1>
<p>If you can see this, it means that the redirect script installed
on this server is working correctly!</p>
<p>Your language type is: HTML</p>
</body>
</html>
```

The code of this page is fairly straightforward; you probably don't even need to put it into a browser to know exactly how it will look (Figure 8.6)!

Figure 8.6 Output of index.html

Code for index.wml (also refer to Figure 8.7):

```
<?xml version="1.0"?>
<!DOCTYPE wml PUBLIC
"-//WAPFORUM//DTD WML 1.1//EN"
      "http://www.wapforum.org/DTD/wml_1.1.xml">
<wml>
<card id="congrats" title="Congratulations">
<p>
Congratulations!<br/>
Your redirect script is working!
<br/></p>
<p>Your language type is: WML</p>
</card>
</wml>
```

Figure 8.7 Output for index.wml

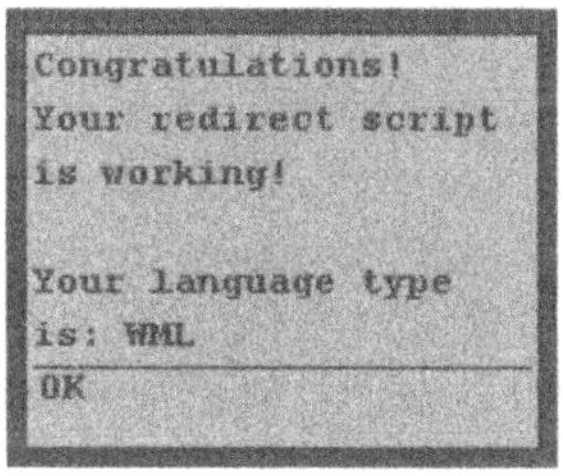

As noted throughout this book, one very important thing to note about WML documents is that they must contain valid markup. Unlike in HTML, there can be no stray or misplaced tags in your document. You'll find this out very quickly when you start to code your own WML on a regular basis!

Code for index.hdml (also refer to Figure 8.8):

```
<hdml version=3.0>
<display>
Congratulations!<br>
Your redirect script is working!<br>
<br>
Your language type is: HDML
```

```
/display>
</hdml>
```

Figure 8.8 Output for index.hdml

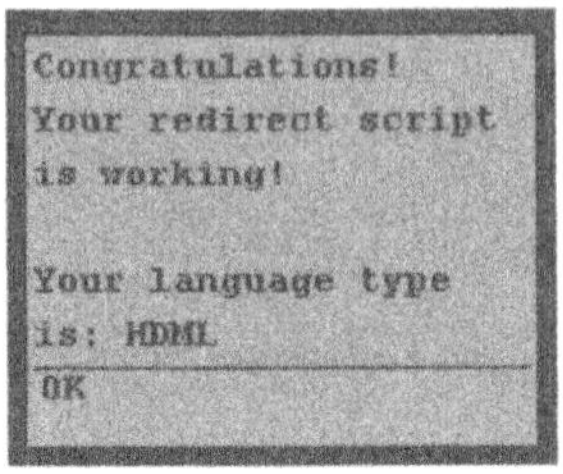

The third markup language that we will use is Handheld Device Markup Language (HDML), which is used by many of the legacy phones available in the United States. It is entirely up to you to decide which languages to support, but we suggest that if you want to reliably deliver content to users in the United States, build at least minimal HDML support into your site.

The first element of this document specifies that it is an HDML document and that it is written in HDML 3.0. All HDML documents require a version statement in the first line. The next element, <display>, is a type of card that can be rendered with HDML. The other two types of cards that can be used are <nodisplay>, which does not display anything to the user, and <choice> cards, which allow the user to pick from a list of options. The HDML that you deliver does not need to be validated against a DTD (like WML), but it is always recommended that you code cleanly.

Support for HDML is waning as support for WML grows, but there are a great many phones still in use that are only capable of rendering HDML. Some WAP gateways do on-the-fly transcoding of HDML to WML and vice-versa, for phones that do not natively support either language. Some gateways will even code HTML to WML, which we will touch on in the next section.

Optimizing Content Distribution

Just as you take care to manage the file system of your existing Web site, you should put some thought into the organization of your wireless site. You may wish to maintain two Web sites running on the same machine, one with the name of www.yoursite.com, and one with the name of wap.yoursite.com. This offers some benefits, as long as your users know where they are supposed to go.

On the other hand, you could install the redirection script covered above to send your users to the correct location, wherever that may be.

Regardless of the technical issues of how you manage your content, it makes sense to take a critical look at your current Web site, and to consider what you want to provide to your wireless users on your wireless Web site. In this section, we will ask the important questions that surround building a wireless Web site, and discuss the issues surrounding the conversion of existing sites to the wireless Internet.

Choosing Mobile Content

One of the first steps of building any site is choosing what content to display on the site. This concept is of particular importance when we consider taking our existing Web site to the wireless Internet. The primary questions that arise in adapting a large existing site to the wireless Internet are the following:

1. What content/services might our users want to access while they are mobile?
2. What limitations are there to the existing mobile interfaces that we must consider?

Most likely, you will not be able (or will not want) to deliver all of your existing site to mobile users. Critically examine your content and applications to ensure that they are useful to the mobile user. For example, if you run a portal site, you may want to deliver wireless news, weather, and email to your mobile users, as this information is of most value to them. Content such as book reviews, in-depth coverage of intricate issues, and user message boards or forums are best left to the desktop browsers.

Remember that mobile users often have a very small window on your site as well as a small-bandwidth connection, and that they will not benefit as greatly from the high-bandwidth components of your site (such as images) or have the ability to scroll through pages and pages of links. Try not to overwhelm the user. Provide a small list of useful actions they can perform on your site, and the wireless portion of your site will be more successful.

Convert or Redevelop?

There are several approaches to adapting existing Web content to the wireless Internet, and the optimal approach depends largely on the nature of the existing content. There are roughly three options for enabling your site for wireless consumption:

1. You could run a program that automatically traverses the HTML document area of your site and produces HTML that is valid. You could then use Extensible Style Language Transformations (XSLT) to transform the valid HTML into a WML version according to an XSL ruleset.
2. Alternately, you might write a 'wrapper' program that will take a request from a wireless browser and act as a proxy to the Internet. This program, upon receiving a request, would retrieve and format the resulting content for a handheld device.
3. You could rebuild a new wireless version of your site, taking into consideration the needs of wireless users and the nature of your content.

So how do you decide what to do? The first option is useful if you need to get your site on the wireless Internet as soon as possible, and if your site is made up primarily of text-based content with minimal formatting. The downside of this option is that you cannot assure that your XSL, which operates on a static rule set, will generate a user-friendly version of your site. If your site is already coded in XML, then you can eliminate the first step of this solution and go straight to XSLT.

The second solution is a good idea if you are familiar with the existing content and can reliably translate it on-the-fly. It certainly helps if the content is generated by a machine rather than by a human being, and is best suited for low-bandwidth applications, such as entertainment calendars, traffic and weather information, and movie listings. Another upside is that you can extract only the elements that your users need, something that they will certainly appreciate. The downside of this solution is that the actual request will be much slower to the user because they are not only waiting for your server to return content, but they are also waiting for your server to retrieve, convert, and deliver content. Depending on the amount of formatting you must do, and the speed of the HTML-based application, this delay may render your application too slow for the mobile user.

We favor the third option because it is most likely to generate a user-friendly wireless site. Many of the existing complaints about the wireless Internet could have been avoided if the early adopters took this strategy rather than the first two options. The problems associated with this option primarily have to do with development time and resources because it is not always economically feasible to start from scratch. Nonetheless, it makes the most sense for you to consider the needs and desires of your users, and build your site around those needs.

NOTE

Google (www.google.com) has developed an intelligent on-the-fly converter that will allow WML browsers to view HTML sites. It works for small, basic, text-based sites, but ultimately fails on sites that contain large amounts of graphic-based navigation elements or form-based content. Using this converter should be enough to convince you that any automated conversion system, no matter how intelligent, fails when compared to a wireless site designed with human usability in mind.

It is certainly possible to convert HTML (even bad HTML) to WML, but is it desirable to do so? Most notably, existing translation mechanisms do not readily allow for the file-size limitations of mobile devices. Furthermore, not all elements of HTML are supported in WML, and any user interface will certainly be sub-optimal unless re-engineered and re-coded by a human being. It is our recommendation that you consider your application from the user's perspective. Ask yourself: would I want to have my content available on a handheld device? Does it provide some utility to my users? Do the benefits outweigh the costs of development? If the answer to any or all of those questions is no, then you should skip to the next chapter!

Delivering Wireless Data

Making data available to mobile users is a key advantage that building a wireless Web site can provide. If we are providing information from a database to users on the WWW, we can make this same data available to users on wireless devices.

If your Web site is database-driven and content is separated from presentation, you should be able to generate an effective wireless Web site fairly painlessly. You will certainly have an easier time building a site from a database of content than by building one from many static pages of HTML that have been hacked together over a long period of time by multiple people with varying skill-levels and coding styles.

In this section, we will cover the coding of a module that will allow you to adapt your existing data application to the wireless Internet. The theories and issues covered here will make sense for any existing Web site that separates content from presentation.

Making Your Applications Accessible

The first step to delivering wireless data is determining what type of device is requesting the content. We have covered the means of detecting devices and redirecting users previously in this chapter, but now we will apply this detection scheme as a means of selecting an interface to your application.

We will cover the basics of building a library that can be accessed from many applications, and return a result that contains the language to be used, and the type of device in order to apply some logic to the presentation of the retrieved data. The routines, regardless of the programming language used, look something like this pseudocode example:

```
IF device_supports_wml AND device_does_not_support_hdml
      $language = "wml"
ELSE IF device_supports_hdml
      $language = "hdml"
ELSE IF device_supports_html
      $language = "html"
ELSE
      $language = "unknown"

IF device_is_phone
      $devicetype = "phone"
ELSE IF device_is_PDA
      $devicetype = "PDA"
ELSE IF device_is_Web_browser
      $devicetype = "Web_browser"
ELSE
      $devicetype = "unknown"
```

Once we have authored this routine and provided a means for it to be called from our applications, we can use it to determine how and in what quantities to display our content. For example, if the request for data came from a mobile telephone, we can assume that our final deck of results should not contain more than 1397 bytes of data. If the same request came from a PDA, we might enable more chunks of the data to be displayed on a given card in the deck (but still minimize the size of the deck because PDA users pay 'per-byte'.) If the request came from a Web browser, we might be able to send back all of the results in one page, with extensive formatting.

The example in Figure 8.9 is provided in Perl, but you should be able to adapt it to the server-side scripting language of your choice.

Figure 8.9 Language and Device Detection in Perl

```
#!/usr/bin/perl
use strict;
my $device    = &detect_device;
my $language  = &detect_language;

#detects language according to HTTP_ACCEPT
sub detect_language {
my $lang;
my $accept = $ENV{HTTP_ACCEPT};
if ( $accept =~ m%text/vnd\.wap\.wml% ) {
$lang = "wml";
} elsif ( $accept  =~ m%text/x-hdml% ) {
$lang = "hdml";
} elsif ( $accept  =~ m%text/x-html% ) {
$lang = "html";
} else {
$lang = "";
}
return $lang;
}

#detects device against known UA list (from device.cgi)
sub detect_device {
my $type;
my $uagent = $ENV{HTTP_USER_AGENT};
open(DB,'<ualist.txt');
while(<DB>) {
```

Continued

Figure 8.9 Continued

```
        my($ua,$dev) = split(/:/,$_);
        if ($uagent eq $ua) {
        $type = $dev;
        }
}
close(DB);
return $type;
}
```

The script in Figure 8.9 provides the basic building blocks to detect both the language that the client can accept and the type of device requesting the content (against a predefined list of user agents and device types). By using the results of these two subroutines, it is possible to alter the presentation of retrieved data depending on the properties of the client.

You could add additional methods to this library to extract the number of softkeys a device has, or to collect device-specific identification strings (such as the subscriber_no displayed in the header for the UP.Browser, or the %deviceid of a Palm VII PDA.) Which environmental variables you choose to examine and how you branch your code is implementation-specific, and it is possible to build WML that works on all devices, but most instances will benefit from some code branching or redirection.

Implementing Wireless Graphics

In general, wireless images will be of lower resolution, color depth, and file size than their WWW counterparts. We will discuss the common file formats for images sent over the wireless Internet, how to maintain accessibility when images may not be available, and some of the more common methods for creating images in the appropriate wireless format.

File Formats

Several different image file formats are supported on mobile devices. Two formats with which any Webmaster will be familiar are GIF and JPEG. A format with which traditional Webmasters may not be familiar is that of the Wireless Bitmap (WBMP), a one-bit depth (two-color) bitmap. Which particular device supports any particular image format is a much harder thing to discern. Some devices support only WBMP images, and others support GIF and JPEG and not WBMP. WML that is transcoded to HDML via a gateway may have all of the images stripped out of it.

Maintaining Accessibility

It is important to maintain accessibility of our site to devices that do not support the technologies that we are using. This applies to images as well. It is absolutely imperative to make use of the ALT attribute of the <IMG> tag when building our site so that users accessing the site with non-image capable browsers can still gain value from the site (after all, we're building it for the users, right?).

Converting Your Images

There are several means for creating images that are viewable by mobile devices. Teraflops (www.teraflops.com/wbmp/) provides an online converter that converts images uploaded via a Web browser. A search for "WBMP" on Tucows (www.tucows.com) will turn up a wide variety of free and/or shareware tools available for download.

Summary

While it may not be possible to magically convert your existing Website in all its glory to a wireless version, it is certainly possible to add wireless capabilities to an existing Website without a complete overhaul.

In this chapter, we have covered the means of adding wireless capabilities at the directory, site, and server level to existing Web server environments for both Apache and Microsoft IIS; and discussed the issues involved with making an existing site available to mobile users.

We have discussed the means of detecting wireless devices and redirecting users to appropriately formatted content, using PHP and Perl, and based on information contained in the environmental variables HTTP_USER_AGENT and HTTP_ACCEPT. We also examined a small library written in Perl that can be used to detect language types and devices in order to branch display code according to the user's browser.

In addition, we discussed the issues surrounding the automated conversion of HTML to WML, and discussed wireless graphics and some tools available for graphics conversion.

Solutions Fast Track

Defining WAP MIME Types

☑ It is important to consider the market for which you are delivering content, and to define the appropriate MIME types for the devices used by your users.

☑ There are several options for defining MIME types under the most common Web servers on the market. MIME types may be defined and Wireless content may be deployed at the directory, site, or server level.

☑ WAP MIME types are defined in the same manner as any other MIME type.

Detecting WAP Devices

☑ WAP devices send the same type of header information to Web servers as desktop browsers do.

☑ HTTP_ACCEPT can be used to detect the language that a given browser can accept.

☑ HTTP_USER_AGENT can be used to differentiate browsers depending on the reported name of the browser.

☑ A combination of HTTP_ACCEPT and HTTP_USER_AGENT can be used to redirect devices to appropriate content, or to profile devices for formatting.

Optimizing Content Distribution

☑ Regardless of the technical issues of how you manage your content, take a critical look at your current Web site and consider what you want to provide to your wireless users.

☑ It is possible to automatically format existing sites, but with dubious results.

☑ WAP sites may be set up with the same flexibility as Web sites.

Delivering Wireless Data

☑ Mobile users are more often in need of data rather than content.

☑ It is important to separate content from presentation for data applications.

☑ Build modules that enable device profiling and accordingly allow for different presentations of dynamic data from the same source.

Implementing Wireless Graphics

☑ Several different formats are supported, including common Web formats for some devices.

☑ Ensure accessibility by using <ALT> tags on all images, and conserve bandwidth by only using graphics when necessary.

☑ Online and desktop converters are available to automatically convert your existing images.

Frequently Asked Questions

The following Frequently Asked Questions, answered by the authors of this book, are designed to both measure your understanding of the concepts presented in this chapter and to assist you with real-life implementation of these concepts. To have your questions about this chapter answered by the author, browse to **www.syngress.com/solutions** and click on the **"Ask the Author"** form.

Q: Will I need to install a WAP gateway to serve out my site?

A: No. You only need to configure your Web server to deliver the appropriate content.

Q: What kind of server-side scripting languages can I use to create wireless content?

A: You can use ASP, PHP, JSP, Perl, Python, Ruby, or any other server-side scripting language to print WML to a browser.

Q: Do I need to branch my WML code for different browsers?

A: Not necessarily. If your code is well designed and valid, it should display on any browser that supports WML. However, there are some differences between browsers that do affect usability. Depending on the nature of your implementation, you may want to branch your code for a better user experience.

Chapter 9

Microsoft Mobile Internet Toolkit

Solutions in this chapter:

- Overview of the .NET Mobile Architecture
- Introduction to ASP.NET
- Developing Mobile Web Forms
- Accessing Data with ADO.NET

☑ Summary

☑ Solutions Fast Track

☑ Frequently Asked Questions

Introduction

In the earlier chapters you have seen the use of the Wireless Markup Language (WML) and WMLScript for creating mobile applications and services. In this chapter, we will take a look at the Microsoft Mobile Internet Toolkit and how it can aid in mobile application development. The Microsoft Mobile Internet Toolkit is a set of mobile framework extensions that have been added to ASP.NET Web Forms. With these extensions, a mobile application developer can create compelling mobile applications without worrying unduly about the limitations of the various target devices. The current situation in mobile application development is that various devices have a very different look and feel, and often developers have to spend huge amounts of time tailoring their applications to run on the target devices. A typical solution is to code the content of your application in XML and use XSLT to transform the content into a target markup language like WML.

Rather than focusing on the user interface issues, the Microsoft Mobile Internet Toolkit provides a set of APIs to let the developer concentrate on the functionality of the application. During runtime, the Microsoft Mobile Internet Toolkit API will automatically detect the kind of device accessing the application and generate the appropriate codes to run on it.

To get the full benefit from this chapter, you should know the basics of Microsoft ASP for developing Web applications.

Overview of the .NET Mobile Architecture

The Mobile Internet Toolkit is built on the Microsoft ASP.NET Web Forms (which we'll discuss in the next section). It is an extension to the ASP.NET model. The toolkit includes a set of Mobile Controls that is executed by the Mobile Internet Controls runtime during the execution phase. The key feature of the runtime is its ability to recognize the different types of devices accessing the forms and to generate dynamically the codes that the device can understand.

The toolkit supports such controls as Calendar, Label, SelectionList, and Textbox. Since the toolkit is an extension of ASP.NET Web Forms, it supports languages like VB .NET, C#, and JScript.NET.

Devices Supported by the Microsoft Mobile Internet Toolkit

According to Microsoft, the Microsoft Mobile Internet Toolkit SDK has been tested with the following devices:

- Mitsubishi T250
- Nokia 7110
- Pocket PC with Microsoft Pocket Internet Explorer version 4.5
- Siemens C-35i

The following additional devices and simulators have had limited testing:

- Ericsson R380
- Microsoft Internet Explorer 5.5
- Microsoft Internet Explorer 6.0
- Mitsubishi D502i
- NEC N502i
- Nokia 6210
- Palm VIIx
- Palm V
- Panasonic P502i
- RIM Blackberry 950
- RIM Blackberry 957
- Samsung 850
- Siemens S-35i
- Sprint Touchpoint phone

System Requirements

To develop mobile applications using the Mobile Internet Toolkit, your system requirements are as follows:

- Microsoft Windows 2000 Server/Advanced Server/Professional SP1
- Internet Information Server
- Microsoft Internet Explorer 6.0
- .NET Framework Beta 2 (including ASP.NET)
- Mobile Internet Toolkit Beta 2

NOTE

Microsoft Internet Explorer 6.0 is installed automatically when you installed the .NET framework SDK.

Starting from Beta 2 of the toolkit, you can now make use of the visual tools in Visual Studio .NET (Beta 2) to develop your mobile application. However, all the code in this chapter has been developed using a text editor.

Obtaining and Installing the Microsoft Mobile Internet Toolkit

The current release of the Microsoft Mobile Internet Toolkit is Beta 2. You can download a copy of the Microsoft Mobile Internet Toolkit Beta 2 from the following URL: http://msdn.microsoft.com/downloads/default.asp?URL=/code/sample.asp?url=/MSDN-FILES/027/001/516/msdncompositedoc.xml.

NOTE

The Beta 1 version of the Microsoft Mobile Internet Toolkit was known as the .NET Mobile Web SDK.

To install the toolkit, simply double-click on the downloaded file and follow the instructions from the installation wizard; start by accepting the licensing agreement. In the Setup Type screen, choose to install the Complete setup to install all the program features, rather than choosing the Custom setup. Click the **Next** button, and when the program completes the installation the wizard will bring you to a final screen that allows you to exit by clicking **Finish**. Once the toolkit is installed, you will find a shortcut called Mobile Internet Toolkit Overview created on your desktop.

NOTE

Before installing the Microsoft Mobile Internet Toolkit, you must first install the .NET framework SDK. The .NET framework SDK can be obtained from http://msdn.microsoft.com/downloads/default.asp?URL=/code/sample.asp?url=/msdn-files/027/000/976/msdncompositedoc.xml.

The toolkit comes with documentation as well as sample code. To use the QuickStart Tutorial provided with the toolkit, you must configure a virtual directory on your Web server to point to the correct directory path. Table 9.1 indicates the virtual directory details.

Table 9.1 Virtual Directory to QuickStart Tutorial

Virtual Directory Name	MobileQuickStart
Directory Path	C:\Program Files\Microsoft.Net\Mobile Internet Toolkit\QuickStart (Please specify the default document as Default.aspx)

If the virtual directory is configured correctly, you will see the screen shown in Figure 9.1 using the URL http://localhost/MobileQuickStart.

Introduction to ASP.NET

Since the Microsoft Mobile Internet Toolkit is based on ASP.NET, it is important for you to have a good understanding of how ASP.NET works and how it is different from ASP. Before we look into the technical details of working with ASP.NET, let's consider a typical situation when writing a Web application with ASP.

As you are probably aware, HTTP is a stateless protocol. Although being stateless has its benefits, such as reducing the resources on the server side, it often poses headaches for Web developers. In the following example, we will illustrate one of the problems with statelessness commonly faced by ASP developers. In this example, we have a form and we need users to fill it in and submit it for processing. Our form may look like Figure 9.2.

Figure 9.1 MobileQuickStart Page

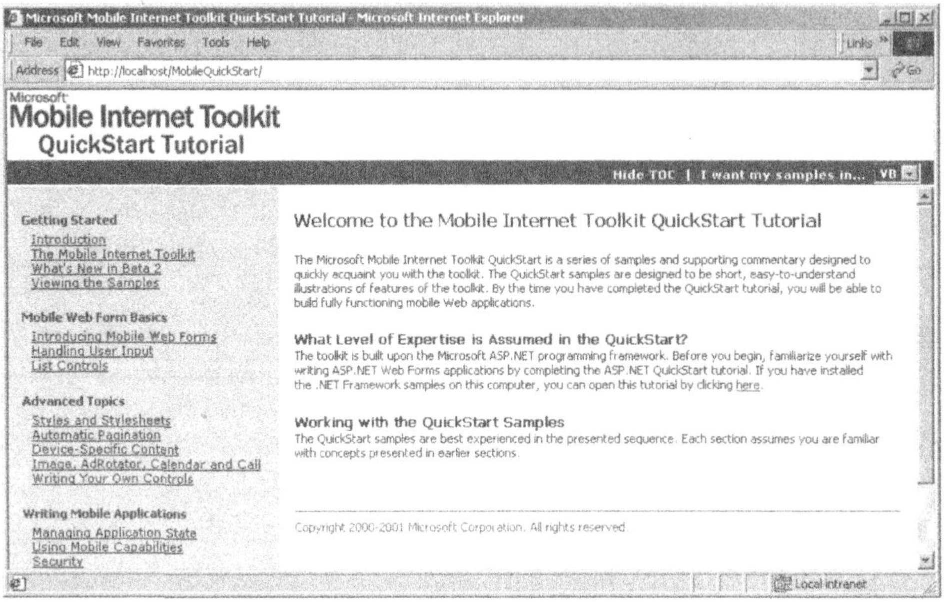

Figure 9.2 Web Application Using ASP

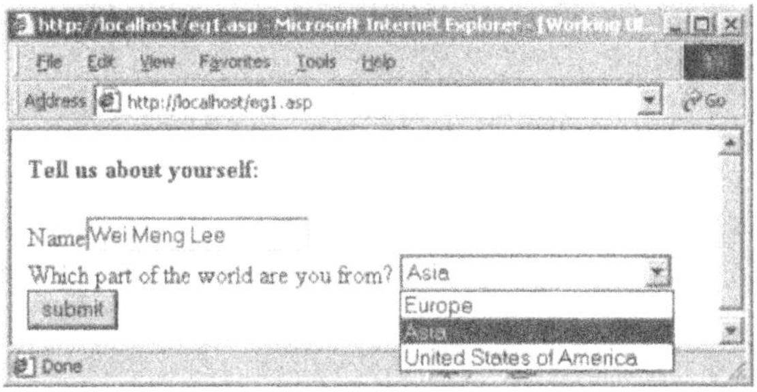

When we click on the **Submit** button, we print a message on the same page, as shown in Figure 9.3.

Notice that the name in the textbox is gone and the item in the selection list has been reset to the first item. Figure 9.4 shows the ASP code for our sample Web application.

Figure 9.3 State Is Lost When the ASP Page Is Submitted

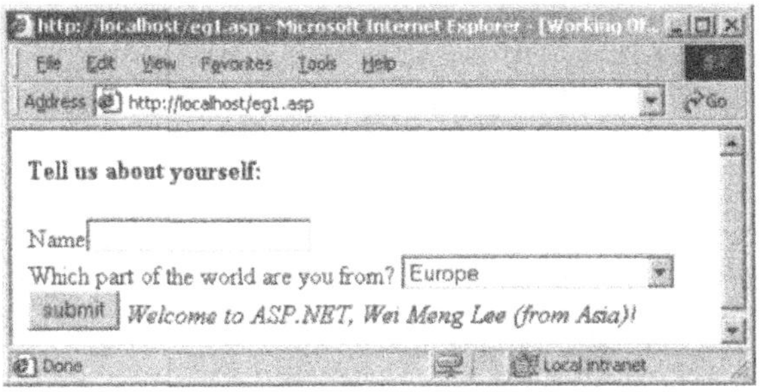

Figure 9.4 Eg1.asp

```
<html>
<b>Tell us about yourself:</b>
<form method="post" action="eg1.asp">
Name<input type="text" name="userName"> <br/>
Which part of the world are you from?
    <select name="partOfWorld">
        <option value="Europe">Europe
        <option value="Asia">Asia
        <option value="United States of America">United States of America
    </select>
<input type="submit" value="submit">
<%
    if Request.Form("userName")<>""then
        Response.Write "<i>Welcome to ASP.NET, " &
Request.Form("userName") & " (from

" & Request.Form("partOfWorld") & ")!</i>"
    end if
%>
</html>
```

To ensure that the name and selection item remains selected after submission, we must modify our codes as shown in Figure 9.5.

Figure 9.5 Eg2.asp

```
<html>
<b>Tell us about yourself:</b>
<form method="post" action="eg2.asp">
Name<input type="text" name="userName" value="<%
=Request.Form("userName") %>"> <br/>
Which part of the world are you from?
   <% itemSelected=Request.Form("partOfWorld") %>
   <select name="partOfWorld">
      <option <%if itemSelected="Europe" then Response.write "SELECTED"
end if %>

value="Europe">Europe
      <option <%if itemSelected="Asia" then Response.write "SELECTED"
end if %> value="Asia">Asia
      <option <%if itemSelected="United States of America" then
Response.write "SELECTED" end if

%> value="United States of America">United States of America
   </select>
<input type="submit" value="submit">
<%
   if Request.Form("userName")<>""then
      Response.Write "<i>Welcome to ASP.NET, " &
Request.Form("userName") & " (from " &

Request.Form("partOfWorld") & ")!</i>"
   end if
%>
</html>
```

And now our Web application will behave as we intend it to, as shown in Figure 9.6.

Figure 9.6 Preserving State in ASP Requires Substantial Effort

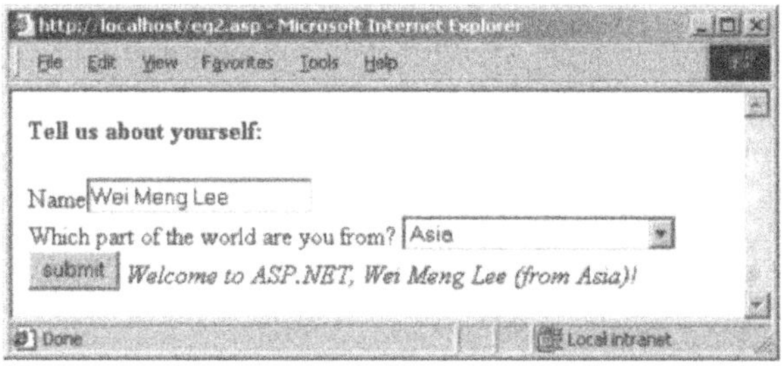

From this simple example, you can see clearly the following problems with the current ASP technology:

- **Mixture of HTML and scripting codes** Our code in Figure 9.4 contains a mixture of display codes (HTML) and application logic (using VBScript). Because building Web applications often involves graphic designers *and* programmers, the current ASP technology does not provide a clean separation of display from content. This often results in bugs and difficulties in post-project maintenance.
- **Extra effort must be spent on maintaining states** In Figure 9.5, look at the amount of code you have to write in order for the server to maintain the state when transiting from page to page. Most of the time spent on maintaining states could be directed toward implementing business logic.

Now let's look at how we can do the same thing using ASP.NET—look at the code shown in Figure 9.7.

NOTE

ASP.NET pages ends with a .aspx extension.

Figure 9.7 Eg1.aspx

```
<script language="vb" runat="server">
   Sub Button1_clicked (sender as Object, e as EventArgs)
```

Continued

Figure 9.7 Continued

```
        message.text = "<i>Welcome to ASP.NET, " & userName.Text &
"(from " & partOfWorld.Value & ") !</i>"
    End Sub
</script>
<html>
<body>
<form runat="server">
    <b>Tell us about yourself : </b><br/>
    Name : <asp:textbox runat="server" id="userName"/><br/>
    Which part of the world are you from?
    <select id="partOfWorld" runat="server">
        <option value="Europe"/>
        <option value="Asia"/>
        <option value="United States of America"/>
    </select>
    <asp:button runat="server" id="button1" onClick="Button1_clicked"
text="Submit"/>
</form>
<asp:label runat="server" id="message"/>
</body>
</html>
```

The ASP.NET code shown in Figure 9.7 deserves our closer attention. We can divide this code into two main parts, *content* and *code*. In the figure, the part related to code rather than content is depicted in in boldface.

The Content Components

Within the user interface (UI) part of Figure 9.7, we can see familiar HTML code. In addition, we also see a few new tags starting with an **asp:** prefix. You might also notice some of the elements have the additional *runat* attribute. Let's define some terms used in ASP.NET. The whole ASP.NET document shown in our example is known as a *Web Form*. A Web Form contains two components: Code and Content. The Content component of a Web Form can contain *Web Form Server controls*. Web Form Server controls contain the following types of controls: *HTML Server control*, *ASP.NET Server control*, *Validation controls*, and *User controls*. The examples in the next section illustrate the first two kinds of controls. (We'll examine the validation controls later in the chapter. User controls are much more complex and won't be addressed here.)

HTML Server Controls

An example of an HTML Server control is as follows:

```
<select id="partOfWorld" runat="server">
```

Notice that HTML Server controls are similar to the normal HTML elements, except that they have the additional *runat* attribute. In ASP.NET, normal HTML elements are converted to HTML Server controls so that they can be programmed on the server. The *id* attribute acts as a unique identifier for the server controls.

NOTE

If you have experience programming Visual Basic, a good way to view ASP.NET programming is to imagine yourself writing VB codes, except that this time your application runs on the Web platform. You can imagine an ASP.NET page as an executable file, producing HTML codes to be sent to the Web browser.

ASP.NET Server Controls

Besides the HTML server controls, ASP.NET provides a different set of server controls known as ASP.NET server controls. You can think of ASP.NET server controls as ActiveX controls in VB. Unlike the HTML Server controls, they do not provide a one-to-one mapping. The following is an example of an ASP.NET Server control:

```
<asp:button runat="server" id="button1" onClick="Button1_clicked"
text="Submit"/>
```

This ASP.NET server control will render itself as an <input> element when viewed using a Web browser. ASP.NET server controls expose properties and events that you can set and service. For example, this ASP.NET server control defines the *onClick* event. When the button is clicked, the *Button1_clicked* subroutine would be serviced (which is covered in the next section).

NOTE

If you are experienced with HTML, think of ASP .NET server controls as another set of tags and elements that you can use to create dynamic Web applications. For example, instead of using the <input> tag for text input, you can also use the <asp:input> element (but with more features!).

The Code Components

The Content component basically concerns itself with display issues. The Code components are the "glue" that binds things up. Our example shows a subroutine defined in the Code section. This subroutine is fired when the user clicks on the **Submit** button. It then displays a welcome message by referencing the controls defined in the Content section.

```
<script language="vb" runat="server">
   Sub Button1_clicked (sender as Object, e as EventArgs)
      message.text = "<i>Welcome to ASP.NET, " & userName.Text &
"(from " & partOfWorld.Value & ") !</i>"
   End Sub
</script>
```

NOTE

Again, the processing model of ASP.NET should be very familiar to VB programmers.

Figure 9.8 shows what our ASP.NET page looks like on the Web browser.

After a page has been submitted, it will retain its state before the submission. To see the HTML codes generated by the ASP.NET runtime, select **View Source** (see Figure 9.9).

Figure 9.8 ASP.NET Preserves the State Automatically

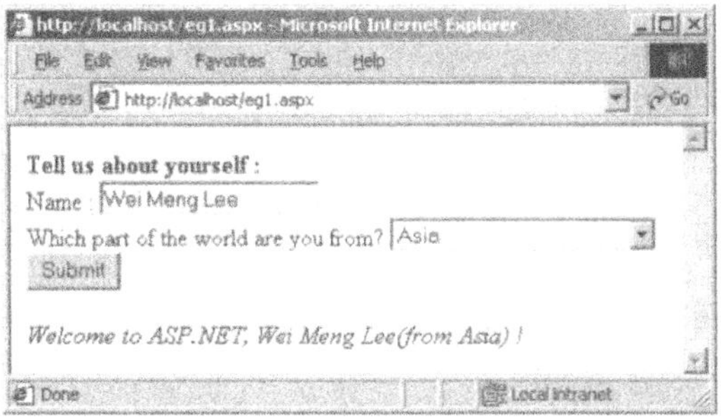

Figure 9.9 Our Example's HTML Output

```
<html>
<body>

<form name="ctrl1" method="post" action="eg1.aspx" id="ctrl1">
<input type="hidden" name="__VIEWSTATE"
value="YTB6OTY0MzM4NTkzX2Ewel9oejV6M3hfYTB6YTB6aHpUZVx4dF88aT5XZWxjb211I
HRvIEFTUC5ORVQsIFdlaSBNZW5nIExlZShmcm9tIEFzaWEpICE8L2k+eF9feF9feHhfeF9fe
A==f77c15df" />

   <b>Tell us about yourself : </b><br/>
   Name : <input name="userName" type="text" value="Wei Meng Lee"
id="userName" /><br/>
   Which part of the world are you from?

   <select name="partOfWorld" id="partOfWorld">
     <option value="Europe">Europe</option>
     <option selected value="Asia">Asia</option>
     <option value="United States of America">United States of
America</option>
</select>

   <input type="submit" name="button1" value="Submit" id="button1" />

</form>
```

Continued

Figure 9.9 Continued

```
<span id="message"><i>Welcome to ASP.NET, Wei Meng Lee(from Asia)
!</i></span>

</body>
</html>
```

What is interesting in this HTML output is the hidden input element, indicated in Figure 9.9 in boldface.

The *__VIEWSTATE* hidden element is the one that performs all the magic. It is responsible for "maintaining" states between pages. The value of this hidden element is used by the ASP.NET runtime to recall the previous state the page was in.

NOTE

The concept of using a hidden element to maintain state is somewhat similar to that of using a browser session, with a sessionid passed as a hidden form value, or of using a cookie.

ASP.NET Architecture

Figure 9.10 illustrates the architecture of ASP.NET. The Web client first interacts with Internet Information Server (IIS). If the Web client is accessing HTML pages, IIS will communicate with the underlying operating system to fetch the HTML pages. If the Web client is accessing an ASP.NET application, the ASP.NET application will first be compiled to produce a .NET runtime class. The .NET runtime class is then compiled and invoked to produce HTML to be sent to the client side.

One important difference between ASP.NET and ASP is that ASP.NET applications are parsed and compiled once and then cached, so that subsequent requests do not go through the same time-consuming steps. This creates a positive impact on the performance of ASP.NET applications.

Figure 9.10 Architecture of ASP.NET

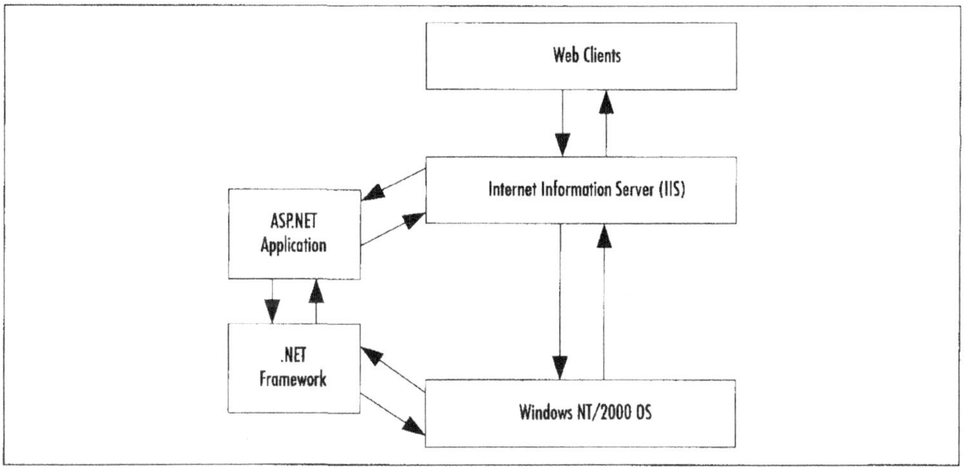

Developing Mobile Web Forms

Now that you have seen how ASP.NET works, it is time to take a look at a very simple Mobile Web Form and the components it contains (Figure 9.11).

Figure 9.11 Welcome.aspx

```
<%@ Page Inherits="System.Web.UI.MobileControls.MobilePage"
Language="VB" %>
<%@ Register TagPrefix="Mobile" Namespace="System.Web.UI.MobileControls"
Assembly="System.Web.Mobile" %>


<Mobile:Form id="FormOne" runat="server">
   <Mobile:Label runat="server">Welcome to the Microsoft Mobile
Internet Toolkit!</Mobile:Label>
</Mobile:Form>
```

Figure 9.12 shows the code from Figure 9.11 displayed in different kinds of browsers: Pocket PC, UP.SDK 4.1, and IE 5.5.

If you have been developing WAP application using WML and ASP, you would be surprised that the same application can be displayed on all these different devices, with no effort on your side for customization. That's the power of the Microsoft Mobile Internet Toolkit SDK.

Figure 9.12 Viewing the Mobile Web Form on the Various Devices

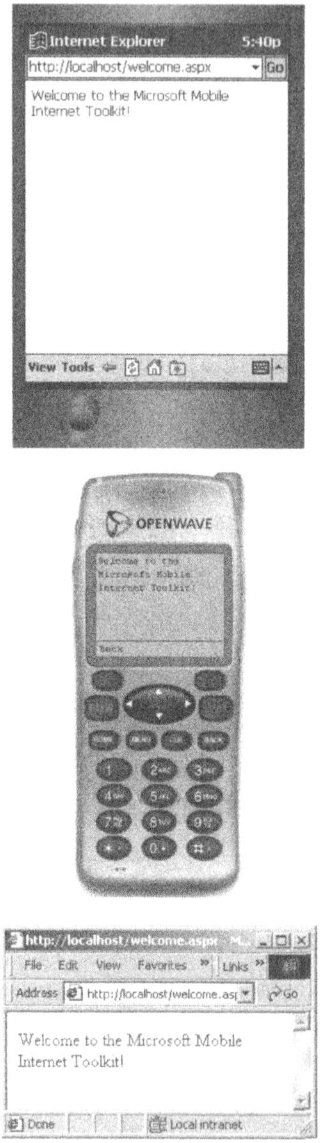

Let's now take a closer look at the Welcome.aspx page. The first few lines of a Mobile Web Form contains the standard header directives:

```
<%@ Page Inherits="System.Web.UI.MobileControls.MobilePage"
Language="VB" %>
<%@ Register TagPrefix="Mobile" Namespace="System.Web.UI.MobileControls"
Assembly="System.Web.Mobile" %>
```

The *@ Page* directive defines page-specific attributes used by the ASP.NET page parser and compiler. The *Inherits* attribute specifies that the page is inherited from the "System.Web.UI.MobileControls.MobilePage" class, which itself is inherited from the ASP.NET Page class. The *Language* attribute specifies the language to be used in the page. For our example, we have used VB.NET. The *@ Register* directive associates aliases with namespaces and class names. In the preceding Mobile Web form, we use the tagprefix of *Mobile* to associate with the System.Web.UI .MobileControls namespace. The assembly in which the namespace you are associating with tagprefix resides is specified in the *assembly* attribute.

Next we have the *<Mobile:Form>* element. This element acts as a container to group controls together logically.

```
<Mobile:Form id="FormOne" runat="server">
```

In our case, we have a *<Mobile:Label>* control, which simply provides a label for text to be displayed.

```
   <Mobile:Label runat="server">Welcome to the Microsoft Mobile
Internet Toolkit!</Mobile:Label>
```

That's all there is to it! As you can see, during runtime when the form is requested, the .NET runtime will automatically detect the type of devices requesting that page and perform a dynamic generation of the target markup languages. In our case, the Pocket PC and IE 5.5 both receive HTML (as shown in Figure 9.13), and the UP.SDK receives WML (as shown in Figure 9.14).

Figure 9.13 HTML Receives by Pocket PC and IE 5.5

```
<html><body><form id="FormOne" name="FormOne" method="post"
action="welcome.aspx?__ufps=631315933684236256">
<input type="hidden" name="__EVENTTARGET" value="">
<input type="hidden" name="__EVENTARGUMENT" value="">
<script language=javascript><!-
function __doPostBack(target, argument){
  var theform = document.FormOne
  theform.__EVENTTARGET.value = target
```

Continued

Figure 9.13 Continued

```
  theform.__EVENTARGUMENT.value = argument
  theform.submit()
}
// ->
</script>
<span>Welcome to the Microsoft Mobile Internet Toolkit!</span><br>
</form></body></html>
```

Figure 9.14 WML Received by the UP.SDK 4.1

```
<?xml version='1.0'?>
<!DOCTYPE wml PUBLIC '-//WAPFORUM//DTD WML 1.1//EN'
'http://www.wapforum.org/DTD/wml_1.1.xml'>
<wml>
   <head>
      <meta http-equiv="Cache-Control" content="max-age=0" />
   </head>
   <card id="FormOne">
      <p>Welcome to the Microsoft Mobile Internet Toolkit!<br/>
      </p>
   </card>
</wml>
```

Debugging...

Known Issues with the Pocket PC Emulator

For readers using the Microsoft Embedded Visual Toolkit 3.0, take note that the Pocket PC emulator by default does not support JScript. This feature will pose a problem for mobile applications that make use of JScript for page navigations. To enable JScript support, you should download the JScript.dll component from Microsoft's Web site.

Continued

Once the component is downloaded, copy the component into the directory that contains the Embedded Visual Toolkit 3.0 (for example, C:\Windows CE Tools\wce300\MS Pocket PC\emulation\palm300\windows).

After copying the component, open a command window and switch into the directory where the component is copied and execute the following command:

```
C:\Windows CE Tools\wce300\MS Pocket PC\emulation\palm300\
windows>regsvrce jscript.dll
```

If the component is installed correctly, you should see the Pocket PC emulator and the window shown in Figure 9.15.

Figure 9.15 Registering the jscript.dll

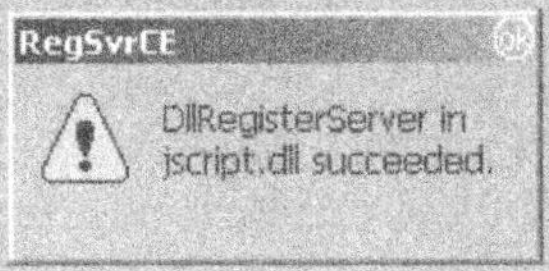

NOTE

For the remainder of this chapter we will illustrate examples using the Pocket PC emulator and the UP.SDK 4.1.

Using Multiple Forms in a Single Page

In ASP.NET pages, there can be only a single form; however, you can have multiple mobile forms in a Mobile Web form. In this section, we will discuss having multiple forms in a page and how to link them up. Consider the example in Figure 9.16.

Figure 9.16 Multiple_forms.aspx

```
<%@ Page Inherits="System.Web.UI.MobileControls.MobilePage"
Language="VB" %>
<%@ Register TagPrefix="Mobile" Namespace="System.Web.UI.MobileControls"
Assembly="System.Web.Mobile" %>
```

Continued

Figure 9.16 Continued

```
<Mobile:Form id="FormOne" runat="server">
    <Mobile:Label runat="server">This is the first form</Mobile:Label>
    <Mobile:Link runat="server" navigateURL="#FormTwo">Goto Form
Two</Mobile:Link>
</Mobile:Form>

<Mobile:Form id="FormTwo" runat="server">
    <Mobile:Label runat="server">This is the second form</Mobile:Label>
</Mobile:Form>
```

In Figure 9.16, we have two forms in a page. To link the two forms, use the *<Mobile:Link>* control. The *navigateURL* attribute contains the ID of the form to link to. Note that the ID is preceded by a number character (#).

Linking to Forms on Other Pages

Even though you may have multiple forms on a page, it is common to have forms located in different pages. With Mobile Web Forms, linking to forms on another page is not so straightforward. Consider the two pages in Figures 9.17 and 9.18.

Figure 9.17 Page1.aspx

```
<%@ Page Inherits="System.Web.UI.MobileControls.MobilePage"
Language="VB" %>
<%@ Register TagPrefix="Mobile" Namespace="System.Web.UI.MobileControls"
Assembly="System.Web.Mobile" %>

<Mobile:Form id="FormOne" runat="server">
    <Mobile:Label runat="server">This is the first form on Page
1</Mobile:Label>
    <Mobile:Link runat="server" navigateURL="Page2.aspx">Goto Form
two</Mobile:Link>
</Mobile:Form>
```

Figure 9.18 Page2.aspx

```
<%@ Page Inherits="System.Web.UI.MobileControls.MobilePage"
Language="VB" %>
<%@ Register TagPrefix="Mobile" Namespace="System.Web.UI.MobileControls"
Assembly="System.Web.Mobile" %>

<Mobile:Form id="FormTwo" runat="server">
   <Mobile:Label runat="server">This is the second form on Page
2</Mobile:Label>
</Mobile:Form>

<Mobile:Form id="FormThree" runat="server">
   <Mobile:Label runat="server">This is the third form on Page
2</Mobile:Label>
</Mobile:Form>
```

The form in the first page (Page1.aspx, Figure 9.17) links to the second page (Page2.aspx, Figure 9.18) by specifying the filename in the *navigateURL* attribute:

```
   <Mobile:Link runat="server" navigateURL="Page2.aspx">Goto Form
two</Mobile:Link>
```

This will link to the FormTwo on Page2.aspx, as shown in Figure 9.19.

Figure 9.19 Linking to Forms on Other Pages

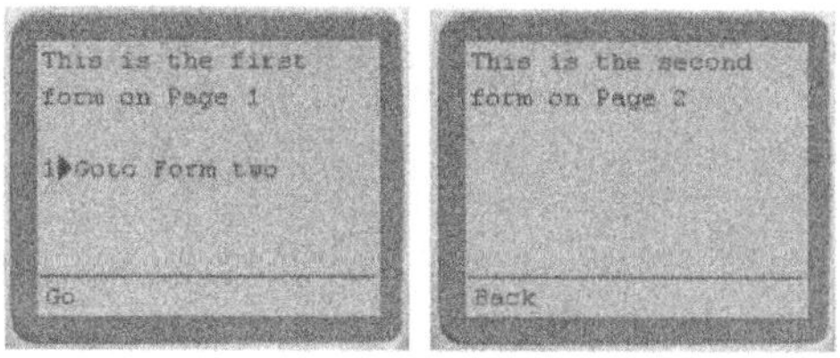

However, if we want to link to FormThree in Page2.aspx, we have a problem. Readers who are familiar with WML might recall using the number character (#) to link directly to a card in a deck. So we might have something like the following:

```
   <Mobile:Link runat="server" navigateURL="Page2.aspx#FormThree">Goto
Form two
```

```
</Mobile:Link>
```

However, this is not going to work! It actually turns out to be more involved than just using the #character. Here is the solution:

```
<Mobile:Link runat="server"
navigateURL="Page2.aspx?Form=FormThree">Goto Form three</Mobile:Link>
```

We have added an additional parameter called *Form* and set it to a value of FormThree. In Page2.aspx, we then added this snippet ofVB code:

```
<script runat="server" language="vb">
    Sub Page_Load(sender as Object, e as System.EventArgs)
        Dim formName = Request.QueryString("Form")
        if formName=FormThree.ID then
            ActiveForm = FormThree
        end if
    End Sub
</script>
```

FormThree is now loaded directly; see Figure 9.20.

Figure 9.20 Jumping Directly to a Form in Another Page

Dissecting Code

Let's take a more detailed look at the code to see how it works:

```
    Sub Page_Load(sender as Object, e as System.EventArgs)
        Dim formName = Request.QueryString("Form")
        if formName=FormThree.ID then
            ActiveForm = FormThree
        end if
    End Sub
```

When the page is first loaded, the *Page_Load* event is first triggered. As the URL contains the parameter *Form*, we can retrieve the value of it using the *Request.QueryString* collection. We then verify that the value is actually the ID of Form three. If it is, we then set the current active form to be Form three using the *ActiveForm* property. The *ActiveForm* property sets and returns the page currently active.

User Inputs

Now that we have looked at linking forms, let's turn our attention to user inputs. The Microsoft Mobile Internet Toolkit supports the following user input controls, with their HTML and WML counterparts shown in Table 9.2:

- TextBox
- Command
- List

Table 9.2 User Input Controls

Input Controls in Mobile Internet Toolkit	Equivalent Tags in HTML	Equivalent Tags in WML
TextBox	<input>	<input>
Command	<input>	<do>
List	<a>	<select><option>

Text and Password Input

To input text into a Mobile Web Form, use the *<Mobile:TextBox>* control provided, as illustrated in Figure 9.21.

Figure 9.21 Password.aspx

```
<%@ Page Inherits="System.Web.UI.MobileControls.MobilePage"
Language="VB" %>
<%@ Register TagPrefix="Mobile" Namespace="System.Web.UI.MobileControls"
Assembly="System.Web.Mobile" %>

   <script runat="server" language="vb">
```

Continued

Figure 9.21 Continued

```
        Sub ComparePassword(sender as Object, e as EventArgs)
            if Password1.Text.Length <8 then
                message.Text = "Password must have at least 8 characters"
                Exit sub
            end if

            if Password1.Text <> Password2.Text then
                message.Text = "Your passwords do not match."
            else
                welcomeMessage.Text += UserName.Text
                ActiveForm = Welcome
            end if
        End sub
    </script>

<Mobile:Form runat="server" id="RegisterForm">
     <Mobile:Label runat="server">Select a user name?</Mobile:Label>
     <Mobile:TextBox runat="server" id="UserName" />
     <Mobile:Label runat="server">Password?</Mobile:Label>
     <Mobile:TextBox password="true" runat="server" id="Password1" />
     <Mobile:Label runat="server">Confirm Password</Mobile:Label>
     <Mobile:TextBox password="true" runat="server" id="Password2" />
     <Mobile:Command runat="server"
onClick="ComparePassword">Register</Mobile:Command>
     <Mobile:Label runat="server" id="message"/>
</Mobile:Form>

<Mobile:Form runat="server" id="Welcome">
     <Mobile:Label id="welcomeMessage" runat="server">Welcome,
</Mobile:Label>
</Mobile:Form>
```

This page contains two forms, one for allowing the user to input his or her username and passwords, and one for displaying a message.

The output from Figure 9.21 displayed on the Pocket PC and the UP.SDK is shown in Figure 9.22 and Figure 9.23, respectively.

Figure 9.22 User Inputs on Pocket PC

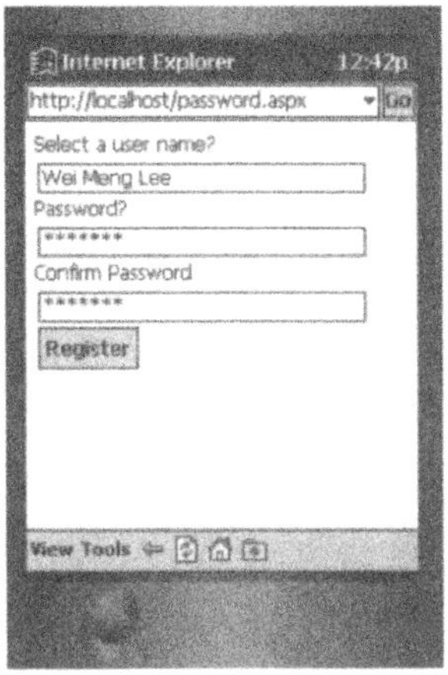

Figure 9.23 User Inputs on UP Emulator

The *<Mobile:TextBox>* control allows text input:

```
<Mobile:TextBox runat="server" id="UserName" />
```

To mask the text input (as in the case of entering passwords), specify the *password* attribute as **"true"**.

```
<Mobile:TextBox password="true" runat="server" id="Password1" />
```

We also saw an additional control, *<Mobile:Command>*. The *<Mobile: Command>* control displays a command button so that an action can be performed.

```
    <Mobile:Command runat="server"
onClick="ComparePassword">Register</Mobile:Command>
```

The *onClick* attribute indicates the subroutine to call when the user clicks on it. In this case, the subroutine to be invoked is *ComparePassword.*

```
Sub ComparePassword(sender as Object, e as EventArgs)
    if Password1.Text.Length <8 then
        message.Text = "Password must have at least 8 characters"
        Exit sub
    end if

    if Password1.Text <> Password2.Text then
        message.Text = "Your passwords do not match."
    else
        welcomeMessage.Text += UserName.Text
        ActiveForm = Welcome
    end if
End sub
```

Within the subroutine, you can simply reference the controls using their IDs. For example, if you want to check for the length of the password that the user has entered, you can simply reference the control using:

```
Password1.Text.Length
```

If the length of the password is less than eight, we set the *Text* property of the *Label* control named **message** to contain the error message:

```
message.Text = "Password must have at least 8 characters"
```

We also check to see if the two passwords entered are the same. If they are, we print a welcome message on the second form:

```
welcomeMessage.Text += UserName.Text
```

The second form is invoked by using the *ActiveForm* property:

```
ActiveForm = Welcome
```

List Selection

Another form of user input is via a selection list. Consider the example in Figure 9.24.

Figure 9.24 Lists.aspx

```
<%@ Page Inherits="System.Web.UI.MobileControls.MobilePage"
Language="VB" %>
<%@ Register TagPrefix="Mobile" Namespace="System.Web.UI.MobileControls"
Assembly="System.Web.Mobile" %>

<Mobile:Form runat="server">
   <Mobile:Label runat="server">Membership Types</Mobile:Label>
   <Mobile:List runat="server" id="Membership">
      <Item value="STU" text="Students"/>
      <Item value="PRO" text="Professionals"/>
      <Item value="LIB" text="Libraries"/>
   </Mobile:List>
</Mobile:Form>
```

The *<Mobile:List>* control provides the ability to display lists of items either as a static list or interactive selection. The page in Figure 9.24 causes the screens on the Pocket PC and the UP.SDK (see Figure 9.25 and Figure 9.26, respectively) to be displayed.

Figure 9.25 Viewing the List on the Pocket PC

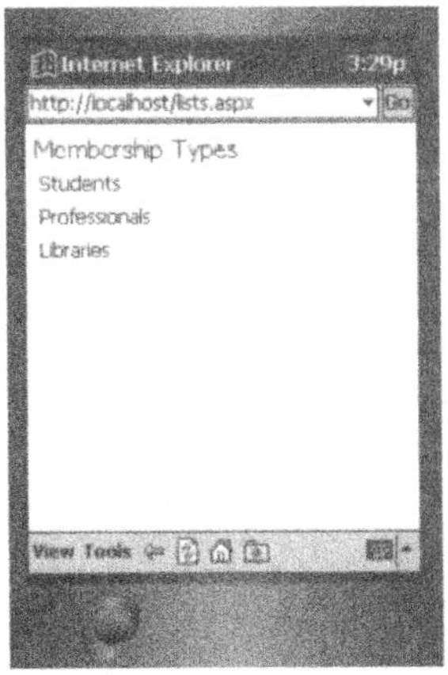

Figure 9.26 Viewing the List on the UP.SDK

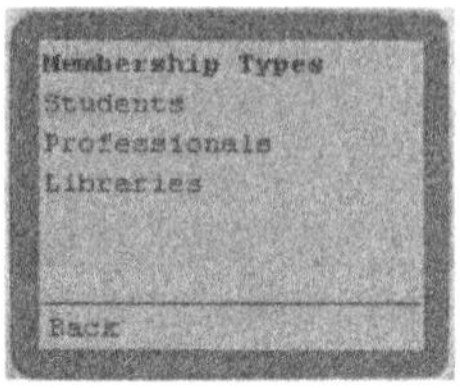

Selecting from a List

A static list is not very exciting, not to mention not very useful. A list is useful only if the user can choose from it. In the example in Figure 9.27, we have modified the previous program to make the list item selectable.

Figure 9.27 Selectlists.aspx

```
<%@ Page Inherits="System.Web.UI.MobileControls.MobilePage"
Language="VB" %>
<%@ Register TagPrefix="Mobile" Namespace="System.Web.UI.MobileControls"
Assembly="System.Web.Mobile" %>

<script runat="server" language="vb">
   Sub Select_Item(sender as Object, e as ListCommandEventArgs)
      Dim Fees as integer
      Dim MembershipType as String = e.ListItem.Value
      Select Case MembershipType
         Case "STU"
                  Fees = 38
         Case "PRO"
                  Fees = 95
         Case "LIB"
                  Fees = 1995
      End Select
      FeesPayable.Text = "The fees payable for " & e.ListItem.Text & "
is $" & Fees
      ActiveForm = FormTwo
   End Sub
```

Continued

Figure 9.27 Continued

```
</script>

<Mobile:Form runat="server" id="FormOne">
   <Mobile:Label runat="server">Membership Types</Mobile:Label>
   <Mobile:List runat="server" id="Membership"
OnItemCommand="Select_Item">
      <Item value="STU" text="Students"/>
      <Item value="PRO" text="Professionals"/>
      <Item value="LIB" text="Libraries"/>
   </Mobile:List>
</Mobile:Form>

<Mobile:Form runat="server" id="FormTwo">
   <Mobile:Label runat="server" id="FeesPayable" />
</Mobile:Form>
```

Note that we have added another attribute, *OnItemCommand*, to the *<Mobile:List>* control. This attribute contains the name of the subroutine to be invoked when the list item is selected (see Figure 9.28).

Figure 9.28 List Items Are Selectable

```
   Sub Select_Item(sender as Object, e as ListCommandEventArgs)
      Dim Fees as integer
      Dim MembershipType as String = e.ListItem.Value
      Select Case MembershipType
         Case "STU"
                     Fees = 38
         Case "PRO"
```

```
                        Fees = 95
                Case "LIB"
                        Fees = 1995
            End Select
            FeesPayable.Text = "The fees payable for " & e.ListItem.Text & "
is $" & Fees
            ActiveForm = FormTwo
        End Sub
```

Within the subroutine, we use a Select-Case statement to find the fees payable; the results are shown in Figure 9.29.

Figure 9.29 Displaying the List Item Selected

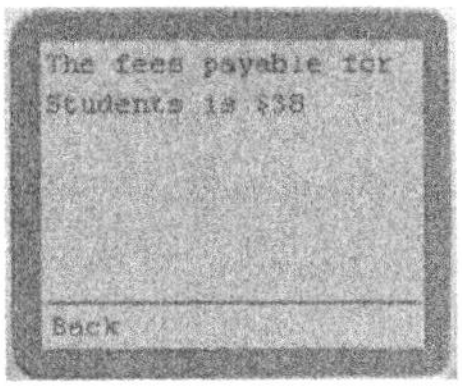

Data Binding List Items

A list is much more useful if you can dynamically bind it to a list of items. The code in Figure 9.30 illustrates how you can bind a list of items using the **ArrayList** class in VB.NET.

Figure 9.30 Databind.aspx

```
<%@ Page Inherits="System.Web.UI.MobileControls.MobilePage"
Language="VB" %>
<%@ Register TagPrefix="Mobile" Namespace="System.Web.UI.MobileControls"
Assembly="System.Web.Mobile" %>

<script runat="server" language="vb">

    Sub Menu_Item(sender as Object, e as ListCommandEventArgs)
        message.Text = "Fees for " & e.ListItem.Text & " membership is
$" & e.ListItem.Value
        ActiveForm = FormTwo
```

Continued

Figure 9.30 Continued

```
End Sub

Private Class Member
  Dim mType as String
  Dim mFees as Single

  Public Sub New(t as String, f as Single)
     mType = t
     mFees = f
  End Sub

  Public Property Type
     Get
        Type = mType
     End Get
     Set
        mType = Value
     end Set
  End Property

  Public Property Fees
     Get
        Fees = mFees
     End Get
     Set
        mFees = Value
     end Set
  End Property
End Class

Sub Page_Load (send as Object, e as EventArgs)
   if not (IsPostBack) then
      Dim array as new ArrayList()
```

Continued

Figure 9.30 Continued

```
          array.Add(new Member("Students", 38))
          array.Add(new Member("Professionals", 95))
          array.Add(new Member("Libraries", 1995))

          Menu.DataSource = array
          Menu.DataBind()
       end if
   End Sub

</script>

<Mobile:Form runat="server" id="FormOne">
   <Mobile:Label runat="server" id="test">Membership
Types</Mobile:Label>
   <Mobile:List runat="server" id="Menu" DataTextField="Type"
DataValueField="Fees" onItemCommand="Menu_Item"/>
</Mobile:Form>

<Mobile:Form runat="server" id="FormTwo">
   <Mobile:Label runat="server" id="message"/>
   <Mobile:Link runat="server"
navigateURL="#FormOne">Back</Mobile:Link>
</Mobile:Form>
```

When the page is loaded, the result is the screen shown in Figure 9.31.

Figure 9.31 Data Binding a List

Dissecting the Codes

We first create an array (using the **ArrayList** class) when the page is loaded. An **ArrayList** class is a single dimensional array that can grow dynamically when elements are added to it.

```
Sub Page_Load (send as Object, e as EventArgs)
    if not (IsPostBack) then
        Dim array as new ArrayList()
        array.Add(new Member("Students", 38))
        array.Add(new Member("Professionals", 95))
        array.Add(new Member("Libraries", 1995))
```

In our case, we have added three **Member** objects to the array. Once the objects are added to the array, we bind the array to the list:

```
        Menu.DataSource = array
        Menu.DataBind()
```

You may have noticed that we have this line:

```
    if not (IsPostBack) then
```

The *IsPostBack* property contains a Boolean value that indicates whether the page is loaded in response to the client's postback, or if the page is loaded for the first time. The *IsPostBack* property will be true if the user clicks on the **Back** link to return to the main page. We want to make sure that the array is not recreated when the user posts back the page (though it is harmless in this case to recreate the array).

NOTE

The .NET framework automatically sets the IsPostBack property. There is no need for the programmer to set it.

The *<Mobile:List>* control also contains two additional attributes—*DataTextField* and *DataValueField.*

```
<Mobile:List runat="server" id="Menu" DataTextField="Type"
DataValueField="Fees" onItemCommand="Menu_Item"/>
```

The *DataTextField* attribute binds the *Type* property of the **Member** class to the List item's *Text* property. The *DataValueField* attribute binds the *Value* property of the **Member** class to the List item's *Value* property. This is evident from the following line:

```
        message.Text = "Fees for " & e.ListItem.Text & " membership is
$" & e.ListItem.Value
```

Events

Mobile controls (like any other ASP.NET server controls) respond to events. You have seen the various events associated with the controls shown in the earlier examples, for example the following:

```
      <Mobile:Command runat="server"
onClick="ComparePassword">Register</Mobile:Command>
```

In this example, the *onClick* attribute represents the *onClick* event. The *ComparePassword* subroutine is invoked when the command button is clicked. In this case, the event is related to the control. Page-level events are also available. Look at this next line as an example:

```
    Sub Page_Load(sender as Object, e as System.EventArgs)
```

In this case, the event (*Page_Load*) is fired when the page is loaded. Form-level events are also possible using the *OnActivate* attribute of the *<Mobile:Form>* control. To see the sequence in which these two events are fired, consider Figure 9.32.

Figure 9.32 OnActivate.aspx

```
<%@ Page Inherits="System.Web.UI.MobileControls.MobilePage"
Language="VB" %>
<%@ Register TagPrefix="Mobile" Namespace="System.Web.UI.MobileControls"
Assembly="System.Web.Mobile" %>

<script runat="server" language="vb">
    Sub Page_Load(sender as Object, e as System.EventArgs)
        message.Text += "Page Loaded. "
    End Sub

    Sub Form_Activate(sender as Object, e as EventArgs)
```

Continued

Figure 9.32 Continued

```
        message.Text += "Form Activated. "
    End Sub
</script>

<Mobile:Form id="FormOne" runat="server" onActivate="Form_Activate">
    <Mobile:Label runat="server" id="message"/>
</Mobile:Form>
```

When the page in Figure 9.32 is loaded, the screen shown in Figure 9.33 is displayed.

Figure 9.33 Demonstrating the Sequence of Events

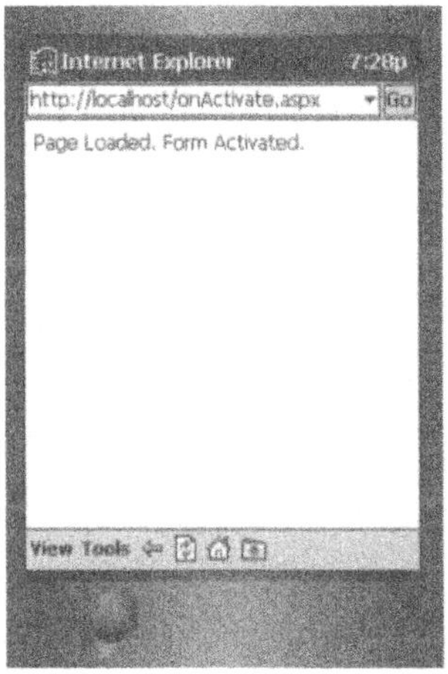

It thus can be seen that the *Page_Load* event is fired first, followed by the *OnActivate* event of the *<Mobile:Form>* control.

Displaying Images

To display images, you can use the *<Mobile:Image>* control. Because various mobile devices display images of differing format, it is important to send the correct image type to the right device. To solve this problem, you can use the *<DeviceSpecific>* control as shown in Figure 9.34.

Figure 9.34 Image.aspx

```
<%@ Page Inherits="System.Web.UI.MobileControls.MobilePage"
Language="VB" %>
<%@ Register TagPrefix="Mobile" Namespace="System.Web.UI.MobileControls"
Assembly="System.Web.Mobile" %>

<Mobile:Form runat="server">
   <Mobile:Label>Photo of myself</Mobile:Label>
   <Mobile:Image runat=server alternateText="[My Photo here]">
    <DeviceSpecific>
      <Choice Filter="isHTML32" ImageURL="myself.bmp" />
      <Choice Filter="isWML11"  ImageURL="myself.wbmp" />
    </DeviceSpecific>
   </Mobile:Image>
</Mobile:Form>
```

Within the *<DeviceSpecific>* control, you have the *<Choice>* elements. In the preceding program, each choice element contains two attributes—*Filter* and *ImageURL*. So in this case, if the user were using a Web browser, the BMP file would be displayed, as shown in Figure 9.35.

Figure 9.35 Displaying the BMP File in a Web Browser

On the UP.SDK, the WBMP file would be selected, as shown in Figure 9.36.

Figure 9.36 Displaying the WBMP File in a WAP Browser

The *<Choice>* elements are evaluated according to the order in which they appear in the *<DeviceSpecific>* control. If none of the *<Choice>* elements evaluates true, the string "[My Photo here]" would be displayed. The *Filter* attribute contains values that are matched from the *<deviceFilters>* element in the web.config configuration file (see Figure 9.37).

The web.config file contains the various device filters. Figure 9.37 shows a portion of the web.config file. A device may match several *<filter>*s. For example, a Web browser satisfies the *isHTML32* and the *prefersGif* filter. The *compare* attribute of the *<filter>* element specifies the capability evaluated by the comparison evaluator and the *argument* attribute specifies the argument against which the capability should be compared.

To illustrate using the preceding example, a WAP device will match the *isWML11* filter, which will in turn match the second *<Choice>* element:

```
<Choice Filter="isHTML32" ImageURL="myself.bmp" />
<Choice Filter="isWML11"  ImageURL="myself.wbmp" />
```

Figure 9.37 Web.config

```
<deviceFilters>
   <!— Markup Languages —>
   <filter name="isHTML32" compare="preferredRenderingType"
                              argument="html32" />
   <filter name="isWML11" compare="preferredRenderingType"
                              argument="wml11" />
   <filter name="isCHTML10" compare="preferredRenderingType"
                              argument="chtml10" />
   <!— Device Browsers —>
   <filter name="isGoAmerica" compare="browser"
```

Continued

Figure 9.37 Continued

```
                                argument="Go.Web" />
    <filter name="isMME" compare="browser"
                                argument="Microsoft Mobile Explorer" />
    <filter name="isMyPalm" compare="browser"
                                argument="MyPalm" />
    <filter name="isPocketIE" compare="browser"
                                argument="Pocket IE" />
    <filter name="isUP3x" compare="type"
                                argument="Phone.com 3.x Browser" />
    <filter name="isUP4x" compare="type"
                                argument="Phone.com 4.x Browser" />
    <!— Specific Devices —>
    <filter name="isEricssonR380" compare="type"
                                argument="Ericsson R380" />
    <filter name="isNokia7110" compare="type"
                                argument="Nokia 7110" />
    <!— Device Capabilities —>
    <filter name="prefersGIF" compare="preferredImageMIME"
                                argument="image/gif" />
    <filter name="prefersWBMP" compare="preferredImageMIME"
                                argument="image/vnd.wap.wbmp" />
    <filter name="supportsColor" compare="isColor"
                                argument="true" />
    <filter name="supportsCookies" compare="cookies"
                                argument="true" />
    <filter name="supportsJavaScript" compare="javascript"
                                argument="true" />
    <filter name="supportsVoiceCalls" compare="canInitiateVoiceCall"
                                argument="true" />
</deviceFilters>
```

Validation Controls

There are quite a few validation controls available in the Microsoft Mobile Internet Toolkit SDK:

- **CompareValidator** Compares two controls using a specified operator.
- **CustomValidator** Allows customized validation of controls.
- **RangeValidator** Validates the value of a control to ensure that it falls within a specified range.
- **RegularExpressionValidator** Validates the value of a control by specifying a regular expression.
- **RequiredFieldValidator** Ensures that a field is supplied a value.
- **ValidationSummary** Displays the summary of all errors that occurred during the rendering of a form.

To see how they work, let's consider the example shown in Figure 9.38.

Figure 9.38 Validation.aspx

```
<%@ Page Inherits="System.Web.UI.MobileControls.MobilePage"
Language="VB" %>
<%@ Register TagPrefix="Mobile" Namespace="System.Web.UI.MobileControls"
Assembly="System.Web.Mobile" %>

<script language="vb" runat=server>
   Sub Submit_OnClick(sender as Object, e as EventArgs)
      if (Page.IsValid) then
         ActiveForm = Form2
         Result.Text = "The month you have entered was " & month.Text
      end if
   End sub
</script>

<Mobile:Form id="Form1" runat=server>
    <Mobile:RangeValidator runat=server
       ControlToValidate="month"
       Type="Integer"
```

Continued

Figure 9.38 Continued

```
        MaximumValue="12"
        MinimumVaLue="1">
        The month is not correct. Please try again.
    </Mobile:RangeValidator>
    <Mobile:Label runat=server>Please enter your birth
month</Mobile:Label>
    <Mobile:TextBox id="month" Numeric="true" runat=server/>
    <Mobile:Command OnClick="Submit_OnClick"
runat=server>Submit</Mobile:Command>
</Mobile:Form>

<Mobile:Form id="Form2" runat=server>
    <Mobile:Label id="Result" runat=server/>
    <Mobile:Link Text="Back" navigateURL="#Form1" runat=server/>
</Mobile:Form>
```

In this example, we use the *<Mobile:RangeValidator>* control to validate the range of a number.

```
<Mobile:RangeValidator runat=server
    ControlToValidate="month"
    Type="Integer"
    MaximumValue="12"
    MinimumVaLue="1">
    The month is not correct. Please try again.
</Mobile:RangeValidator>
```

Once the number is entered and the button is clicked, the *Submit_OnClick()* subroutine is invoked. The *IsValid* property will validate the range of the number entered. If the validation fails, the message "The month is not correct. Please try again" is displayed; otherwise Form2 will be loaded.

```
Sub Submit_OnClick(sender as Object, e as EventArgs)
    if (Page.IsValid) then
        ActiveForm = Form2
        Result.Text = "The month you have entered was " & month.Text
```

```
    end if
End sub
```

Figure 9.39 and Figure 9.40 show the output as displayed by the Pocket PC emulator and the UP.SDK, respectively.

Figure 9.39 Using the Validator Controls on the Pocket PC

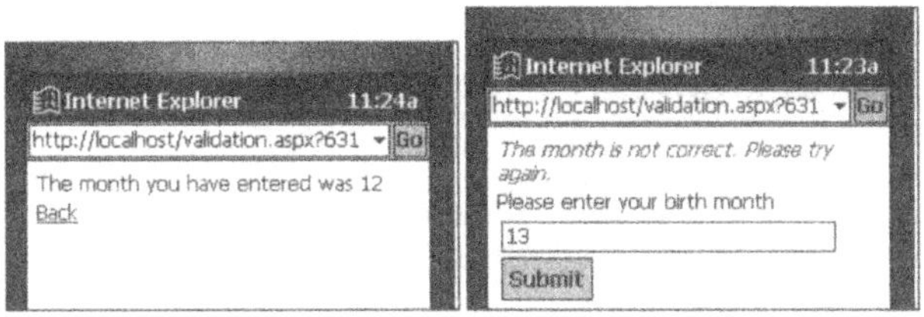

Figure 9.40 Using the Validator Controls on the UP.SDK

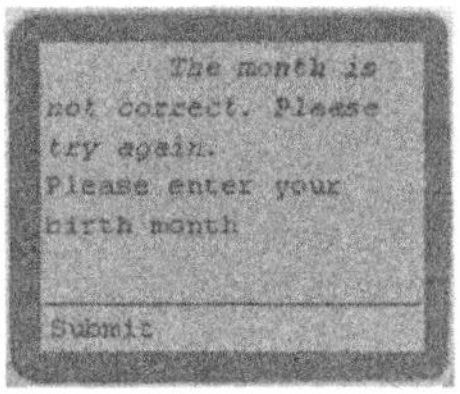

Paginations

In an earlier section we saw the use of the *<Mobile:List>* control. It is possible that the list of items within the control might be long. Anyone who has written a WAP application can attest to the importance of keeping the list short, at least per screen. A common technique is to display the list in multiple pages, and as such this technique is commonly known as *records paging*. One of the great features of the Mobile API is its auto-paging capability. Consider the example shown in Figure 9.41.

Figure 9.41 Paginate.aspx

```
<%@ Page Inherits="System.Web.UI.MobileControls.MobilePage"
Language="VB" %>
<%@ Register TagPrefix="Mobile" Namespace="System.Web.UI.MobileControls"
Assembly="System.Web.Mobile" %>
```

Continued

Figure 9.41 Continued

```
<script language="vb" runat=server>
    Sub Select_Item (sender as Object, e as ListCommandEventArgs)

    End Sub
</script>

<Mobile:Form runat="server" id="form1"
                     paginate="true"
                     PagerStyle-NextPageText="Go to Page {0}"
                     PagerStyle-PreviousPageText="Back to Page {0}">
    <Mobile:Label runat="server" StyleReference="title" Text="Books in
the .net Developer Series" />
    <Mobile:Label runat="server" id="PageNo"/>
    <Mobile:List runat="server" id="titles"
OnItemCommand="Select_Item">
        <Item value="1" text="VB .net Developer's Guide"/>
        <Item value="2" text="XML Developer's Guide to Web Based EDI"/>
        <Item value="3" text="C#.net Developer's Guide"/>
        <Item value="4" text="ASP.net Developer's Guide"/>
        <Item value="5" text=".net Mobile Web Developer's Guide"/>
        <Item value="6" text="ADO.net Developer's Guide"/>
        <Item value="7" text="Web Services Developer Guide"/>
    </Mobile:List>
</Mobile:Form>
```

Our list contains seven items. When loaded using the UP.SDK, we see that the list is displayed in multiple cards (see Figure 9.42).

Figure 9.42 Paginating a Form

To allow for paging, simply insert the *Paginate* attribute into the *<Mobile:Form>* control and set it to "**true**". Additionally, the *PagerStyle-NextPageText* and the *PagerStyle-PreviousPageText* attributes allow you to set the message for displaying the next and previous page, respectively.

```
<Mobile:Form runat="server" id="form1"
                         paginate="true"
                         PagerStyle-NextPageText="Go to Page {0}"
                         PagerStyle-PreviousPageText="Back to Page {0}">
```

Calendar Control

Apart from those regular controls like *Label* and *Textbox*, the Microsoft Mobile Internet Toolkit also includes some interesting controls like the *Calendar* and *AdRotator* controls. We will illustrate the use of the Calendar control in this section.

Date selection is a commonly used feature of mobile applications and in the past, great efforts have gone into making date selection as easy and error-proof as possible. Instead of spending time in building the date selection module, the Mobile API has included the Calendar control. Consider the example shown in Figure 9.43.

Figure 9.43 Birthdate.aspx

```
<%@ Page Inherits="System.Mobile.UI.MobilePage" Language="VB" %>
<%@ Register TagPrefix="Mobile" Namespace="System.Mobile.UI" %>

<script language="VB" runat="server">
   Sub date_Changed(sender as Object, e as EventArgs)
      message.Text = "So your birthdate is " & birthdate.SelectedDate
   End Sub
</script>

<Mobile:Form id="Form1" runat="server">
     <Mobile:Label runat="server" styleReference="Title" Text="Tell me
your birthdate!"/>
     <Mobile:Calendar id="birthdate" OnSelectionChanged="date_Changed"
runat="server"/>
```

Continued

Figure 9.43 Continued

```
    <Mobile:Label runat="server" id="message"/>
</Mobile:Form>
```

Figure 9.44 and Figure 9.45 shows how our code appears in the various emulators.

Figure 9.44 Using the Calendar Control on the Pocket PC

Figure 9.45 Using the Calendar Control on the UP.SDK

When a date has been selected, the message in Figure 9.46 is printed.

Figure 9.46 Printing the Birth Date

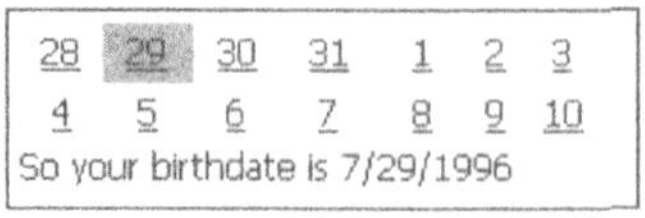

If you want the individual day, month and year printed instead (it is restricted to mm/dd/yyyy format), you can use the following properties:

```
message.Text = "So your birthdate is " & birthdate.SelectedDate.day
```

or

```
message.Text = "So your birthdate is " & birthdate.SelectedDate.month
```

or

```
message.Text = "So your birthdate is " & birthdate.SelectedDate.year
```

Accessing Data with ADO.NET

Today, most applications of any respectable size involve database access in one way or another. Developers are familiar with using the ActiveX Data Objects (ADO) for accessing databases thorough OLE DB and ODBC. In anticipation of the increasing trend of distributed computing and the need to access data remotely, ADO.NET was evolved to support disconnected data access. Actually, ADO.NET is more of an evolution, rather than a revolution. If you are familiar with ADO, chances are you will find most of the concepts in ADO.NET similar.

In the next section, we will take a closer look at ADO.NET and at how you can get started with it quickly.

A Brief Look at ADO.NET

If you are familiar with ADO, you should know that the Recordset object in ADO is no longer available in ADO.NET. Figure 9.47 sums up the architecture of ADO.NET.

In place of the Recordset object, in ADO.NET there are two new objects for data access. They are:

- Dataset
- DataReader

A Dataset object basically represents a complete set of data including related tables, constraints, and relationships among the tables. Think of a Dataset object as a static cursor in ADO, but instead of storing only a single table, it stores multiple tables. A DataReader object is used for reading records in a forward-only fashion. Think of a DataReader object as a forward-only cursor in ADO.

Figure 9.47 ADO.NET Architecture

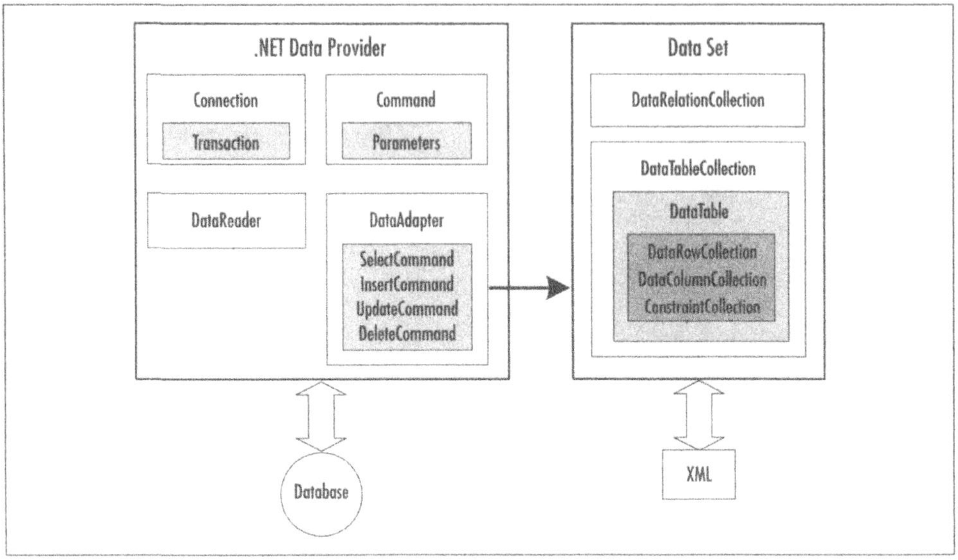

Data Providers

In ADO, communication with the data source is through the OLE DB providers. In ADO.NET, the communication is through Data providers. ADO.NET contains two Data providers:

- SQL Data provider
- OLEDB Data provider

If your backend database is SQL Server, you should use the SQL Data provider as it talks natively (using TDS) to SQL server. This results in immediate performance gains, as there is no need to go through the OLE DB layer. However, if you are not using SQL Server, you should use the OLEDB Data provider.

The OLEDB Data provider is engineered to work with most OLE DB providers. The providers listed in Table 9.3 have been tested and are known to work with ADO.NET.

Table 9.3 Supported OLE DB Providers

Driver	Provider
SQLOLEDB	Microsoft OLE DB Provider for SQL Server
MSDAORA	Microsoft OLE DB Provider for Oracle
Microsoft.Jet.OLEDB.4.0	OLE DB Provider for Microsoft Jet

NOTE

It is possible to use the OLEDB Data provider even if you are using SQL server. In this case, you are foregoing the benefits of talking directly to SQL server by going through additional layers by first going to the OLEDB Data provider and then going through the OLEDB provider.

Figure 9.48 summarizes the discussion so far.

Figure 9.48 Comparing SQLData Provider and OLEDB Data Provider

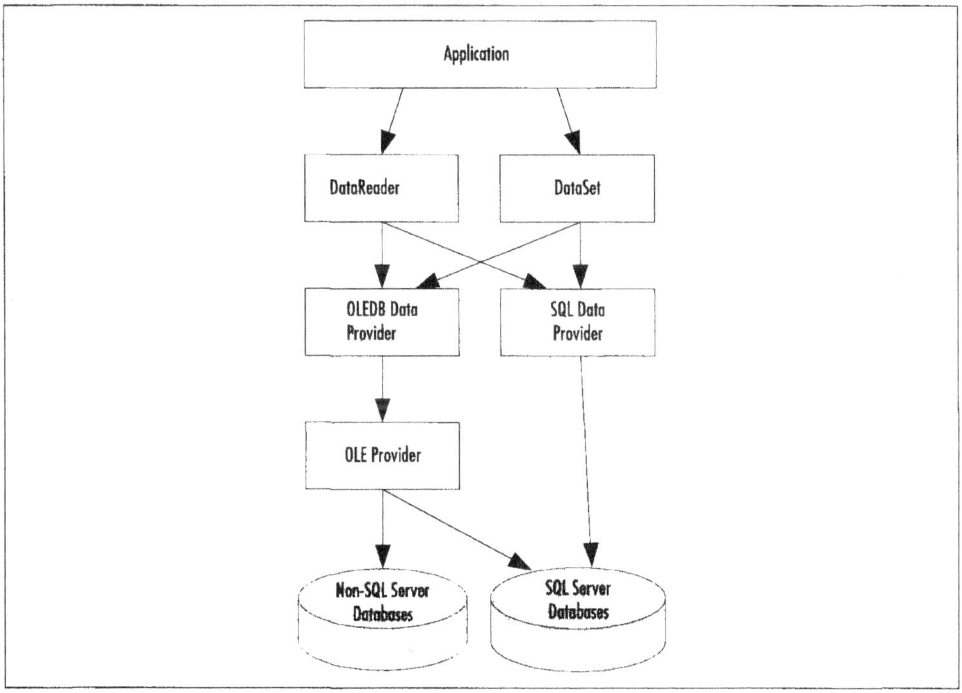

ADO.NET DataReader

A huge portion of our database access is on retrieving records and simply displaying them on the client side. For this reason, ADO.NET provides the DataReader. The DataReader is a read-only, forward-only stream returned from the database. In order to prevent storing a huge number of records in memory (resulting from multiple users performing the data retrieval at the same time, typical of Web access patterns), the DataReader stores only a single record in memory at any one time. The example in Figure 9.49 illustrates the use of the DataReader.

Figure 9.49 DataTitles.aspx

```
<%@ Page Inherits="System.Web.UI.MobileControls.MobilePage"
Language="VB" %>
<%@ Register TagPrefix="Mobile" Namespace="System.Web.UI.MobileControls"
Assembly="System.Web.Mobile" %>

<%@ Import namespace="System.Data" %>
<%@ Import namespace="System.Data.SQLClient" %>

<script language="vb" runat=server>
    Sub Page_load (sender as Object, e as EventArgs)
        Dim connStr As String = "server=localhost; User ID=sa;
password=;database=Pubs"
        Dim conn As New SQLConnection(connstr)
        Dim comm As New SQLCommand("SELECT * FROM Titles", conn)
        Dim dataReader As SQLDataReader
        Try
            conn.Open()
            dataReader = comm.ExecuteReader
            '---reads the record one by one and add to list---
            While datareader.Read
                titles.Items.add  (datareader("Title"))
            End While
        Catch any_exception As Exception '---catching any exception
and displaying it---
```

Continued

Figure 9.49 Continued

```
                errorMessage.Text = "Error!"
            Finally
                '---close the connection and frees the datareader---
                conn.Close()
                datareader = Nothing
            End Try
        End Sub
</script>

<Mobile:Form runat="server" paginate="true">
    <Mobile:Label runat="server" StyleReference="title" Text="Books in
the Pubs table" />
    <Mobile:List runat="server" id="titles"/>
    <Mobile:Label runat="server" id="errorMessage"/>
</Mobile:Form>
```

When this code is run, the screen shown in Figure 9.50 will appear.

Figure 9.50 Accessing Records Using the DataReader Object

Dissecting the Codes

The first thing to note when using ADO.NET is that we need to import two namespaces:

```
<%@ Import namespace="System.Data" %>
<%@ Import namespace="System.Data.SQLClient" %>
```

We next create three objects—conn, comm, and dataReader. The SQLConnection object is for making a connection to the database and the

SQLCommand object is used for setting a command. The SQLDataReader object is used for reading records in a read-only, forward-only fashion.

```
        Dim connStr As String = "server=localhost; User ID=sa;
password=;database=Pubs"
        Dim conn As New SQLConnection(connstr)
        Dim comm As New SQLCommand("SELECT * FROM Titles", conn)
        Dim dataReader As SQLDataReader
```

We next have a Try, Catch, and Finally block:

```
Try

        Catch any_exception As Exception

        Finally

        End Try
```

Within the Try block, we open a connection to the database and execute the command. To read the individual record, we use the *Read()* method of the DataReader and then add it to the list control.

```
            conn.Open()
            dataReader = comm.ExecuteReader
            '---reads the record one by one and add to list---
            While datareader.Read
                titles.Items.add  (datareader("Title"))
            End While
```

Within the Catch block, we want to display any exception that occurs as a result of executing the codes in the Try block.

```
            errorMessage.Text = "Error!"
```

And in the Finally block, we close the connection and free the **DataReader** object:

```
            '---close the connection and frees the datareader---
            conn.Close()
            datareader = Nothing
```

NOTE

Note that in VB.NET, the Set keyword is no longer in use. Also, notice the ability to pass parameters to a class at the moment of instantiation.

ADO.NET Dataset

From the last section you can see that the DataReader object provides a quick and easy way to retrieve records from a table. In this section, we will look at the more powerful and flexible Dataset object.

Let's take a look at the following example and see how we can use a Dataset object to access three different tables in the database. We will use the Pubs database that comes installed with Microsoft SQL Server 2000. We will specifically use the following three tables:

- Titles
- Authors
- TitleAuthor

The relationship between the three tables is shown in Figure 9.51.

Figure 9.51 Relationships between the Three Tables

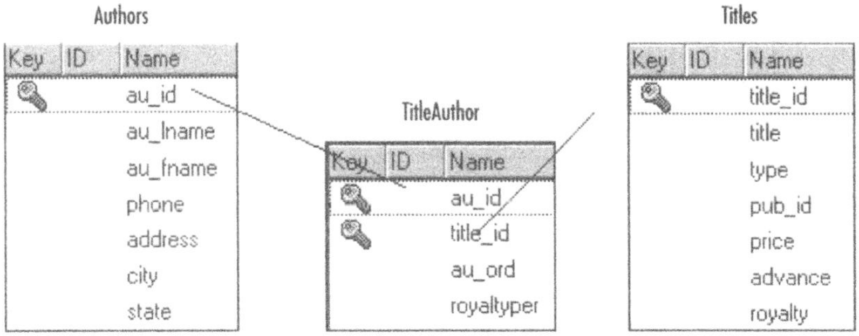

We want to print out all the titles stored in the Title table as well as the associated authors.

We have the following code:

```
<%@ Page Inherits="System.Web.UI.MobileControls.MobilePage"
Language="VB" %>
<%@ Register TagPrefix="Mobile" Namespace="System.Web.UI.MobileControls"
Assembly="System.Web.Mobile" %>


<%@ Import namespace="System.Data" %>
<%@ Import namespace="System.Data.SQLClient" %>


<script language="vb" runat=server>
    Sub Page_load (sender as Object, e as EventArgs)
        '---using dataset---
        Dim connStr As String = "server=localhost; User ID=sa;
password=;database=Pubs"
        Dim conn As New SQLConnection(connstr)
        Dim comm As New SQLCommand("SELECT * FROM Titles", conn)
        Dim sql As String = "SELECT * FROM TitleAuthor INNER JOIN
Authors ON TitleAuthor.au_id=Authors.au_id"
        Dim adapter as New SQLDataAdapter (comm)
        Dim ds As New DataSet("Pubs")
        Dim titleToAdd as String
        Dim count as short

        Try
          '---using the dataset command to fill a table from a
dataset---
           adapter.Fill(ds, "Titles_table")
          '---setting the dataset command to another Command object---
            comm.CommandText = sql
          '---filling another table in the dataset---
          adapter.Fill(ds, "TitleAuthor_table")

          '---set a relationship between the two tables---
          Dim titleID_titles_Column As DataColumn
          Dim titleID_titleauthor_column As DataColumn
```

```
            '---relationship between the titles and titleauthors
tables-
            titleID_titles_Column =
ds.Tables("titles_table").Columns("title_id")
            titleID_titleauthor_column =
ds.Tables("titleauthor_table").Columns("title_id")
            Dim TitleToAuthor As New DataRelation("TtoA",
titleID_titles_Column, titleID_titleauthor_column)

            Dim childrow As DataRow
            Dim row As DataRow

            '---add a relation to the dataset---
            ds.Relations.Add(TitleToAuthor)

            For Each row In ds.Tables("titles_table").Rows
                titleToAdd = row("title") & " by "
                count = 0
                For Each childrow In row.GetChildRows("TtoA")
                   count += 1
                   if count>1 then
                      titleToAdd += ", "
                   end if
                   titleToAdd += childrow("au_fname") & " " &
childrow("au_lname")
                Next
                titles.items.Add (titleToAdd)
            Next

        Catch any_exception As Exception '---catching any exception
and displaying it---
            errorMessage.Text = "Error!"
        Finally
            '---close the connection and frees the dataset---
            conn.Close()
            ds = Nothing
```

```
        End Try

    End Sub
</script>

<Mobile:Form runat="server" Paginate="true">
    <Mobile:Label runat="server" StyleReference="title" Text="Titles
and Authors" />
    <Mobile:List runat="server" id="titles"/>
    <Mobile:Label runat="server" id="errorMessage"/>
</Mobile:Form>
```

Now let's take a closer look at the preceding code. We first create an SQLConnection object to connect to our database:

```
        Dim connStr As String = "server=localhost; User ID=sa;
password=;database=Pubs"
        Dim conn As New SQLConnection(connstr)
```

Next we create a SQLCommand object:

```
        Dim comm As New SQLCommand("SELECT * FROM Titles", conn)
```

This SQLCommand object simply retrieves all the titles in the Title table. The second SQL statement performs an *INNER JOIN* between the TitleAuthor table and the Authors table. The joining field is "au_id". This join is performed to retrieve the names of authors.

```
        Dim sql As String = "SELECT * FROM TitleAuthor INNER JOIN
Authors ON TitleAuthor.au_id=Authors.au_id"
```

We next create an SQLDataAdapter object for executing the command. The SqlDataAdapter serves as a bridge between a Dataset and SQL Server for retrieving and saving data. We also create a Dataset object:

```
        Dim adapter as New SQLDataAdapter (comm)
        Dim ds As New DataSet("Pubs")
```

Within the Try block, we first fill the Dataset's Tables collection with records from the Titles table using the SQLDataAdapter object and named it Titles_table. We next fill another table within the Tables collection and name it TitleAuthor_table. This table contains records from the TitleAuthor table.

```
'---using the dataset command to fill a table from a dataset---
adapter.Fill(ds, "Titles_table")
'---setting the dataset command to another Command object---
comm.CommandText = sql
'---filling another table in the dataset---
adapter.Fill(ds, "TitleAuthor_table")
```

Since there is a relationship between the Titles_table and TitleAuthor_table tables, we proceed to create a relationship between them.

```
'---set a relationship between the two tables---
Dim titleID_titles_Column As DataColumn
Dim titleID_titleauthor_column As DataColumn
'---relationship between the titles and titleauthors tables---
titleID_titles_Column = ds.Tables("titles_table").Columns("title_id")
titleID_titleauthor_column =
   ds.Tables("titleauthor_table").Columns("title_id")
Dim TitleToAuthor As New DataRelation("TtoA", titleID_titles_Column,
   titleID_titleauthor_column)
```

Figure 9.52 shows the relationship between the tables.

Figure 9.52 Relationship between the Two Tables

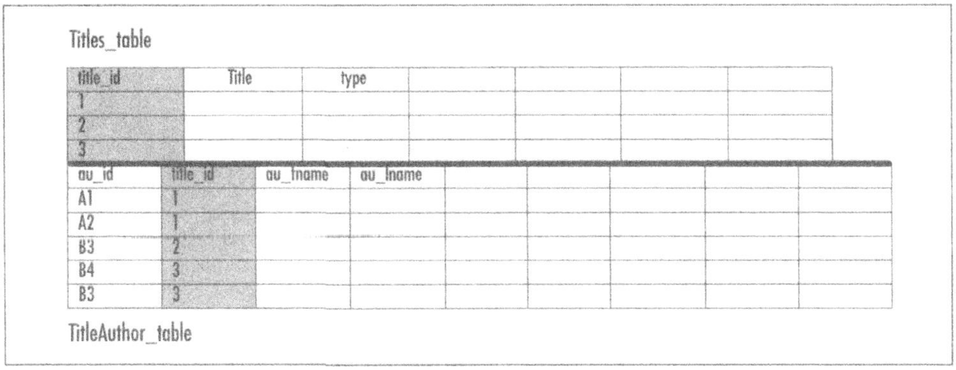

You can view the Titles_table as the parent and the TitleAuthor_table as a child. Each title in Titles_table has some (or no) rows in TitleAuthor_table. Using this parent-child relationship, we add the relationship into the dataset and then print out all the titles and authors name.

```
        Dim childrow As DataRow
        Dim row As DataRow

        '---add a relation to the dataset---
        ds.Relations.Add(TitleToAuthor)

        For Each row In ds.Tables("titles_table").Rows
            titleToAdd = row("title") & " by "
            count = 0
            For Each childrow In row.GetChildRows("TtoA")
                count += 1
                if count>1 then
                    titleToAdd += ", "
                end if
                titleToAdd += childrow("au_fname") & " " &
childrow("au_lname")
            Next
            titles.items.Add (titleToAdd)
        Next
```

When viewed using the Pocket PC emulator, you should see the screen shown in Figure 9.53.

Figure 9.53 Using the Dataset Object

Summary

This chapter has covered quite a lot of ground for developers wishing to utilize the Microsoft .NET Framework for mobile application development. In particular we have introduced you to how ASP.NET works and how you can use the Microsoft Mobile Internet Toolkit and ADO.NET to develop compelling mobile applications.

The current version of the Mobile Internet Toolkit is Beta 2. Since the .NET Mobile Architecture is an extension of the ASP.NET Web Forms, developing mobile applications is very similar to developing Web applications. In the early part of this chapter, we have seen how ASP.NET addresses the problem of HTTP statelessness using HTML and Web Server Controls. Using the architecture in ASP.NET, the Mobile Internet Toolkit allows developers to write mobile applications using the mobile controls, and during runtime it automatically will generate the appropriate codes for the mobile devices.

The set of mobile controls the Mobile Internet Toolkit provides offers a rich set of functionalities for mobile developers. The nicest feature is that the runtime frees the developer from the arduous tasks of customizing the application for the myriad devices available in the market.

In these days, any application that is of any use makes use of databases. Developing mobile applications is no different. In the last section of this chapter, we cover data access using ADO.NET. ADO.NET is part of the .NET framework and is an evolution (rather than revolution) of ADO.

Solutions Fast Track

Overview of the .NET Mobile Architecture

☑ The Mobile Internet Toolkit is built on the Microsoft ASP.NET Web Forms and supports languages like VB .NET, C#, and JScript.NET. It is an extension to the ASP.NET model.

☑ The toolkit includes a set of Mobile Controls that is executed by the Mobile Internet Controls runtime during the execution phase.

☑ The key feature of the runtime is its ability to recognize the different types of devices accessing the forms and to generate dynamically the codes that the device can understand.

- ☑ The current release of the Microsoft Mobile Internet Toolkit is Beta 2. Before installing the Microsoft Mobile Internet Toolkit, you must first install the .NET framework SDK.

Introduction to ASP.NET

- ☑ Current ASP technology contains a mixture of HTML and scripting codes and does not provide a clean separation of display from content, which often results in bugs and difficulties.
- ☑ HTTP is a stateless protocol. Preserving state in ASP requires substantial effort by the developer.
- ☑ In ASP.NET, normal HTML elements are converted to HTML Server controls so that they can be programmed on the server. Besides the HTML Server controls, ASP.NET provides a different set of server controls known as ASP.NET server controls.
- ☑ A Web Form in ASP.NET contains two components: Code and Content.
- ☑ The Content component of a Web Form can contain Web Form Server controls. Web Form Server controls contain the HTML Server control, ASP.NET Server control, Validation controls, and User controls.
- ☑ One important difference between ASP.NET and ASP is that ASP.NET applications are parsed and compiled once and then cached, so that subsequent requests do not go through the same time-consuming steps.

Developing Mobile Web Forms

- ☑ During runtime when the form is requested, the .NET runtime automatically will detect the type of devices (our examples use Pocket PC, IE 5.5 and UP.SDK) requesting that page, and will perform a dynamic generation of the target markup languages. Unlike WAP applications developed using WML and ASP, the same ASP.NET application can be displayed on different devices, with no effort on your part for customization.
- ☑ In ASP.NET pages, there can be only a single form; however, you can have multiple mobile forms in a Mobile Web form. To link the two

forms, you use the *<Mobile:Link>* control. The *navigateURL* attribute contains the ID of the form to link to.

- ☑ Linking to forms on another page is not so straightforward. The form in the first page links to the second page by specifying the filename in the *navigateURL* attribute. Subsequent steps involve adding another parameter called *Form*, retrieving its value using the *Request.QueryString* collection, verifying the form ID in that value, and using the *ActiveForm* property to set and return the active page.
- ☑ The Microsoft Mobile Internet Toolkit supports user input controls TextBox, Command, and List.
- ☑ To input text into a Mobile Web Form, use the *<Mobile:TextBox>* control. To display a command button so that an action can be performed, use the *<Mobile:Command>* control. To display lists of items either as a static list or interactive selection, use the *<Mobile:List>* control. You can also dynamically bind a list of items using the **ArrayList** class.
- ☑ To display images, you can use the *<Mobile:Image>* control. Because various mobile devices display images of differing format, use the *<DeviceSpecific>* control (within which are the *<Choice>* elements) to send the correct image type to the right device.
- ☑ Validation controls available in the Microsoft Mobile Internet Toolkit SDK include CompareValidator, CustomValidator, RangeValidator, RegularExpressionValidator, RequiredFieldValidator, and ValidationSummary.
- ☑ Other features of the Mobile API are its records paging capability, using the *Paginate* attribute, and also its *Calendar* control for date selection.

Accessing Data with ADO.NET

- ☑ Developers are familiar with using the ActiveX Data Objects (ADO) for accessing databases through OLE DB and ODBC. ADO.NET was evolved to support the need for remote data access.
- ☑ In ADO, communication with the data source is through the OLE DB providers. In ADO.NET, the communication is through Data providers.

ADO.NET contains two data providers—SQL Data providers and OLEDB Data providers.

- ☑ It is possible to use OLEDB Data provider even if you are using SQL server.
- ☑ ADO.NET provides the DataReader for retrieving records as a read-only, forward-only stream returned from the database for display on the client side. The DataReader stores only a single record in memory at any one time to prevent storing a huge number of records in memory.
- ☑ The more powerful Dataset object is used to access different tables in the database. The requested data can be retrieved, saved, and printed with the use of Tables collections.

Frequently Asked Questions

The following Frequently Asked Questions, answered by the authors of this book, are designed to both measure your understanding of the concepts presented in this chapter and to assist you with real-life implementation of these concepts. To have your questions about this chapter answered by the author, browse to **www.syngress.com/solutions** and click on the **"Ask the Author"** form.

Q: What are the main differences between Beta 1 and Beta 2 of the Microsoft Mobile Internet Toolkit?

A: Besides the name change, you can now develop mobile application using Visual Studio.NET. Also, more devices are supported in Beta 2. For more information about the changes from Beta 1 to Beta 2, refer to the documentation that comes with the Toolkit.

Q: I am developing WAP applications using the Mobile Internet Toolkit. Do my users still need a WAP gateway?

A: Yes, the Mobile Internet Toolkit simply provides an easier way to develop mobile applications that runs on multiple devices. Your user still needs to use a WAP gateway to access your application.

Q: Do I need to know VB to build for mobile.NET?

A: Since the Mobile Internet Toolkit is based on ASP.NET Web forms, you can use any of the languages supported by ASP.NET; that is, Visual Basic .NET, C#, or JScript.NET.

Q: Do I need to know XML to build for mobile.NET?

A: No. You need not learn XML or other languages like WML since the Mobile Controls runtime automatically will generate the appropriate codes for the target device.

Chapter 10

Securing Your Wireless Web

Solutions in this chapter:

- Comparing Internet and Wireless Security
- Security Challenges of the Wireless Web
- Security Models of the Wireless Web
- WTLS and Point-to-Point Security Models
- PKI Technology and End-to-End Security Models
- The Future of Security on the Wireless Web

☑ Summary

☑ Solutions Fast Track

☑ Frequently Asked Questions

Introduction

Today's wireless landscape is highly fragmented and lacks a standard security solution. As a wireless Webmaster, you must choose from three methods of securing the information under your care: the first is to ensure that information has a low security requirement, which is compatible with the currently deployed security model; (2) severely limit access to devices and networks by implementing a custom high-security solution; (3) wait for newer third generation (3G) devices and networks that will support end-to-end Secure Sockets Layer (SSL) protection.

The most important weapon in your arsenal is SSL. Using SSL to limit access to Web Servers and applications is the best short-term solution, but this does nothing to fix potential security flaws in the Wireless Application Protocol (WAP). Implementing a Public Key Infrastructure (PKI) will result in the highest level of security, but PKI security limits the devices that can be used and poses deployment challenges, particularly for phones. If you require a level of security higher than that required by e-mail, deploying a PKI on Personal Digital Assistants (PDAs) or standardizing on devices that support end-to-end SSL are the best options.

The applications driving the wireless Web provide access to time-critical information and transactions using mobile devices such as WAP phones, 2-way pagers, and wireless PDAs. An investor might receive a wireless message informing him or her of a merger or stock split, or that a stock has reached a given price. He or she might wish to browse immediately to a brokerage account and place a trade using a wireless phone or PDA. A traveling credit card holder might be notified that their credit card has reached its balance. He or she may then browse to his or her bank account and place an electronic payment, or access another credit card company's wireless application to transfer the balance. A consumer may receive a message reminding him or her of a relative's birthday and wish to place an order to have flowers delivered. An avid user of eBay could be notified that a coveted item is about to be sold, and place a last-second bid from a wireless phone or two-way pager. In all of these situations, time is critical, money is involved, and the information or the transaction absolutely *must* be secure.

Security for both the conventional and wireless Webs involves client applications or devices, physical networks, transport protocols, and server-based applications (see Figure 10.1). Security technology involves privacy, data integrity, and authentication. There are various security technologies in the wireless Web; putting all the pieces together is a challenge not only for the wireless Webmaster but for the wireless and security industries as well. Secure wireless applications must interoperate with existing security standards and technologies while seamlessly incorporating new wireless security technologies as they become available. This chapter explores the major technologies and debates in wireless security, and gives practical advice for securing your wireless Web setup. The best place to start is with a comparison of Web and wireless technologies. Wireless security implementations fall in two categories: point-to-point security models and end-to-end security models. Understanding the pros and cons of both models will prepare you to design a secure wireless Web presence. This chapter introduces the major issues and challenges of wireless Web security and discusses the two general security models that are in use today, as well as covering the specific ways those models attempt to overcome security challenges.

Comparing Internet and Wireless Security

The Internet security landscape is far from simple, and adding wireless into the mix hardly makes things easier. Wireless security involves several interconnected components that are often in different locations, for example: a private corporate network, the public Internet, and a Wireless Application Service Provider (WASP). Wireless Web security introduces new technologies while using existing major security technologies that are used on the Web and in Internet-accessed corporate applications. This means that a number of different protocols, connection mechanisms, and networks—each with its own security technologies and features—have to come together to provide security on the wireless Web.

The Internet provides a fairly coherent model for applications and security by using ubiquitous standards like Transmission Control Protocol/Internet Protocol (TCP/IP), Hypertext Transfer Protocol (HTTP) and Hypertext Markup Language (HTML). On the conventional Web there are three major operating systems (Windows, UNIX, and Mac OS), and two major Web browsers (Netscape Navigator and Microsoft Internet Explorer). On the *wireless* Web there are many networks using different standards (Advanced Mobile Phone System [AMPS], Code Division Multiple Access [CDMA], Time Division Multiple Access [TDMA], Global System for Mobile Communication [GSM], Integrated Digital Enhanced Network [iDEN] and so forth) and there are multiple browser protocols, including WAP and NTT DoCoMo's i-mode protocol (which has been widely deployed in Japan), as well as many different browsers. Perhaps the best illustration of the disparate standards on the wireless Web is that in contrast to

HTML there are several wireless markup languages, including Handheld Device Markup Language (HDML), Wireless Markup Language (WML), Compact Hypertext Markup Language (cHTML), Mobile Markup Language (MML), Extensible Hypertext markup Language (XHTML) and ordinary HTML; as well as multiple technologies to extend browser functionality including WML Script, Java 2 Micro Edition (J2ME), and Qualcomm's Binary Runtime Environment for Wireless (BREW) which enable remote execution of application code on arbitrary mobile devices. 3G wireless networks and a convergence of standards will eventually result in a relatively homogenous environment for wireless applications, but it will be many years from the time of this writing before this transition is complete—and legacy devices and networks must be supported throughout these changes.

Security on the conventional Web is less complex than wireless security because the Web represents a single paradigm for both application development and security. (Figure 10.1 illustrates the differences in security models between the wired Internet and the wireless Web.) On the Internet, there is one protocol for Web sites and Web-based applications (HTTP), one transport protocol (TCP/IP), and one dominant security standard, SSL, also known as secure HTTP or SHTTP). Higher levels of security can be deployed with relative ease by distributing X.509 digital certificates that are already supported by Web browsers in a PKI security model. On the Web there is only one markup language (HTML) and a small number of standardized technologies to enable client-side application logic (Java and ActiveX). Web browsers also have a standard plug-in API so that third-party program enhancements can be added to Web browsers. Virtual private networks (VPNs) are also used to enable access to private corporate networks from remote locations or machines over the Internet through a secure encrypted connection. Access can be further controlled by technologies, such as Security Dynamics SecureID, that are relatively easy to integrate with applications and to deploy.

There are multiple security technologies available on the web. These technologies are used where and when they are appropriate. High levels of security, such as 128-bit SSL and Web-based PKIs using X.509 digital certificates provide strong authentication and encryption, and are widely used for e-commerce and to protect private information transmitted over the Internet (A digital certificate is like a passport that proves the identity of the certificate holder and enables strong encryption between the user and a server on the Web). Internet and Web security is a relatively mature field with a few central standards and readily available expertise.

Figure 10.1 Security on the Wired Internet versus the Wireless Web

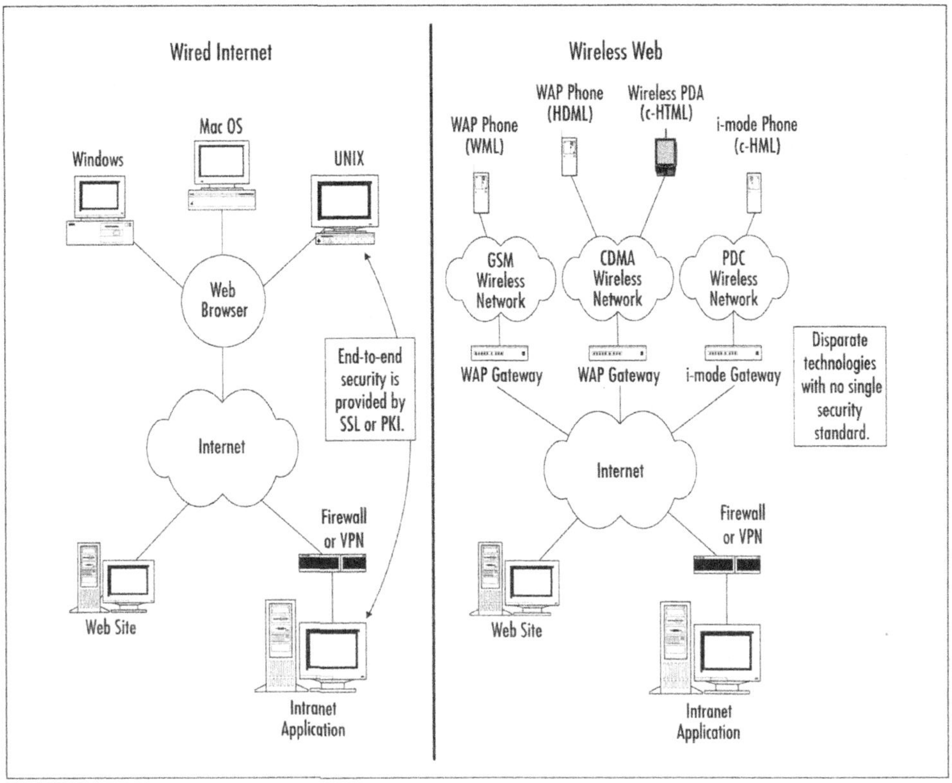

Common standards on the wired Internet mean that secure access to the Web is available wherever Internet access is available. In stark contrast, access to the wireless Web, if security is a requirement, is limited in many ways. The many devices, operating systems, browsers, markup languages, and protocols of the wireless Web pose a variety of challenges from a security standpoint.

Security Challenges of the Wireless Web

The lack of a dominant standard and the difficulty of deploying new security technologies (such as a PKI) to a wide range of disparate mobile devices mean that security on the wireless Web is inherently limited. Straightforward concepts, like VPNs, that work easily over the Internet do not directly apply to the wireless Web. On the one hand, the wireless Web involves new security technologies such as the Wireless Transport Layer Security protocol (WTLS) and new standards for lightweight digital certificates and PKIs that can be supported on low-power mobile devices. On the other hand, these technologies are limited in terms of deployment: without the benefit of a single global wireless security standard, access to applications and information remains limited to the specific networks and devices where a given security technology is available.

Lack of Standards

Unlike SSL and the x.509 standard for PKIs on the Internet today, there is no single standard for wireless digital certificates or browser plug-ins. As a result, each wireless end-to-end security solution uses a combination of devices, browsers, and digital certificate technology, and while Internet access is the same everywhere, applications that employ PKI security cannot work globally because of the simple fact a user cannot travel worldwide using the same mobile device for data access. This is due to the different and incompatible networks and devices used around the world. Since the same devices and browsers are not available everywhere, digital certificate technologies that are already limited to specific browsers and devices don't work worldwide. Users that travel internationally, for example, typically use different devices for wireless messaging and data access in Europe, North America and Japan. WTLS security, along with WAP, is available in North America and Europe but not in Japan or other parts of Asia. Stronger PKI security is limited to specific browsers and devices that are invariably available only on certain networks. There is no single wireless browser or common PKI technology than covers all the bases. Users must either switch to a non-secure mode of communication or be denied access until they return to their home continent or network.

Horsepower, Bandwidth, and Weak Encryption

While the PCs of today are like the supercomputers of decades past, the same cannot be said of mobile devices. The main limitation in wireless security is the low processing power and memory capacity of mobile devices, which means that wireless encryption and digital certificate technologies must be very small and efficient. This also means that there are practical limits as to how secure information can be, although mobile devices will become more powerful in the future. Even today's fastest PDAs cannot efficiently provide the same level of encryption that desktop PCs can handle, and wireless phones are far less powerful. Device power and capacity need not be great to have vulnerabilities or run malicious code, but they must be powerful and sophisticated to provide strong encryption and have the capacity for embedded anti-virus technology. Where wireless devices are concerned, you can either shop around for devices that meet your criteria or you can wait for 2.5G or 3G mobile devices with enhanced software and increased power and capacity to hit the market.

Most wireless networks are limited to data rates of 19.2Kbps (Cellular Digital Packet Data or CDPD). The pseudo-random patterns of encrypted data make it almost impossible to conserve bandwidth via compression, which tends to expand the total size of the information in transit. This imposes the limitations that wireless protocols must be very efficient and that the amount of data communicated must be kept to a minimum. Until 2.5G and 3G network standards replace existing wireless infrastructures, there is no solution to this problem.

The relatively weak encryption provided by wireless security technologies (such as WTLS and lightweight wireless PKIs) is directly related to the length of the keys used and the sophistication of the encryption algorithms. These in turn are a function of device capacity, processing power, and wireless network bandwidth. As with other device limitations, you can buy the most powerful devices currently available to use the best available encryption technology, or you can wait for more powerful devices and more mature wireless security technologies.

User Awareness and Unsecure Devices

One of the biggest challenges in wireless security is making users aware of the issues and risks. In this, the best defense is a good offense. In the case of users who are generally unaware of security issues, this means controlling devices and device configurations; and providing users with clear policies for wireless access. Example policies might include things like observing standard password criteria and procedures, making sure that devices are password protected or locked when shut off, and providing guidelines for handling confidential information, both inside the company and when traveling.

Lost and stolen mobile devices are a fact of life for reasons that are much more mundane than the loss or theft of a notebook computer. Controlling device configurations is the key to minimizing the risks when devices are lost or stolen. Advising users of the risks can reduce losses if they are also provided with guidelines. You need to make sure that the devices under your control are password protected and that you are in a position to have devices or wireless modems cut off immediately if lost or stolen. With PDAs there are third-party security and encryption programs that you can incorporate into your standard configuration.

Mistrust of Wireless ASPs

Many of the available wireless solutions in the market are services rather than products. WASPs reduce customer infrastructure investment but require customers to trust their data to a network outside their control. VPNs can help to solve this problem, but they don't provide end-to-end security from mobile devices to applications behind firewalls on secure corporate networks. There are two approaches to managing WASPs. The first is to determine your own desired security architecture and standards, then audit the WASP. The second approach, which is not recommended, is to trust them. Of course, the best alternative is not to use a WASP at all. If you must use one, make sure you have a secure connection to their network and that server-to-server communication on the service provider's network is also secure. This model is generally acceptable for corporate applications but not necessarily for financial transactions.

Potential for New Viruses

Managing the potential risks posed by viruses, Trojan horses and worms is a matter of device strategy. Limiting the risks means standardizing on devices that have anti-virus capabilities, such as an embedded scanning engine. The inevitability of the threat is not in dispute, but the scope of problem and the difficulty of handling it are unknown at this point. One temporary advantage is that the same diversity of devices, browsers and standards that hampers security can also hamper the spread of viruses and worms. Built-in interpreters such as the J2ME virtual machine and a convergence of browser standards will eventually change this, but not before 2.5G and 3G devices replace the devices deployed today.

Debugging...

Wireless Viruses?

In two to three years, the introduction of third-generation wireless networks will make viruses as large a problem on mobile phones and PDAs as they are today on desktop computers and Internet-based servers. As mobile phones and wireless PDAs continue to grow in popularity, mischievous programs will inevitably emerge. Virus and e-mail scanning technologies that are popular today have already begun to migrate to mobile devices. As devices grow in power and capacity, they will also

Continued

move from having simple firmware to having true operating systems. The most powerful PDAs today have many times the processing power and capacity of the first Apple and IBM personal computers; operating systems like Palm OS, Symbian, and EPOC are becoming more sophisticated, and PDAs are even available running embedded Linux.

Phones and PDAs also have integrated messaging and e-mail capabilities that could be used (as has happened with certain phones) to exploit vulnerabilities in devices, to reprogram them, or to introduce and execute programs that potentially include viruses, worms, and Trojan horses. As the messaging capabilities of mobile devices become more feature-rich and support more types of attachments, the introduction of mischievous and malicious programs to take advantage of these capabilities is inevitable. A case in point is that of a popular PDA operating system that has introduced the capability of programmatically transmitting data files or actual programs from device to device by tunneling them through existing wireless messaging. While you can imagine many good uses for this technical feature, it could in theory be used to propagate a virus or similar program.

In the near future, anti-virus technology is likely to be embedded in all major phone and PDA operating systems. In the mean time, one thing to look for in the devices ypon which you standardize your organization is the history of viruses or malicious compromises related to messaging, as well as the availability of anti-virus technology for that platform. It's not too soon to consider shying away from devices if the operating system vendor does not either have built-in anti-virus technology or concrete plans to embed anti-virus technology in future versions of their product.

Understanding Your Security Objectives

Creating a secure wireless intranet or application requires that you evaluate your goals and security requirements. E-mail, for example, is often sent in the clear over the Internet and via mail relays outside the control of corporate IT. If that risk is deemed acceptable in your business, then wireless e-mail posses no special risks for you. On the other hand, if you require VPNs, private extranets, or PKIs to exchange e-mail with your customers or business partners, then wireless e-mail is likely to be less secure than you require. The economic forces driving wireless are of course related to time-critical data where there are financial implications. Financial information such as stock trading, bank transfers, business-to-business exchanges, or the day-to-day operations of investment bankers all demand a high standard of security. While there's no silver bullet, each of the security problems of the wireless Web can be addressed with varying degrees of satisfaction. Once you've determined what you're going to make available wirelessly and how secure it needs to be you can determine what steps you need to take to provide an appropriate degree of security, bearing in mind that the more secure the solution is the less accessible information is to legitimate users and the less flexibility you'll have to provide access to information and applications.

Security Models of the Wireless Web

as mentioned, there are two basic models for wireless security: *point-to-point* and *end-to-end*. In a wireless Web application there are many legs in the journey data makes from a mobile device to an application or through to transaction. *Point-to-point* security means that information is protected at each leg of transit by the appropriate security technologies for that part of the communication. Collectively this patchwork of security technologies can cover the entire journey from mobile device to an application and back again. Unfortunately, at the points where one type of security leaves off and another begins, there is a vulnerability that couldtheoretically be exploited. To make matters worse, it takes only one weak link to break the chain; point-to-point security is only as strong as the weakest link. Add to this the question of using a WASP and most companies are unwilling to risk corporate data or financial transactions to a point-to-point security model. Corporate security czars are correct in viewing security on the wireless Web as immature and problematic compared to security on the Web.
End-to-end security means that a single security technology is at work all the way from the end device to the application regardless of the various networks that the communication may traverse. In this security model, point-to-point security mechanisms may still be in place, but only as a secondary line of defense. With end-to-end security, wireless applications can be as secure as Web-based applications. Unfortunately, this cannot be accomplished without placing limitations on the wireless applications, devices and browsers that are used. Like SSL and PKI technologies on the Web, end-to-end security means that information is encrypted before it leaves the mobile device and remains encrypted until after it reaches a server on a secure network. Unlike the Web, however, there are several different PKI technologies, each supported only in specific mobile devices, browsers and applications.

Public and Private Key Cryptography

Point-to-point and end-to-end security solutions both involve some form of cryptography. *Cryptography* is the science of taking ordinary information such as a plain text message and converting it into something that can only be understood by the intended recipient of a message. The intermediate data, or *cipher text*, appears to be random and is indecipherable to anyone without knowledge of how to convert the information back to an understandable form. Methods of encrypting and decrypting data using mathematical algorithms are called *cryptosystems*. Most of the algorithms that encrypt and decrypt data do so by systematically using a particular piece of information known as a *key*. Once the data is encrypted, it can only be decrypted again by a party that knows both the encryption algorithm *and* the encryption key. This makes it exceedingly difficult for unauthorized parties to intercept information in transit. On the Internet, keys are often generated and distributed in the form of *digital certificates*.

There are two basic kinds of cryptography that use keys. The first is *private-key* cryptography (see Figure 10.2), which uses symmetric algorithms to encrypt and decrypt data using the same key. This is sometimes called *secret key* cryptography because a shared secret or key is used on both ends of the communication. The method of exchanging keys is critical for both public and private key cryptography since keys must be exchanged securely in order for the cryptosystem to be effective. Methods of key exchange are defined in established cryptosystems such as the Rivest Shamir Adelman (RSA), Diffie-Hellman, and Elliptic Curve Diffie-Hellman systems.

Figure 10.2 Private or Secret Key Encryption

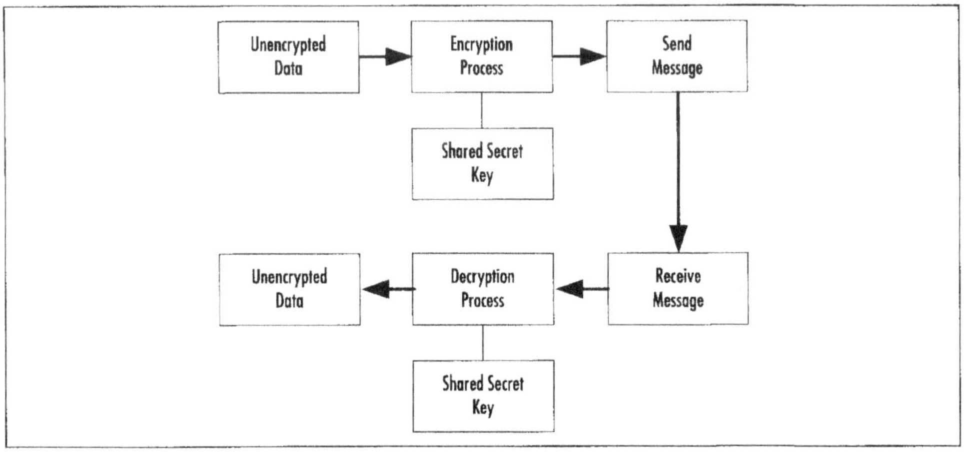

The second type of cryptography is *public-key* cryptography (see Figure 10.3), which uses *asymmetric* algorithms, meaning that information is encrypted using one key (a public key), but decrypted using another key (a private key). In public key cryptography there are actually two keys on each end: a private key known only to the recipient of information and a public key known to the sender, as well as anyone else. Information is encrypted using the public key but it can only be decrypted using the recipient's private key. Since only the recipient of a message can decrypt that message, public key cryptography can also be used to verify the identity of the recipient. This is referred to as *digital authentication*.

Figure 10.3 Public Key Encryption

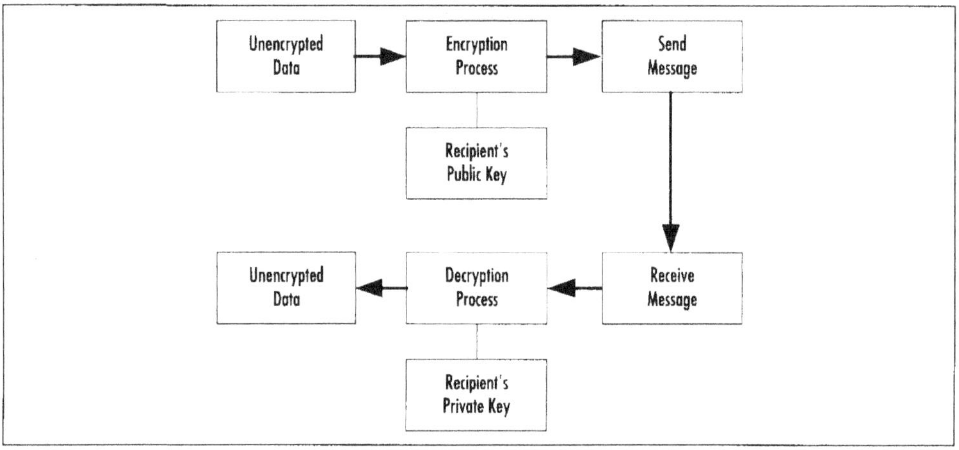

For both private and public key encryption, the degree of security depends on the algorithms and on the length of the key. The method of using a key to encrypt data is referred to as *cipher*. *Block ciphers* break up information into blocks that have a fixed length (normally 64 bits), and then encrypt each block using the shared secret key. Block ciphers use the same key for all encryption. *Stream ciphers* encrypt small units of data using a series of keys generated by a separate shared key or generator key. The received data are then decrypted by the recipient with the same series of keys. Stream ciphers use different ciphers, built using a common generator key, for each block of the encrypted information.

SSL uses several well-defined encryption ciphers, including RC5, the Data Encryption Standard (DES), 3DES and the International Data Encryption Algorithm (IDEA). DES, for example, is a cipher that encrypts 64-bit blocks of data with a 56-bit shared secret key, which was originally developed by IBM and later adopted as a standard by the US government.

Developing & Deploying...

Security Cheat Sheet

- **Authentication** Authentication means that access to information is restricted to users that can verify their identity. The simplest form of authentication is logging in to a system with a user ID and password pair. Authentication can also use a third factor, such as SecureID, or be based on public key encryption algorithms (the client verifies its identity by decrypting a token encrypted with the user's public key using the user's private key, thus verifying the presence of the user's private key without disclosing it.
- **Authenticity** Authenticity means that the recipient of a message can verify the origin of the message and thus ensure that it is genuine and that it has not been replaced with a substitute.
- **Certificate Authority** Any organization that has its own root certificate from which other certificates are derived and by which they are digitally signed. A certificate signed by a known certificate authority (such as an established software vendor) is regarded as legitimate.
- **Digital Certificate** A digital certificate is an electronic document used to store keys such as a user's private key. Messages sent by a user can be digitally signed using the user's public key and digital signature.
- **Encryption** Encryption means systematically altering information in a way that only the intended recipient of the information can reverse. Privacy is accomplished by encrypting data using an encryption algorithm such as elliptic curve cryptography (ECC) or RSA.
- **In the Clear** Information in the clear is the opposite of secure information. It is plain (clear) text that can be read by anyone who intercepts it. Communications in the clear are inherently insecure.
- **Integrity** Data integrity means that transmitted information has not been altered or tampered with. For example, a simple way of verifying data integrity is through the use of a

Continued

cyclic redundancy check (CRC) algorithm, which represents the integrity of information as a number.

- **Privacy** Privacy means that information communicated between two people or computers is inscrutable to third parties. Encrypting information so that only the sender and recipient understand it ensures privacy.
- **Public Key** In public-key cryptography the sender and recipient each get two keys: a private key and a public key. The public key is made accessible while the private key remains secret. The sender of a message encrypts the information using the recipient's public key but the information can only be decrypted using the recipient's private key.
- **Secret Key** In secret key cryptography the sender and recipient use the same method of encrypting and decrypting information. A shared piece of information or secret known only to a message's sender and recipient can be used to encrypt and decrypt the message. This is known as secret key or symmetric cryptography.
- **Trojan** A program that appears to be legitimate but is designed to have destructive effects on the programs and data of the computer onto which the Trojan program has been loaded.
- **Virus** A program that replicates itself by infecting other programs. Viruses are typically programmed to append their executable code to other programs, resulting in their propagation.
- **Worm** A malicious program that replicates itself over a network and that typically fills all of the storage space or network capacity. Worms typically exploit a specific vulnerability, such as a buffer overflow in a particular network application, in order to execute their own code on remote machines.

WTLS and Point-to-Point Security Models

The term *point-to-point security* describes an approach where information is protected at each leg of the journey from a user to a Web server by the appropriate security technology for each part of the communication. As we have seen, this approach has inherent weaknesses at the points where the security methods change between legs of the data's journey. The most important technology in the point-to-point security model is WTLS. WTLS is the equivalent of SSL for WAP, and it provides encryption between wireless browsers and WAP gateways. The most standard form of WTLS (WTLS Class I) is designed to work together with SSL so that WTLS operates on the wireless network side of the WAP gateway and SSL operates on the Internet side. WTLS and SSL together ensure that information is encrypted from point to point all the way from a wireless browser to a Web server (see Figure 10.4).

Figure 10.4 Point-to-Point Security Model

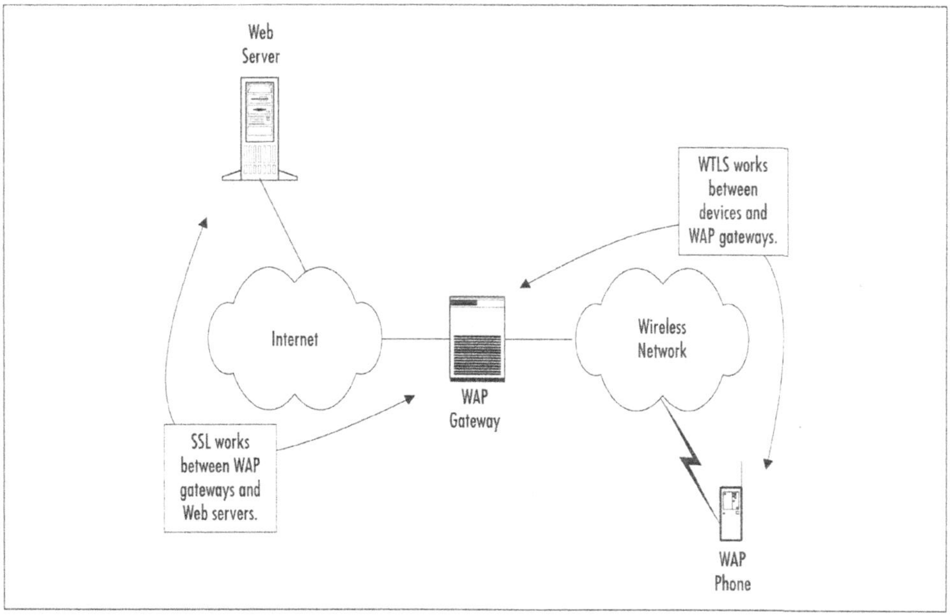

How WTLS Works

WTLS is the part of the WAP specification designed to ensure the privacy, authenticity, and integrity of communication. Communications traffic in the air may also be encrypted depending on the wireless network and air-connect technology but, like WTLS, this does not provide true end-to-end encryption.

The three main components of WTLS are: (1) the handshaking protocol that provides for key exchange; (2) a record structure for encrypted information; and (3) the Wireless Identity Module (WIM). The handshaking protocol is used when a client and server (a WAP gateway) initiate a session. During the handshaking process, the client lists supported cryptographic and key exchange methods, and the server chooses a preferred method. After authenticating each other ,the client and server select a protocol version and cipher. WTLS borrows from the SSL standard and supports the RC5, DES, 3DES and IDEA ciphers, although the DES and 3DES ciphers are the more typically used. Three key exchange methods are supported including RSA, Diffie-Hellman, and Elliptic Curve Diffie-Hellman, with the RSA method being the most commonly used. WTLS also provides a way keys to be exchanged anonymously based on the servier's public key. When authenticating anonymously, the client encrypts a secret key using the server's public key, and sends a Client Key Exchange message. The record structure of WTLS provides a mechanism for the data's privacy and integrity to be checked, and the WIM is the core software logic that performs all of the actual cryptography, including handshaking, authentication, and encryption.

WTLS Classes

The version 2.0 WAP specification incorporates three classes of WTLS security, offering successively stronger levels of security. WTLS Class I only provides encryption between the wireless browser and the WAP gateway, after which the gateway is responsible for the data's security. WTLS Class II is a close analog of SSL on the Internet because it allows SSL-like encryption directly between wireless browsers and Web servers. WTLS Class III provides a framework for PKI security.

The WAP Gap

Mobile devices using WAP do not connect directly to Web sites or applications nor do they directly support the HTTP protocol or SSL. In effect, WAP gateways act like proxy servers for mobile devices. A gateway translates one kind of communication to another kind. In this case a WAP gateway translates communication from the WAP protocol to HTTP over the Internet. When a WAP gateway relays a request to a Web server on behalf of a mobile device, it uses the WAP protocol to communicate with the device and HTTP to communicate with the Web server. Like Web browsers, WAP gateways support SSL, which is the standard method of encrypting HTTP communications. SSL is normally used between Web browsers and Web servers. Communication between a mobile device and a WAP gateway is secured using WTLS. and communication between the WAP gateway and Web servers is secured using SSL. WAP gateways decrypt WTLS communication and then re-encrypt the communication using SSL. This means that inside the WAP gateway, the information is unencrypted at one point. It is theoretically possible for the WAP gateway to malfunction and establish unencrypted HTTP communication rather than using SSL. This flaw is referred to as the *WAP gap* (see Figure 10.5) and it is the ideal point for a *man-in-the-middle* attack.

Figure 10.5 The WAP Gap

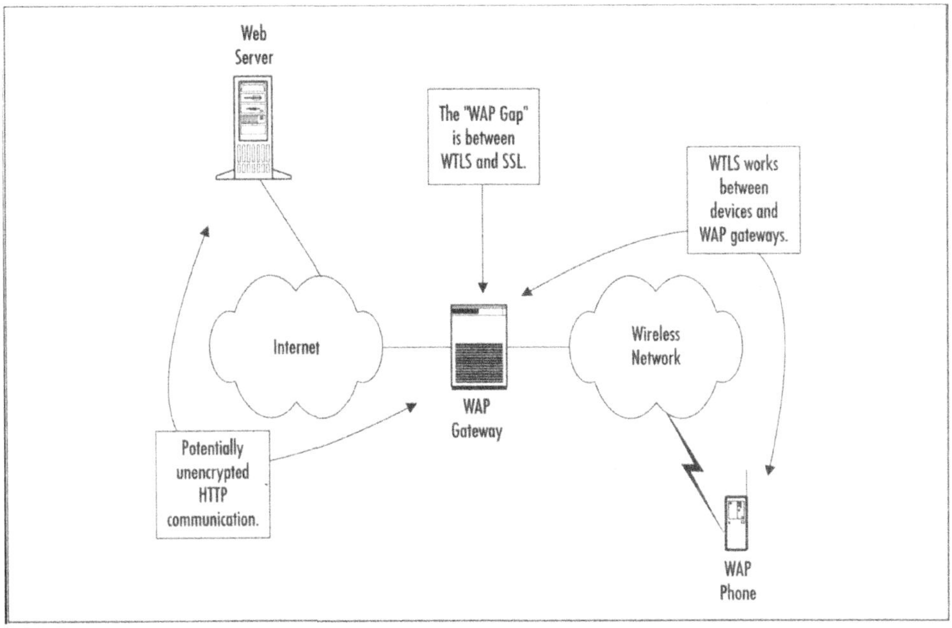

How Likely is a WAP Gateway Compromise?

WTLS Class I is the most widely deployed security standard on the wireless Web for WAP devices (there are currently many more DoCoMo i-mode devices in use). WTLS Class I communication is theoretically flawed because it is possible, however improbable, that a mobile operator's WAP gateway can be compromised or that it might not initiate SSL connections over the Internet. However, what is more important to you as a wireless Webmaster , is that the software and configuration of the mobile operator's WAP gateway and the security of the WAP gateway itself are totally outside your control; you have no way of knowing if one or more of these machines has been compromised or if you are being victimized by a man in the middle attack. Experts disagree about how serious the WAP gap really is or whether it can be successfully exploited. However, the fact that the WAP gap exists means that the design of WTLS Class I, and of the wireless Web today, is imperfect at best.

SECURITY ALERT

There are two methods of testing SSL between a WAP gateway and a Web server or Web-based application. The first is to directly enter an HTTPS Universal Resource Locator (URL) on the device and see if the WAP gateway successfully connects. The more secure method is to restrict all communications to SSL (TCP/IP port 443). Enforcing SSL at the Web server is the best way to guarantee that information is secure.

The Seven Layers of Point-to-Point Security

Point-to-point security can be broken down into seven layers, corresponding to the steps in the communication path between mobile devices and Web servers or applications. Despite concerns like the WAP gap and mistrust of WASPs, these seven security layers provide practical assurance that applications and transactions are reasonably secure. For most organizations, content and information such as e-mail that are made available through wireless devices are adequately served by a point-to-point security model. This is only because the security requirements are low. For banking solutions such as consumer banking and mobile credit card applications, point-to-point security as it exists today (primarily using WTLS Class I security) is not acceptable. Nonetheless, in the fierce competition to reach the wireless market first, even a theoretically flawed security solution may pose an acceptable risk when balanced with other business considerations. Device limitations and the lack of common global standards mean that relatively high levels of security cannot be widely deployed today. Point-to-point security forms the only real alternative because it can be widely deployed. The seven layers of point-to-point security are:

1. Embedded Security Technology
2. Secure Air-Connect Technologies
3. Mobile Operator Network Security
4. Secure Mobile operator Gateways
5. Authentication
6. Data Center and Network Security
7. Secure Application Interfaces

Embedded Security Technology

The first layer of defense in a computer system is always the end terminal. Physical access to the device must be controlled. If the device is a phone, it will often have a lock code or password feature that prevents it from being used unless a code is entered. PDAs such as Palm OS devices have password and lock features to prevent unauthorized access in the event that the device is lost or stolen. Notebook computers have the same capabilities either as a Basic Input/Output System (BIOS) feature orbuilt in to the operating system. In order to be effective, all of these features require configuration. As a wireless Webmaster, it is up to you to set security policies and to define standard configurations for the devices used to access your network and servers. Unlike desktop workstations, you have to expect that mobile devices will inevitably be lost or stolen. Guidelines covering what and how to communicate can protect confidential information when all else fails. Security policies are your final line of defense: users must be told what can be communicated through mobile devices and what can be stored on mobile devices such as PDAs. Users should be advised to treat their wireless communications in the same way they would a private conversation with a coworker in a public place.

Developing & Deploying...

Security Policies

An excellent example of security guidelines comes from the world of investment banking, where security is of supreme importance because of the ramifications for transactions. Unlike most corporate users, investment banking professionals are keenly aware of security issues and that the ultimate responsibility for confidentiality rests upon the bankers themselves.

Investment banking professionals must observe a strict standard and adhere to protocols that ensure the highest level of confidentiality possible. They must always use caution when discussing business, particularly in a public place such as an airport, elevator, or restaurant. As with products that are not yet announced in other industries, investment bankers often use code names for their projects and clients even in internal discussions.

Continued

When using mobile devices to communicate, investment banking professionals must rely first and foremost upon the established best practices within their field and observe the same precautions they would when sending e-mail outside the company or when traveling. Regardless of the security technology used, any communication technology is only as secure as the policies and practices observed by users.

Mobile Operator Network Security

WTLS extends security beyond the inherent air-connect security, across the entire mobile operator network, right to the edge of the Internet at the WAP gateway. Once traffic leaves the WAP gateway it is no longer secured by the air-connect technology, WTLS, or the network operator's internal network security. At the same time, users may roam to areas where they do not have the same coverage or may use a less secure air-connect technology like the analog AMPS system. The security technologies implemented in air interfaces such as CDMA are designed to protect the network and subscribers from misuse such as stolen phone numbers or unauthorized network use. Security of the air interface itself and the mobile operator's network enhances the security of wireless data services such as WAP browsing, but were designed to protect data communications.

Secure Mobile Operator Gateways

The WAP gap and the potential for man-in-the-middle attacks mean that the security of mobile operator WAP gateways is critical. Inside the WAP gateway, information encrypted through WTLS Class I security is decrypted and then re-encrypted using SSL. The information is vulnerable at that point; ss a wireless Webmaster you have no control of the mobile operator's WAP gateway and no way of knowing if one or more of these machines has been compromised. For organizations buying network service from a carrier, it is reasonable to request a description of network security as would normally be provided by an Internet service provider. The only way to be certain that WAP gateway security is not an unmanaged risk is not to depend on it, relying instead on end-to-end SSL or PKI security.

Authentication

Exposing applications and information on the Web means providing more than one line of defense against unauthorized access and malicious hacking. The simplest strategy is to support a single authentication standard such as Remote

Authentication Dial-In User Service (RADIUS) or Lightweight Directory Access Protocol (LDAP)-based user ID/password authentication. Technologies such as SecureID can easily be added to wireless applications but are cumbersome for users because of the constraints of entering information quickly using a mobile phone or wireless PDA.

SECURITY ALERT

As with local area network (LAN) or host access user IDs and passwords, wireless user IDs and passwords should follow standard guidelines for length and composition. Users may wish to simplify their passwords to make wireless applications more usable, but as a wireless Webmaster you must consider that cracking will be done over the Internet and not from mobile devices. Weak passwords can be quickly broken, and this is especially true for numeric personal identification number (PIN)-based passwords, which are the easiest passwords to enter on a phone.

Data Center and Network Security

If you are using a WASP you must make sure that the WASP data center facility is secure. This means physical security, security policies, operational methodology and procedures, and tools to detect and protect against intrusion attempts. Your WASP should be able to clearly articulate their security architecture and practices including:

1. Secure Data Center Design
2. Customer Network Isolation
3. Secure Router Configurations
4. VPNs and Private Pipes
5. Secure Methodology
6. Security Management
7. Security Auditing

Secure Data Center Design

A secure data center design involves a physical network architecture (see Figure 10.6) that isolates servers and customer information from access over the Internet. This is commonly accomplished through a double firewall scheme where Internet-accessible servers are separated from other machines, and where access to machines through a second firewall is restricted in any of several ways, such as being limited to a particular network address and application.

Figure 10.6 Typical Secure Data Center Network Design

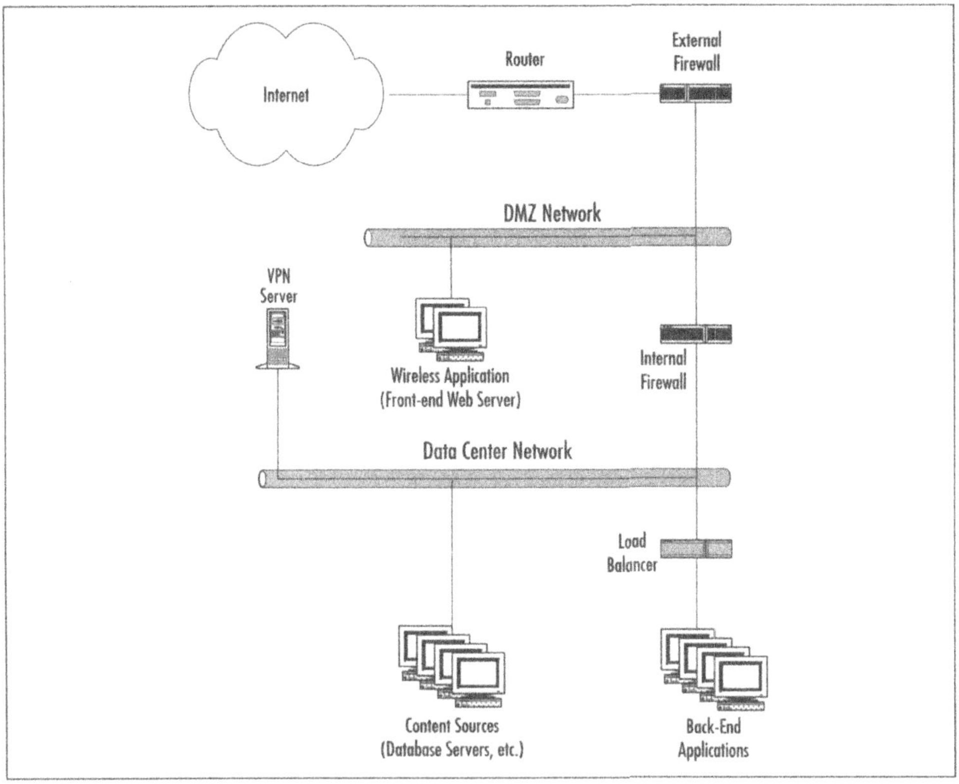

Customer Network Isolation

Isolating customer networks means that firewalls are configured to compartmentalize each customer's servers and data. This mitigates the risk that another customer's application might receive secure information if it were unencrypted for any reason within the service provider's network.

Secure Router Configurations

Like any service provider, a WASP must have secure network router and device configurations. This means that devices are properly configured following well-defined security guidelines. The best way to ensure that your WASP's network router configurations are secure is through an independent audit.

VPNs and Private Pipes

Availability of Virtual Private Network technology or private network connections ("private pipes") is an important consideration. A VPN acts like a conduit over the Internet. Information passing through the conduit is encrypted, but the encryption is transparent to applications on either end of the connection. VPNs allow information to be passed over the Internet with no practical risk of a compromise. Another method involves establishing private network connections between the WASP data center and customer networks. This approach is more costly than a VPN, but is also theoretically more secure since it bypasses the Internet completely.

Secure Methodology

Secure deployment methodologies and remote administration protocols such as SSH are necessary to ensure that there is no exposure of secure information or systems at any point, even when new system components are being deployed. Secure methodology can include administration procedures and tools so that only authorized personnel can perform administrative tasks. Secure methodology guards against accidental exposure and malicious activity within the WASPs network.

Security Management

Designing and deploying a secure system does not mean that it will remain secure indefinitely. Security flaws in software applications and computer or network router operating systems are discovered and corrected over time. Monitoring and timely deployment of security patches will correct known vulnerabilities, and all service providers should have clear procedures to accomplishing this on an ongoing basis.

Security Auditing

You should negotiate independent auditing as a term of your contract with a WASP. A WASP will not give you direct access to their network, firewalls, or routers, therefore you must rely on their self-report or obtain the contractual right to an independent audit. Some service providers will provide an independent audit report, but it is still necessary to consider the scope and the age of an audit report.

Secure Application Interfaces

Wireless applications and servers typically communicate with back-end data sources and applications such as databases and legacy applications. In a typical three-tier architecture (Web browser, Web server plus middleware, and back-end application) a Web server is exposed to the Internet while back-end applications reside within more secure regions of the network. Communication with back-end systems should be implemented using secure protocols and, if possible, through private networks. If an ASP is used, a VPN or private network connection may be configured, but this does not provide security through to the Web or server or mobile application; only to the service provider's network.

The best way to address the issue of secure communications between applications is for servers to communicate using a secure protocol such as SSL. If this is not possible, a VPN and a private WAN connection is the best solution when using a service provider and a private LAN between machines at the data center is recommended (This can be accomplished by adding a secondary network interface card to each server and explicitly configuring the IP addresses or network route to the sister servers.

Problems of a Point-to-Point Security Model

Theoretically, the problem of point-to-point security architectures can never be fully resolved. The only solution is end-to-end security. Of course, point-to-point security can provide additional layer of security as a conduit for communications secured through a PKI. The advantage of going with the flow on point-to-point security is that you retain complete flexibility with respect to devices and the locations of users as they travel, assuming that your mobile application software operates globally.

Sniffing and Spoofing

Sniffing is the process of collecting raw information from a network then filtering it for information related to specific users, machines, or applications. Spoofing refers to simulating a node on a network in order to redirect users to a replica of an application and deceiving them into unknowingly revealing passwords or credit card numbers. As a rule, unencrypted communication can be observed and falsified without detection. PKI security eliminates this possibility.

Session Management and URL Rewriting

On the Web, cookies are used to maintain state between Web browsers and Web servers. On the wireless Web not all browsers support cookies. In the absence of a PKI, less secure methods of maintaining state, such as URL rewriting, must therefore be used. URL rewriting allows applications to maintain their last state independent of cookies by rewriting the URLs sent to the browser in such a way that when the user browses to the rewritten URLs within an application, the server is able determine that the request has come from a specific user. This method poses a security risk since URLs of this kind could be sniffed off the wire and used by hackers to bypass normal authentication before accessing the application. If the algorithms for URL rewriting can derived by a hacker, arbitrary information or transactions can be accessed for a given server or application.

Man-in-the-Middle Attack

A man-in-the-middle is a person who intercepts communications passing through a point where it is unencrypted (such as a WAP gateway), and then replaces the original communication with a false communication that is made to appear legitimate. When the recipient of the false communication responds, they believe that they are dealing with the person who originated the communication rather than the man in the middle. In practice, exploiting this theoretical vulnerability would require a combination of specialized software either installed on a mobile operator's WAP gateway or interposed in the communication path through spoofing.

Security Alert

- **Cracking** Cracking is the practice of guessing a user's password. Since most users choose weak passwords, the best way to crack a password is to know things about the user such as important dates or names of children or pets. Systematic guessing can be automated by writing a program that attempts to enter things such as the words in the dictionary as a user's password. The best defense is a good password and a system that does not tolerate failed login attempts.
- **Hacking** Hacking is a much overused term and it has more than one meaning. The original and most common use refers to programming or working with computers in an obsessive way, especially if the result of this work is ingenious. In the 1980's the

terms was applied to people who broke into computer systems or wrote malicious programs such as computer viruses.

- **Sniffing** Capturing raw network traffic and filtering it to look for specific information. Information in the clear can be read by anyone with the hardware and software necessary to sniff the or network.
- **Spoofing** Spoofing refers to methods of simulating the identity of a machine or application in a network. This can be done either at the hardware level (assuming control of a network route) or a physical or logical level (network address and software applications). The best defense is a PKI because end-to-end security technologies can detect if one end of the communication has is inauthentic.

No Complete Solution

Although a point-to-point security model sounds reasonable, it is a fundamentally flawed and limited approach. Whenever data is unencrypted it is vulnerable, and from a security standpoint it would be clearly incorrect to assume that accidentally transmitting data over the Internet in the clear because of an improper WAP gateway configuration is a worthwhile risk. Similarly it would be a mistake to assume that all WAP gateways or WASP data centers are secure. WTLS may be secure, but the question is irrelevant if the security it provides stops at the WAP gateway. Each juncture within the current wireless security patchwork is a vulnerability that can, at least in theory, be exploited. One key to good security is the attitude that even the most obscure vulnerabilities are unacceptable if there is any way that they can be avoided.

PKI Technology and End-to-End Security Models

The promise of Public Key Infrastructure security is complete end-to-end security where communications remain secure even if intercepted. This is because there is no point between the mobile device and the Web server or mobile application where data are unencrypted. In contrast to the point-to-point WTLS security model, PKI security provides end-to-end security (see Figure 10.7) by deploying digital certificates to client applications such as wireless browsers. A PKI may be used to provide strong security within an enterprise or between businesses since a PKI provides the security necessary for secure business transactions over the Internet.

Figure 10.7 End-to-End Security Model

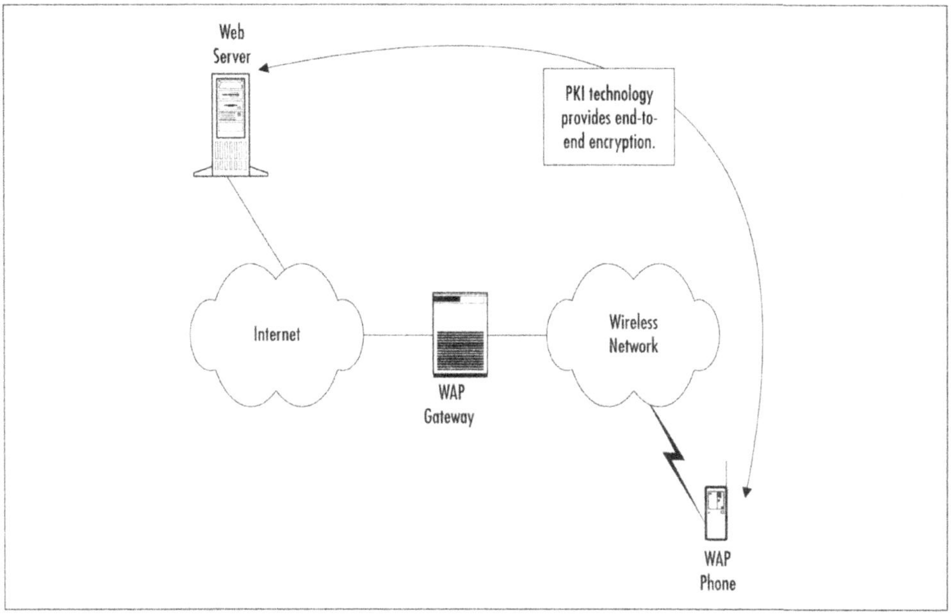

Although PKIs are relatively common within large corporate networks and on the Internet, certificate-based encryption technologies and PKIs are not widely deployed on the wireless Web. For several reasons, there is no dominant standard for wireless digital certificates and PKI technologies.

- Different PKI security technologies and competing vendors
- Different wireless browsers
- Limited bandwidth, device capacity, and processing power
- Albatross of incompatible legacy devices already deployed
- Lack of global standards for browsers and devices

In the past, the adoption of PKI security on the Web has concentrated on industries and focused only on applications that deal with the most sensitive data, rather than becoming ubiquitous. The wireless Web is no different, and you, the wireless Webmaster, need to decide if there is a return on investment for the expense and overhead of deploying a PKI.

How to Deploy a PKI

Devices that support PKI security technology are not widely deployed today. Every PKI implementation is unique to the organization or application that requires security. For this reason, PKI technology is not an off-the-shelf product or turnkey solution. To deploy a PKI you have to first select a wireless PKI technology and a vendor. The technology and vendor you select depends on the application and on the wireless browser and devices that you wish to deploy.

Server Side PKI Integration

Most wireless PKI vendors provide a server-side Software Development Kit (SDK) that allows their technology to be integrated with wireless applications, and some wireless application platforms and WASPs already support one of the leading PKI solutions.

Client Side Devices

PKI technologies must be supported both in a client application, such as a wireless browser, and in a server application. Deploying a PKI for the wireless Web means standardizing on a specific wireless browser and on the devices that support the selected browser. There are several available wireless browsers that support PKI technologies, but this by itself is not a complete solution because the server must support the same technology as the browsers and the PKI must deployed in order to be used . As a rule, existing devices cannot be upgraded to support the latest PKI security technologies so deployment of new mobile devices along with a PKI solution is a routine approach.

Choosing a Certificate Authority

Deployment of a PKI for both the Web and the wireless Web depends on the deployment of a Certificate Authority (CA). When a client certificate is generated, the algorithm uses the creator's root certificate and digitally signs the client certificate. The root certificate is the basis for trust between clients and servers that share certificates with a common root. Every organization that deploys a PKI must decide what CA to use. For your organization's CA, you can choose either a commercial security technology vendor such as Certicom, Diversinet, or Baltimore, or you can use their software to establish you own CA. For interoperability between systems it is best to use a common CA so that organizations can easily grant access to one another's users. The decision of whether to use a commercial CA or become a CA is not only a question of technology but also a function of company size and organizational goals. There is also a political component for mobile commerce since there are a growing number of a laws related to digital signatures.

Certificate Management Framework

PKI technology vendors provide tools for the creation, management and deployment of certificates. Certificate management is the process of choosing or becoming a certificate authority, of creating and securely deploying certificates, of keeping them in escrow in case they are lost or destroyed, and of controlling their expiration and renewal. Since certificates expire, there must be a straightforward way of replacing certificates that are deployed on mobile devices.

Certificate Deployment

PKI deployment involves server-side integration, mobile device or browser selection, certificate creation, and client-side certificate deployment. PKI solutions require users, IT administrators, or both to create and install or renew client-side certificates. The certificate deployment process can be problematic for mobile devices because they are typically in the hands of users who are dispersed within and outside the organization. Certificate deployment must be done securely: if a user's certificate is intercepted, it could grant unauthorized access to an intruder.

Practical Limits of PKI Technology

The largest problem with deploying a PKI is the lack of standards; it is not possible to deploy a PKI technology on the server side and accommodate the devices that users already have to allow users much choice of devices. For practical reasons, the lack of standards also limits geographical coverage. For example, a PKI may be deployed in a specific c-HTML browser on a wireless PDA platform such as Palm OS in North America, but wireless connectivity for the device may not be available in Europe. Another example would be if a specific model of phone implementing current WAP security standards were issued to mobile workers. Users traveling to Asia cannot use these devices, and the available Asian devices (such as NTT DoCoMo i-mode phones) do not use WAP. In many companies it is not practical to standardize mobile devices throughout the organization. To avoid replacing or standardizing on a single wireless phone, the best approach may be to deploy a PKI in conjunction with PDAs, particularly where this reduces the need for notebook computers since reduced cost is a key reason for using both PDAs and wireless access.

Using PDAs with PKI Security

The most powerful handheld mobile devices with the most capacity, flexibility, and readily available security technologies are PDAs. PDAs also support installable software and have the ability to synchronize with desktop PCs. In situations where wireless PDA users sync their PDAs to desktop workstations, administrators have some control over what software is installed, and have the ability to update that software. These managers should specifically ensure that wireless browsers are kept up-to-date. If a management solution such as Microsoft's System Management Server is in place, this can be used to exert centralized control of PDAs by indirectly manipulating PDA configurations. Although PDAs are more involved than phones, using wireless PDAs is the most manageable solution because wireless browsers with digital certificate support are already available, and the software on a PDA such as a Palm Pilot or PocketPC can be easily upgraded. PDAs with expansion slots, such as the Handspring Springboard slot or Pocket PC Card adapter can accommodate more than one type of wireless modem, so PDAs can be configured to go to wherever users travel as long as there is a wireless network to provide data access. In the future, the problems of PKI security will be eased by the introduction of new networks such as General Packet Radio Service (GPRS) and new mobile phones with either with built-in digital certificate support or flexible software configurations similar to today's PDAs.

The Future of Security on the Wireless Web

The future of wireless security lies in its convergence with Internet and Web security. For example, a future PDA with a direct IP connection and HTML browser supporting SSL need not pass through a WAP gateway. In the interim there will be further standardization on wireless browsers, and hopefully a single dominant PKI standard. More to the point, there should be a standard means of installing digital certificates and of managing wireless PKIs from an IT perspective. Mobile devices have a long way to go before corporate IT personnel and wireless Webmasters will find them configurable and manageable.

The Internet and telecommunications marketplaces will continue to converge in the wireless Web, but this will be driven more by enterprise applications than by Web content. Mobile operators and device manufacturers will continue to evolve their alliances with systems integrators and wireless software companies, pursuing enterprise business directly with solutions based on their selected devices and wireless network and security infrastructures, although this does not solve the problem of global security standards. For a global solution there are two options. The first, which is currently available, is a sophisticated software solution that eliminates the complexities of disparate devices, networks and standards but does not solve the problem of creating a globally viable PKI. The second is to wait for 2.5G and 3G networks and devices.

PDAs are generally a better overall solution for corporate users, though not the lowest in cost. In North America, however, there is limited coverage for wireless PDAs. It remains to be seen how these solutions will fare against the coming 2.5G and 3G networks and devices. In the meantime, PDAs are morphing into miniature Web pads. The adoption of PDAs, particularly in the corporate IT sector, will continue alongside that of wireless phones over the next few years.

Summary

The adoption of wireless technologies and applications is driven significantly by the exchange of information and financial transactions that must be secure. Wireless promises to extend corporate data, applications, and the Web to mobile devices. without security that promise is rendered hollow, but security on the wireless Web is far from simple. Unlike the Internet, the wireless Web is a patchwork of different and incompatible standards. There are two basic approaches to security on the wireless Web: point-to-point and end-to-end. Point-to-point security provides the widest choice of mobile devices and browsers, and is the only way to achieve a truly global solution. End-to-end security is synonymous with PKI security technologies, and while PKIs are clearly the better approach, there are many barriers to successful deployment, not the least of which is that using a PKI severely limits the devices that can be deployed. The fundamentals or security technologies (private or secret key and public key encryption) are identical on both the conventional and wireless Web, but there are several problematic areas in wireless Web security. Most of these problems can be managed with varying degrees of assurance with respect to minimizing risks through careful analysis, planning, and management of the wireless solution; and by balancing security requirements with the need for flexibility in mobile device, browser, and network support. In the future, many of the current limitations in wireless Web security will be resolved. However, It remains to be seen if, or to what extent, the adoption of wireless and the introduction of faster networks and more powerful devices will outrun the maturation of wireless security technologies, while wireless and Internet security standards and technologies simultaneously converge.

For ordinary Web content and applications like e-mail that enjoy limited security over the Internet, point-to-point security and WTLS Class I are clearly adequate solutions. For financial applications and sensitive corporate information, the enforcement of SSL on Web servers and applications is a necessary step that must be taken today. Newer implementations of WTLS will improve security in this case. A PKI solution is necessary for highly secure applications,, and the best way to secure your organization's wireless communications via a PKI solution is to use PDAs rather than mobile phones. Many of the issues that are seen as challenging today will be resolved when 2.5G and 3G networks replace the current wireless infrastructure on a large scale. 3G networks and the devices that will run on them will provide better and more manageable security because they will support end-to-end SSL and installable software through technologies such as J2ME.

Solutions Fast Track

Comparing Internet and Wireless Security

☑ Security on the Web is less complex than security on the wireless Web because the Web represents a single paradigm both for application development and for security.

☑ The Internet and the Web provide a somewhat coherent model for applications and security with a handful of ubiquitous standards. On the wireless Web there are many networks using different standards, multiple browser protocols, and several wireless markup languages.

Security Challenges of the Wireless Web

☑ Unlike Secure Sockets Layer (SSL) and the x.509 standard for Public Key Infrastructures (PKIs) on the Internet today, there is no single standard for wireless digital certificates or wireless browser plug-ins.

☑ The relatively weak encryption provided by wireless security technologies such as the Wireless Transport Layer Security (WTLS) protocol and lightweight wireless PKIs is directly related to the length of the keys used and the sophistication of the encryption algorithms. These in turn are a function of device capacity, processing power, and wireless network bandwidth.

☑ User awareness and insecure devices pose a large challenge to the wireless Webmaster. Password protection, encryption programs, and device configuration control are the keys to minimizing the risks when devices are lost or stolen.

☑ Wireless Application Service Providers (WASPs) reduce customer infrastructure investment but require customers to trust their data to a network outside their control.

☑ Along with the spread of new technologies comes the potential for new viruses, but the same diversity of wireless devices, browsers and standards that hampers security can also hamper the spread of viruses and worms.

☑ Once you've determined what you're going to make available wirelessly and how secure it needs to be, you can determine what steps you need to take to provide an appropriate degree of security; bear in mind that the more secure the solution is, the less accessible information is to legitimate users.

Security Models of the Wireless Web

- ☑ There are two basic models for wireless security: *point-to-point*, and *end-to-end*. *Point-to-point* security means that information is protected at each leg of the journey by the appropriate security technologies for that part of the communication. *End-to-end* security means that a single security technology is at work all the way from the end device to the application regardless of the various networks that the communication may traverse.
- ☑ Point-to-point security is only as strong as the weakest link.
- ☑ With end-to-end security, there are several different PKI technologies supported only in specific mobile devices, browsers and applications.
- ☑ Point-to-point and end-to-end security solutions both involve some form of cryptography.
- ☑ SSL uses several well-defined encryption ciphers including RC5, the Data Encryption Standard (DES), 3DES and the International Data Encryption Algorithm (IDEA).

WTLS and Point-to-Point Security Models

- ☑ The most important technology in the point-to-point security model is WTLS. WTLS is the WAP equivalent of SSL, and it provides encryption between wireless browsers and WAP gateways.
- ☑ The most standard form of WTLS (WTLS Class I) is designed to work together with SSL so that WTLS operates on the wireless network side of the WAP gateway and SSL operates on the Internet side. WTLS and SSL together ensure that information is encrypted from point to point all the way from a wireless browser to a Web server
- ☑ The three main components of WTLS are the handshaking protocol that provides for key exchange, a record structure for encrypted information, and the Wireless Identity Module (WIM).

- ☑ WAP gateways decrypt WTLS communication and then re-encrypt the communication using SSL. This means that inside the WAP gateway the information is at one point unencrypted. It is possible, at least in theory, for the WAP gateway to malfunction and establish unencrypted Hypertext Transfer Protocol (HTTP) communication rather than using SSL. This flaw is referred to as the *WAP gap*.
- ☑ The seven layers of point-to-point security are Embedded Security Technology, Secure Air-Connect Technologies, Mobile Operator Network Security, Secure Mobile operator Gateways, Authentication, Data Center and Network Security, and Secure Application Interfaces.
- ☑ Although a point-to-point security model sounds reasonable, it is a fundamentally flawed and limited approach. Whenever data is unencrypted it is vulnerable.

PKI Technology and End-to-End Security Models

- ☑ In contrast to the point-to-point security model of WTLS, PKI security provides end-to-end security by deploying digital certificates to client applications such as wireless browsers.
- ☑ There is no dominant standard for wireless digital certificates and PKI technologies. The lack of standards also limits geographical coverage.
- ☑ To deploy a PKI, you have to first select a wireless PKI technology and a vendor. The technology and vendor you select depends on the application and on the wireless browser and devices that you wish to deploy.
- ☑ Every organization that deploys a PKI must decide what Certificate Authority (CA) to use.
- ☑ The most powerful handheld mobile devices with the most capacity, flexibility, and readily available security technologies are Personal Digital Assistants (PDAs), not phones. In the future, the problems of PKI security will be eased by the introduction of new networks, such as General Packet Radio Service (GPRS), and of new mobile phones either with built-in support for digital certificates or flexible software configurations similar to today's PDAs.

The Future of Security on the Wireless Web

- ☑ The future of wireless security lies in its convergence with Internet and Web security.
- ☑ There will hopefully be further standardization on wireless browsers and a single dominant PKI standard—there should also be a standard means of installing digital certificates and of managing wireless PKIs.
- ☑ Many of the issues that are seen as challenging today will be resolved when 2.5G and 3G networks replace the current wireless infrastructure on a large scale. 3G networks and the devices that will run on them will provide better and more manageable security because they will support end-to-end SSL and installable software through technologies such as Java 2 Micro Edition (J2ME).

Frequently Asked Questions

The following Frequently Asked Questions, answered by the authors of this book, are designed to both measure your understanding of the concepts presented in this chapter and to assist you with real-life implementation of these concepts. To have your questions about this chapter answered by the author, browse to **www.syngress.com/solutions** and click on the **"Ask the Author"** form.

Q: Is the wireless Web as secure as the Internet?

A: Not currently. However, 2.5G and 3G networks will eventually offer equivalent security. Wireless PKIs can be considered as secure as SSL over the Internet, but they are not yet widely deployed.

Q: What's the most important factor in wireless security?

A: Users. Users need to be careful with their mobile devices, follow security guidelines put forth by IT organizations, and be discrete in their communications. No technology can protect information against careless users.

Q: Why does wireless security seem more complex than security on the Internet?

A: Because it *is* more complex. Challenges such as limited device horsepower are exacerbated by a lack of standards on more than one level and by competing commercial interests.

Q: What are the main security concerns for mobile applications?

A: The main issues are unencrypted communication over the public Internet, the security risks facing wireless ASPs, and standardisation of WAP security models.

Q: What's the difference between public key and secret key cryptography?

A: In public key cryptography, users have two keys: one that is public (to encrypt data) and one that is private and known only to the user (to decrypt data). In secret key cryptography users have single key known both to them and to the party with whom they are communicating.

Q: Why are so-called point-to-point security models bad?

A: A point-to-point security model is where the *best available* security technology is used for each part of the communication. The problem is that wherever there is a change in security technology the data must be unencrypted. At that point the data are potentially vulnerable. The more hops there are from point A to point B, the greater the overall risk.

Q: Are wireless PDAs more secure than WAP phones?

A: Yes. PDAs are more configurable and manageable for IT. PDAs can be easily upgraded to support new browsers, and PKIs can currently be deployed on PDAs with relative ease compared with phones.

Q: What's the best way to make sure that my wireless Web is secure?

A: Deploy SSL on your servers and support only SSL connections. Standardize on devices and browsers if possible and consider a standard wireless PDA configuration.

Appendix

Webmaster's Guide to the Wireless Internet Fast Track

This Appendix will provide you with a quick, yet comprehensive, review of the most important concepts covered in this book.

❖ Chapter 1: Moving from the Web to Wireless

Explaining Wireless

☑ The emphasis on mobility is one of the defining characteristics of this new wireless paradigm, and from a Webmaster's point of view this mobility, not simply the lack of wires, is likely to be the most important aspect you have to deal with.

☑ Low bandwidth, differing standards, multiple network carriers, and a multitude of radically different devices means that the job of the wireless Webmaster just got immensely more complicated.

Types of Wireless Connectivity

☑ The Wireless Application Protocol (WAP) is the first widely available method of accessing Internet content from a mobile device. WAP gateways enable legacy browsers to understand WML content. However, due to differences in the WAP gateway configuration, and the particular microbrowser installed on the handset, a WAP page may display differently on different handsets.

☑ With Short Message Service (SMS), users can send short text messages to each other at a fraction of the cost of a voice call. SMS can also be used to send configuration settings to your phone. SMS is a huge success in Europe, and it is gradually becoming available on U.S. wireless phone plans, although in a limited fashion.

☑ Japan's NTT DoCoMo mobile data service i-Mode offers users the ability to browse a huge range of Web sites with cheap, full-color handsets that maintain an always-on connection to the Internet. It could possibly become an alternative to WAP but currently is in use only in Japan.

☑ The European wireless standard, Global System for Mobile Communications (GSM), is available on a limited basis in the US. The General Packet Radio System (GPRS) will soon offer higher data speeds and an always-on connection worldwide; it is already available in some European countries, and on a trial basis in a few U.S. cities.

Chapter 1 Continued

- ☑ A recent option for wireless connectivity in the U.S. is Cellular Digital Packet Data (CDPD), a packet-switched network this is an always-on connection. The major drawback of CDPD is limited availability.
- ☑ The 802.11b standard has found ready acceptance as a short-range radio replacement for traditional Ethernet connections. Bluetooth is another short-range wireless standard.

Evolving Mobile Devices

- ☑ The three main categories of mobile devices, mobile phones, PDAs, and laptop computers, are differentiated by connectivity, screen size, memory, and processing power.
- ☑ Data-capable phones use the WAP protocol, and content needs to be coded in Wireless Markup Language (WML). They have minimal requirements for memory and processing power. A mobile phone never communicates directly with your Web server; there is always a WAP gateway acting on its behalf (the gateway may alter the content somewhat on its way through).
- ☑ The market for Personal Digital Assistants (PDAs) is split mainly between those running the Palm operating system from both Palm, Inc. and its licensees, and devices based on Microsoft's Pocket PC or Windows CE. One feature of Pocket PCs that's especially relevant to wireless is that most come with an industry-standard expansion slot, either CF or PCMCIA Type II.
- ☑ PDAs come in a wide range of configurations of connectivity, screen size, memory, and processing power.
- ☑ Several manufacturers have begun shipping laptops with built-in wireless LAN (802.11b) cards, with antennas integrated into the casing. These same manufacturers will soon begin offering Bluetooth-equipped laptops. However, with larger screens, keyboards, and more memory and storage, Handheld PCs are beginning to offer a viable alternative to bulky laptops.
- ☑ Also, several devices are available that seek to combine aspects of each category—a mobile phone with an integrated Palm screen, PDAs that can be used as phones, and laptop-size devices without keyboards that you use by writing directly on the screen.

Chapter 1 Continued

Something Old, Something New

☑ TCP/IP has been able to adapt and grow with the increasing demands of the Internet; both the Palm and Pocket PC use the same HTTP to communicate with your content server; and HTML has also proven to be extremely adaptable and long-lasting. Another Web concept that has been maintained in the wireless realm is the browser.

☑ WAP provides for a mapping between all layers of HTTP and the corresponding layers of WAP. This translation is performed transparently by the WAP gateway, so as a Webmaster you really don't have to worry too much about it.

☑ Microbrowsers installed on mobile phones tend to be proprietary to the handset manufacturer and impossible to change, but in the future it's likely that they will coalesce around a common standard, and be user-changeable.

Moving from a Wired to a Wireless Internet

☑ The new wireless medium requires a change in perspective from a large-screen desktop browser to a small mobile device with limited user-interaction mechanisms and, for now, a slow wireless connection.

☑ Probably the main adjustment Webmasters will need to make to the wireless Web is to realize that users of mobile devices need quick access to relevant information only.

☑ You'll need to test and verify your code on a variety of handsets, through as many carrier gateways as you can. Similarly, Web Clipping applications can look quite different depending on the transcoding proxy server used. On Pocket Internet Explorer, you'll need to test how your content looks with the different view settings and different user preferences.

☑ The best way to deal with differing browser capabilities, and build a truly scalable Web site publishing system, is to completely separate content from presentation.

❖ Chapter 2: Wireless Architecture

Components of a Wireless Network

- ☑ You can use your existing Web server to provide WAP services with only minor configuration changes.
- ☑ WAP introduces a gateway between your server and the WAP browser. The gateway helps the limited memory, low bandwidth device browse the Internet by validating WML files and compiling them for quicker transmittal.

Adjusting the Metaphor for the Wireless Internet

- ☑ Just as the Web required a different approach than print publishing, the wireless Internet requires a different approach than the Web. The capabilities of the mobile device are quite different than that of a desktop computer.
- ☑ The mobile user is, by definition, on the move and will not tolerate difficult-to-navigate sites or extra fluff that just gets in the way of helping her find what she is looking for.
- ☑ Your Web site and WAP site should work together to provide an experience that never inconveniences the user. Long signup forms and surveys should be reserved for the Web site, and the WAP site should help the user find the information he is looking for as quickly as possible.

Accepting the Challenge of WAP-Enabled Devices

- ☑ The form factor and capabilities of WAP devices can vary greatly—ranging from pocket-sized to handheld, and possibly to the size of a large-screen television.
- ☑ Some components are in place to help you determine device capabilities as they hit your site. These are not pervasive yet, but may be in the near future.
- ☑ Testing is important. Each device has its own peculiar set of "features" that make it behave differently from every other browser.

Chapter 2 Continued

Adopting Wireless Standards

☑ Many wireless standards are out there. Find out what your audience has access to and build your site accordingly.

☑ WAP is the standard that currently has the most momentum, but this could change as companies experiment and roll out other technologies

Noting the Market for Wireless Browsers and Other Applications

☑ A variety of applications are available for mobile devices. The one you can almost guarantee will be available is the WAP browser, however.

☑ Java2 Micro Edition is poised as an interesting player in the mobile data arena. You can write an application once that can run on any brand of phone and on any network.

☑ Old technologies such as SMS are still going strong. Device manufacturers are slowly overcoming the limitations of SMS, and the concept of SMS is being expanded on to include multimedia capabilities.

❖ Chapter 3: A New Markup: WML

A Brief History of Wireless Content

☑ The Intelligent Terminal Transfer Protocol (ITTP) was developed by Ericsson in 1995. Unwired Planet developed the Handheld Device Markup Language (HDML) in mid-1996 and made it available to developers. The Tagged Text Markup Language (TTML), developed by Nokia Corporation, and the Extensible Markup Language (XML) had become available around the same time.

☑ In June 1997, Nokia and Unwired Planet formed The WAP Forum, also bringing together Motorola and Ericsson. These initial founders represented over 90 percent of the wireless market. The WAP Forum's primary goal was to develop a protocol that could be built on any platform to allow users to interact with services and information as fast and efficiently as possible and to promote product interoperability.

Chapter 3 Continued

- ☑ The WAP Forum examined the various markup languages being offered by the different companies and took the best aspects of each to form the Wireless Markup Language (WML), which was released in 1999.
- ☑ Those devices that contained HDML browsers gained the ability to browse WML content from HDML version 3.1 onwards.

WML Overview

- ☑ WML is an application of XML.
- ☑ A WML document contains *elements* that have a *start tag* and an *end tag*. If the element isn't a container for data, the element must be self-closing (indicated by a backslash).
- ☑ WML files consist of a deck containing one or more cards. Each file can be thought of as a deck, within which can be any number of cards. Each card is a single page that can be displayed on the device.
- ☑ WML is constructed hierarchically. Files must be well-formed and valid XML documents. Validity is achieved by the inclusion of a Document Type Definition (DTD).

WML Elements

- ☑ WML elements specify the structure of the content.
- ☑ WML is quite similar to HTML in its use of elements and attributes to describe the content within each file. There are relatively few elements in comparison to HTML.

Creating WML Content

- ☑ Dynamic applications are applications that build content "on the fly" in response to requests made. A single template file filled with dynamically-served content can replace hundreds of similar HTML pages.
- ☑ Openwave extensions to WML allow further context and better error handling to be introduced to your WML application.
- ☑ WML provides a number of navigation aids that are more flexible than those available in HTML.

Chapter 3 Continued

- ☑ Tasks allow the user to perform actions dependent on the situation encountered.

WML Editors, WAP SDKs, and Emulators

- ☑ WAP editors allow the quick and easy creation of WML files. Most of the popular HTML editors support editing WML.
- ☑ WAP editors can also sometimes contain a built-in emulator to preview work.
- ☑ You should always check WML content on the target device wherever possible.

❖ Chapter 4: Enhancing Client-Side Functionality with WMLScript

What Is WMLScript?

- ☑ WMLScript is loosely based on the ECMAScript (ECMA262).
- ☑ Most devices in the market support WMLScript.
- ☑ WMLScript programs are compiled into bytecode by WAP gateways.
- ☑ WMLScript is activated by WML decks.

Understanding Basic Elements of WMLScript

- ☑ WMLScript contains libraries.
- ☑ Within each library are functions that provide most commonly needed functionality.

Learning to Interpret WMLScript

- ☑ WMLScript functions that are preceded by the *extern* keyword are callable by WML decks.

Chapter 4 Continued

Performing Mathematical Operations Using WMLScript

- ☑ Variables are declared in WMLScript using the *var* keyword.
- ☑ WMLScript handles data type internally.
- ☑ WMLScript supports looping using the for construct.

Using WMLScript for Input Validation

- ☑ The **compare()** function in the String library compares two strings.

Credit Card Validation

- ☑ WMLScript does not support arrays.
- ☑ Use a string to improvise an array if needed.

Using WMLScript and Microsoft ASP: A Case Study

- ☑ A server-side technology like ASP can be used to generate dynamic WMLScript programs.
- ☑ WMLScript programs are cached on the client-side.
- ☑ Use the HTTP directives to control caching behavior on the client-side.

❖ Chapter 5: Wireless Development Kits

The Openwave UP.SDK 4.1

- ☑ The UP.SDK provides emulation for a variety of mobile devices. You can use it to test your application on a variety of phones from multiple device manufacturers as long as they use the UP.Browser in their phones.
- ☑ You can download the UP.SDK from the Openwave Developer Program Web site (http://developer.openwave.com) in the Downloads section.

Chapter 5 Continued

- ☑ The UP.SDK does not provide any text editing or IDE-style capabilities. It is useful for testing applications only, and you must have a separate program to create and edit your WAP files.
- ☑ The error messages reported by the UP.SDK are fairly helpful in finding syntactical problems. They will point you in the correct direction but are not explicit enough to make finding errors a simple task.

The Nokia WAP Toolkit 2.1

- ☑ The WAP Toolkit provides a prototype-like mobile phone for development.
- ☑ You can download modules that emulate actual Nokia phones from the Forum Nokia Web site (http://forum.nokia.com)
- ☑ The WAP Toolkit is a full-featured IDE. You can create and edit WML and WMLScript files as well as WBMP images using the built-in tools.
- ☑ The error messages reported by the WAP Toolkit are geared more towards machines than humans, but the line numbers they report are usually very close to the source of the problem.

The Motorola Mobile Application Development Kit 2.0

- ☑ The Mobile ADK includes support for a large variety of Motorola mobile phones. The Mobile ADK is the only SDK we looked at that also supports voice applications through VoxML and VoiceXML as well as Microsoft ASP support.
- ☑ You can download the Mobile ADK from the Motorola Applications Global Network (MAGNET) Web site at www.motorola.com/developers/wireless in the Tools & Downloads section.
- ☑ The Mobile ADK and Wireless IDE provide a complete development environment for your mobile needs. You can integrate with source control products and develop for a variety of environments using the same IDE.
- ☑ The error reporting in the Mobile ADK is entirely subpar when compared to the other SDKs. The only thing you will find out is that an error occurred with your file. You will have to do all the work of figuring out where the error actually is.

Chapter 5 Continued

The Ericsson Mobile Internet WAP-IDE 3.1

☑ The WAP-IDE includes support for three Ericsson mobile phones. You can use the emulator independent of the environment for building and debugging applications, which provides a good mechanism to demo your WAP applications.

☑ You can download the Ericsson WAP-IDE from the Ericsson Developer Zone Web site at www.ericsson.com/developerzone.

☑ The WAP-IDE includes an Application Designer that helps you build WML decks that are syntactically correct as well as compile and debug the ones that aren't.

☑ The error reporting is quite descriptive although the line numbers don't tend to match up that well. Also, it displays a lot of error messages for one error (three in our case), which makes tracking down problems a little more difficult.

The Yospace SmartPhone Emulator 2.0

☑ The SmartPhone Emulator can emulate a variety of mobile devices from a large variety of manufacturers. Viewing source files in multiple emulators—either individually or at the same time—is quite easy with the layout of the SmartPhone Emulator. It is also written entirely in Java, making it the only emulator that you can use on operating systems other than Microsoft Windows.

☑ You can download the SmartPhone Emulator from the Yospace Web site (www.yospace.com) in the Products section.

☑ The SmartPhone Emulator includes no editing capabilities, but it does provide good debugging facilities for viewing variables, history stacks, and other portions of the running WAP browsers.

☑ The error reporting is the most accurate of the group. It pinpoints the cause of the problem rather than the effect. The error messages are cluttered with a lot of information pertaining to the internal implementation of the SmartPhone Emulator, which makes finding the actual error message a little difficult. Once you do find it however, it points you directly to the error.

❖ Chapter 6: Web Clipping

What Is Web Clipping?

☑ Web clipping refers to a proprietary network that allows Palm-compatible handheld devices to connect to the Internet by browsing compressed HTML contained in special files installed on the device. The Web Clipping Application Viewer is also called the Clipper browser.

☑ Web clipping differs from Web browsing both in usage patterns and the actual technology used to access the Internet. WCA users are mobile, and deal with limited input mechanisms.

☑ A Web clipping application is installed on a device, and cannot be updated until the user installs a new version. This means that extra thought should be put into what interactions are included in a WCA.

☑ A subset of HTML 3.2 is used to build Web clipping applications. Not all elements of the specification are supported, but many elements are.

What Types of Hardware Support Web Clipping

☑ Devices running the Palm Operating System version 3.5 or higher can take advantage of Web clipping.

☑ Many devices can access the Internet via Web clipping, including the Palm VII/VIIx connected via Mobitex and other Palm-compatible handhelds connected via the CDPD Network or Mobile Internet Kit.

☑ The RIM 957 (Blackberry) Pager can browse the content of a WCA if it is accessed via a direct link over the Internet. These devices are unable to follow links to, or display images that the WCA expects to be found locally on the device, such as links using the file: protocol.

Working with the Palm OS Emulator

☑ The Palm Operating System Emulator (POSE) is freely available from the Palm Web site at www.palm.com/dev/tech/tools/.

☑ In order to use the POSE, first you need to install the emulator to emulate the hardware, and then install a ROM image of the OS to start the emulator or run any software.

Chapter 6 Continued

- ☑ There are two ways to obtain ROM images: transfer one from a device that you own, or download one from the Palm Resource Pavilion. You must register as a Palm developer to obtain ROM images from Palm.
- ☑ It is necessary to configure the emulator to access the Internet via the network interface of the computer upon which it is installed. The emulator must be set to redirect network requests to TCP/IP, and the emulator software must be configured to use a Palm.net Proxy Server.

Creating a Web Clipping Project with the Web Clipping Application Builder

- ☑ The Web Clipping Application (WCA) Builder, like the POSE, can be downloaded from the Palm Web site at www.palm.com/dev/tech/tools/.
- ☑ The WCA Builder is used to compile device-resident Web clipping applications from HTML and images.
- ☑ The WCA Builder automatically will scan HTML from a single index page and automatically include any linked pages or referenced images. It will do some basic error checking, but it is not foolproof, and code should be validated externally.
- ☑ Custom icons may be used for your Web clipping applications. These can be selected in the **Build PQA** dialog box, which is the final step in the application building process.

Web Clipping Basics and Examples

- ☑ Many of the more common tags from the HTML 3.2 specification are available, but many other recent developments are not. Any elements that require client-side processing, such as animated images, imagemaps, and client-side scripting have been eliminated due to device constraints.
- ☑ Some useful features are unique to Web clipping, including variables that relay information about the location of the user and a unique device identifier. Two other elements are available: datepicker and timepicker. These elements help to offset the device constraints of Web clipping.
- ☑ Data transmitted over the air should be minimized as much as possible, and local resources on the device should be leveraged to minimize network

Chapter 6 Continued

traffic. This can be accomplished by linking to local images on the device, and by including content that is not time-sensitive on the device.

❖ Chapter 7: Deck of Cards: Designing Small Viewpoint Content

Thinking In the Hand, not On the Web

☑ The wireless Internet provides us with a smaller viewpoint for content, and it is not possible to represent the typical pyramidal site structure of the WWW on handheld devices.

☑ It is difficult to provide both horizontal and vertical navigation on a mobile device due to a lack of screen real estate.

☑ The needs of the mobile user necessitate a fairly linear, task-based navigational scheme, with a frequency of access-based segregation of tasks.

☑ Working within the bandwidth and input constraints of the wireless medium can prevent the mistakes that are typically made by many Webmasters.

Stacking a Deck of Cards

☑ It is possible to make many small refinements to your markup that will have a cumulative effect on the final size of your content.

☑ A hub-and-spoke metaphor can be used effectively within the framework of WML. Users have full freedom of vertical navigation, though this metaphor does not use horizontal navigation.

☑ Minimizing the number of server connections can greatly increase a site's usability, and one of the easiest ways to do this for small sites is to send one deck consisting of navigation, and, on request, send decks that contain the sections' content.

☑ WML variables are stored on the device (similar to cookies), and are persistent between decks as well as cards. You should be aware of the state of the user's variables in your application, and clear them as appropriate.

Chapter 7 Continued

Examining Display Differences Between Browsers

☑ One of the most notable differences between the UP.Browser and the Nokia browser is in the rendering of the <SELECT> and <INPUT> elements. On average, the Nokia browser user will need to enter twice as many keystrokes.

☑ The 4thpass Kbrowser (for the Palm OS) renders WML differently than either the Nokia or the UP.Browser. If you are supporting this browser in your site, you should take care to branch your code and test your application thoroughly.

❖ Chapter 8: Wireless Enabling Your Big Bandwidth Site

Defining WAP MIME Types

☑ It is important to consider the market for which you are delivering content, and to define the appropriate MIME types for the devices used by your users.

☑ There are several options for defining MIME types under the most common Web servers on the market. MIME types may be defined and Wireless content may be deployed at the directory, site, or server level.

☑ WAP MIME types are defined in the same manner as any other MIME type.

Detecting WAP Devices

☑ WAP devices send the same type of header information to Web servers as desktop browsers do.

☑ HTTP_ACCEPT can be used to detect the language that a given browser can accept.

☑ HTTP_USER_AGENT can be used to differentiate browsers depending on the reported name of the browser.

☑ A combination of HTTP_ACCEPT and HTTP_USER_AGENT can be used to redirect devices to appropriate content, or to profile devices for formatting.

Chapter 8 Continued

Optimizing Content Distribution

☑ Regardless of the technical issues of how you manage your content, take a critical look at your current Web site and consider what you want to provide to your wireless users.

☑ It is possible to automatically format existing sites, but with dubious results.

☑ WAP sites may be set up with the same flexibility as Web sites.

Delivering Wireless Data

☑ Mobile users are more often in need of data rather than content.

☑ It is important to separate content from presentation for data applications.

☑ Build modules that enable device profiling and accordingly allow for different presentations of dynamic data from the same source.

Implementing Wireless Graphics

☑ Several different formats are supported, including common Web formats for some devices.

☑ Ensure accessibility by using <ALT> tags on all images, and conserve bandwidth by only using graphics when necessary.

☑ Online and desktop converters are available to automatically convert your existing images.

❖ Chapter 9: Microsoft Mobile Internet Toolkit

Overview of the .NET Mobile Architecture

☑ The Mobile Internet Toolkit is built on the Microsoft ASP.NET Web Forms and supports languages like VB .NET, C#, and JScript.NET. It is an extension to the ASP.NET model.

☑ The toolkit includes a set of Mobile Controls that is executed by the Mobile Internet Controls runtime during the execution phase.

Chapter 8 Continued

☑ The key feature of the runtime is its ability to recognize the different types of devices accessing the forms and to generate dynamically the codes that the device can understand.

☑ The current release of the Microsoft Mobile Internet Toolkit is Beta 2. Before installing the Microsoft Mobile Internet Toolkit, you must first install the .NET framework SDK.

Introduction to ASP.NET

☑ Current ASP technology contains a mixture of HTML and scripting codes and does not provide a clean separation of display from content, which often results in bugs and difficulties.

☑ HTTP is a stateless protocol. Preserving state in ASP requires substantial effort by the developer.

☑ In ASP.NET, normal HTML elements are converted to HTML Server controls so that they can be programmed on the server. Besides the HTML Server controls, ASP.NET provides a different set of server controls known as ASP.NET server controls.

☑ A Web Form in ASP.NET contains two components: Code and Content.

☑ The Content component of a Web Form can contain Web Form Server controls. Web Form Server controls contain the HTML Server control, ASP.NET Server control, Validation controls, and User controls.

☑ One important difference between ASP.NET and ASP is that ASP.NET applications are parsed and compiled once and then cached, so that subsequent requests do not go through the same time-consuming steps.

Developing Mobile Web Forms

☑ During runtime when the form is requested, the .NET runtime automatically will detect the type of devices (our examples use Pocket PC, IE 5.5 and UP.SDK) requesting that page, and will perform a dynamic generation of the target markup languages. Unlike WAP applications developed using WML and ASP, the same ASP.NET application can be displayed on different devices, with no effort on your part for customization.

Chapter 9 Continued

☑ In ASP.NET pages, there can be only a single form; however, you can have multiple mobile forms in a Mobile Web form. To link the two forms, you use the *<Mobile:Link>* control. The *navigateURL* attribute contains the ID of the form to link to.

☑ Linking to forms on another page is not so straightforward. The form in the first page links to the second page by specifying the filename in the *navigateURL* attribute. Subsequent steps involve adding another parameter called *Form*, retrieving its value using the *Request.QueryString* collection, verifying the form ID in that value, and using the *ActiveForm* property to set and return the active page.

☑ The Microsoft Mobile Internet Toolkit supports user input controls TextBox, Command, and List.

☑ To input text into a Mobile Web Form, use the *<Mobile:TextBox>* control. To display a command button so that an action can be performed, use the *<Mobile:Command>* control. To display lists of items either as a static list or interactive selection, use the *<Mobile:List>* control. You can also dynamically bind a list of items using the **ArrayList** class.

☑ To display images, you can use the *<Mobile:Image>* control. Because various mobile devices display images of differing format, use the *<DeviceSpecific>* control (within which are the *<Choice>* elements) to send the correct image type to the right device.

☑ Validation controls available in the Microsoft Mobile Internet Toolkit SDK include CompareValidator, CustomValidator, RangeValidator, RegularExpressionValidator, RequiredFieldValidator, and ValidationSummary.

☑ Other features of the Mobile API are its records paging capability, using the *Paginate* attribute, and also its *Calendar* control for date selection.

Accessing Data with ADO.NET

☑ Developers are familiar with using the ActiveX Data Objects (ADO) for accessing databases through OLE DB and ODBC. ADO.NET was evolved to support the need for remote data access.

☑ In ADO, communication with the data source is through the OLE DB providers. In ADO.NET, the communication is through Data providers.

Chapter 9 Continued

ADO.NET contains two data providers—SQL Data providers and OLEDB Data providers.

☑ It is possible to use OLEDB Data provider even if you are using SQL server.

☑ ADO.NET provides the DataReader for retrieving records as a read-only, forward-only stream returned from the database for display on the client side. The DataReader stores only a single record in memory at any one time to prevent storing a huge number of records in memory.

☑ The more powerful Dataset object is used to access different tables in the database. The requested data can be retrieved, saved, and printed with the use of Tables collections.

❖ Chapter 10: Securing Your Wireless Web

Comparing Internet and Wireless Security

☑ Security on the Web is less complex than security on the wireless Web because the Web represents a single paradigm both for application development and for security.

☑ The Internet and the Web provide a somewhat coherent model for applications and security with a handful of ubiquitous standards. On the wireless Web there are many networks using different standards, multiple browser protocols, and several wireless markup languages.

Security Challenges of the Wireless Web

☑ Unlike Secure Sockets Layer (SSL) and the x.509 standard for Public Key Infrastructures (PKIs) on the Internet today, there is no single standard for wireless digital certificates or wireless browser plug-ins.

☑ The relatively weak encryption provided by wireless security technologies such as the Wireless Transport Layer Security (WTLS) protocol and lightweight wireless PKIs is directly related to the length of the keys used and the sophistication of the encryption algorithms. These in turn are a function of device capacity, processing power, and wireless network bandwidth.

Chapter 10 Continued

- ☑ User awareness and insecure devices pose a large challenge to the wireless Webmaster. Password protection, encryption programs, and device configuration control are the keys to minimizing the risks when devices are lost or stolen.
- ☑ Wireless Application Service Providers (WASPs) reduce customer infrastructure investment but require customers to trust their data to a network outside their control.
- ☑ Along with the spread of new technologies comes the potential for new viruses, but the same diversity of wireless devices, browsers and standards that hampers security can also hamper the spread of viruses and worms.
- ☑ Once you've determined what you're going to make available wirelessly and how secure it needs to be, you can determine what steps you need to take to provide an appropriate degree of security; bear in mind that the more secure the solution is, the less accessible information is to legitimate users.

Security Models of the Wireless Web

- ☑ There are two basic models for wireless security: *point-to-point*, and *end-to-end*. *Point-to-point* security means that information is protected at each leg of the journey by the appropriate security technologies for that part of the communication. *End-to-end* security means that a single security technology is at work all the way from the end device to the application regardless of the various networks that the communication may traverse.
- ☑ Point-to-point security is only as strong as the weakest link.
- ☑ With end-to-end security, there are several different PKI technologies supported only in specific mobile devices, browsers and applications.
- ☑ Point-to-point and end-to-end security solutions both involve some form of cryptography.
- ☑ SSL uses several well-defined encryption ciphers including RC5, the Data Encryption Standard (DES), 3DES and the International Data Encryption Algorithm (IDEA).

Chapter 10 Continued

WTLS and Point-to-Point Security Models

☑ The most important technology in the point-to-point security model is WTLS. WTLS is the WAP equivalent of SSL, and it provides encryption between wireless browsers and WAP gateways.

☑ The most standard form of WTLS (WTLS Class I) is designed to work together with SSL so that WTLS operates on the wireless network side of the WAP gateway and SSL operates on the Internet side. WTLS and SSL together ensure that information is encrypted from point to point all the way from a wireless browser to a Web server

☑ The three main components of WTLS are the handshaking protocol that provides for key exchange, a record structure for encrypted information, and the Wireless Identity Module (WIM).

☑ WAP gateways decrypt WTLS communication and then re-encrypt the communication using SSL. This means that inside the WAP gateway the information is at one point unencrypted. It is possible, at least in theory, for the WAP gateway to malfunction and establish unencrypted Hypertext Transfer Protocol (HTTP) communication rather than using SSL. This flaw is referred to as the *WAP gap*.

☑ The seven layers of point-to-point security are Embedded Security Technology, Secure Air-Connect Technologies, Mobile Operator Network Security, Secure Mobile operator Gateways, Authentication, Data Center and Network Security, and Secure Application Interfaces.

☑ Although a point-to-point security model sounds reasonable, it is a fundamentally flawed and limited approach. Whenever data is unencrypted it is vulnerable.

PKI Technology and End-to-End Security Models

☑ In contrast to the point-to-point security model of WTLS, PKI security provides end-to-end security by deploying digital certificates to client applications such as wireless browsers.

☑ There is no dominant standard for wireless digital certificates and PKI technologies. The lack of standards also limits geographical coverage.

Chapter 10 Continued

- ☑ To deploy a PKI, you have to first select a wireless PKI technology and a vendor. The technology and vendor you select depends on the application and on the wireless browser and devices that you wish to deploy.
- ☑ Every organization that deploys a PKI must decide what Certificate Authority (CA) to use.
- ☑ The most powerful handheld mobile devices with the most capacity, flexibility, and readily available security technologies are Personal Digital Assistants (PDAs), not phones. In the future, the problems of PKI security will be eased by the introduction of new networks, such as General Packet Radio Service (GPRS), and of new mobile phones either with built-in support for digital certificates or flexible software configurations similar to today's PDAs.

The Future of Security on the Wireless Web

- ☑ The future of wireless security lies in its convergence with Internet and Web security.
- ☑ There will hopefully be further standardization on wireless browsers and a single dominant PKI standard—there should also be a standard means of installing digital certificates and of managing wireless PKIs.
- ☑ Many of the issues that are seen as challenging today will be resolved when 2.5G and 3G networks replace the current wireless infrastructure on a large scale. 3G networks and the devices that will run on them will provide better and more manageable security because they will support end-to-end SSL and installable software through technologies such as Java 2 Micro Edition (J2ME).

Index

C

E

F

G

H

I

J

K

N

O

P

Q

T

U

V

X

Y

Z